Becoming a Better
Elementary Science Teacher

Becoming a Better Elementary Science Teacher

A Reader

edited by

Robert B. Sund
University of Northern Colorado

Rodger W. Bybee
New York University

CHARLES E. MERRILL PUBLISHING COMPANY
A Bell & Howell Company
Columbus, Ohio

For the Marsh family:
Bob and Nancy, David, Kamela and Benta

Published by
CHARLES E. MERRILL PUBLISHING COMPANY
A Bell & Howell Company
Columbus, Ohio 43216

International Standard Book Number: 0-675-09059-8

Library of Congress Catalog Card Number: 72-90162

Printed in the United States of America

1 2 3 4 5 6 7 8 — 78 77 76 75 74 73

PREFACE

Individuals preparing to teach and those teaching elementary science want to become excellent instructors. It is our belief that the readings in this book contribute to the individual's growth as an elementary science teacher. The organization of the sections of the book reflects the research on good teaching. First, excellent teachers have healthy personalities. Second, their perception of others, especially children, is positive; and third, their classroom interaction is characterized by a helping, facilitating relationship based on an understanding of curriculum materials and teaching procedures such as questioning and inquiry. An individual can develop existing competencies and *Become a better elementary science teacher* by more fully and deeply:

UNDERSTANDING SELF
UNDERSTANDING CHILDREN
UNDERSTANDING ALL CHILDREN ARE SPECIAL
UNDERSTANDING THE CURRICULUM
UNDERSTANDING THE FACILITATION OF
    LEARNING
UNDERSTANDING THE ROLE OF LISTENING,
    LEARNING, AND QUESTIONING
UNDERSTANDING CREATIVITY, DISCOVERY, AND
    INQUIRY

This reader can be used as a complement to elementary methods texts such as *Teaching Science Through Discovery* (Carin and Sund,

Charles E. Merrill Publishing Co., 2nd ed., 1970) and *Teaching Modern Science* (Carin and Sund, Charles E. Merrill Publishing Co., 1971), or as a basic text for graduate and undergraduate seminars, workshops, and in service training in elementary science.

We have attempted to focus on the positive aspects of teaching with special emphasis given to teaching elementary science. Many articles are from sources other than those traditionally reviewed by science educators. Several of these have been selected as the lead articles for the sections. Following the leads are readings that attempt to show how their ideas can be applied in the elementary science classroom. Each of the seven sections is preceded by an introduction elaborating the emphasis, ideas, strengths, and weaknesses of the articles.

Particular attention was given to selecting readable articles for elementary teachers. Our colleagues have stressed the importance of doing this. It has also been our experience that many articles that stimulate science educators dull and bore elementary teachers. For this reason we have avoided using specific research and other highly technical materials.

Finally, we feel education is entering an era of greater recognition of the affective aspects of instruction. Developing an individual's self-concept, identity, attitudes, and values is as important as learning subject matter. During the last decade science education responded to the needs for curriculum reform. Many new innovative elementary science curriculums were developed as a result. In this decade we believe that science education is continuing to evolve with the needs of society by increasingly emphasizing the affective domain, as partially demonstrated in several of the articles. Today, a truly professional elementary science teacher tends to have a more global view of the individual, one including the realization that the child is a bundle of potential talents and a *person* in the process of *becoming* a mature human.

We wish to express our sincere appreciation to the authors, publishers, and journals for their cooperation in preparation of this book.

RBS
RWB

CONTENTS

Becoming a Better
Elementary Science Teacher

Becoming a Better Elementary Science Teacher Through Understanding of Self

You are in the process of becoming a better elementary science teacher. Along with most people, you probably want to evolve toward human excellence and professional competence. To aid you in the journey, the following articles have been selected. They describe outstanding persons, various personality types, and the characteristics of good science teachers. From the beginning it is important to remember you do not have to be a bad teacher to become a better teacher.

Socrates said, "Know thyself." How well do you know yourself? For example: What do you hope to achieve through science education? What attitudes, values, and prejudices, both positive and negative, do you hold that might help or hinder your science teaching? How do you see your teaching contributing to the development of a fully functioning person?

Dr. Abraham Maslow's work can help you answer some of these questions. He devoted much of his life to investigating individuals manifesting the highest levels of psychological health. From this work he described what could well be an ideal toward which teachers and students might strive. Maslow's term for the mentally healthy individual was *self-actualizer*. A self-actualized person is one who is utilizing the maximum of his potentials, capabilities, and talents. He has become all that he is capable of becoming. Teachers have a role in assisting people to actualize their potentials. They help unfold, reveal, draw out, and develop individuals as fully and completely as possible. Interestingly, the teacher that helps others develop their potentials grows toward self-actualization in the process.

Behavior, both positive and negative, is a function of our beliefs. Dr. O. J. Harvey has investigated the area of belief for a number of years and has found that individuals fall into roughly four major behavior and personality types: authoritarian, anti-authoritarian, peer oriented, and inquiry or neutral/free. These types of individuals are not necessarily good or bad, but are just different personalities. Teachers must learn to accept and value all types of children. An Instructor should assess his own personality and modify it where he thinks it is appropriate.

The characteristics of good teachers are discussed in the closing article of this section. Generally these individuals have good perceptions of themselves, others and the helping relationship. This should provide a good base from which to start a greater understanding of education. Hamachek sets the theme for teachers, as well as this book of readings, when he states:

> Research is beginning to tell us what common sense has always told us; namely, people grow, flourish and develop much more easily when in relationship with someone who projects an inherent trust and belief in their capacity to become what they have the potential to become (see p. 32).

After reading these articles, outline several things you particularly want to change in your behavior so as to better assist children in "Becoming" through science involvement.

1

SELF-ACTUALIZATION AND BEYOND

A. H. Maslow

What I plan to discuss today are ideas that are in midstream rather than ready for formulation into a final version. I find that with my students, and with other people with whom I share these ideas, the notion of self-actualization gets to be almost like a Rorschach ink blot: it frequently tells me more about the person using it than about reality. What I would like to do today is explore some of the nature of self-actualization, not as a grand abstraction, but in terms of the operational meaning of the self-actualizing process. What does self-actualization mean in moment to moment terms? What does it mean on Tuesday at four o'clock?

My investigations on self-actualization (to my horror, dismay, shock, and surprise—the only ones in existence) were not planned to be research and did not start out as research. They started out as the effort of a young intellectual in his twenties to try to understand two of his teachers whom he loved, adored, and admired, and who were very very wonderful people. It was a kind of high IQ devotion. I could not be content simply to adore, but sought to understand why these two people were so different from the run-of-the-mill of people in the world. These two people were Ruth Benedict and Max

Reprinted from an address delivered at the Workshop on the Training of Adult Counselors in Chatham, Massachusetts, May, 1965. The address was printed in Don E. Hamachek (ed.), *Human Dynamics in Psychology and Education—Selected Readings*. Boston: Allyn & Bacon, Inc., 1968, pp. 173–83. Dr. Abraham H. Maslow is deceased. He was Professor of Psychology at Brandeis University.

3

Wertheimer. They were my teachers after I came with a Ph.D. from
the West to New York City, and here were these most remarkable
human beings. My training in psychology equipped me not at all for
understanding them. It was as if they were not quite people but something more than people. My own investigation began as a pre-scientific
thing. I made descriptions and notes on Max Wertheimer, and I made
notes on Ruth Benedict, and when I tried to understand, write about,
and think about my own journal and my own notes, I realized in one
wonderful moment that their two patterns could be generalized. I was
talking about a kind of person, not about two non-comparable individuals. There was wonderful excitement in that. I tried to look to see
if this pattern could be found elsewhere, and I did find it elsewhere,
in one person after another.

By ordinary standards of laboratory research, of rigorous and controlled research, this simply was not research at all. My generalizations
grew out of *my* selection of certain kinds of people. Obviously, other
judges are needed. So far, one man has selected perhaps two dozen
people whom he liked, or admired very much, and thought were wonderful people and then tried to figure them out and found that he was
able to describe a syndrome—the kind of pattern that seemed to fit
all of them. These were people only from Western cultures, people
selected with all kinds of build-in biases. But unreliable as it is, that
was the only operational definition of self-actualizing people as I
described them in my first publication on the subject. After I published
the results of my investigations there appeared perhaps six, eight, or
ten other lines of evidence that supported the findings, not by replication
but by an approach from a different angle. Carl Rogers' findings and
those of his students add up to corroboration for the whole syndrome.
The new work with LSD, all the studies on the effects of therapy,
(good therapy that is), some test results—in fact everything I know
adds up to corroborated support, though not replicated support, for
that study. I personally feel very confident about its major conclusions.
I cannot conceive of any research that would make major changes
in the pattern, though I am sure there will be minor changes. I have
made some of those myself. But my confidence in my rightness is
not a scientific datum. If you question the kind of data I have from
my researches with monkeys and dogs, you are bringing my competence
into doubt or calling me a liar, and I have a right to object. If you
question my findings on self-actualizing people, you may do so because
you don't know very much about the man who selected the people
on whom all the conclusions are based. The conclusions are in the
realm of pre-science, the realm of affirmations that are set forth in
a form that can be put to test. In that sense, they are scientific.

The people I selected for my investigation were older people, people who had lived much of their lives out and were visibly successful. We do not yet know about the applicability of the findings to young people. We do not know what self-actualization means in other cultures, though a study of self-actualization in China is now in process, as well as one in India. We do not know what the findings of these new studies will be but of one thing I have no doubt: when you select out for careful study very fine people, strong people, creative people, saintly people, sagacious people—in fact, exactly the kind of people that I picked out, then you get a different view of mankind. You are asking how tall people can grow, what can a human being perhaps become? And these are the Olympic gold medal winners—the best we have got. Now the fact that somebody can run a hundred yards in less than ten seconds means that in potentiality any baby that is born into the world is, in theory, capable of doing so too. In that sense, any baby that is born into the world can in principle reach the heights that actually exist and can be described. When you look at mankind this way, your thinking about psychology and psychiatry changes radically. For example, 99 percent of what has been written on so-called learning theory is simply irrelevant to a grown human being. Learning theory does not apply to a human being growing as tall as he can. Most of the literature on learning theory deals with what I call "extrinsic learning" to distinguish it from "intrinsic learning." Extrinsic learning means collecting acquisitions to yourself like keys in your pocket or coins that you pick up. Extrinsic learning is adding another association or adding another craft. The process of learning to be the best human being you can be is another business altogether. The far goals for adult education, and for any other education, are the processes, the ways in which we can help people to become all they are capable of becoming. This I call intrinsic learning and I am confining my remarks today entirely to it. That is the way self-actualizing people learn. To help the client achieve such intrinsic learning is the far goal of counseling.

These things I *know* with certainty. There are other things that I feel very confident about—"my smell tells me" so to speak. Yet I have even fewer objective data on these points than I had on those above. Self-actualization is hard enough to define. How much harder it is to ask the question, "Beyond self-actualization, what?" Or, if you will, "Beyond authenticity, what?" Just being honest is, after all, not sufficient in all this. What else can we say of self-actualizing people?

Self-actualizing people are, without one single exception, involved in a cause outside their own skin, in something outside of themselves.

They are devoted, working at something, something which is very precious to them—some calling or vocation in the old sense, the priestly sense. They are working at something which fate has called them to somehow and which they work at and which they love, so that the work-joy dichotomy there disappears. One devoted his life to the law, another to justice, another to beauty or truth. All, in one way or another, devote their lives to the search for what I have called the "Being" values, (B for short), the ultimate values which are intrinsic, which cannot be reduced to anything more ultimate. There are about fourteen of these "B" values including truth and beauty and goodness of the ancients, and perfection, simplicity, comprehensiveness, and several more. These "B" values are described in the appendix to my book, "Religions, Values, and Peak Experiences," which came out about six months ago. They are the values of being. The existence of these "B" values adds a whole set of complications to the structure of self-actualization. These "B" values behave like needs. I have called them *meta-needs*. Deprivation of them breeds certain kinds of pathologies which have not yet been described. I call them *"meta-pathologies"*— the sickness of the soul which comes, e.g., from living among liars all the time and not trusting anyone. And just as we need counselors to help people with the simpler problems of unmet needs, so we may need *meta-counselors* to help the soul-sickness that grows from the unfulfilled *meta-needs*. In certain definable and empirical ways, it is necessary for man to live in beauty rather than ugliness, as it is necessary for him to have food for an aching belly or rest for a weary body. In fact, I would go so far as to claim that these "B" values are the meaning of life for most people, but many people don't even recognize that they have these meta-needs. Part of our job as counselors may be to make them aware of these needs in themselves, just as the classical psychoanalyst has made his patients aware of their instinctoid basic needs. Ultimately, perhaps, we will come to think of ourselves as philosophical or religious counselors.

We try to help our students move and grow toward self-actualization. These youngsters are all wrapped up in value problems. These youngsters are, *in principle,* very wonderful people, though in actuality they often seem to be little more than snotty kids, but I assume (in the face of all behavioral evidence sometimes) that they are in the classical grand sense, idealistic. I assume that they are looking for values and that they would love to have something to devote themselves to, to be patriotic about, to worship, adore, love. These youngsters are making choices from moment to moment of going forward or retrogressing, moving backward or moving toward self-actualization. As a counselor, or a meta-counselor, what can you tell them about becoming more fully themselves? What do you do when you self-actualize? Do you grit your teeth and squeeze? What does self-actualization mean in terms of actual behavior, actual procedure?

First of all, self-actualization means experiencing fully, vividly, selflessly, with full concentration and total absorption. It means experiencing without the self-consciousness of the adolescent. At this moment of experiencing, the person is wholly and fully human. This is a self-actualization moment. This is a moment when the self is actualizing itself. As individuals, we all experience such moments occasionally. As counselors, you can help clients to experience them more often. You can encourage them to become totally absorbed in something and to forget their poses and their defenses and their shyness—to go at it whole hog. From the outside, we can see that this can be a very sweet moment. In these youngsters who are trying to be very tough and cynical and sophisticated, we can see the recovery of some of the guilelessness of childhood, some of the innocence and sweetness of the face can come back as they devote themselves fully to a moment and throw themselves fully into the experiencing of it. The key word for this is "selflessly," and our youngsters suffer from too little selflessness, too much self-consciousness, self-awareness.

Second, let us think of life as a process of choices, one after another at various choice points. At each point there is a progression choice and a regression choice. There may be a movement toward defense, toward safety, toward being afraid, but over on the other side is the growth choice. To make the growth choice instead of the fear choice a dozen times a day is to move a dozen times a day toward self-actualization. Self-actualization is an on-going process; it means making each of the many single choices about whether to lie or be honest, whether to steal or not steal at a particular point, to make each of these choices as a growth choice. This is movement toward self-actualization.

Third, to talk of self-actualization implies that there is a self to be actualized. A human being is not a *tabula rasa,* not a lump of clay or plastocene, but a something which is already there, at least a cartilaginous structure of some kind. A human being is at minimum, his temperament, his biochemical balances, and so on. There is a self, and what I have sometimes referred to as "listening to the impulse voices" means letting the self emerge. Most of us, most of the time (and especially does this apply to children, young people), listen not to ourselves but to Mommy's voice being introjected or Daddy's voice, or to the voice of the Establishment of the Elders, of authority or tradition. As a simple first step toward self-actualization, I sometimes suggest to my students that when they are given a glass of wine and asked how they like it, they don't look at the label on the bottle in order to get the cue about whether or not they should like it, but that instead they close their eyes if possible, and they make a hush, and they look within themselves and try to shut out the noise of the world and then to savor it on their tongues and look to the Supreme Court inside there and *then* come out and say, "I like it" or "I don't like it." That statement is different from the usual kind of phoniness that we all indulge in. At a party recently, I caught myself looking at the label on a bottle and assuring my hostess that she had indeed selected a very good Scotch. But then I caught myself—what was I saying? I knew little about Scotches. I had no idea whether this was good or not, but this kind of thing we all do. Refusing to do it is part of the on-going process of actualizing yourself. Does *your* belly hurt? Or does it feel good? Does this taste good on *your* tongue? Do *you* like lettuce?

Fourth, when in doubt, be honest rather than not. I am covered by that phrase "when in doubt..." so that we need not argue too much about diplomacy. Frequently, when we are in doubt we are not honest. Our college students are not honest much of the time. They are playing games and posing. The boys swagger around trying to look like something out of a movie, and the girls are trying to appear glamorous. They do not take easily to the suggestion to be honest. But looking within one's self for many of the answers implies taking responsibility. That is in itself a great step toward actualization. This matter of responsibility has been little studied. It is not a part of the American Psychological Association's psychology. It doesn't turn up in our textbooks, for who can investigate responsibility in white rats? It is an almost tangible part of psychotherapy. In psychoanalysis you can see it, you can feel it, you know this moment of responsibility. You know what it feels like. This is one of the great steps. Each time one takes responsibility, this is an actualizing of the self.

Fifth, we have talked so far of experiencing without self-awareness, of making the growth choice rather than the fear choice, of listening to the impulse voices and of being honest and taking responsibility. All these things are steps toward self-actualization and all of them guarantee better life choices. Do each of these little things each time the choice point comes and they will add up to better choices about what is constitutionally right for you, what your destiny is, who your wife or husband will be, what your mission in life will be. You cannot choose wisely for a life unless you dare to listen to yourself, *yourself,* at each moment in life, and to say calmly, "No, I don't like such and such."

The art world, in my opinion, has been captured by a small group of opinion and taste makers, whom I feel suspicious about. That is an *ad hominem* judgment, but it seems fair enough for people who set themselves up as able to say, "You like what I like or else you are a fool." We must teach people to listen to their own tastes. Most people don't do it. You rarely hear before a puzzling painting, "That is a puzzling painting." We had a dance program at Brandeis a few nights ago—a weird thing altogether, with electronic music, tapes, and people doing surrealistic and dada things—and when the lights went up everybody looked stunned and nobody knew what to say. In that kind of situation most people will make some smart chatter instead of saying, "I would like to think about this." Making an honest statement involves daring to be different, unpopular, non-conformist. If we cannot teach our students, young or old, about being prepared to be unpopular, we might just as well give up right now at anything. To be courageous rather than afraid is another version of the same thing.

Sixth, self-actualization is not only an end state but it is also the process of actualizing your potentialities at any time, in any amount. It is a matter of becoming smarter by studying if you are an intelligent person, as our college students are. Self-actualization means using your IQ, using your intelligence. It does not mean doing some far-out thing necessarily, but it may mean going up to your dormitory room and sweating, studying, getting the mathematics or physics. Self-actualization can consist of finger exercises at a piano keyboard. Self-actualization means working to do well the thing that you want to do. To become a second-grade physician is not a good path to self-actualization. You want to be first-rate, or as good as you can be.

Seventh, peak experiences are transient moments of self-actualization. They are moments of ecstasy which you cannot buy, cannot guarantee, cannot even seek. You must be as C. S. Lewis wrote, "surprised by joy." But you can set up the conditions so that peak experiences are more likely, or you can perversely set up the conditions so that they are less likely. You can reassure young people about discovering things they do not like to do. Some of our youngsters at Brandeis have come in prepared to be astronauts, and they take physics and math and find out that it's not what they thought. Breaking up an illusion, getting rid of a false notion, learning what they are not good at, learning what their potentialities are *not*—this is also part of discovering what yourself is in fact.

Practically everyone does have peak experiences, only not everyone knows it. Some people wave these small mystical experiences aside. Helping people to recognize these little moments of ecstasy when they happen is one of the jobs of the counselor—or meta-counselor. But, how does one's psyche, with nothing external in the world to point at—there is no blackboard there—look into another person's secret psyche and then try to communicate? You have to work out a new way of communication. I have tried one. It is described in another appendix in that same book, under the title, "Rhapsodic Communications." I think that kind of communication may be more of a model for teaching, counseling, for helping adults to become as fully developed as they can be than the kind we are used to when we see teachers writing on the board. If I love Beethoven, and I hear something in a quartet that you don't, how do I teach you to hear? The noises are there, obviously. But I hear something very, very beautiful and you look blank. You hear the sounds. How do I get you to hear the beauty? That is more our problem of teaching than teaching the A, B, C's, or demonstrating arithmetic on the board, or pointing to a dissection of the frog. These things are external to both people, and one has a pointer and you can both look at the same time. This kind of teaching is easy, the other one much harder, but it is part of our job as counselors. It is meta-counseling.

Eighth, finding out who you are, what you are, what you like, what you don't like, what is good for you and what is bad, where you are going and what your mission is—opening yourself up to yourself, means the exposure of psycho-pathology. It means identifying defenses, and after defenses have been identified, it means encouraging people to give them up. And this is painful, for defenses are against something which is unpleasant, but it is worth while. If the psycho-analytic literature has taught us nothing else, it has taught us that repression is not a good way of solving problems. Let me talk about one defense mechanism that is not mentioned in the psychology text-books, though it is a very important defense mechanism to the snotty and yet idealistic youngster of today. It is the defense mechanism of *de-sacralizing*. These youngsters mistrust the possibility of values and virtues. They feel themselves swindled or thwarted in their lives. Most of them have, in fact, dopey parents whom they don't respect very much, parents who are quite confused about values themselves, and who frequently are simply terrified of their children and who never punish them or stop them from doing things that are wrong. So you have a situation where the youngsters simply despise their elders—often for good and sufficient reason. And the youngsters have learned to make a big generalization and they won't listen to anybody who is grown up, especially if the grownup uses the same words which they've heard from the hypocritical mouth. They have heard their fathers talk about being honest or being brave or being bold and seen their fathers being the opposite of all these things. The youngsters have learned to reduce the person to the concrete object, and to refuse to see what he might be, or refuse to see him in symbolic values, or refuse to see him or her eternally. Our kids have de-sacralized sex, for example. Sex is nothing, it is a natural thing and they have made it so natural that it has lost its poetic qualities in many instances, which means that it has lost practically everything. Self-actualization means giving up this defense mechanism and learning, or being taught, to re-sacralize. (I have had to make up these words because the English language is rotten for good people. It has no decent vocabulary for the virtues. Even the nice words get all smeared up. Love, for instance.)

Re-sacralizing means being willing, once again, to see a person "under the aspect of eternity," as Spinoza says, or to see him in the medieval Christian unitive perception, that is, being able to see the sacred, the eternal, the symbolic. It is to see Woman with a capital W and everything that that implies even when one looks at a particular woman. Another example: you go to medical school and dissect a brain. Certainly something is lost if you don't get awed, but see the brain only as one concrete thing without the unitive perception. Open to re-sacralization, you see it as a sacred object also, see its symbolic value, see it as a figure of speech, see it, so to speak, in its poetic aspects.

Re-sacralization often means an awful lot of corny talk—"very square," the kids would say. But for the counselor, especially for the counselor of older people, where these philosophical questions about religion and the meaning of life come up, this is a most important way of helping the person to move toward self-actualization. The youngsters may say that it is square, the logical positivists may say that it is meaningless, but for the person who seeks your help in this process it is obviously very meaningful and very important and you'd better answer him or you're not doing what it is your job to do.

Put all of these points together and we see that self-actualization is not a matter of one great moment. It is not true that on Thursday at four o'clock the trumpet blows and one steps into the Pantheon forever and altogether. Self-actualization is a matter of degree, of little accessions accumulated one by one. Our students are inclined to wait for some kind of inspiration to strike and then to say that, "At 3:23 on this Thursday I became self-actualized!" People who can be selected as self-actualizing subjects, people who fit the criteria, go about it in these little ways: they listen to their own voices, they take responsibility, they are honest, and they work. They find out who they are and what they are in terms not only of their mission in life but of the way their feet hurt when they wear such and such shoes and whether they do or do not like eggplant or stay up all night if they drink too much beer. All this is what the real self means. They find their own biological natures, their congenital natures which are irreversible or difficult to change.

These are the things people do as they move toward self-actualization. Who, then, is a counselor? And how can he help the people who come to him to make this movement in the direction of growth?

Counseling is not concerned with training nor with molding, nor with teaching in the ordinary sense of telling people what to do and how to do it. It is not concerned with propaganda. It is a Taoistic uncovering. Taoistic means the non-interfering, the "let be." Taoism is not a *laissez-faire* philosophy nor a philosophy of neglect nor of refusal to help or care. As a kind of model of this process we might think of a therapist who, if he is a decent therapist and also a decent human being, would never dream of imposing himself upon his patients or propagandizing in any way, or trying to make the patient into an imitation, or to use himself as a model. What he does, the good clinical therapist, is to help his particular client to unfold, to break through the defenses against his self-knowledge, to recover himself and get to know himself. Ideally, the therapist's rather abstract frame of reference, the textbooks he has read, the schools that he has gone to, his beliefs about the world—these should never be perceptible to the patient. Respectful of the inner nature, the being, the essence of this "younger brother," he would recognize that the best way for him to lead a good life is to be more fully himself. The people we call sick are the people who are not themselves, the people who have built up all sorts of neurotic defenses against being human. And just as it makes no difference to the rosebush whether the gardener is Italian or French or Swedish, so it should make no difference to the younger brother how his helper learned to be a helper. What the helper has to give are certain services that are independent of his being Swedish or Catholic or Mohammedan or Freudian or whatever he is.

These basic concepts include, imply, and are completely in accord with the basic concepts of Freudian psycho-dynamics. It is a Freudian principle that unconscious aspects of the self are repressed and that the finding of the true self requires the uncovering of these unconscious aspects. Implicit is a belief that truth heals much. Learning to break through one's repressions, to know one's self, to hear the impulse voices, to uncover the triumphant nature, to reach knowledge, insight, and the truth—these are the requirements.

A ten-year-old paper by Lawrence Kubie, "The Forgotten Man in Education," originally published in the *Harvard Education Review,* made long ago the point that one ultimate goal of education is to help the person become a human being, as fully human as he can possibly be. If you do not accept the importance of the unconscious and work to do away with repression and defenses, then education is missing its ultimate goal.

I have used the words "therapy," "psychotherapy," and "patient." Actually, I hate all those words and I hate the medical model that they imply because the medical model suggests that the person who comes to the counselor is a sick person, beset by disease, by illness, seeking a cure, whereas, actually, of course, we hope that the counselor will be the person who helps to foster the self-actualization of people rather than helping to cure a disease.

The helping model has to give way, too; it just doesn't fit. It makes us think of the counselor as the person or the professional who knows, reaching down from his privileged position above to the poor jerks below who don't know and have to be helped in some way, the poor cripples who don't talk back much. Nor is the counselor to be a teacher, in the usual sense, because what teachers have specialized in and gotten to be very good at, is what I have called "extrinsic learning," whereas the process of growing into the best human being you can be is, instead, intrinsic learning.

The existential therapists have wrestled with this question of models, and I can recommend to you James Bugental's book, *Beyond Authenticity, What?,* for a discussion of the matter. Jim Bugental suggests that we call counseling or therapy "ontogogy" which means trying to help people to grow to their fullest possible height. Perhaps that's a better word than the one I once suggested, a word derived from a German author, *"psychogogy,"* which means the education of the psyche. Whatever the word we use, I think that the concept we will eventually have to come to is one that Alfred Adler suggested a long, long time ago when he spoke of the "older brother." The older brother is the loving person who takes responsibility, just as you do for your young kid brother. Of course you know more, you've lived longer, but you are not qualitatively different, you are not in another realm of discourse, and you help him in particular ways. Earlier I used the word "horticultural." I hope you caught the reference there, the idea of helping onions to grow to be onions and not trying to change them over into turnips. Let me give you another example of the kind of thing I am talking about:

If a young man wants to be a professional prizefighter, he goes to some professional gymnasium, offers himself to the manager, and says, "I would like to be a boxer." And then the manager, characteristically, I'm told (I don't know, I've never tried this myself), will get one of his experienced fighters and say, "Take him into the ring and try him out." The instructions are always "stretch him." That is, let him go as far as he can, see how hard he can hit, find out the hardest he can possibly hit, find out how much he can take, see how fast he is, see how good his reflexes are—stretch him to his fullest capacity and get some notion there of the real self—the intrinsic self I was talking about before. This is the job of finding capacity, of determining whether this young man does seem to have promise (and that itself is an instinctoid statement). Now suppose he's good, he's fast, he's strong, he's powerful, and so on. If he looks good, do you think that the manager gives him a manual to read and tells him, "Now you forget everything you know and you start at Point 1 and you go on to Points 2 and 3 and 4? No. He takes this young man and tries to train him to be the best possible kind of fighter that he already is. He tries to improve him and he tries to make him better than he is, *in his own style*. See how different this is from the "teaching somebody who doesn't know nothin'," model! A child comes along, one who doesn't know any French at all. You pour it into him. You start from scratch. But especially with adults we are not in that position. We already have a start, we already have capacities, talents, directions, missions, callings, and then the job is, if we are to take this model seriously, to help them to be more perfectly what they already are, to be more full, more actualizing, more realizing in fact what they are in potentiality.

2

BELIEFS AND BEHAVIOR:
SOME IMPLICATIONS FOR EDUCATION

O. J. Harvey

As one who has "backed" into education, I have become convinced that, if the social psychologist wants to have any influence on society, the school system has to be among his crucial concerns. It is obvious that the importance of the school is increasing as other institutions in our society undergo rapid change and some move toward their possible demise. As a result of great personal and social changes, man is facing questions and problems he has never faced before, ones for which past approaches and solutions are wholly inappropriate, but ones which must be solved if man and his institutions are to survive in ways which we now understand and value.

Clearly, education is one institution that should concern itself with these problems. I have observed in many schools throughout this country an eagerness to tackle these problems and an openness to their implications for change. I believe I have observed this eagerness and openness to be highest at the elementary level, decreasing as the college level is approached and stopping almost altogether in graduate schools. As I see it, universities not only have not initiated changes aimed at fostering attitudes toward flexibility and change, they have responded slowly and grudgingly to others' efforts at change. If true, this is rather

Reprinted from *The Science Teacher, 37*, December 1970, pp. 10–73. Dr. O. J. Harvey is Professor of Social Psychology, University of Colorado, Boulder. Colorado.

tragic, since universities, at least as they would have the public believe, are supposed to spearhead such educational innovations.

When we talk about change in education, however, we must first answer the question: "Education for what?" The answer depends, of course, on the objectives we have for education, more particularly, on the kinds of product we wish to turn out in terms of capacities and skills. Perhaps the most crucial skills we need to impart are those that equip our students with the ability to cope with the world of tomorrow. At first glance this sounds sophomoric, in that we have no idea of what tomorrow will bring. But the very fact that we do not know provides us with crucial information. It tells us, for example, that the only things of which we can be certain are uncertainty, the occurrence of the unexpected, and stress from the incompatibility of old solutions with the demands of new problems. It says, therefore, that education should aim at developing attitudes in both students and teachers that foster openness, sensitivity to change, and the ability to withstand stress and to behave adaptively, flexibly, and creatively.

In an attempt to understand how these skills operate and how they may be developed, we have conducted experiments in the laboratory that involve such skills and have examined classroom environments that enhance and retard them.

In our research we have focused mainly on how an individual's *belief system* (i.e., his deeply held attitudes or values) affect these skills, how such belief systems come to be formed, and ways in which they may be changed in the direction of greater openness, stress tolerance, and creativity.

We have examined belief systems in terms of two basic aspects, *content* and *structure*. Content includes the referents toward which one holds beliefs or attitudes, such as God, oneself, a stone, or any object of direct or indirect experience. Structure relates to *how we organize* our beliefs and includes such attributes as openness-closedness, consistency-inconsistency, and complexity-simplicity. By considering content and structure together, Dave Hunt, Harry Schroder, and I in our 1961 book, *Conceptual Systems and Personality Organization,* deduced and treated several such systems. However, here I will discuss only the four major systems on which most of my own research has concentrated, indicating how they operate, the environments that seem to produce them, and some of their implications for education: for classroom environments, student-teacher interaction, and teacher selection, training, and retraining.

System 1 is characterized by such things as high concreteness of beliefs; high absolutism toward rules and roles; a strong tendency to view the world in an overly simplistic, either-or, black-white way; a strong belief in supernaturalism and inherent truth; a strongly positive attitude toward tradition, authority, and persons of power as guidelines to thought and action; an inability to change set, role play, put oneself in another's boots, and to think and act creatively under conditions of high involvement and stress.

One illustration of the absolutism with which System 1 representatives conceive rules is provided by Piaget in his study of moral development in children. When asked why they played marbles the way they did, the young children replied in essence:

> "That's the way marbles are played."
> "What do you mean, that's the way they are played?"
> "Those are the rules."
> "Why are those the rules?"
> "Well, that's just the way they are."

This tautological circularity, this attribution of inherent truth, this incapacity to step outside the system and look at things from a different point of view is, to say the least, deplorably unpragmatic. For example, I often have students write papers on "How can I know that I know?" The answers of those with a System 1 orientation center around something like "Certitude equals validity." That is, "I feel strongly; therefore, it's right." I try to point out that while this seems to be a pervasive assumption, its oversimplification and divorcement from outside points of view have led to great atrocities under its guise, such as those of Hitler and other zealots.

Evidence of role absolutism and deference toward status and power is manifested by the System 1 representative in his tendency to pay little attention to the logic of what is being said or to the expertise of the one saying it, but instead to make his decisions and actions conform to those espoused by a person of power and high status, irrespective of the latter's expertise and informational basis for his espousal. The old adage that "It's not what is said but who says it that matters" seems to be particularly valid for the person of System 1 beliefs.

Representatives of System 2 are only slightly less dogmatic, evaluative, and inflexible than System 1 individuals. However, they tend to have strong negative attitudes toward institutions, traditions, and the social referents toward which System 1 persons are strongly positive. Also, representatives of System 2 are the lowest of the four groups in self-esteem and the highest in alienation and cynicism, wanting and needing keenly to trust and rely upon authority and other persons, but fearing to do so because of potential loss of personal control and exploitation. Thus, for example, Rupert Brooke found that while Alcoholics Anonymous was quite effective in controlling the alcoholism of persons from Systems 1 and 3, it failed almost completely in this objective for the System 2 representative. Whereas the emphasis of AA upon religion and dependency on God appeared to assist the System 1 alcoholic, and the stressing of friendship and interpersonal dependencies seemed to help control the drinking of the System 3 person (for reasons to be noted), these same factors appeared to reduce the effectiveness of AA to almost nothing for the System 2 alcoholic. As I hope to elaborate later, we have observed in our classroom studies that the placement of a System 2 student with a teacher from System 1 or System 3, especially the former, almost invariably results in severe interpersonal conflict and social discord, with the System 2 student being more likely than others to resolve the conflict by dropping out of school.

One other interesting and seemingly paradoxical behavior of the System 2 representative centers around his use of authority and power. While he denounces power figures and their use of power when he is of low status and without power, he appears to use authority and power quite rigidly and abusively once he gets them. Espousal of the cause of the weak and disenfranchised by the System 2 individual when he is of low power doesn't seem to stop him from using power unfairly once he acquires it. In line with this is the finding by Kaats that upperclassmen at the Air Force Academy classified as System 2 were rated by lower classmen as using their authority more unfairly than were representatives of any other belief system. Similarly one is reminded of Camus's observation in *The Rebel,* as well as the fact that System 2 leaders in the French Revolution spearheaded the introduction of the Reign of Terror.

A System 3 belief system is reflected in a strong outward emphasis upon friendship, interpersonal harmony, and mutual aid. This takes the more subtle form of efforts at manipulation through establishing dependency, of oneself on others, and of others on oneself. Those whom the System 3 representative would have dependent upon him are persons of low status and low power, the underdog whom the System 2 representative extols and then abuses. Those on whom the System 3 individual would be dependent are individuals of high status, power, and expertise. The apparent need of the System 3 person to control others through dependency relations tends to be guised under the desire and need to help others. Thus we should expect, and some of our evidence supports this, that members of the helping professions, such as clinical psychology, social work, etc., overly represent the System 3 orientation. While I have no hard data on which to base an opinion, my casual observations lead me to suspect that the majority of persons spearheading the drive for widespread sensitivity training represent System 3 functioning.

System 4, the most abstract and open-minded of the four belief systems, manifests itself in information seeking, pragmatism, a problem-solving orientation, and a higher ability to change set, withstand stress, and behave creatively. Representatives of this system are neither pro-rule, like System 1 persons, nor anti-rule, like System 2 individuals. They are for rules, structure, and organization when these are utilitarian and instrumental to problem solving and attaining an objective; but they want none of these for its own sake.

As I will elaborate later, System 4 representatives comprise a very small minority, no more than 7 percent, of the several thousand individuals, mainly college students and teachers, whom we have studied.

Let me turn now to a brief description of the social conditions and developmental histories that seem to produce these different belief systems or ideologies.

System 1 evolves from a training history in which the individual is restricted in the exploration of his environment, especially those aspects having to do with values and issues of great personal and social involvement. The individual's rewards and approval are contingent upon his responses conforming to omnipotently and omnisciently imposed standards which emanate from social prescriptions and not firsthand experience. Consequently, representatives of this system develop ways of placating omnipotence, shown often by superstition, supernaturalism, rigid adherence to rules, high evaluativeness and punitiveness toward "deviant" values and behavior, and a strong reliance upon the defense of institutional authority.

The System 2 representative also appears to come from a background in which, like System 1, the parents have behaved omnipotently and omnisciently, but, unlike System 1, in an inconsistent and, to the child, capricious and arbitrary manner, causing the child to distrust authority, fear uncertainty, and to be suspicious of even acts of friendliness until an unquestionable basis of trust has been established. While needing structure, on the one hand, the System 2 individual is so distrustful of its source that he tends to rebel against, even attempts to destroy, it in many of its manifestations, including religion, patriotism, and other institutional expressions.

I would like to add parenthetically (and my parenthetical addition may be more important than anything else I say here) that the conditions fostering System 2 functioning are extremely rampant in our society today. From the point of view of the blacks, the Mexican-American, the college student, and many other minority groups—including the public school teacher, let me add—the wielders of power and social control in this country tend to behave omnipotently, omnisciently, and highly arbitrarily. Indeed, there is a basis for such perception, at least a psychological basis if not a logical one.

In America we are taught that men are created equal. Parents teach it. Schools teach it. Institutions proclaim it. And wars, holy wars, are fought under its banner. Yet all around us, men are not equal. Aspirations of minority groups are fanned. Within sight, almost within reach of goals of equality, minority members are told that they must wait. They are encouraged to participate in mainstream America; and then their efforts at achieving along these lines are blocked and frustrated by a variety of obstacles, some imposed deliberately and others, the inadvertent consequences of our social system. It is true that, in an objective sense, many more freedoms are enjoyed by minority group members today than were available a few years ago, before the 1954 Supreme Court decision on segregation, for example. But in relation to the aspirations that have been encouraged, *less* freedom exists. This is a condition social psychologists speak of as *relative deprivation*. In a large-scale study during World War II, for example, it was found that while Army Aircorpsmen were actually promoted almost twice as rapidly as Military Policemen, the former were much more dissatisfied with the promotion rate than were the latter. Moreover, psychologists have demonstrated in a wide variety of studies the *goal gradient phenomenon*, the tendency for the pull or attraction of a goal to increase as its attainment becomes closer. Also, of course, the closer one gets to the goal, the greater the frustration from failure. Thus blocking the goals of participation of minority groups just when first class citizenship is within sight and possible grasp is more devastating psychologically than blockage when the goal is not in sight.

Clearly, it is incumbent upon all of us with any power at all to help remove the disparity between the aspirations our society creates and the freedom it allows to certain people in achieving those aspirations. Otherwise we are guilty of hypocrisy, a hypocrisy that results from a disparity between espoused values and actual practices. It is this disparity that constitutes the generation gap; not the disparity between ages; nor the disparity between espoused values. It is the gap between what we are taught to dream as Americans and the way we fail to carry out these values that has disenchanted and embittered so many in this country. In line with this, our own research has found an increased incidence of System 2 belief systems.

System 3 functioning tends to result from overprotection of the developing child in which one or both parents, more often the mother, serves as a buffer between the child and the environment, preventing him from getting realistic feedback from his world and fostering in him methods of coping through dependency and manipulation. The mother tends to have a great need to be needed and to control the child, which she achieves through trying to convince the child that he will fail without her help, often creating a situation in which the child actually fails in order to reinforce her contention of indispensability. She exercises control by creating a need for the child and then satisfying this need which the child otherwise would not have had.

Unlike the environment that produces System 1, in which the father is the dominant parent, in environments producing System 2 and System 3 the mother is more dominant. In the case of System 2, the parents tend to be in strong disagreement and conflict over most involving issues, with the father making only occasional forays into the child-rearing arena, and then mainly in a punitive or divisive way. In the case of System 3, the father tends more to leave the field and passively leave the child rearing to the mother.

System 4 evolves from an environment in which the child is encouraged to explore both his physical world and the world of values and to derive his own beliefs and personal standards from his own reasoning and direct experience instead of from omnipotently and arbitrarily imposed social norms. Such exploration takes place within the context of family warmth and where the child is valued in his own right rather than in terms of the reflections he can cast upon the family. Both parents participate fairly equally in the child-rearing decisions, interpersonal disagreements are dealt with openly, explanation is used frequently as both punishment and reward for the child. When punishing the child, the parents distinguish between the child and the act for which he is being punished.

Let me turn now to some of our research findings and theorizing on belief systems and education.

First, you might be interested in the distribution of systems we have found. From the study of several thousand liberal arts students approximately 35 percent have been found to represent System 1, 15 percent to represent System 2, 20 percent to represent System 3, and 7 percent to represent System 4. Among undergraduate education majors approximately 45 percent are System 1, 5 percent are System 2, 25 percent are System 3, and 5 percent are System 4. Among practicing teachers the percentage of System 1 goes up to 55; the incidence of System 2 practically disappears; System 3 reduces to 15 percent and the percentage of System 4 shrinks to 4. Seventy-five percent of principals and 90 percent of superintendents in Colorado, Wyoming, Utah, and New Mexico have been found to represent System 1. I am sure you won't be surprised to learn that not a single representative of System 2 has been found among principals and superintendents in this area. You might be surprised, however, that from among several hundred teachers only one representative of System 2 has been found in our area, and he was busily engaged in trying to form a teachers union. One suspects that the only school system in which System 2 representatives will exist in any sizable numbers is one in which the teachers organization is strong and thus serves as a protective buffer between the teachers and the administration, whose top members, at least, are likely to represent System 1.

Liberal arts students as well as Air Force Academy cadets have been found to become slightly, but significantly, more abstract from the freshman to the senior year. On the other hand, studies carried out at two major teacher-training institutions, one in Colorado and one in Illinois, found that the highest incidence of System 4 functioning occurred at the sophomore level and decreased from there all the way through graduate training. This last result, moreover, appears to be the consequence not of student attrition but of the socializing influences of the schools of education investigated.

A study of LeMarr on the relationship of principals' belief systems to their hiring preferences found that System 1 principals gave more weight to the clubs and organizations to which prospective teachers belonged than to their academic credentials.

We have conducted a series of studies on how teachers' belief systems influence both the classroom environments and the students.

In the first study, carried out by Harvey, White, Prather, Alter, and Hoffmeister (2), kindergarten and first-grade teachers representing Systems 1, 3, and 4 were rated by trained observers on 26 dimensions having to do with such things as enlistment of student participation, encouragement of student responsibility, teaching of concepts instead of isolated facts, perceptiveness, rule orientation, and punitiveness. A factor analysis of the rating scale yielded two major factors, Fostering Exploration and Dictatorialness. The first one included such items as attention to the individual child, teaching of concepts, ingenuity in use of resources, and encouragement of creativity and diversity. Dictatorialness included such items as personal need for structure, use of rules without explanation, and coldness and inflexibility. System 4 teachers scored the highest on Fostering Exploration and the lowest on Dictatorialness; the reverse was true for System 1 teachers; and System 3 teachers scored in between.

A second study by Harvey, Prather, White, and Hoffmeister (1) replicated the preceding one and in addition showed the differential influence of teachers of different belief systems upon their students, who again were kindergartners and first-graders. A factor analysis of the ratings made of the students on 30 dimensions by trained observers yielded seven factors, which we termed (1) Cooperation, (2) Student Involvement, (3) Activity Level, (4) Nurturance Seeking, (5) Achievement Level, (6) Helpfulness, and (7) Concreteness of Response. Students of System 4 teachers, in contrast especially to students of System 1 teachers, were more cooperative, more involved in classroom activities, more active, higher in achievement, more helpful, less nurturance seeking, and less concrete in their responses.

To answer the question of whether or not students themselves perceive teachers of different belief systems much as trained observers do, Misha Prather, Carolie Coates, and I had students, from kindergarten through the sixth grade, make ratings of teachers classified as System 1, 3, or 4 on dimensions akin to those used by trained observers. Without elaborating either the methodology or the results, I can say the answer to our question was affirmative. A factor analysis of the ratings made by the students yielded five factors: (1) Fostering Exploration, which included such items as "She likes to have us think of new approaches," "She explains 'why' we should learn the work," and "We often help plan the work." (2) Fostering Rigidity, comprised of such items as "She only talks about things that are in the books," "We have to do things the same way all the time," and "She thinks she is always right." (3) Fostering Hostility, containing such items as "When she leaves the room we get noisy," "We fight a lot when we are in her class," and "Some children play tricks when they think she isn't looking." (4) Fostering Cooperation, consisting of such items as "She lets us help each other," "She often lets us talk to each other in class," and "She lets us think up our own projects." and (5) Fostering *Esprit de Corps,* constituted by such items as "She is fun to be with in school," "Most of the children in our class like her," and "We like to work hard when working with her."

System 4 teachers were rated the highest by their students on Fostering Exploration, Fostering Cooperation, and Fostering *Esprit de Corps.* System 1 teachers were rated the highest on Fostering Rigidity, and System 3 teachers were rated the highest on Fostering Hostility. Supplementary evidence suggests that System 3 teachers, more than the others, tended to pursue a classroom policy of *laissez faire* which, among other things, resulted in less structure and greater absence of direction than most of the students could utilize effectively.

This brings us to what I consider to be one of the most crucial questions in education: What kind of classroom environment best fosters growth toward System 4 functioning in different kinds of children?

This, I think, is the heart of individualized instruction, not the policy of *laissez faire* nor indiscriminate permissiveness which many, especially System 3 representatives, apparently mistake for individualized instruction. One of our long-range objectives, still largely unrealized, is to assign students to teachers in terms of the belief systems and other personality attributes of both. Let me stress that, with the exception of System 4, this does *not* mean putting together teachers and students of the same belief systems. For example, a System 1 teacher would be likely to increase the need of the System 1 child for structure, rules, and external guides. The System 2 teacher would be likely to increase the rebellious and destructive tendencies of the System 2 child. The System 3 teacher probably would reinforce the need for dependency and the manipulative tendencies of the System 3 child.

Yet an environment needs to be provided which will meet these individual needs in such a way that the children can grow out of them. This probably means providing the child one kind of environment earlier and a different kind later. To foster growth in a System 1 child, for example, one should probably give him, at the outset, high structure and detailed teacher guidance. Gradually the external guides and pressures should be removed and the child encouraged to be independent and to react to the absence of external guides and constraints by generating his own approaches and solutions. A System 2 child should also be provided a great deal of structure at the outset, but it *must* be coupled with warmth, fairness, and functional explanations for rules and the teacher's behavior instead of these being imposed and exercised without apparent reason. Gradually, but at a pace probably faster than that for a System 1 child, the System 2 child is moved toward independence—the inclinations toward which he already strongly possesses. Similarly the System 3 child should not be forced to give up his dependency behavior abruptly but should be encouraged more and more to be independent and do things for himself.

These are but brief examples. Yet they suffice to illustrate the complexity of the problem and the need for a teacher to wear many hats, as it were, to give one kind of child one thing and another child another. This is the kind of problem Prime Minister Nehru had in mind in his concept of *guided democracy,* which implied his provision to the Indian people of more freedom than they were comfortable with at the beginning but less than he and others wanted them to have, with a gradual movement toward more and more freedom. Figuratively, this might be like wading in the water that was so deep one had to tiptoe to keep the water out of his nose but in the process grew taller.

Our observations would indicate that only a System 4 teacher is multifaceted and flexible enough to provide the kind of individualized environments needed by children of different belief systems. Yet any thought of filling the classroom with System 4 teachers, as attractive as that might be to many of us, is wholly unrealistic, if for no other reason than that there aren't that many System 4 individuals around. While I feel certain that we should make strong efforts at bringing System 4 individuals into teaching, we must also proceed with teacher retraining programs aimed, at least, at imparting some of the skills necessary for individualized instruction along the lines suggested. Some of the seemingly simple yet significant things we might help a System 1 teacher to achieve, for example, are to become less rule oriented, to offer explanations for why things are to be done in certain ways, to become less upset and punitive when a rule is violated and to become comfortable with less structure and guidance herself. So far we have had some success along these lines, although our efforts in teacher retraining are only getting underway.

To attain the proper pairing of students and teachers by belief systems requires, among other things, adequate measures for both. We presently have two quite good tests for classifying teachers into different belief systems, one called the "This I Believe" Test (TIB) and the other the Conceptual Systems Test (CST). The TIB requires the individual to write his beliefs about 12 or so referents of high involvement, such as "the American way of life," "religion," "marriage," "hippies," and "extra-marital sex." From the novelty, openness, and number of alternatives expressed in these responses individuals can be scored into one of the four major belief systems I discussed or into some combination of two or more systems. The CST is an objective test, with the respondent indicating on a six-point scale his degree of agreement or disagreement with each item. Seven major factors have been extracted from the CST: Supernaturalism or Divine Fate Control; Need for Structure-Simplicity; Need for Sociability or Contact with Others; Need to Help Others; Moral Absolutism; Interpersonal Aggression; and General Distrust.

These two measures are quite good down through high school but inadequate below that. Misha Prather, Carolie Coates, and I have developed the first version of an objective test, using 900 kindergartners through sixth-graders, that looks promising for the younger children, the level of greatest concern if we are to try early to pair students and teachers in terms of their belief systems.

Omitting the methodology, let me say that we obtained four factors from this scale, each one of which appears to coincide with one of the four belief systems: The factor that sounds much like System 1 is the one we might term Need for Structure which consists of such items as "I do not like to work by myself," "I do not like to find things out for myself," and "I like to be told exactly what to do."

What we think may be a System 2 factor we have termed Hostility, and it consists of such items as "I'd like to fight anyone who pushes me around," "If I could I'd fight with lots of people," and "I don't get along well with my teacher." The apparent System 3 factor we have labeled Sociability, and it contains such items as "I like almost everybody in class," "I like to work with other children," and "I feel bad when other children get mad at me." The probable System 4 factor, termed Independence, consists of such items as "The class doesn't bother me when it is noisy," "I don't get worried when I don't know what is going on," and "I don't like to be told exactly what to do."

Using these measures, we found that children of different personalities reacted differently to teachers of different belief systems. For example, students with a high need for structure and guidance reacted negatively to System 3 and even System 4 teachers, reporting that these teachers did not give them freedom. The reverse was true for children low in need for structure and high in independence. These interesting findings suggest that, from a subjective definition, freedom is the provision of an environment that meets the person's individual needs—whether this means (from an outside point of view) providing external structure and restraints or allowing the person largely to make his own decisions.

References

(1) Harvey, O. J., M. Prather, B. J. White, and J. Hoffmeister, "Teachers' Beliefs, Classroom Atmosphere and Student Performance." *American Educational Research Journal, 5,* 1968, pp. 151–66.

(2) Harvey, O. J., B. J. White, M. Prather, R. Alter, and J. Hoffmeister, "Teachers' Belief Systems and Preschool Atmospheres." *Journal of Educational Psychology, 57,* December 1966, pp. 373–81.

3

CHARACTERISTICS OF GOOD TEACHERS AND IMPLICATIONS FOR TEACHER EDUCATION

Don Hamachek

It is, I think, a sad commentary about our educational system that it keeps announcing both publicly and privately that "good" and "poor" teachers cannot be distinguished one from the other. Probably no issue in education has been so voluminously researched as has teacher effectiveness and considerations which enhance or restrict this effectiveness. Nonetheless, we still read that we cannot tell the good guys from the bad guys. For example, Biddle and Ellena (2) in their book, *Contemporary Research on Teacher Effectiveness,* begin by stating that "the problem of teacher effectiveness is so complex that no one today knows what *The Competent Teacher* is." I think we *do* know what the competent—or effective, or good, or whatever you care to call him—teacher is, and in the remainder of this paper I will be as specific as possible in citing *why* I think we know along with implications for our teacher-education programs.

What the Research Says

By and large, most research efforts aimed at investigating teacher effectiveness have attempted to probe one or more of the following dimensions of teacher personality and behavior: 1) personal characteristics,

Reprinted from *Phi Delta Kappan,* February 1969, pp. 341–45. Mr. Don Hamachek is Associate Professor of Educational Psychology, Michigan State University, East Lansing, Michigan.

27

2) instructional procedures and interaction styles, 3) perceptions of self, 4) perceptions of others. Because of space limits this is by no means an exhaustive review of the research related to the problem, but it is, I think, representative of the kind and variety of research findings linked to questions of teacher effectiveness.

Personal Characteristics of Good Versus Poor Teachers

We would probably agree that it is quite possible to have two teachers of equal intelligence, training, and grasp of subject matter who nevertheless differ considerably in the results they achieve with students. Part of the difference can be accounted for by the effect of a teacher's personality on the learners. What kinds of personality do students respond to?

Hart (7) conducted a study based upon the opinions of 3725 high school seniors concerning best-liked and least-liked teachers and found a total of 43 different reasons for "liking Teacher A best" and 30 different reasons for "liking Teacher Z least." Not surprisingly, over 51 percent of the students said that they liked best those teachers who were "helpful in school work, who explained lessons and assignments clearly, and who used examples in teaching." Also, better than 40 percent responded favorably to teachers with a "sense of humor." Those teachers assessed most negatively were "unable to explain clearly, were partial to brighter students, and had superior, aloof, overbearing attitudes." In addition, over 50 percent of the respondents mentioned behaviors such as "too cross, crabby, grouchy, and sarcastic" as reasons for disliking many teachers. Interestingly enough, mastery of subject matter, which is vital but badly overemphasized by specialists, ranked sixteenth on both lists. Somehow students seem willing to take more or less for granted that a teacher "knows" his material. What seems to make a difference is the teacher's personal style in *communicating* what he knows. Studies by Witty (14) and Bousfield (3) tend to support these conclusions at both the high school *and* college level.

Having desirable personal qualities is one thing, but what are the results of rigorous tests of whether the teachers having them makes any difference in the performance of students?

Cogan (4) found that warm, considerate teachers got an unusual amount of original poetry and art from their high school students. Reed (10) found that teachers higher in a capacity for warmth favorably affected their pupils' interests in science. Using scores from achievement tests as their criterion measure, Heil, Powell, and Feifer (8) compared various teacher-pupil personality combinations and found that the well-integrated (healthy, well-rounded, flexible) teachers were most effective with *all* types of students. Spaulding (12) found that the self-concepts of elementary school children were apt to be higher and more positive in classrooms in which the teacher was "socially integrative" and "learner supportive."

In essence, I think the evidence is quite clear when it comes to sorting out good or effective from bad or ineffective teachers on the basis of personal characteristics. Effective teachers appear to be those who are, shall we say, "human" in the fullest sense of the word. They have a sense of humor, are fair, empathetic, more democratic than autocratic, and apparently are more able to relate easily and naturally to students on either a one-to-one or group basis. Their classrooms seem to reflect miniature enterprise operations in the sense that they are more open, spontaneous, and adaptable to change. Ineffective teachers apparently lack a sense of humor, grow impatient easily, use cutting, ego-reducing comments in class, are less well-integrated, are inclined to be somewhat authoritarian, and are generally less sensitive to the needs of their students. Indeed, research related to authoritarianism suggests that the bureaucratic conduct and rigid overtones of the ineffective teacher's classroom are desperate measures to support the weak pillars of his own personality structure.

Instructional Procedures and Interaction Styles of
Good Versus Poor Teachers.

If there really are polar extremes such as "good" or "poor" teachers, then we can reasonably assume that these teachers differ not only in personal characteristics but in the way they conduct themselves in the classroom.

Flanders (6) found that classrooms in which achievement and attitudes were superior were likely to be conducted by teachers who did not blindly pursue a single behavioral-instructional path to the exclusion of other possibilities. In other words, the more successful teachers were better able to range along a continuum of interaction styles which varied from fairly active, dominative support on the one hand to a more reflective, discriminating support on the other. Interestingly, those teachers who were *not* successful were the very ones who were inclined to use the same interaction styles in a more or less rigid fashion.

Barr (1) discovered that not only did poor teachers make more assignments than good teachers but, almost without exception, they made some sort of textbook assignment as part of their unyielding daily procedure. The majority of good teachers used more outside books and problem-project assignments. When the text was assigned they were more likely to supplement it with topics, questions, or other references.

Research findings related to interaction styles variously called "learner-centered" or "teacher-centered" point to similar conclusions. In general, it appears that the amount of cognitive gain is largely unaffected by the autocratic or democratic tendencies of the instructor. However, when affective gains are considered, the results are somewhat different. For example, Stern (13) reviewed 34 studies comparing nondirective with directive instruction and concluded:

> Regardless of whether the investigator was concerned with attitudes toward the cultural out group, toward other participants in the class, or toward the self, the results generally have indicated that nondirective instruction facilitates a shift in a more favorable, acceptant direction.

When it comes to classroom behavior, interaction patterns, and teaching styles, good or effective teachers seem to reflect more of the following behaviors:

1. Willingness to be flexible, to be direct or indirect as the situation demands
2. Ability to perceive the world from the student's point of view
3. Ability to "personalize" their teaching
4. Willingness to experiment, to try out new things
5. Skill in asking questions (as opposed to seeing self as a kind of answering service)
6. Knowledge of subject matter and related areas
7. Provision of well-established examination procedures
8. Provision of definite study helps
9. Reflection of an appreciative attitude (evidenced by nods, comments, smiles, etc.)
10. Use of conversational manner in teaching—informal, easy style.

Self-Perceptions of Good Versus Poor Teachers

We probably do not have to go any further than our own personal life experiences to know that the way we see, regard, and feel about ourselves has an enormous impact on both our private and public lives. How about good and poor teachers? How do they see themselves?

Ryans (11) found that there are, indeed, differences between the self-related reports of teachers with high emotional stability and those with low emotional stability. For example, the more emotionally stable teachers 1) more frequently named self-confidence and cheerfulness as dominant traits in themselves, 2) said they liked active contact with other people, 3) expressed interests in hobbies and handicrafts, 4) reported their childhoods to be happy experiences.

On the other hand, teachers with lower emotional maturity scores 1) had unhappy memories of childhood, 2) seemed *not* to prefer contact with others, 3) were more directive and authoritarian, 4) expressed less self-confidence.

We can be even more specific. Combs (5), in his book *The Professional Education of Teachers,* cites several studies which reached similar conclusions about the way good teachers typically see themselves, as follows:

1. Good teachers see themselves as identified with people rather than withdrawn, removed, apart from, or alienated from others.
2. Good teachers feel basically adequate rather than inadequate. They do not see themselves as generally unable to cope with problems.
3. Good teachers feel trustworthy rather than untrustworthy. They see themselves as reliable, dependable individuals with the potential for coping with events as they happen.
4. Good teachers see themselves as wanted rather than unwanted. They see themselves as likable and attractive (in a personal, not a physical sense) as opposed to feeling ignored and rejected.
5. Good teachers see themselves as worthy rather than unworthy. They see themselves as people of consequence, dignity, and integrity as opposed to feeling they matter little, can be overlooked and discounted.

In the broadest sense of the word, good teachers are more likely to see themselves as good people. Their self-perceptions are, for the most part, positive, tinged with an air of optimism and colored with tones of healthy self-acceptance. I dare say that self-perceptions of good teachers are not unlike the self-perceptions of any basically healthy person, whether he be a good bricklayer, a good manager, a good doctor, a good lawyer, a good experimental psychologist, or you name it. Clinical evidence has told us time and again that *any* person is more apt to be happier, more productive, and more effective when he is able to see himself as fundamentally and basically "enough."

Perceptions of Others by Good Versus Poor Teachers

Research is showing us that not only do good and poor teachers view themselves differently, there are also some characteristic differences in the way they perceive others. For example, Ryans (11) reported several studies which have produced findings that are in agreement when it comes to sorting out the differences between how good and poor teachers view others. He found, among other things, that outstandingly "good" teachers rated significantly higher than notably "poor" teachers in at least five different ways with respect to how they viewed others. The good teachers had 1) more favorable opinions of students, 2) more favorable opinions of democratic classroom behavior, 3) more favorable opinions of administrators and colleagues, 4) a greater expressed liking for personal contacts with other people, 5) more favorable estimates of other people generally. That is, they expressed belief that very few students are difficult behavior problems, that very few people are influenced in their opinions and attitudes toward others by feelings of jealousy, and that most teachers are willing to assume their full share of extra duties outside of school.

Interestingly, the characteristics that distinguished the "lowly assessed" teacher group suggested that the relatively "ineffective" teacher is self-centered, anxious, and restricted. One is left with the distinct impression that poor or ineffective teachers have more than the usual number of paranoid defenses.

It comes as no surprise that how we perceive others is highly dependent on how we perceive ourselves. If a potential teacher (or anyone else for that matter) likes himself, trusts himself, and has confidence in himself, he is likely to see others in somewhat this same light. Research is beginning to tell us what common sense has always told us; namely, people grow, flourish, and develop much more easily when in relationship with someone who projects an inherent trust and belief in their capacity to become what they have the potential to become.

It seems to me that we can sketch at least five interrelated generalizations from what research is telling us about how good teachers differ from poor teachers when it comes to how they perceive others.

1. They seem to have generally more positive views of others— students, colleagues, and administrators.
2. They do not seem to be as prone to view others as critical, attacking people with ulterior motives; rather they are seen as potentially friendly and worthy in their own right.
3. They have a more favorable view of democratic classroom procedures.
4. They seem to have the ability and capacity to see things as they seem to others—i.e., the ability to see things from the other person's point of view.
5. They do not seem to see students as persons "you do things to" but rather as individuals capable of doing for themselves once they feel trusted, respected, and valued.

Who, Then, Is a Good Teacher?

1. A good teacher is a good person. Simple and true. A good teacher rather likes life, is reasonably at peace with himself, has a sense of humor, and enjoys other people. If I interpret the research correctly, what it says is that there is no one best better-than-all-others type of teacher. Nonetheless there are clearly distinguishable "good" and "poor" teachers. Among other things, a good teacher is good because he does not seem to be dominated by a narcissistic self which demands a spotlight, or a neurotic need for power and authority, or a host of anxieties and tremblings which reduce him from the master of his class to its mechanic.

2. The good teacher is flexible. By far the single most repeated adjective used to describe good teachers is "flexibility." Either implicitly or explicitly (most often the latter), this characteristic emerges time and again over all others when good teaching is discussed in the research. In other words, the good teacher does not seem to be overwhelmed by a single point of view or approach to the point of intellectual myopia. A good teacher knows that he cannot be just one sort of person and use just one kind of approach if he intends to meet the multiple needs of his students. Good teachers are, in a sense, "total" teachers. That is, they seem able to be what they have to be to meet the demands of the moment. They seem able to move with the shifting tides of their own needs, the student's, and do what has to be done to handle the situation. A total teacher can be firm when necessary (say "no" and mean it) or permissive (say "why not try it your way?" and mean that, too) when appropriate. It depends on many things, and good teachers seem to know the difference.

The Need for "Total" Teachers

There probably is not an educational psychology course taught which does not, in some way, deal with the highly complex area of individual differences. Even the most unsophisticated undergraduate is aware that people differ in readiness and capacity to handle academic learning. For the most part, our educational technology (audio-visual aids, programmed texts, teaching machines, etc.) is making significant advances designed to assist teachers in coping with intellectual differences among students. We have been making strides in the direction of offering flexible programs and curricula, but we are somewhat remiss when it comes to preparing flexible, "total" teachers. Just as there are intellectual differences among students, there are also personality and self-concept differences which can have just as much impact on achievement. If this is true, then perhaps we need to do more about preparing teachers who are sensitive to the nature of these differences and who are able to take them into account as they plan for their classes.

The point here is that what is important for one student is not important to another. This is one reason why cookbook formulas for good teachers are of so little value and why teaching is inevitably something of an art. The choice of instructional methods makes a big difference for certain kinds of pupils, and a search for the "best" way to teach can succeed only when learners' intellectual *and* personality differences are taken into account. Available evidence does not support the belief that successful teaching is possible only through the use of some specific methodology. A reasonable inference from existing data is that methods which provide for adaptation to individual differences, encourage student initiative, and stimulate individual and group participation are superior to methods which do not. In order for things of this sort to happen, perhaps what we need first of all are flexible, "total" teachers who are capable of planning around people as they are around ideas.

Implications for Teacher Education

Research is teaching us many things about the differences between good and poor teachers, and I see at least four related implications for teacher education programs.

1. If it is true that good teachers are good because they view teaching as primarily a human process involving human relationships and human meanings, then this may imply that we should spend at least as much time exposing and sensitizing teacher candidates to the subtle complexities of personality structure as we do to introducing them to the structure of knowledge itself. Does this mean personality development, group dynamics, basic counseling processes, sensitivity training, and techniques such as life-space interviewing and encounter grouping?

2. If it is true that good teachers have a positive view of themselves and others, then this may suggest that we provide more opportunities for teacher candidates to acquire more positive self-other perceptions. Self-concept research tells us that how one feels about himself is learned. If it is learned, it is teachable. Too often, those of us in teacher education are dominated by a concern for long-term

goals, while the student is fundamentally motivated by short-term goals. Forecasting what a student will need to know six months or two years from now, we operate on the assumption that he, too, perceives such goals as meaningful. It seems logical enough, but unfortunately it doesn't work out too well in practice. Hence much of what we may do with our teacher candidates is non-self-related—that is, to the student it doesn't seem connected with his own life, time, and needs. Rather than talk about group processes in the abstract, why can't we first assist students to a deeper understanding of their own roles in groups in which they already participate? Rather than simply theorize and cite research evidence related to individual differences, why not also encourage students to analyze the individual differences which exist in *this* class at *this* time and then allow them to express and discuss what these differences mean at a more personal level? If one values the self-concept idea at all, then there are literally endless ways to encourage more positive self-other perceptions through teaching strategies aimed at personalizing what goes on in a classroom. Indeed, Jersild (9) has demonstrated that when "teachers face themselves," they feel more adequate as individuals and function more effectively as teachers.

3. If it is true that good teachers are well-informed, then it is clear that we must neither negate nor relax our efforts to provide them with as rich an intellectual background as is possible. Teachers are usually knowledgeable people, and knowledge inculcation is the aspect of preparation with which teacher education has traditionally been most successful. Nonetheless, teachers rarely fail because of lack of knowledge. They fail more often because they are unable to communicate what they know so that it makes a difference to their students. Which brings us to our final implication for teacher-education programs.

4. If it is true that good teachers are able to communicate what they know in a manner that makes sense to their students, then we must assist our teacher candidates both through example and appropriate experiences to the most effective ways of doing this. Communication is not just a process of presenting information. It is also a function of discovery and the development of personal meanings. I wonder what would happen to our expectations of the teacher's role if we viewed him less as dispenser, answerer, coercer, and provoker and more as stimulator, questioner, challenger, and puzzler. With the former, the emphasis is on "giving to," while with the latter the focus is on "guiding to." In developing ability to hold and keep attention, not to mention techniques of

encouraging people to adopt the reflective, thoughtful mood, I wonder what the departments of speech, theater, and drama on our college and university campuses could teach us? We expose our students to theories of learning and personality; perhaps what we need to do now is develop some "theories of presentation" with the help of those who know this field best.

This paper has attempted to point out that even though there is no single best or worst kind of teacher, there are clearly distinguishable characteristics associated with "good" and "bad" teachers. There is no one *best* kind of teaching because there is no *one kind* of student. Nonetheless, there seems to be enough evidence to suggest that whether the criteria for good teaching is on the basis of student and/or peer evaluations or in terms of student achievement gains, there are characteristics between both which consistently overlap. That is, the good teacher is able to influence both student feeling and achievement in positive ways.

Research is teaching us many things about the differences between good and bad teachers and there are many ways we can put these research findings into our teacher-education programs.

Good teachers do exist and can be identified. Perhaps the next most fruitful vineyard for research is in the classrooms of good teachers so we can determine, by whatever tools we have, just what makes them good in the first place.

References

(1) Barr, A. S., *Characteristic Differences in the Teaching Performance of Good and Poor Teachers of the Social Studies.* Bloomington, Ill.: The Public School Publishing Co., 1929.

(2) Biddle, B. J. and W. J. Ellena, *Contemporary Research on Teacher Effectiveness.* New York: Holt, Rinehart, & Winston, Inc., 1964, p. 2.

(3) Bousfield, W. A., "Student's Rating on Qualities Considered Desirable in College Professors." *School and Society,* February 24, 1940, pp. 253–56.

(4) Cogan, M. L, "The Behavior of Teachers and the Productive Behavior of their Pupils." *Journal of Experimental Education,* December 1958, pp. 89–124.

(5) Combs, A. W., The Professional Education of Teachers." Boston: Allyn & Bacon, Inc., 1965, pp. 70–71.

(6) Flanders, N. A. *Teacher Influence, Pupil Attitudes and Achievement: Studies in Interaction Analysis.* University of Minnesota, U. S. Office of Education Cooperative Research Project No. 397, 1960.

(7) Hart, W. F., *Teachers and Teaching.* New York: The Macmillan Company, 1934, pp. 131–32.

(8) Heil, L. M., M. Powell, and I. Feifer, *Characteristics of Teacher Behavior Related to the Achievement of Children in Several Elementary Grades.* Washington, D. C.: U. S. Office of Education, Cooperative Branch, 1960.

(9) Jersild, A. T., *When Teachers Face Themselves.* New York: Bureau of Publications, Teachers College, Columbia University, 1955.

(10) Reed, H. B., "Implications for Science Education of a Teacher Competence Research." *Science Education,* December 1962, pp. 473–86.

(11) Ryans, D. G., "Prediction of Teacher Effectiveness." *Encyclopedia of Educational Research,* 3rd ed. New York: The Macmillan Company, 1960, pp. 1486–90.

(12) Spaulding, R., "Achievement, Creativity, and Self-Concept Correlates of Teacher-Pupil Transactions in Elementary Schools." University of Illinois, U. S. Office of Education Cooperative Research Project No. 1352, 1963.

(13) Stern, G. C., "Measuring Non-Cognitive Variables in Research on Teaching." In *Handbook of Research on Teaching,* N. L. Gage (ed.), Chicago: Rand McNally & Co., 1963, p. 427.

(14) Witty, P., "An Analysis of the Personality Traits of the Effective Teacher." *Journal of Educational Research,* May 1947, pp. 662–71.

Becoming A Better Elementary Science Teacher Through Understanding Children

Many teachers think of children as being miniature adults. In fact, children vary considerably from adults—a child's mind is not an adult mind. A maturing child is in the process of becoming—becoming able to perform logical tasks, be more sensitive, aware, artistic, creative, ethical, etc. Since each child has a diversity of genetic and environmental background, he varies from other children and differs from them in what interests, motivates, and has personal meaning for him. In this section the first two articles deal primarily with the affective portion of a child's education. The latter two are concerned with the cognitive development.

Arthur Combs stresses the need for teachers to realize that learning only occurs when there is personal meaning in combination with knowledge. If something is not meaningful to the individual, it is not remembered for long. Combs says: "The school that does not concern itself with personal meaning is a school where nothing is happening" (see p. 43).

Material becomes meaningful to an individual when it helps to increase his self-image positively. Ben Strasser suggests that the significance of science may be increased by having children become involved in activities where they have opportunities to use their minds to identify problems, and generate and test hypotheses. In the process of so doing they learn to use their minds to solve problems and develop their mental ability; as a result, they increase their self-images.

Dr. Jean Piaget believes minds will only develop if they have the input requiring them to build methods of handling information. Piaget has also found that there is a marked difference in how children at various ages of development handle information. He believes that children pass through four stages of mental development. Three of these stages, pre-operational, concrete operational, and formal operational, may emerge during the elementary years. Unfortunately, because many teachers are not aware that many classrooms have children at different levels of mental development, they doom some children to failure. These teachers require achievement at higher cognitive levels than the children are capable of, causing feelings of frustration and poor self-images. The relevance of this problem becomes keenly aware to teachers when they administer Piagetian tasks to children to investigate the variation in their abilities to think. The tasks outlined in the last part of this section are exciting, easy to administer, and are fun for the child, in addition to leading to insight on the part of the teacher. We strongly suggest that you use these tasks as a basis for interviewing children. Your perceptions of them will almost assuredly change. These interviews can be used, furthermore, to give you insights on how to determine children's comprehension of concepts. For example, teachers often accept answers to questions as an indication that the child understands what he is learning, but it is the child's justification of answers, as Piaget has pointed out, that reveals his true comprehension.

4

AFFECTIVE EDUCATION—OR NONE AT ALL

Arthur W. Combs

Many people regard the whole question of affective education as a frill. Some even get hysterical about it. They think it is an invasion of home, family, and the sacred right of parents to do as they please with children. Other people think it is an unwarranted interference with the school's goal of "excellence." Along with Max Rafferty, they scream, "Do you want education for intellect or education for adjustment?" as though we had to make a choice between well-adjusted dopes or smart psychotics! I have news for these people. We are going to have affective education or none at all. We need to recognize *all* behavior is affective and any educational system that rules out affect is making itself absolutely ineffective. Why is this so?

To understand why, we need first to understand the nature of emotion in psychological terms. We usually think of emotion as something separate, a dynamic in itself; but, to the psychologist, emotion is simply a question of the degree of a person's involvement, a question of the importance of something to himself. It may be plus or it may be minus; but it has to do with the closeness of some event to one's self. For example, let us talk about rattlesnakes: Now, rattlesnakes in Texas don't upset me. Rattlesnakes on the other side of the glass in the zoo make me feel rather uneasy. Rattlesnakes in the grass in front of me create a great deal of emotion. Take another example:

Reprinted from a speech given at the National Conference on Affective Education, Chicago, Ill., May 2–4, 1971. Dr. Arthur Combs is Director, Center for Humanistic Education, University of Florida, Gainesville, Florida.

Think of a young woman who has a lover in North Vietnam; she
hears that he is coming home in six months. Then, a letter says he
will be home next month. The day comes when he's on his way.
He's back in the country! It is time to go to the airport. Here comes
his plane! There he is! "Oh, John! John! John!" I would be willing
to bet there was an increase in emotion as you read these words.

Learning Equals Information *Plus* Personal Meaning

When we talk about affect we are talking about the degree of closeness
to one's self . . . of whatever idea you hold. Emotion had a tremendous
survival value in the course of history because it made it possible
for us to have the energy available to either fight or run. It is also
important today in its relationship to learning. Learning always has
two aspects: one aspect has to do with some kind of new experience;
the other aspect has to do with the discovery of the meaning of that
experience. Let's take an example: I read in the paper about an increase
in the number of cases of pulmonic stenosis. I do not even know
what pulmonic stenosis is, and so it goes in one ear and out the other.
Now, let's suppose a little later I hear a friend of mine talking about
pulmonic stenosis. That bothers me because I don't know what it
means; so I go and look it up and find out that it has to do with
the closing up of the pulmonary artery. It's a condition which causes
"blue babies." Well, that is interesting. It raises my temperature a
little, but not much. Now I get a letter about one of the children
in my class from a mother who says, "Dear Mr. Combs, We have
taken Ellen to the clinic this past week and we find that she has pulmonic
stenosis and she will have to be operated on in two years. Meantime,
we would appreciate it if you would look out for her." Now—the
same bit of information which before had no meaning for me has much
more meaning because *it is happening to one of my children.* It is
closer to me and it affects my behavior more. So I talk about it to
other people. I say, "Did you hear about little Ellen? It is a terrible
thing." I talk about it; I find ways of protecting her in class and so
on. Let's go one step further now. Let's suppose I have just learned
that my daughter has pulmonic stenosis. Now the same piece of information affects my behavior tremendously in everything I do.

The basic principle I am stating here is the basic principle of
learning as it is understood in a perceptual orientation. We could state
it formally as follows: *Any information will have an effect upon an
individual's behavior only to the degree to which he has discovered
the personal meaning of that information for him.* Now let's go back
to the illustration above. Notice as I talked about pulmonic stenosis

how the amount of emotion arose from the beginning to the end of the illustration which I used. Again the emotion experienced is only a question of the degree of importance of any event to an individual. This explains why so much of what we do in school fails when we say to a child, "I am not interested in what you think about that. What does the book say?"

Education as we know it has been immensely successful with the information half of the learning equation. We have been very successful in providing people with information and experience, but we have failed miserably in helping children discover the personal meaning of information for them. We pay almost no attention to meaning; we are almost exclusively preoccupied with the information half of the problem. Perhaps we do it because it's easier. It is easier to control information than it is to help people discover personal meaning.

In the light of the principle I am talking about, we need to understand that there is only cognition plus the degree of closeness that information has to one's self. Emotion is indicative of meaning. It is simply an artifact, an indication of the degree to which a particular idea has meaning for the individual. Your children, I can be very objective about—my children I cannot. If it doesn't matter to oneself, then it doesn't matter at all. The school that does not concern itself with personal meaning is a school where nothing is happening; and the degree of affect or emotion in any situation is an indication of the degree of involvement. Let me provide an illustration from what happens in a good discussion group as people begin to get involved. They start out the discussion group by talking at fingertip length: "I saw"; "I went to"; "Did you see that?" "I read where." Then as things get a little closer to themselves they begin to talk in descriptive terms; they tell you a story about something that happened to somebody else. After a while they come a little closer and talk about things they are "wondering" about. A little closer than that and they talk about things they have "some doubts about." Closer still they talk about a "concern" which they have, then how they "feel about" something. When they really get close to themselves they may even talk about "I hate that" or "I love her" or "That makes me so mad!" The degree of involvement, you see, is a question of the degree of closeness to self.

Education for Personal Meaning

In the light of this understanding, that emotion is the degree of personal meaning, I suggest that we throw out the term "affective education" entirely and begin to talk about the question of personal meaning.

That will save us a lot of headaches too because at the present time when we talk about education for emotion or feeling or affect, we run into all kinds of difficulties with people who object strenuously to such thoughts. But who can be against education for personal meaning? Who can be against education which is relevant? And who can be against education which has to do with the development of a more positive self? I think we could get rid of a lot of problems if we stopped talking about affective education and began to talk about the question of *meaningful education*. It is the same thing, but we don't have to use such fighting language.

Education, to be meaningful, must produce change. But here we run into the problem of a current fallacy that the way to go about helping people change is to concentrate on their behavior. Behavior, we need to understand, is only a symptom. The behavior that you observe at any moment is not a cause; it is a result. How the person is behaving is a consequence of what is going on within him. When you and I attempt to deal with other people by concentrating on their behavior we are in the same position as the doctor who doesn't do anything but treat your symptoms. Behavior is a symptom, and few of us would be content to go to a doctor who did nothing but help us with our symptoms while ignoring the causes of our illness. Treating symptoms may sometimes make you feel better but they don't really solve problems.

Educators, everywhere, seek a direct attack upon behavior these days; and the most notable example of this is the current insanity over behavioral objectives. We have gone overboard with this matter. Our preoccupation with behavioral objectives is concentrating on what people do, but this is only a symptom of the causes with which we ought to be concerned. What we do is apply industrial techniques to the problems of education. We apply industrial techniques to deal with people as though they were things and we ought to know better. When we did that in industry, when we applied the industrial approach to the workers, what happened? What happened was the workers rose up in revolt. They formed unions and fought systems—and I would like to point out to you, that is exactly what has happened in education today. Students are rising in revolt and fighting against the system. They are demonstrating what Maslow so beautifully said, "The screams of the tortured at the crushing of their psychological bones!"

Behavior Is a Function of Perceptions

We need to understand that how a person behaves is a function of his perceptions of himself and his world. That means somehow we have to find ways of dealing with people's self-concepts and with the relevance of the events in the world to those self-concepts.

Let me take a moment to talk about each of these. The self-concept, as everybody knows these days, is terribly important. It determines a person's adjustment or maladjustment. It also determines the likelihood of his intelligence. It also determines the chances of his success in all kinds of fields. We know from our research at the University of Florida on good and poor helpers that it also determines in very large measure whether the person will be a good teacher or a bad one. Incidentally one of the things we've been finding in that research on effective helpers in all fields like counseling, teaching, and nursing is that objectivity correlates negatively with effectiveness! Yet, currently we are going all out in education to become more and more objective!

We also know that the self-concept is terribly important in that it lies at the heart of many of our social problems. Literally millions of people think they can only do "x" much so that's all they do. The rest of us, seeing they do "x" much, say, "Well, that's an "x" much person," which just proves what they already thought in the first place! We know that the self-concept is learned from experience; and in order to change the self-concept, it is necessary to change the experiences people have. The self-concept changes as a result of the feedback we get from other people.

Now another of the fallacies we have at the present time is the assumption that the way to get a person to change is to have him look at himself. Logically, people assume you should take a good look at yourself, decide what you want to be, then go ahead and make yourself that. That's a nice logical approach to the problem of changing the person except it never works. As Earl Kelley once said, "Logic is often only a systematic way of arriving at the wrong answers." If a person wants to change himself, what he ought *not* to do is pay attention to himself. My clients in therapy do not get better when they look at themselves. They get better when they look at how they feel about their wives, their husbands, their children, their co-workers, the people they associate with. Let me give you an illustration of why it is a fallacy that the way to get a person to change his self-concept is to look at himself. Let's suppose I want to make myself a more lovable person. Now the way for me to make myself more lovable is not to sit around and think about my lovableness. What I have to do is think about how I feel about you, about my students, about my job, about the people I know and come in contact with, about the Blacks in our society, about the poor. As I feel better about these people, I behave better toward them. And as I behave better toward them they like me better and so treat me as a more likeable person.

Eventually I wake up someday and find that I have become more lovable. But I did not get that way by looking at myself!

What we have to do in order to help people to develop better self-concepts is to create situations which help them to feel in the ways we have in mind. Healthy self-concepts have been pointed out to us by psychologists who have worked with the problems of self-actualization. They tell us that effective, efficient people, self-actualizing, self-fulfilling people see themselves in essentially positive ways. Now, if you know that, you don't have to be an expert to know what to do. What we have to do is to ask ourselves the question, "How can a person feel wanted unless somebody wants him? How can a person feel acceptable unless somebody accepts him? How can a person feel he is a person of dignity and integrity unless somebody treats him so? And how can a person feel able unless somewhere he's had some success?" In the answers that you and I find to these questions we will find what we need to do about the self-concept. A child's self-concept is not something that he parks at the door. He brings it right on in with him into the classroom; and whatever we are doing in that classroom is affecting his self-concept whether we know it is doing so or not. It goes right on happening in spite of us.

Teaching and the Helping Relationship

We know that the self-concept is basically a product of the kinds of relationships people have. I recently began to understand the importance of relationships in a different way than formerly. I began my professional career with Carl Rogers back at Ohio State years ago. In those first days of developing what we then called *non-directive therapy* we thought it was the method that was the important thing. Accordingly we were so non-directive that, believe me, if you asked me in those days, "What time is it?" I would say to you, "You are wondering what time it is!" After a while we began to discover that it was the relationship that was the important thing. And most recently it has become quite clear to me that it is not the relationship just because it's a nice idea to have a good relationship; instead, the relationship is important because of what it *teaches* to the person who is experiencing it. When a client says to me, "Dr. Combs, do you think I can?" And I say to him, "Look, I am sure you can, but I am not sure if you will," I am giving him an experience in can-ness, an experience that somebody believes he can. When he says, "You know, I am not sure if I can talk about this." And I say, "Well, I can see that you are concerned about that, but it is all right with me. You can talk about it if you wish." I am saying to him that even very frightening things can be looked at. Or, I recall a very paranoid client who never loved anybody in her life, who said to me, "Dr. Combs, is it all right if I love you?" When I reply, "Well, yes, indeed; I am glad and honored that you feel so," this is an experience in caring. So the relationships we create with other people are teaching them something about themselves, and we need to be aware of what we are teaching by the relationships that we are creating. We are beginning to understand that these relationships may be more important than anything else that happens in the public schools. A good example of this is to be seen in Rosenthal's finding that if you believe that children are able then, somehow, they are more able, as a consequence of your belief about them. I repeat, these relationships need to be carefully looked at, not just because you want to have nice relationships, but because of what they are teaching. Such relationships are much more important than anything else that is going on in school, certainly more important than arithmetic or reading. One young woman who did a study at the University of Florida found that the self-concept is a better predictor of success in reading than the intelligence level. We ignore the self-concept at our peril. If we pay no attention to it we make the educational process sterile and futile. We cannot ignore what makes us human, and self-concept is a vital aspect of our humanness.

Relevance, Recognition, and Acceptance in Education

Behavior is a function of the person's concept of himself and the relevance of the world as he sees it to that self; the more relevant, the more emotional; the more relevant, the more feeling. When you say "I feel" what you are talking about is the personal meaning of something to you. I say "I love you." That's my personal meaning of you and me. When we talk about feeling we are talking about the personal meaning of something to us. An important technique in psychotherapy is called "the recognition and acceptance of feeling." It could just as well be called "recognition and acceptance of personal meaning." That's what it is.

Let us look now at the question of relevance. Again we find the terrible preoccupation with information and content throughout the entire system is dehumanizing our schools. I think, for example, of Don Snygg's beautiful quotation, "The problem of American education is we are busily teaching students answers to problems they ain't got yet." This is true. If we are going to find ways of making education relevant we are going to have to begin by accepting the problems of youth as they are. Unfortunately, we don't approve of young people. We say to them, "Here is a new teen town; go dance some more." "Here is a playground; go play some more." But the message is clear. "Go away and don't bother us." If we are really going to deal with affective education, we must begin with the problems people have. We must begin by accepting them where they are. Too many of us simply do not approve of the problems of young people. We don't begin by accepting them. Instead we are so busy trying to make them into something else that we fail to accept them where they are as they are. For example, when a juvenile delinquent comes into our office and he's surly and slouches in his chair and we say, "Now look here young man, you behave yourself. Sit up and be polite." Now, in the society of a real tough delinquent, being polite would ruin him! Being polite is what we hope someday to help him become. But we begin by demanding that he be what we want him to be today. It is like going to the doctor and the doctor says, "Go away and get better and come back and I'll help you." Is it any wonder that we find that the young people today opt out, cop out, drop out of the system? The kids who have those options are lucky. That can happen if you are a high schooler. But what if you're a junior high schooler and you don't even know that it's a screwed up system. Or what if you're an elementary student or a kindergartner or a nursery schooler. You don't have the option of copping out. You have to deal with it and you have to live with it.

If we are really going to make education relevant, we are going to have to take young people in as partners. We are going to have to involve them in self-direction and responsibility. You never learn to be responsible by having it withheld. Responsibility is learned from having been given responsibility. I think, for instance, of the school at which I arrived just after they had had an election for student body president. All the teachers were in a tizzy because the young man who got elected president had run on a platform of no school on Friday, free admissions to the football games, extra desserts for lunch, etc. "It's a travesty on democracy," the teachers said. "Don't you think we should call the election off and make them do it over?" I said "No! How else are these kids ever going to discover the terrible price you have to pay for electing a "jackass" to office? Better they should learn it early. Look at the mess the rest of us are in."

Somehow we have to find ways of helping young people to get committed. They don't get committed to things that have no relevance, that have no meaning for them. I don't know if we could have done a better job of creating irrelevance if we had set out purposely to design a system which would turn people off. I asked a class of young people learning to be teachers, "How come you don't get committed?" This is what they told me: They said, "Teachers and students ought to be friends but they're not; they're enemies." The only thing that matters is conformity. It's details, details, details. That's all that matters or grades, grades, grades, as though they mattered. They feed us a Pablum diet all chewed over until there is no life left in it. The only good ideas are the old ideas. The only things that matter is what somebody else wrote or what somebody else said. Nobody cares what we think. Nobody believes that we can do anything right ourselves. These were things they named and they ended this discussion by voting 100 percent for the following statement. "The things worth getting committed to don't get you ahead in school." I think that is a terrible indictment. Apparently the things that make life worthwhile are not things the school regards as important as these young people see it.

The Logical, Objective Approach to Education

We are caught up at present in the worship of objectivity. We come by it honestly. This nation was made great by conquering the wilderness and conquering things. We admire our great industrial production, magnificent examples of accomplishment by control and direction of the stream of events. We adore the scientific method technique of approaching problems logically and objectively. Even our religious tradition leads us in this direction as our Christian philosophy takes the position that you must make yourself be good. Work on your behavior. Small wonder we worship the logical approach to dealing with things.

The logical approach is the technique of approaching problems in which we say, "Let us define our objectives, analyze the situation, set up the machinery, then put it in action and measure whether you did it." That's the technique we use everywhere in our society in dealing with "things" but it doesn't work with people. It certainly isn't appropriate for affective education. Instead, the approach we have to use is one I would describe as the "get-with-it approach." In this you don't decide on what the answers are in advance. That worked very badly in dealing with problems of the ghettos. We sat in our nice air-conditioned offices and decided what those poor devils needed down there. Then we went down and tried to do it to them but they didn't want any part of it. That's the logical approach. The "get-with-it approach" means we have to get into the problems with people. We have to get involved in the problems they face and *together* we search. The people who operate this way are also likely to be much nicer people to get along with. Operating in the logical way of approaching questions you can never afford to be wrong. This is the medical model. In the medical model the doctor knows and the patient doesn't. But when we are talking about human behavior we have to switch that around. In teaching and counseling it is my client or student who knows how things are with him and I don't. I am on the outside; he is on the inside. The logical objective way simply is not appropriate if we are really going to deal with the affective aspects of education.

Affective Education—Or None at All—A Summary

Let me review what I have been saying. Affective education is not some special domain. When we talk about *affect* we mean the importance or relevance of any event to self, the personal meaning of ideas. As ideas are more important or closer or more relevant to the self or more threatening to the self, emotion increases. Our problem is not to increase emotion. Our problem is to help students discover the personal meaning of events for them, and in this sense *all learning is affective*. Affective learning is a question of relevance. It has to do with discovery of the personal meaning of events to the person. This is something we cannot ignore. You cannot suspend the laws of learning because they are inconvenient. If it's true that a person's self-concept affects his behavior we have to deal with that. If it's true that relevance and personal meaning are at the heart of the problem we're confronted with, we have to deal with that. If we don't, we are in the position of the mechanic who says, "I know my car needs a carburetor to run, but I'm going to run mine without one." It's about that silly for us to say we are not going to be concerned about affective problems.

We have to recognize that the self and the relevance of things are basic. It's the heart of the problem and if we don't attend to it then we will have failed our society; we will have failed the parents; we will have failed the schools; but most important of all we have failed the children.

5

SELF-IMAGE GOALS FOR SCIENCE EDUCATION

Ben B. Strasser

The talk about goals and objectives for science education continues. Currently the trend is to develop objectives in such a way that evidence of the attainment of each objective may be readily observed in the student's overt behavior. Call them behavioral or performance objectives, and color them difficult to formulate. Of course, the real issue is, *what happens when such objectives are used as a base for instruction?* What happens to the students: to their feelings about their growing scientific knowledge and about their ability to solve problems of a scientific nature?

In an informal discussion several years ago, Richard Feynman of Cal Tech commented that "Science is coming to think you're clever by yourself." Statements such as this invite us to reconsider our objectives in whatever way they are written and however they are taught. The process of objectifying instruction is highly analytical. It involves taking the curricula apart, bit by bit. Each bit is then subjected to the question, "What will the students do to demonstrate attainment of the objective?" In this process—which can undoubtedly upgrade any science curriculum—a danger is that we lose sight of the *net effect* we want the science program to have on each of our students. That is, *what should the student be able to say about himself as bit by*

Reprinted from *The Science Teacher, 38,* May 1971, p. 48. Dr. Ben B. Strasser is a consultant in curriculum and instruction at the Office of Los Angeles County Superintendent of Schools, Los Angeles, California.

bit the wide-eyed child is transformed into the scientifically literate adult?

We've given some thought to this question—as I'm certain many have. We call the product of our efforts "Self-Image Goals for Science Education." Here is our list:

I can identify some problems of my own to work on.

I can generate some of my own theories about "why" things happen as they do, and I am able to test out these theories.

There are some things I know something about.

There are some problems or questions I have identified which I cannot solve—to my satisfaction—at this time.

Hopefully these goals represent the kinds of statements a student is able to *make about himself* as a product of his experiences and learnings in the science program.

It is apparent that these goals were designed to speak both to content and process. Our students should learn some of the history, data, and theories of science, for these are the "food" for scientific thought. However, without equal emphasis on the more dynamic theory-building and theory-testing side of the discipline, it's questionable that the development of both valued attitudes toward scientific knowledge and of the student's ability to use scientific knowledge to solve his own problems would take place.

As these goals statements are read, some may wish we had included more discussion of each one in order to communicate, in further depth, the meaning each of these goals has for us. However, it is our belief that if any of these specific goal statements has no meaning for a teacher or school district, it probably should not be among his or its goal statements.

Perhaps there are changes in the wording of these goal statements which should be made to make them more definitive. Make the changes. Perhaps there are goal statements which should be added. Add them. For example, these statements speak to issues of "I can..." Some may want to add statements such as, "I like to...." Or better yet, "I want to...."

(Perhaps these self-image goals speak to several areas of the curriculum in addition to science. So much the better.)

But goals for science education, indeed for any area of the curriculum, are more than some word to be included in the frontispiece of the district curriculum guide or hung on the wall of the science center. *They must come alive in the classroom,* for they live only in the feelings, thoughts, attitudes, and actions of our students.

How will the students know they can...? As far as we know, *the only way they'll know they can do what each of the Self-Image Goals suggests is when they are able to say, "I have done so."* That is,

I have identified some problems of my own...

I have generated and tested some of my own theories about...

I have learned that...

I have these problems I want to explore...

Thus, these goals come alive only as students have continuing opportunities to practice them in their day-by-day bit-by-bit living and learning.

6

PIAGET AND THE TEACHER

Robert B. Sund
Rodger W. Bybee

Imagine you are an elementary teacher correcting and grading first grade math problems. The following worksheet emerged from the mountain of papers.

$$
\begin{array}{cccccc}
3 & \boxed{\mathcal{E}} & \boxed{3} & 1 & 2 & \boxed{q} \\
+\boxed{7} & +2 & +1 & +\boxed{4} & +\boxed{6} & +4 \\
\hline
4 & 5 & 2 & 3 & 4 & 5
\end{array}
$$

$$
\begin{array}{cccccc}
\boxed{8} & 2 & 3 & \square & \square & 0 \\
+3 & +\boxed{4} & +\square & +0 & +2 & +\square \\
\hline
5 & 2 & 5 & 4 & 3 & 5
\end{array}
$$

Reprinted from a paper presented at the annual convention of the National Association of Biology Teachers, Denver, Colorado, October 21–24, 1970. Dr. Robert B. Sund is Professor of Science Education, University of Northern Colorado, Greeley, Colorado. Mr. Rodger W. Bybee is presently associated with the TTT Project, School of Education, New York University, New York City.

How many problems would you mark wrong? Seven? Eight? The illustration shows an example of a student's ability to add. He adds from the top down, the bottom up, and either end to the middle, always resulting in the correct answer. The child responds to the concrete symbols, the numbers, and the addition sign. This might be interpreted as indicating the child is unable to deal with the abstraction of completing a subtraction operation in order to arrive at the correct answer. Likewise, it appears as though the child does not understand the function of the line indicating "equal to" or summation. This symbol may have been neglected in the work.

From a Piagetian frame of reference this child is able to perform certain mental operations, i.e., summation, but has not yet reached the level of cognitive development enabling him adequately to conceptualize the series of manipulations necessary to resolve the problems. There are many components of the problem that must be centered on and held simultaneously in the mind; and then operations must be performed on the figures. These mental operations are governed by the symbols. It is possible that the child is unable to complete the operations required by the two symbols, the addition symbol and summation line. In a way, the problem is tricky. Although the symbols tell the child to add, he must, in fact, mentally realize he has to subtract. The child's eventual ability to complete this problem will develop as a result of experience with subtraction in the environment both in and out of school. His understanding can be aided by the teacher through an appreciation for the child's level of logical reasoning.

Many teachers would mark this student's work as wrong, because they failed to realize the operational significance of what the child was doing. Fortunately, there is a wealth of research alerting teachers to a fuller awareness of the mental development of the child. It suggests better ways for teachers to assist children in the evolution of their minds.

Dr. Jean Piaget and his colleagues at the Jean Jacques Rousseau Institute in Geneva, Switzerland, have studied for more than 40 years the mental development of the child. Through extensive investigations into the thinking behavior of children they have slowly evolved a theory of cognitive development. The theory states that as children mature they pass through four major stages of mental development:

> sensory motor — 0–2 years
> preoperational — 2–7 years
> concrete operational — 7–11 years
> formal operational — 11–14 years

The year spans for each stage are true for the majority of children but it should be understood that many individuals will not necessarily reach the stages as indicated. The progression through the stages in sequence, however, never deviates.

What causes mental development? Piaget believes there are four factors contributing to intelligence:

1. Maturation
2. Physical experience
3. Social experience
4. Equilibration

Maturation

It is obvious that as a child lives he grows and develops. There are in the maturation process physiological and anatomical changes, and these contribute to the development of the person.

Physical Experience

In the process of maturing physically, a baby is able to move, crawl, and investigate his environment to a greater extent than possible when he was younger. When the child encounters something in the environment, i.e., a rattle, there is a stimulus entering his mind. He moves, shakes, the rattle. As he performs physical actions on it and has physical experience he learns, as a consequence, that he can have and interact with objects in the environment. Piaget believes physical action—shaking the rattle—enables the organism to later develop mental action, i.e., "I can think in my mind of shaking the rattle." For this reason, Piaget says: "There is no learning without experience." This does not mean that you can't learn from words. But words only have as much value as the experience behind them.

Social Experience

Social experience contributes to intelligence because through social interaction individuals are forced to consider others' views of the world. For example, in a discussion or an argument various ideas are presented. The young child of three or four thinks the way he perceives things is the same for all individuals. Try playing a game with a child of three and you will see how egocentric he is. He won't follow the rules because rules are the way he sees things. As children interact with other humans they slowly come to realize that phenomena may be perceived in various ways. Through argument a child gains mental experience enabling and sometimes forcing his mind to develop new operations or techniques for perceiving and solving problems.

Equilibration

Why does an organism take in information? Why does it develop mental systems for handling information to be retrieved and used in various ways later in life? Piaget has originated the Equilibration Process to explain why a person builds his own mental computer. He believes an organism's nature is to be in a state of equilibrium. When stimuli interact with it, the organism responds and returns to a state of equilibrium. Mentally this means that when an individual encounters something within his environment, he has to use his mind to handle it. The process of the organism reacting to stimuli mentally is equilibration. Piaget breaks the equilibration process down into two categories, assimilation and accommodation. These may be understood by thinking of the mind as if it were a file cabinet. When the mind encounters information—for example, a baby might experience several chairs—it may eventually constitute the concept—chair. In other words he makes a new file—chair. He is said to have accommodated information.

In the future he might see a new type of chair—made from vinyl and containing air. As a consequence of this experience, he has to

FIGURE 1. Cognitive Development as Viewed by Jean Piaget: Assimilation Process

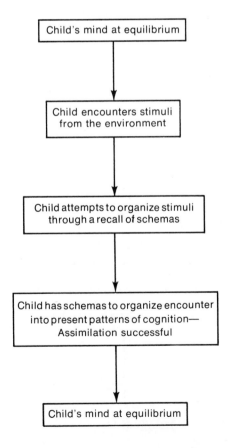

modify his old idea of chairs. He changes or slightly modifies previous concepts. In this case he is said to have assimilated the information. You might think of the assimilation process as adding new information to old files and bringing them up to date. The accommodation process, on the other hand, is the development of new files and schemes for handling information.

FIGURE 2. Cognitive Development as Viewed by Jean Piaget: Accommodation Process

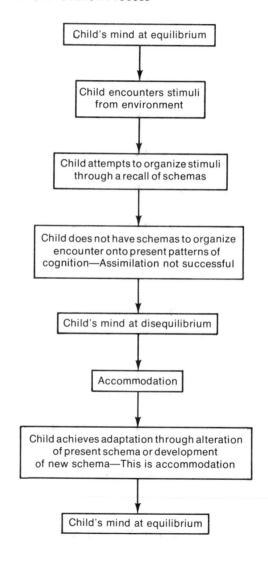

Child's mind at equilibrium

Child encounters stimuli from environment

Child attempts to organize stimuli through a recall of schemas

Child does not have schemas to organize encounter onto present patterns of cognition—Assimilation not successful

Child's mind at disequilibrium

Accommodation

Child achieves adaptation through alteration of present schema or development of new schema—This is accommodation

Child's mind at equilibrium

In order to gain better insights into instructional problems, a teacher needs to become relatively familiar with the characteristics of children at each of the cognitive stages. To facilitate this, a brief synopsis of the cognitive stages appears below.

The Sensory Motor Stage: 0–2 years
A period of discriminating and labeling

The sensory motor stage is called this because the child mainly interacts with the environment with his senses and muscles and is directed by sensations from without. He develops his ability to perceive, touch, move, etc., during this stage. Most of his body motions are in a sense an experiment with the environment. As the child interacts with his surroundings, he slowly learns to handle it better. For example, he eventually perceives depth whereas in the early part of the stage he only sees things as flat.

Behavior is preverbal, and the child concerns himself mainly with organizing and coordinating physical actions. The concept of object permanence has not developed; thus, the child is limited to dealing with definite external stimuli from objects rather than mental pictures of them, which would be possible in the more developed mind. In this sense, he is bound by the stimuli about him rather than originating them from his brain. When an object is hidden from the child's immediate view, he does not search for it. For him, an object not directly perceived does not exist. The conception of object permanence only gradually develops through repeated experience.

The sensory motor child is "space limited" to the immediate environment in which he acts. Life is seen as a series of disconnected individual pictures without understanding relationships within the whole. Rudimentary concepts about time, space, and causality do not develop until the child approaches the end of this period.

The Preoperational Stage
Intuitive, stimulus-limited

Preoperational thought spans approximately ages two to seven years, thus including most children in kindergarten, first grade, and second grade. Though the child can now form mental images and label them verbally, he has not developed the ability to carry out the mental activities Piaget has termed "operations." Operations include abilities to make mental transformations, such as simultaneously thinking about more than one dimension of a problem, ordering a series of events, understanding the quantity, weight, and volume of matter are conserved under ordinary conditions, and knowing that many material changes are reversible. For example, a preoperational child is confused by the following conservation task. Two glasses are placed in front of him, of which one is tall and filled with colored water and the other is short, greater in diameter, and empty. The colored water from the tall glass is then poured into the short glass. The child is asked: "Is there more, less, or the same amount of colored water in the small as there was in the large glass?" Preoperational children usually respond by saying: "There is more in the tall glass." You may then ask: "Was there any water added or taken away from the glasses?" The child will say "no." You might then repeat his statement: "But you think there is more water in the tall glass," and the child will say "yes" once again. The child responds in this apparently illogical manner because he doesn't as yet realize that rearranging matter doesn't affect the amount of material present. He doesn't, therefore, grasp conservation.

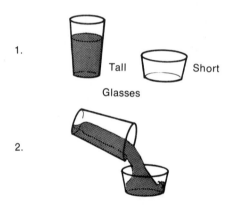

1.

Tall   Short

Glasses

2.

    Most mathematical activities such as adding, subtracting, and multiplying are operations. Because these preoperational children are unable to perform operational functions, they appear illogical to adults.

    During this stage the child is highly egocentric. He finds it difficult to comprehend views other than his own. Understanding of chance and probability is largely absent as he assumes only one truth or one event is possible in any given situation. Animistic and anthropomorphic explanations are commonly expressed for observed natural events. For example, a child might explain a plant's bending toward a window because it "likes light" or it "wants to." "Clouds smile at him."

During the latter part of the stage memory is developed and the child has the ability to think of the past and the future, but is limited in how far he goes in either direction.

The Concrete Operational Stage
Performs operations

During the developmental phase between seven and eleven years of age, the child is able to perform mental operations. Mental processes are incorporated into a coherent system. Thought patterns follow a set of logical rules. The operations are "concrete," because they usually require the presence of actual objects. If the child is given a piece of clay to roll out, he is aware that the amount of clay has not changed by his manipulating it, and that his mental action is reversible. He can get the clay back into the original shape. If he is presented with a problem of changing the form of clay in abstract terms without actually changing it, he still may experience difficulties in answering conservation types of questions.

Problems involving conservation of quantity, weight, and volume are easily solved by the children at the end of this stage, and they can satisfactorily justify their solutions. They can also consider two dimensions of a problem simultaneously, and changing events can be ordered in a chronological sequence. They observe, judge, and evaluate in less egocentric terms and formulate more objective explanations. But they experience difficulty in expressing hypotheses following a long series of related ideas or if concrete referents are not available. While they can form simple groups in classifying objects, it remains difficult or impossible to group classes into more comprehensive groups.

The Formal Operations Stage
Propositional thought

Between twelve and fifteen years of age, the child begins to function intellectually like an adult. This stage marks the child's emancipation from dependence on direct perception of objects as a mediator of thought. In contrast to the concrete operational child, the adolescent thinker can represent his own thoughts by symbols, consider ideals as opposed to realities, form inferences based on stated sets of assumptions (propositional thought), formulate complex and abstract theories, and reflect upon his thought processes. He can carry out "mental" experiments as well as actual ones. Probability is well understood.

He can complete operations on operations. In short, the kind of cognition that is considered adult is now the rule rather than the exception.

Since the work of Piaget gives us new insights into the development of the mind and its characteristics at various stages of growth, the implications of his work for education are many-fold. A few of the more salient considerations are outlined below. Any astute individual who comes to know Piaget's work will certainly originate several more.

Training Elementary Science Teachers

The child's world and thought processes are not those of an adult. A child's mind is not just a diminished version of the adult's. Any individual working with children must understand how their minds function and grow in order to interact with them more effectively. This is true not only for the sake of the child's cognitive development but for mental health as well. For poor perceptual judgment of the child's capabilities can affect the positive relations of the child and the adult.

At the University of Northern Colorado we have investigated the effectiveness of involving both preservice and inservice teachers in the administration of Piagetian tasks to children. Piaget's theory is introduced to them. After this, they perform a series of these tasks with the children.

Both preservice and inservice teachers have been very positive in their reactions to this experience. Responses on questionnaires indicated a change of attitude toward teaching certain concepts, insight into the child's cognitive development, and a projected change in teaching behavior. The change in behavior occurs when the teachers are confronted, operationally, with the fact that children's perceptions are different than adult's perceptions.

As a result of this work we feel college methods and inservice courses can be improved through the inclusion of experiences involving students in the administration of Piagetian tasks to children. This approach gives a two-fold accomplishment: first, teachers gain better insights into the thinking of young children; second, they tend to modify their instructional approaches, relying more on activities than verbalizing and reading.

Evaluation

There is great need for instructors to assess in-depth understanding of concepts. How well do children really understand the material they have been taught? A correct answer on a Piagetian task does not necessarily indicate the child comprehends it. The justification for his answer enables the interviewer to determine his comprehension and level of cognitive ability. Likewise, a correct answer on a test does not indicate the student understands the concept. A teacher performing Piaget's clinical techniques in administering his tasks soon realizes the relevance of this fact and is more likely to modify his evaluations. Furthermore, Piaget's tasks are given free from the traditional pass/fail atmosphere. A child's answer is always accepted. The implication of this for teaching is obvious.

Presently there are instruments that utilize Piaget's stages of development for assessment of intellectual capacity. Although these generally require considerable sophistication to administer and interpret, work continues and better evaluational tests will probably evolve as a result.

Learning Environment

Piaget's work clearly mandates that the learning environment should be rich in physical and social experiences. Involvement is the key to intellectual development, and for the elementary child this includes direct physical manipulation of objects. This implies a minimum of verbalization from the teacher. A primary implication of Piaget's work is that children should be actively involved in both physical and social activities. For example, Piaget believes play is food for the young child's mind. If this is so, many elementary school children may be suffering from malnutrition or are starving cognitively. The learning environment should be rich in materials and time for children to interact with them. Many of the British Infant schools have stressed child-centered activities and report high maturation, interest, and achievement as a result.

It should be stressed further that Piaget believes social interaction is an important aspect of learning and thus should be pursued for a considerable amount of time in the elementary school. The egocentricity of the young child decreases through increased interaction with other individuals. The preoperational child thinks his perception is the only way to see things. Through confrontation with views in opposition to his own the child begins to understand that others have different ways of perceiving the environment. Social interaction through argument, for example, nurtures the development of critical thinking.

Readiness

All students do not progress in their cognitive development at the same rate; yet, for the most part they are treated as though this were true. An assessment of a child's cognitive development can provide considerable insights into his readiness. It is a rare class that includes all individuals at the same cognitive level. We have found most classes have a mix of levels. For example, a typical junior high school class has concrete, formal operational, and several transitional students (those in a state of transition from one stage to the next). Transitional individuals sometimes demonstrate concrete operational limitations in their thinking but at other times appear to use formalistic reasoning. The percentage of formal operational junior high school students generally is low, although this may vary considerably depending upon the class. Preliminary research by us suggests the quality of the general socioeconomical and cultural environment plays a significant role in determining whether there will be a higher or lower number of formal operational students in a class.

Pseudo-learning

Insufficient understanding of Piaget's work undoubtedly contributes considerably to pseudo-learning. Pseudo-learning occurs when a student neither assimilates nor accomodates information. Cognitively the child is not ready for X concept; however, the teacher is unaware and decides to teach X anyway. When asked a question about X the child "reads" the teacher for the correct answer and is thus positively rewarded. From a Piagetian model of intellectual growth the child has neither assimilated nor accommodated the information; thus, learning has not taken place. From the teacher's point of view, the child has answered correctly, thus indicating an understanding of the concept. For the child the concept will have to be relearned, but at the present time the teacher believes "achievement" has occurred.

Curriculum

The curriculum should be designed for individual instruction taking into consideration cognitive differences in children. This is another very strong plea for a curriculum designed for the student, or by the student, and not "fitting" the student to the curriculum. Hans Furth (1) has suggested a theoretical curriculum for thinking based on Piaget's theory of intelligence. He stresses the active process of thinking, and does not attempt to accelerate the stages of development, but suggests thinking activities should be provided at the child's cognitive level. The school should involve games of logical, social, musical, and creative thinking. According to Furth's theoretical curriculum, language, reading, and other activities presently receiving primary emphasis would not be neglected, but would receive secondary emphasis to be utilized at the child's discretion.

Maurice Belanger is of the opinion that schools by the 1980s will be basically Piagetian-based. Their "curriculum" will follow the suggestions described by Furth. Belanger maintains educators have traditionally emphasized the cognitive, but that during the 1970s education will shift to an emphasis of the affective areas. In the late 1970s, gradually there will evolve a more realistic "ecological" view of the child. This view will encompass a greater understanding of the total interaction process that takes place between the total environment and the child. Metaphorically the present environment is somewhat polluted with over emphasis on the 3 *R*'s. The children are not, therefore, in ecological balance with their environment.

Education for the Special Student

"Special students" are individuals in Adult Basic Education, the culturally deprived, and the students within special education. Research indicates that in many cases individuals in areas described above are operating at levels lower than expected for their age. In some cases they will never achieve formal operations, in others this is possible if enough experiences are provided.

Direct manipulative experience should become the model for many of these individuals. Many cannot operate very well verbally, yet they can learn many concepts and understand them even though they cannot talk about them very well. Recent studies in science, for example, have shown that when these individuals are given paper-pencil written tests they do relatively poorly compared to when they are tested by pictures or concrete objects.

Creativity and Problem Solving

Piaget's model for the intellect includes within it creative and problem-solving ability. Creativity is usually defined as the ability to generate new and novel patterns of thought. Problem solving is similar except that it has a specific or immediate goal. In the Piagetian model both activities utilize a restructuring of mental schemes or the development of new schemes. Fluency and flexibility in the assimilation and accommodation process naturally influence the creative and problem-solving abilities. It is apparent that students should be in an environment encouraging activity. Considerable time should be available for play and social interaction, particularly in the elementary and middle grades. Piaget has consistently pointed out that the acquisition of knowledge is a result of one's activity. The talents of creativity and problem solving develop only if individuals are involved in a learning environment requiring their manifestation. Instruction emphasizing memorization and regurgitation not only fails to develop these talents but inhibits them.

Summary

Piaget's theory suggests that teaching in the traditional sense needs considerable modification. Teachers must become more aware of cognitive development in order to provide more of a meaningful learning environment for the student. However, acceptance of Piaget's work should not lead an instructor to emphasize cognition at the expense of all of the other talents composing a person. Too many teachers already commit this error. Teachers must constantly remember that students are persons having over 120 talents, only a few of which are related to the cognitive realm. The richness of the educational experience comes to fruition when instructors perceive and interact with students to maximize their total human potential. Understanding that children's minds evolve and are not adult in form is a first step toward helping children *become* as persons and build better mental health as a result.

Reference

(1) Furth, Hans G., *Piaget for Teachers*. Englewood Cliffs, N. J.: Prentice-Hall, Inc., 1970.

Bibliography

Belanger, Maurice, "Focus on Knowledge." Speech given to Jefferson County, Colorado, teachers, December 7, 1970.

Bybee, Rodger W. and Alan McCormack, "Applying Piaget's Theory." *Science and Children, 8,* December 1970, pp. 14–17.

Duckworth, Eleanor, "Piaget Rediscovered." *Journal Research In Science Teaching, 2,* 1964, pp. 172–75.

Elkind, David, "Children and Adolescents." *Interpretive Essays on Jean Piaget.* New York: Oxford University Press, 1970, p. 15.

Piaget, Jean, "Cognitive Development In Children: The Piaget papers." In *Piaget rediscovered: A Report of the Conference on Cognitive Studies and Curriculum Development,* March, 1964, R. E. Ripple and U. N. Rockcastle (eds.). Ithaca, N. Y.: Cornell University, School of Education, 1964, pp. 11–12.

7

PIAGET *IS* PRACTICAL

John W. Renner
Judith Brock
Sue Heath
Mildred Laughlin
Jo Stevens[1]

We were interested in employing Piaget's theory in a practical way in our elementary classrooms. In order to do that, however, we needed information about where in Piaget's model, children in the elementary school really are operating. We began our inquiry concerning its usefulness by administering six conservation tasks[2] to 252 children in the Norman, Oklahoma, Public Schools with the results shown in Table 1.

The data shown in Table 1 demonstrate that all children do not become concrete thinkers on all tasks at the same time. Piaget has said:

> We have followed the accepted custom of considering a test successfully passed when at least 75% of the children of the same age have answered correctly. (1)

If Piaget's procedure is followed, the children in the sample all conserved number by the age of 84 months (7 years). We believe that

[1]The authors express their gratitude to Leticia Bautista, Norris Grant, James Nickel, Mary Smith, Shirley Stone and Alta Watson, Science Education Center, College of Education, University of Oklahoma for their valuable assistance.
[2]For a description of the tasks used, see the explanation at the end of this article.

Reprinted from: *Science and Children, 9,* October 1971, pp. 23–26. Dr. John W. Renner is Professor of Science Education, University of Oklahoma, Norman, Oklahoma. Ms. Judith Brock, Ms. Sue Heath, Ms. Mildred Laughlin, and Ms. Jo Stevens are teachers at John F. Kennedy Elementary School, Norman, Oklahoma.

to thoroughly understand the concept of number, as opposed to memorizing the digits or how to count, a child must conserve number. Perhaps this will help to explain why some children have trouble with mathematics in the primary grades.

The children in the sample exercised conservation reasoning on solid amount and liquid amount by the age of 88 months (7 years, 4 months). Those two tasks require that a child hold the image of an object in his mind while it is distorted and then be able to recognize that the distorted object still has many of the same properties as the nondistorted one.

These conservation tasks also are excellent indications of the child's ability to reverse his thinking; i.e., to start at one point (equal amounts of liquid), think ahead to another point (same amounts in different-sized vessels), do a thinking reversal, and see that the two amounts are still the same. Perhaps that characteristic sheds some light on why some children have difficulty with subtraction. Piaget has stated that not being able to reverse one's thinking is a characteristic of a preoperational thinker.

The data in Table 1 show that the children in the sample were not consistent (even using Piaget's 75 percent rule) in their development of the ability to conserve length until 128 months (10 years, 8 months) of age, area until 132 months (11 years), and weight until 120 months (10 years). These data might indicate why elementary school mathematics teachers become frustrated in trying to teach that area = length × width, why trying to teach the use of a ruler to young children is difficult, and why some children seem unable to master a system of weights and measures. Studying when children conserve can influence one's expectations in the classroom; it influenced ours.

The age at which children begin to use conservation reasoning, which means that they are understanding thoroughly any concepts the tasks include, makes a teacher question our present curricula. This teacher might even become thoroughly discouraged and say, "Why do anything if the children are not capable?" Such reasoning is fallacious under our present instructional scheme. The responsibility still lies with the teacher to provide growth experiences for each child. As the data in Table 1 show, the preoperational child will eventually become concrete in his thinking, but what can his teacher do presently?

The data clearly show that just because a child is 7 years old, he has not necessarily left the preoperational stage. Let us consider the following five characteristics of thinking which are characteristics of the preoperational child; i.e., centering, irreversibility, egocentrism, inability to see states in a transformation, and transductive reasoning. There are many activities during the course of a normal day which can encourage a child to lose his preoperational characteristics and

TABLE 1. The number shown in each cell is the number of children at that particular age who demonstrated conservation reasoning on a particular task. The total number of children in the sample was 252.

Age-Months	Sample	Number	Solid Amount	Liquid Amount	Length	Area	Weight
60– 64	12	3	2	2	–	1	1
65– 68	12	7	2	–	2	2	3
69– 72	12	6	3	4	1	2	1
73– 76	12	8	7	7	3	6	3
77– 80	12	8	5	5	3	2	6
81– 84	12	9	5	5	–	3	5
85– 88	12	11	11	9	6	9	10
89– 92	12	11	9	11	9	8	11
93– 96	12	9	9	8	7	6	8
97–100	12	12	12	11	9	8	11
101–104	12	12	11	8	5	7	8
105–108	12	11	9	9	7	8	10
109–112	12	11	10	10	7	7	6
113–116	12	11	11	10	7	7	7
117–120	12	12	12	10	7	6	9
121–124	12	9	12	11	7	8	9
125–128	12	11	11	10	9	7	11
129–132	12	12	11	11	12	10	10
133–136	12	12	12	12	8	7	12
137–140	12	12	10	10	10	10	12
141–144	12	12	12	12	12	12	12

pass into the state of concrete thinking. A few such experiences which have been successful for us are these:

Treating all points on a continuum equally encourages divergent thinking and thus releases the child from centering.

1. Play "Simon says." This will give the child an opportunity to respond to another point of view.
2. Draw a heavy dot on a sheet of paper. Lightly sketch a familiar object such as a Christmas tree around the dot. Ask the child what he sees. Observe how many children center on the dot. These children need further experiences.
3. Make a ball out of clay or play dough. Flatten it. Give the children an opportunity to make different objects out of the same amount of clay. Discuss which object has the most clay. Children who still have the tendency to center may think that a tall thin or a short flat shape have different amounts of clay.

4. Serve the children equal amounts of Kool-Aid in glasses of different sizes and shapes. Have each child choose a glass of Kool-Aid. The children will discuss the reasons for the choice of a particular glass. Have measuring cups available so that the children can measure their Kool-Aid before drinking it. You may be surprised at the number of children who center on the shape of the glass.

5. Have the children classify different colored objects of the same size and shape; i.e., jaw breakers or wooden cubes. This gives them an opportunity to consider more properties than merely size and shape.

A child who cannot continually transpose as he moves forward in his thinking exhibits irreversibility.

1. This activity can be done with a seesaw or a smaller balance device inside the school. Begin with the equipment in balance. Add a child to the seesaw or an object to the balancing device. Ask the child to put it in balance again. If the child can make it even again, he is reversing his thinking.

2. Arrange a group of children in different positions so that one has his hand raised; another has his foot extended. Have a child observe the positions and then leave the area. Another child then changes the positions. The first child comes back and tries to return the children to their original positions. His ability to do this shows a reversal in his thinking.

3. Plant seeds and watch the growth. Later, have the children draw what was planted. Children who cannot reverse their thinking will not picture the original seed.

4. Observing a whole pumpkin, have the children make a jack-o-lantern. Ask one of the children to make the pumpkin look like it did before.

5. Allow the group to observe a container of water. Pour the water into an ice tray and freeze it. A child who is reversing will be able to describe the original state of the water.

Egocentric children need experience in observing from different frames of reference.

1. Place a box somewhere in the classroom. After the children have drawn the box as they observe it from their position, they will move to a new location and draw the box again. By performing this task, the child will be observing an object from a different frame of reference.

2. Have a child stand facing an object in the center of the room. Ask him to stand as he would if he were on the opposite side of the room without actually changing his location. Unless the child is now standing with his back to the object he is not able to observe from a different frame of reference.

3. Give the following directions for a relay game. Place your left arm in the proper sleeve of a coat. Run to the opposite end of the area and return to face the next player. Continue facing the next player until you have removed the coat and he has placed his arm in the proper sleeve. Children who have right and left confusion because they are facing a partner cannot cope with a change in reference frame, but such experiences will help them to develop reversibility in their thinking.

4. Ask the child to record his views on a pertinent problem. Have him interview five people and record their views. It's obvious in this case that the child will be exposed to other points of view.

States in a transformation involve a continuum of thinking in which motion and stages are realized as well as the beginning and ending.

1. Let the children build towers with clay and push them over. Ask them to draw what happened. If the child draws only the beginning and the end and shows no intermediate stages, he does not see states in a transformation.

2. Show a candle to your class. Light it and let it burn. Give the children an opportunity to describe what they saw.

3. Give a child a set of dominoes. Suggest that he stand them on end. Push them over. The child may draw what happened.

4. Mix batter from a cake mix and bake it. As a follow up the children may record data of what happened through sequential pictures.

5. Place a stick of celery in water to which red food coloring has been added. Ask the children to record what they saw.

A child who practices transductive reasoning cannot equate seemingly unrelated parts of a continuum. For example:

Teacher: I wear many green clothes. My car is green. Much of the furniture in my home is green. Keeping this in mind, what do you know about me?

Pupil: You wear glasses.

Some children need activities involving pure logic. You might say or do the following:

1. Encyclopedias are stored in alphabetical order. You are returning Volume C. Where does it go?

2. People wear special clothes for certain activities. As the teacher shows pictures of a football player, nurse, etc., she asks, "What does each person do?"

3. Litmus paper turns red when dipped into an acid. Vinegar is an acid. If I dip litmus paper into vinegar, what color will it be?

4. A quart holds two pints of water. I poured three pints of water into a quart jar. Draw what happened.

5. Select a reel full of tape. Place it on a tape recorder. Have a child choose a take-up reel of the appropriate size from a group of 3-, 5-, and 7-inch black reels.

6. Abe Lincoln and Robert E. Lee lived in the same century. Lee lived in the 1800's. When did Abe Lincoln live?

With statistical data in mind, and activities such as these as a beginning, the practicality of Piaget's ideas is limited only by imagination.

Reference

(1) Piaget, Jean, *Judgement and Reasoning in the Child*. Totowa, N. J.: Littlefield, Adams and Company, 1966, p. 100.

Description of Conservation Tasks Used*

1. Conservation of number

Six black checkers in one row and six red checkers in another row were arranged for the child.

The child was asked if he agreed that there was the same number of red checkers as there were black checkers. After he agreed to this fact, the red checkers were stacked, one on top of the other, and the black checkers were left as they were:

The child was then asked if there was still the same number of black checkers as there were red checkers and why.

2. Conservation of solid amount

[Present the child with a ball of clay. Ask the child to observe it. Then roll the clay into a long cylinder. Ask—"Does the snake have less, more, or the same amount of clay as the ball?" (If the child is confused say, "Was the ball bigger, smaller, or the same size as the snake?" Justification—Ask the child, "Why do you think the snake was bigger, smaller, or the same?"]

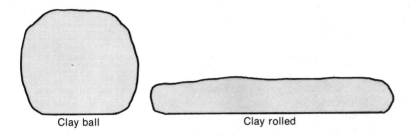

Clay ball   Clay rolled

3. Conservation of liquid amount

[Use two jars (a baby food jar and a tall cylinder) and enough colored water to fill the tall jar. Present the jars with the water in the short jar. Ask—"What will happen if I pour the water into the tall jar? Will I have more, less, or the same amount of water? Pour the water into the second container. Is there less, more or the same amount of water?" Justification—Ask the child, "Why do you think the amount of water was (more, less, the same)?"]

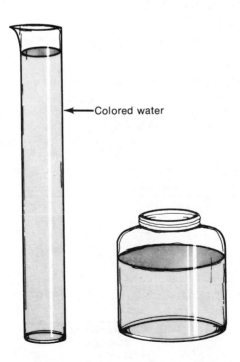

←—Colored water

We agree with this test and its use as explained by Bybee and McCormack but believe it reflects conservation of amount rather than volume. There is a specific text designed by Piaget for the conservation of volume.

4. Conservation of length

Place a rod 12 inches long and three other pieces each 4 inches long next to each other. These rods represent two roads. Next, place a toy car at the beginning of each road:

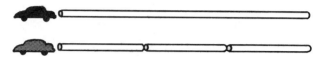

Ask the child if he agrees that both roads are the same length. After he agrees to this fact, pose the problem: "If the cars travel the same speed, which car, the red one or the black one, will read the end of the road first? Or will they reach the end of the road at the same time?" Record the child's answers. Then move one piece of the three-piece road ahead of the other two pieces, ask the same question, and why.

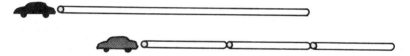

5. Conservation of area

[Present the child with two identical pieces of green construction paper. Tell him these represent fields or pastures. Place one toy animal on each piece of paper.

Ask the child to compare the fields. Note they are the same size. Comment that since the fields are the same size each animal will have the same amount of grass to eat. Tell the child you are going to use blocks to represent barns.

Place four barns on each field as shown in [the first drawing]. (Leave the animal on the field.) Ask, "Now which animal will have the most grass to eat or will the amount of grass be the same?" Justification—"Why do you think this is true?" Continue adding equal numbers of barns to each field. Each time repeat the question, "Which animal will have the most grass to eat?"]

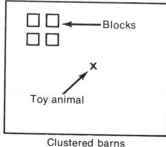

Clustered barns
Field A

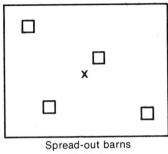

Spread-out barns
Field B

6. Conservation of weight

Form two balls of clay equal in size and let the child experience that they weight exactly the same:

Deform one of the balls of clay to make a pancake and do not let the child handle the clay.

Ask the child which would weigh more, the ball or the pancake, or would they both weigh the same and why.

[*In the original article tasks 2, 3, and 5 were only cited in reference. They are reprinted here from Rodger Bybee and Alan McCormack, "Applying Piaget's Theory." *Science and Children, 8,* December 1970, pp. 14–17.]

Becoming a Better Elementary Science Teacher Through Understanding All Children Are Special

Dr. Calvin Taylor says that every individual is a composite of multiple talents: academic, creative, social, planning, organizing, communicating, etc. To become a fully functioning individual a child should be assisted by his school to maximize his talents. Dr. Taylor has, as a result, helped schools to set up multi-talent approaches to education.

Children differ widely in their abilities. Because a child is strong in academic talent does not mean he will be creative. Teachers traditionally have emphasized academic talent at the expense of other talents. If a child has a talent potential he probably needs to demonstrate and be rewarded for it. Yet, schools with their narrow academic view of a person may hinder and reject individuals for attempts to manifest talent. Robert Samples points out how this occurred in the case of Kari, a creative child. In fact, Samples maintains that the way some schools are now operated Kari's creative ability is a handicap. How can such a beautiful talent be a handicap? What will you do to insure that children under your care are not handicapped?

If you perceive children only from an academic reference, many of them will be failures. However, if you see them as talent pools, then they all will be, as Dr. Taylor has pointed out, above average in at least one area. This is an important concept for a teacher to realize. Failure causes the demeaning of a child's self-concept. Dr. William Glasser's article dealing with the unmotivated student confronts directly the problem of failure. He believes teachers should stop failing children and provide an environment where there are always options for success. He suggests that teachers can have schools without failure if they get children involved, provide relevant material, and stimulate critical thinking.

Dr. Glasser's suggestions have been particularly successful in working with the culturally deprived child. Samuel Malkin describes these children and suggests how elementary science teaching may help to develop reading and other basic academic skills. As you read his article, apply his ideas to the way you think you operate your classroom.

The latter part of this section describes programs for children with acute special needs. They are in special education programs: blind, retarded, or handicapped by deafness. The articles are included because little has been done concerning science for special education; and teaching these children provides a model of a good learning environment for *all* children. This model emerges because the teacher must take the child from where he is and help him progress. How do they differ from normal classroom instructors?

Boekel and Bybee believe involvement, communication, attention span and self-concept need particular attention in teaching science to retarded children. One of their major points, "self-fulfilling prophecy," can be either positive or negative. Adapting teaching behavior to the needs of mentally retarded students is more important than adapting a curriculum; it is also harder.

Dr. Herbert Thier of the Science Curriculum Improvement Study has adapted SCIS materials for the blind. His article describes the actual work with physical and life science units.

What if you were suddenly required to teach a science lesson without talking—what would you do? The concluding article is about science for preschool deaf children. The importance of other avenues of communication becomes paramount and mandatory in teaching deaf children. There are some valuable lessons for all teachers derived from teaching the deaf. Teachers should consider how they would teach science concepts without resorting to verbal discourse.

You would not be in teaching if you didn't think children were special. By actualizing this belief in your teaching, you will move toward becoming an exciting elementary science teacher. After reading this section outline several ways you specifically want to modify your teaching behavior and work on them.

8

THE HIGHEST TALENT POTENTIALS OF MAN

Calvin W. Taylor

No. 1. Recommendation of 1970 White House Conference on Children: To provide opportunities for every child to learn creatively, to grow creatively, and to live creatively—by reordering national priorities.

Some of man's greatest inner powers and resources are his multiple high-level talents. The challenge is how we can teach people to use more of their brain cells, i.e., more of their many brain talent processes, and thus more of their potential talent powers.

If a composer were asked to create a new tune using only eight notes or keys on the piano or if an accomplished pianist were asked to perform on only eight notes, they could both undoubtedly do a respectable job. But consider how much less restricted they would be and how much better they could do if they were allowed to use all eighty-eight keys or notes covered by the piano. This analogy holds for the extent to which we are now having students use all their known talent powers in classes. Both we as teacher and they as students could do considerably better if we would deliberately try to have them use all of their known talents or all of the keys of their mind.

Thurstone was the first to come up scientifically with this insight about multiple talents, subdividing the intelligence test into about seven

Reprinted from revision of a speech given at the 15th Annual Conference for the National Association for Gifted Children, Chicago, Illinois, May 1–3, 1968. Dr. Calvin W. Taylor is a Professor of Psychology at the University of Utah, Salt Lake City, Utah.

or eight primary mental abilities. Then, with the help of his students, he pushed beyond the intelligence test composite to find additional primary mental abilities (or high-level talents) up to about twenty in number. These have been extended, especially in recent years by Guilford through his sustained work on a model called the "Structure of Intellect" which is a "periodic table of the mind." The number of talents that can now be measured is about 80 out of the 120 suggested by his model.

In retrospect, it is now painfully obvious that the intelligence test is *not* by any means a full measure of man. In fact, it measures only about seven or eight of the eighty high level talents discovered to date and thus covers only 1/10 of these known talents. In other words, it misses 9/10 of the known talents.

For a third of a century, we have known that there are many different types of intellectual talents. Nonetheless, this evidence can be quite a shocker to those with *the overgeneralized but fixed idea* about what a "general intelligence" test measures. One conclusion strongly supported by a vast and continually growing body of evidence is that there are many types of giftedness, not just the one type implied by the widely used phrasing, "The Gifted." Each of these types of giftedness is, in itself, quite complex and is composed of several different high-level intellectual talents. In other words, there is a particular subset of intellectual talents for each different type of giftedness.

This unfolding approach has been described in a simplified but colorful way by indicating that there are several ways of being smart. The first one is called "School Smart." The second is called "Street Smart" which breaks into two types: one is being smart like a youngster must be to survive in the streets in an extreme poverty, underprivileged, slum area. The other type is to be street smart as an adult by successfully planting a business on the main street and having it survive and thrive so that it tends to become an enduring enterprise, moving toward corporate immortality and toward living in perpetuity. Still another kind of smart is called "Aleck-Smart."

New Talents Provide Many New Hopes for
Reaching the Heretofore Deprived

This talent research provides many new hopes because there are many, many high-level talents and different persons excel in different ones of these talents. This means that if we search for a new type of talent, we will find as the most talented, essentially a new group of people from those at the top of the previous talent ladder. Likewise different subgroups of people are found to have a low degree of each particular talent. Consequently, those heretofore at the bottom of the previous talent ladder will rise as a subgroup to be almost average as far as the new type of talent is concerned—and a fraction of them (a third or more) are likely to be above average in the new talent area. This talent-approach to education therefore yields a beautiful phenomenon, for not only do new star performers emerge from almost all levels of the previous talent ladder but also those who had not been flourishing in the old talent areas will rise as a group toward the middle of their class in each new talent area in turn, and a sizeable number of them will be above average in each case.

Evidence available suggests that grades in our lengthy school programs of twelve to sixteen or more years do not particularly forecast who will have the skills and desire to keep abreast of knowledge on their own after they leave the formal educational system with all of its artificial props. In other words, the fact that a person has attained an educational degree in the present system gives little assurance that he is an independent scholar who has all the necessary abilities and will keep abreast of the knowledge explosion thereafter on his own. We feel that we are not doing very well in preparing students for change, for keeping on the "right side of change," and even for bringing about needed changes in knowledge and practices.

For those who claim that in the talent area, a major problem is lack of testing time, we point out that from our view, talent identification and development is central—not peripheral—to the educational processes. Therefore, all the time in our twelve to sixteen or more years of schooling can be spent in talent development while students are simultaneously working with subject matter knowledge.

Viewing our educational program in this light suggests that our talent searches should occur right in the classroom and that we should develop the talents of students in the regular curriculum while they are simultaneously acquiring knowledge. With the wide variety of talents that we now know how to search for, we can try to use a different approach in the classroom for each new type of talent. Since each new type of talent tends to be unrelated or not highly related to previous talents, this will result in much greater variety in education. It will also provide the best hope of reaching each and every person in the classroom *because almost everyone will be above average in one or more of these high level talents.*[1] This means that at one time or another in this highly varied curriculum we will be reaching almost all the

---

[1] It is also realistic to recognize that contrarily, almost everyone is below average in at least one talent.

heretofore educationally deprived, the goal of the poverty program, as we seek for a wide variety of new talents in our youth.

The role for the teachers is that of a developer of talent as well as a subject matter teacher. In fact, the talent developer role could well be the primary one. Shouldn't each student have the chance during school time to develop each of his multiple talents, since different talent processes still permit subject matter acquisition and are the inner processes that can be used in acquiring knowledge. In fact, we have found that students will grow in subject matter knowledge at least as fast, if not faster, when we have them utilize and develop new talents while they are acquiring the subject matter.

With the current emphasis on knowledge acquisition, a relative narrow band of talents is probably being cultivated. Moreover, there is some suspicion that any increase in the amount of typical programmed instruction might further narrow the band of talents being developed. In sharp contrast, if a multiple talent approach is used in the classroom, the band of talents being developed would not only be deliberately widened, but as an automatic by-product, the scope and type of knowledge being acquired might also widen.

The cultivation of certain talents such as creativity and one of its components, curiosity, would require the student to work at the fringe of knowledge and with unknown areas beyond the fringe, both of which are customarily not experienced much by students in our educational program until they reach advanced levels of graduate study. And the curiosity of students should be encouraged to function in areas that are *as yet unknown* to man (including the teacher and the textbook), as well as in the other areas where the students do not yet know what man (including the teacher) already knows. The teacher must function appropriately with students in both areas or else their curiosity will likely be stifled in both, for students have no way of telling in advance whether their curiosity is in one of man's known areas, merely unknown to themselves, or one of man's unknown areas.

Theory and Evidence on a Multiple Talent Approach

If there were merely one type of talent, only 50 percent of the students would be talented above average (median). If there were two *unrelated* talents with 50 percent above average on each, 25 percent would be above average on both talents, 25 percent above on the first but not the second, and 25 percent on the second but not the first, so that a total of 75 percent would be above average on at least one talent.

For three uncorrelated talents, 87.5 percent would be above average on at least one talent.

This trend continues by splitting the distance to 100 percent in each case, as indicated below in rounded-off percentages:[2]

Number of Unrelated Talents	Percent Above Average in at Least One Talent
1	50.0%
2	75.0
3	87.5
4	93.8
5	96.9
6	98.4
7	99.2
8	99.6

Since high-level talents are not absolutely unrelated but tend to be lowly related in the positive direction, evidence indicates that the actual trends upward toward 100 percent do not climb as rapidly as in the theoretical picture above (based upon the extreme case of zero intercorrelations). In other words, there would be some slippage downward due to some overlapping between talents. In the case of two somewhat correlated talents, the expectation for the percentage above average would be in the high 60's (instead of 75 percent); for three talents it would be in the 70's (instead of 87.5 percent); for four talents in the high 70's or possibly in the low 80's (instead of 93.75 percent), etc. The estimated downward slippage will depend upon the level of correlation found to be present—the more intercorrelation, the more the slippage. One will reach over 90 percent with six lowly intercorrelated talents.

The same type of theoretical approach could be applied to the top end of the talent ladder. For example, considering the top 10 percent as highly gifted and looking across several types of talents of giftedness yields a similar important trend. If only one type of talent is cultivated, only 10 percent will be "highly gifted." If talents are independent and two uncorrelated types are cultivated, 19 percent will be highly gifted. (One percent will be highly gifted in both types of talent and a total of 19 percent will be highly gifted in at least one type of talent.) This percent will likewise increase to 27 with three talents, to 35 with four talents, and will continue upwards at a diminishing rate as each

---

[2] An equation for the extreme case of n uncorrelated talents is $(.50)^1 + (.50)^2 + (.50)^3 + \ldots + (.50)^n = $ the percentage above the median in at least one talent out of the n talents considered.

new type of talent is added, assuming that talents are completely unrelated.

However, in the usual case of talents being somewhat related, this percentage will not rise as rapidly. For example, if creativity is added as a second type of talent, the evidence suggests that a new 7 percent will be found to be in the top 10 percent of the highly talented in creativity along with 3 percent from the previous talent area who will have a high profile across both types of talent. Thus a total of 17 percent will be highly gifted in at least one of the two talent areas. By further taking into account the low interrelationships among different types of giftedness, approximately 22 to 23 percent will be found to be in the top 10 percent of at least one of three types of giftedness. This trend will continue so that if one cultivates at least six different types of giftedness in the classroom, about 30 percent of the students could be found to be highly gifted (in the top 10 percent) in at least one of the six high-level talent areas. We can therefore triple the percent who are highly talented by extending the number of talents to six—that is, to multiple types of giftedness, numbering at least six.[3]

Again this presents a most promising picture for educators, since about a third of the students will be found to be highly gifted in at least one major talent area. This is a very heartening outlook in terms of motivation of students and the potential in our human resources.

Recently I had an interesting experience with a multiple talent approach in working with a Navy team on Project Compass. We tried to insert a computer into the personnel program and eventually did so with success. The Navy has about 60 schools which are the entrance pathways into Navy jobs. With the help of the computer we could readily handle 1500 recruits who had come into the Navy during one week. By processing across the profiles of characteristics of recruits and then looking across a variety of Navy schools, it became possible to try to place each person into one of the better schools for him, though not necessarily into absolutely the best predicted one for him. This process is called differential prediction and placement (or classification). The task is to try to place each person in a job where he would have a good chance of success and so the entire set of placements would yield a maximum in terms of total predicted success for all those entering all the Navy schools. The computer assisted and kept the final placement problem completely open until it had made 60 forecasts for each of the 1500 people (a total of 90,000 forecasts) as to how well they would do in each and every one of the schools. And then it recommended a placement for each person so that all school

---

[3] Darrel Allington has illustrated this multiple talent teaching approach by what he has called "Taylor's Talent Totem Poles" (see Figure 1).

quotas were also completely filled. All this took the computer about twenty minutes to do.

We checked into the final solution and found that something over 80 percent of the people were placed in schools where they would be above average, which has great implications for education and the world of work. This means that at least four talent dimensions are being utilized in their present placement program. By doing further research work on this problem it should be possible to increase this percentage toward 90 percent.

We completed this project almost "in spite of the system," in this large organization. We finished it to the stage of making it operational just a month before the number of enlisted men entering the Navy doubled. We met this deadline only through putting sustained strain on the system, because the system had not budgeted nor otherwise adequately planned to have all this done that year.

The Navy may not fully realize what a good thing they have working. If there were only one kind of talent, there obviously would be no basis on which to capitalize on differential prediction through use of the computer. But since there are multiple types of talent and since jobs likewise differ widely in the types of talents they require, differential prediction and placement can be used to great advantage. This approach deliberately tries to find an area where each person is a hotshot or is at least above-average. It provides great hope both for individuals and for the total manpower problem. And an analogous approach can work in teaching in classrooms to identify and develop new types of talent.

There are many kinds of talents and with these modern facilities we can use techniques which previously have theoretically been available but are now also actually available through the help of computers. These computers are becoming more and more available and economical, so this message is a tremendous one for illustrating the great human resources potentially available in our youth.

This over-all evidence argues not only for an upward lift for those previously at the bottom of a talent ladder but also for new groups rising to the top as each new kind of giftedness is focused upon and cultivated.

We plan to go to three groups of people, in turn, to tell them the message that almost all students are above average in at least one area of talent. First we are going to teachers and other educators. If they do not show sufficient readiness to listen and to react quickly to do something about it, then we are going to the parents who should be glad to know that each one of their children is above average. However, if the parents also are not sufficiently alert to stir action toward greater development of these neglected resources in the midst of their own families, then we will go directly to the students themselves. From all our experiences with them and from our demonstrations on them, we are confident that they will be ready and will not want any delay in having schools become more actively and deliberately dedicated to developing their multiple talents in classrooms.

Many Clues on How to Teach for Creativity

The importance of creativity is possibly best described by Arnold Toynbee in his two fascinating papers on this topic (4). He points out in his first paper, "On the Role of Creativity in History," that creative talent is the talent which, when functioning effectively, can make history in any area of human endeavor. In his second paper he raises the question "Is America Neglecting Her Creative Talents?" (and thus her future history). In it he mentions that creativity is mankind's ultimate capital asset—a matter of life and death for any society.

Then he warns that "Potential creative ability can be stifled, stunted, and stultified by the prevalence in society of adverse attitudes of mind and habits of behavior. What treatment is creative ability receiving in our Western World, and particularly in America?" He states that any society "... has a moral duty to ensure that the individual's potential ability is given free play. If, on the contrary, society sets itself to neutralise outstanding ability, it will have failed in its duty to its members, and it will bring upon itself a retribution for which it will have only itself to blame."

He says it is ironic and tragic that America herself should have become the archconservative power in the world after having made history as the archrevolutionary one and that she turned her back on the very same creative and pioneering characteristics which had led her to attain her position in history.

With a note of hope that America can reverse herself concerning her creative potentials, Toynbee states that "America's need, and the world's need, today is a new burst of American pioneering, and this time not just within the confines of a single continent but all round the globe."

Toynbee adds a final challenge to our nation by saying that "America's manifest destiny in the next chapter of history is to help the indigent majority of mankind to struggle upwards toward a better life than it has ever dreamed of in the past." And if she is to embark successfully upon this mission, he concludes that *"America must treasure and foster all the creative ability that she has in her."*

More recently[4] he wrote that "my impression—and indeed my conviction— is that, if America is to treasure and foster all the creative ability that she has in her, a new and right spirit of change has to be injected into her educational philosophy." To him the rather rigid "models of educational selection and treatment will, I should press, have to be refashioned to include the creative talents of the coming generations."

And he further wrote that "new educational philosophies and new institutions of learning need to be constructed to provide an opportunity for creative individuals to enhance their talents in schools. If the American people, or any other people, are unwilling to change their minds and hearts to remold their educational establishment in ways that foster creative talents, they cannot expect to be able to persist in this negative attitude with impunity. This is surely true, particularly of the American people, conceived, nurtured, and guided, as it has been, for almost two hundred years by its creative leadership. 'Where there is no vision, the people perish.' "

Since creativity is a many faceted topic (a many splendored thing), several different avenues of exploratory development work can and should be tried. One source for suggestions of numerous new approaches that could be tried for developing creativity is in the series of ten articles entitled "Clues for Creative Teaching" (1). We recommend a multi-prolonged attack for implementing creativity into the classroom. Different approaches can be tried, using different teachers and different classrooms with accompanying comparison studies to see what results are yielded by each approach and to determine which approaches are most fruitful.

We have recently published a book on our sixth research conference on instructional media and creativity (2). In this new book the question is raised whether existing instructional media can be used for creativity. According to experts in this area, only a negligible proportion of the vast amount of existing instructional media have ever been designed with the creativity of students in mind. Consequently, there is a vast universe of challenges ahead in the modification of existing media and in the construction and refinement of new media to elicit most effectively creative processes and creative behaviors in students.

In this new book another vast number of clues are given as to how we could produce instructional media designed for creativity and thereby teach more effectively for creativity. The importance of having activities and assignments and media which call upon the inner resources of students is stressed as is the use of multiple media and instructional materials. Another important approach that has been sug-

---

[4]Taken from an April 18, 1968, letter to Calvin W. Taylor.

gested is to identify those teachers who are most masterful in teaching for creative processes and creative behaviors in their students. Then it could be possible through the use of powerful instructional media devices to capture or in other ways to duplicate the approaches of these master teachers which are most effective, so that their teaching can be captured and rapidly spread to reach many many students in classrooms while the other teachers are learning how to teach for creativity at their own pace and in their own ways.

Our traveling Utah task force team has helped several school districts in Western U.S.A. to start learning how to teach for creativity. Our strongest features are the variety of classroom demonstrations, using their own students, plus ways we have devised to get their teachers to gradually join and then to replace us in continuing the demonstrations.

In the eighth grade Joe Maddy dropped out of school because it was not developing his best kinds of talents. In the course of his career, he started new schools at Interlochen, Michigan, of the type that would develop his kinds of talent. Both the National Music Camp and the Arts Academy in Interlochen now describe themselves as one of the great talent developer centers in the world. As a reward for starting and successfully building such schools and also the planning of a new two-year college at Interlochen, Maddy was awarded several honorary doctoral degrees by schools of the type that he still would have dropped out of.

A highly effective, self-made man who is one of the top advisors in the nation has observed that colleges and universities with their high specialization and their sharp boundaries between departments have a problem that they may be good at producing narrow-minded people. In looking for ways to overcome these sharp differences and boundaries, one college believes that creativity can serve them well by providing the unifying theme for their college.

There is also a move afoot to start a college for the creatively talented as a small initial step toward counterbalancing the 2500 colleges and universities available for the academically talented.

All this leads us to the conclusion that what is needed in education is not "just more of the same," but instead to try to develop creative and other high level talents in addition to the customary talents displayed so well by the academically gifted. Do we want to follow the past tradition entirely or do we want to innovate by adding first creative talents to the academic talents now being cultivated? In other words, do we want students to be not merely learners but also thinkers; not only memorizers and imitators but also searchers and innovators; not merely scholars of past knowledge but also producers of new knowledge; not only well versed that "it is written" but also alert that "all is not yet written"; not solely skilled in "knowing the ropes," but capable of "improving the ropes"; not only able to adjust themselves to their environment, but also able to adjust their environment to themselves; not only producers of imitative products but also of creative products; not only high quality performers of an existing pattern, but also composers and creators of new patterns; not merely capable of preserving our past heritage but also capable of creating a better future; and thus able to use not only their gold-like talents but also their uranium-like talents.

Demonstration Studies on
Communication Talents in Language Arts

Communication talents are the next new talent area after creativity that we have been implementing into classrooms. We have been doing basic research on communication abilities intermittently for nearly two decades.[5] Our first finding is that there are many, many different sets of communication talents. These various communication abilities can be very important in a variety of high-level activities in the world of work, including supervisory, administrative, and executive work, professional work, selling, and advertising of all kinds—in fact, in almost every area of human endeavor. We have developed nearly 200 new scores on communication talents based upon the large number of different communication activities sampled from the human roles in communication systems in organizations, i.e., from the human components in the communication systems.

Upon invitation from educators we have constructed many classroom exercises of either paper-and-pencil or situational types.[6] We have built several sets of these educational exercises for classroom use initially in Granite and Jordan School Districts and since then in other places such as Polk County, Iowa; Clark County, Nevada; and Laramie, Wyoming. We have worked with teachers in the English

[5]Our latest support was from the Air Force Office of Scientific Research Project # AF-AFOSR-144-63, Rowena Swanson, monitor, Exploratory Research on Communication Abilities and Creative Abilities, U. S. Government Printing Office, AFOSR 67-1523, 309 pages, April, 1967.

[6]*Communication and Creativity Training Exercises: Training Manual,* Institute for Behavioral Research in Creativity, 1417 So. 11 East, Salt Lake City, Utah, and also at P. O. Box 298 in Greensboro, North Carolina. This nonprofit trusteeship staffed by my former students has been established in order to handle the increased activities in creativity and communication abilities. A main purpose of this Institute is to make research findings and materials available for practical use in classroom situations. For example, this new Institute has also just published the *ALPHA Biographical Inventory,* for identifying creative talent using the biographical approach which has been repeatedly valid and culture-fair. The ALPHA also provides a predicted academic ability score for college work.

programs in helping them learn to use and incorporate these exercises into their regular classroom activities.

These sets of exercises call for new communication talents which students generally have not yet been asked to display in school. Consequently, in the regular English classes we have been reaching many of the presently educationally deprived children with one or more of this great variety of communication tasks. In fact in our comparison studies in eight out of twelve comparisons the group trained with these exercises did significantly better than the control group which had the usual training (and most of the remaining differences were in the expected direction and approaching statistical significance).

We plan to continue to build additional sets of these exercises from others of our communication tests and from additional ideas that have emerged in more recent work and experiences in the communication area. The teachers have also been enthusiastic about these materials and about challenges we have given them to add their own modifications to these exercises and to construct their own new variations of these exercises. Furthermore, we encourage the teachers to ask their students to build their own variations of these exercises and to create new communications exercises based upon their own ideas.

Our research evidence shows that we can select several separate sub-sets of these short, stimulating exercises which collectively will give students practically a parallel experience to the much more complex task of writing a theme. Yet as students are asked to work on these short simpler exercises, practically all of them are able to become involved and deeply interested in each of these exercises. In contrast when they had been given an assignment to write a theme, many students were not nearly so interested and a few of them would no longer even participate in the assignment.

In conclusion, we have demonstrated several times through several different teachers that with the use of these exercises designed to develop communication talents, we can reach most of those who were heretofore academically deprived in the language arts program. More liveliness and enthusiasm has been shown by the entire class as they work with these thinking and communication exercises. At the same time they are mastering subject matter and skills needed in the language arts area.

Human Capabilities Will Grow as New Projects Progress

An important insight into human variables in this bridging process has emerged from a recent Department of Defense investigation entitled "Hindsight." The evolution of each of nearly twenty new military weapons or large complex pieces of equipment, which had been successfully constructed and installed into military operations, was studied in retrospect. On the average across the nearly twenty new pieces of equipment, it was found that only two-thirds of the various types of human know-how and capabilities were present when work was officially initiated. Consequently, the other one-third of the know-how and capabilities had to be created during the course of successful completion of the work on the new weapons system or equipment (a ratio of 2:1). In other words, 50 percent additional human know-how and capabilities, on the average, needed to be generated and were generated during the work on the weapons system or equipment in order to finish these R&D efforts through the stage of official installation.

A major—and perhaps the greatest—accomplishment of these projects, then, was the tremendous and rapid growth in human and organizational capabilities through the course of each R&D project. Knowing this evidence, no judges or critics should complain that a new project cannot be started, "because before we start, we must have available 100 percent of the knowledge and capability to successfully complete the project." In other words, one does not have to foresee all the steps through the project with 100 percent certainty, but instead the project through its existence can stimulate the development of the needed human insights and capabilities that are not yet available.

A project can therefore be a tremendous catalyst toward the development of uncultivated human potentials and can noticeably increase human capabilities. It is even possible that some hotshot, creative R&D individuals and teams may be able to succeed on projects where much less than two-thirds of the required know-how and capabilities are present at the time of decision on whether to initiate the project.

Our main educational thesis in this article is that in deciding about the kinds of classroom projects to initiate, current student capabilities should not prevent us from exploring new areas where talent can be greatly increased. The challenge is to initiate various appropriate types of projects such as those in which less than 100 percent is known and in which students are encouraged to undertake ventures into somewhat unexplored areas of human activities and knowledge—at least partly out into the unknowns.

A tentative generalization recently emerging from our own work is pertinent here. We strongly suspect that whatever activity or responsibility teachers hold closely unto themselves as their *prerogative* will be an activity which the students will be largely deprived of. For example, if the teacher does all the planning or all the decision making, then the students will have little experience or opportunity to grow in their planning or decision-making talents. This trend becomes even more intensified if parents and then their first supervisors on the job, later in life, also deprive them of any opportunity to plan or to make decisions. These tendencies and trends may be overcome by deliberately inserting into the curriculum the planning and decision-making (and other previously withheld) activities for students to experience.

On the Importance of Other High-Level Talents

As indicated earlier, there are at least eight or ten types of giftedness for which students can be tested. Through proper educational engineering work, these tests can be modified into classroom training exercises that are well founded in research studies about human talents. It then becomes possible for a student to learn a great deal about his own talents and the particular talents that are his best ones. Consequently, from these experiences and insights he can become self-directed and whenever he desires, he can steer himself throughout his life into activities which call for his best talent areas.

After students have learned to use their different types of talents, with permission and encouragement from the teacher, each one of them could then use his own best talent as his best way of learning any particular subject matter area. In this way the total subject matter performance of the class would be maximized as a powerful result of helping students to develop their talents and to learn to select and use their best talents when needed. (Then students would practically all find and use their own smiling stage in the Talent Totem Poles.)

Admittedly it is challenging to attempt to bring about changes such as these in educators and in their procedures and practices administratively and in classrooms. One school principal said that he had changed his school as a consequence of a rather full exposure to our research work. The only thing he had changed was his counseling with parents. When parents came into see him about their son who was not doing too well, he would comment that the parents were probably quite capable people living in a good neighborhood, driving a new car, and holding down a good job with a sizeable income. The parents would proudly agree. Then he stated that he would bet on heredity. Therefore, their child should prove to be strong in the same kind of talents that they have, but that schools were not now emphasizing those particular talents. So if they could just be patient until their son struggled through and finished school, his stronger talents would show up when he went out into the world of work and he would probably be very successful like they have been.

We thought this was quite an honest observation of this principal and was an interesting way to have his school adjust, but so far primarily only through his counseling with parents. It may be an important first step, however, for he recognizes that he is leaving almost all talents (except the school-like ones) to be developed later in the world of work as chances there will permit.

Our results indicate that there is preciously little relationship between the talents and other characteristics needed to succeed in the present academic world and those called for in professional career performances in the world of work. In our studies of professional careers of physicians, we have 849 correlations between performance in the academic world and performance in the professional world. The average correlation was zero (.00) and the frequency distribution of these 849 correlations yielded an almost random error (normal curve) distribution around zero (.00) correlation, with only 3 percent of the correlations being significant: 2 percent in the negative direction and only 1 percent in the positive direction. So current academic grades are highly inadequate as substitute criteria for later multiple criteria of career performances as well as being, of course, inadequate as predictors.

Let us illustrate some problems of neglected, dormant, hidden, or stifled talents. We need to try to produce a higher percentage of "can doers" and at the same time reduce considerably the percentage of "can't doers." In effect, greater attention needs to be paid to both the selection and training of students so that a smaller and smaller percentage of them become "can't doers"—persons whose main contribution is to offer and document all the reasons "why it is impossible" to try to accomplish something. Their negative influence can spread to others because their statements imply that no one else can do it, either, not just themselves, and they therefore would not want anyone else to try and perhaps prove they are wrong. It can therefore be very refreshing to find a true leader who is a "can doer," who will find ways to have something good become possible, and who will shoulder foreseeable new missions not in their job descriptions that can lead to improvements and progress, especially when no one else is willing to assume these responsibilities.[7]

Much greater emphasis in training students should be paid on having them focus a sizeable percentage of their attention (5—15 percent) at all times on improving the present system and procedures. Instead of resisting and "fighting off" suggestions and opportunities for improving the system, persons should be alert to and positively prepared to take advantage of such opportunities *whenever* and *however* they arise. Then if transfer of training occurs when they are assigned to key leadership positions, they will again spend up to 15 percent

---

[7]This recommendation is consistent with John Gardner's comment that too many of the people sitting in leadership spots are spending all their energies tending the old system, so that little or no leadership of any important type is really being displayed—let alone either creative leadership or leadership for creativity.

or more of their time and energies on improving the system rather than merely tending the old system and keeping it operating.

Perhaps the world has been oversold on the idea that people must learn to *adjust to their environment*. A new emphasis which describes the creatives is that they have the necessary talents and are interested in *adjusting their environment* to themselves and to their needs.

Studies on research training of science students suggest that the sound rule is "the earlier the better, and the later the worse." In other words, the sooner we can have students using their research talents, the better and the later we postpone their use, the worse. Yet science education has historically violated this recent research finding by postponing the use of research *talents in students* until their seventeenth or eighteenth year of formal education.

This multiple talent approach is a very healthy one indeed and should make our school systems much more efficient in accomplishing another potential goal of education, namely, the development of all the nation's human resources. In our educational theory project (3) [we] proposed that one of the important ways of viewing an educational program was to see it as functioning to identify and develop the nation's important student resources for the over-all benefit of the individuals, the communities, the nation, and the world. The higher the potentials that anyone conceives to be present in students, the more eager and impatient he will be for improvements in education to occur so that more of these total potentials will be developed.

A homely analogy may serve here. In our mining region, some large, efficient mills have been built in order to process literally tons of raw materials from which valuable metals can be extracted as important natural (physical) resources. In fact, a mountainside of rocks and boulders of all sizes is being processed through the mills. These rocks are ground in successive steps until they are so fine that, upon the addition of water, they are turned into a stream of silt. This stream is next processed to yield copper, the metal initially sought. The procedure used to end here, but now the stream is further processed, in several other successive ways, to extract each additional metal that can be found in the current of silt. These metal mining organizations claim that they have been very alert to new and better ways of processing the metals presently recovered out of the stream of raw material.

They also contend that they are very alert to any discoveries, through basic research, of the existence of new and sometimes rare and precious metals. As soon as such a metal is thus discovered, they state that they will immediately try to identify its presence in the residual stream that is being poured into the valley floor as a mere waste product. If the new metal is present, they will rapidly try to find ways of adding other processes in the mill to develop this additional metal out of the total potential in the stream. They will, of course, continue to be interested in extracting and processing the initial metal, copper, but no longer to the exclusion of other important metals, whether known to be present or potentially available, though still to be identified and developed. The extraction of any additional metal might, in large part, become a bonus, because the rock has already been ground, because the total mill is already in existence, and because only minor additions in the processing may be needed to develop this other metal out of the raw materials.

As they look backwards over the years, they realize that they have dumped so-called waste products into the valley floor that may contain various metals of a larger total value than the metals that they have extracted.

Besides focusing on those talents traditionally identified and cultivated in schools, in a similar manner we could be alert to discover other human talents and resources heretofore unrecognized or underdeveloped. We could try to identify as soon as possible the newly recognized potentials in students (such as psychological uranium) and to incorporate suitable additional processes into the educational program in order to develop these additional resources, wherever feasible. Much of the work has already been done, because the students are already here, the organizations are already functioning, and certain processes are already in efficient operation. And as we discover, identify, and process these additional new human resources, we may wonder, like the mining specialists, about how long we have previously been pouring such resources untouched through the mills and out on the world, unnoticed and undeveloped.

Without delay we urge that schools, as well as programs for "The Gifted," move away from ignoring and failing to develop these new hidden talents and move as rapidly as possible toward active programs focused upon talent development both for the sake of the heretofore educationally deprived as well as the heretofore unrecognized and underdeveloped gifted persons in each of the many new talent areas.

During the last year, there was an important White House Task Force on Talents on which I was a senior consultant. The final report delivered recently to the President strongly showed that most organizations and government agencies and educational institutions do *not* put their money directly on talents, but give only lip service and peripheral attention to them. In contrast, our recommendations strongly urged that talents should be right at the center of focus, for highly talented people of various types and in various fields are the ones who solve our most difficult problems and create a better world.

How to Kill Creativity

Recently I was asked to give a short TV speech on an assigned but reversed topic: "How to Kill Creativity." The following nine rules emerged based on our research and the research of others—in fact, from our total experience in working on creativity.

1. Assume there is only one academic (or intelligence) type of talent, only one type of giftedness.
2. As teachers, ignore scientific research results about creative talents.
3. Keep doing what was done to your ideas—and even do it more so.
4. Be very human—*react* quickly and negatively to new ideas. Allow me to be sarcastic on this point. If you, as a supervisor or teacher really want to stop something, be really alert, be sensitive very early to the problem. Nip it in the bud, because not many people will see you kill it—just the person with the idea and you. But if you let it grow into a branch you will have to saw it off, or if you allow it to become a tree, you will have to chop it down. Then many people will hear you sawing and chopping and hear it fall, so they can easily find out who chopped it down.

    If, as another possibility you initially let the idea alone to grow on its own and you don't make a decision one way or another for a while, but later desert it, you may have a problem. Or if it really flourishes, and you try later to actively join, you [may] have a hard time having the idea-person welcome you and find room for you on the band wagon. Psychologically he may then not be eager to have you join if you had earlier failed to back him up when he really needed such support. So you can avoid all these problems by being very alert and sensitive to new ideas and nipping them in the bud.
5. Keep the rule going: "The more highly creative the idea, the more likely it will be *in trouble.*" And the person who created the idea will equally be in trouble, too.
6. Have a deadly negative incentive system for creative persons and ideas. Some workers have developed techniques to use on their boss. When they approach him with an idea, and when he's listening to the new idea, they flash a green card on him. But when he starts producing killers of the idea, they flash a red card on him. Or they might flash a yellow card to indicate he is being cautionary (or just plain yellow).

7. *Organize* creatives in (under your controls)—or organize them *out,* ostracise them.

8. Design all possible *features* into classrooms *that stifle* or kill creativity. (Try this exercise on your teachers or on your students.)

9. Jealously guard, keep prerogatives only to yourself to plan to think, and to create.

As one of my closing comments I want to make the observation that from all the research results I have seen, it is a rare day when a highly creative person is surrounded by much understanding. This is unfortunately a sad comment—though I am confident it is too frequently a true one. As many have noted, the creative person is likely to find himself in a lonely role, and also in the role of an underdog.

Instead of having understanding support, he is surrounded by many techniques, as illustrated above, that are effective as "killers of creativity." Let me arm you with one example of an *anti-killer technique* to combat such killer attempts. At our last creativity research conference one person took a defensive view that perhaps only a very few creative people are really needed in an organization or in a nation. He wondered where we would be if for the next fifteen to twenty years we did everything we could to identify, develop, and encourage creative talent. He asked, "Wouldn't there then be too many creative people and wouldn't this be a problem?" Lindsey Harmon brilliantly replied, "If there were too many creative people and if it were a problem, then there ought to be enough creative people around to solve it." Let's all take this position of hope and stride ahead.

George Washington stated brilliantly that the difficulty in bringing about reforms in an organization is that one must do so through the persons who have been the most successful in that organization, no matter how faulty it is. So these people would tend to say "Look how good an organization it must be because look who succeeded best in it." These persons who usually think of the organization as already being a good system are unfortunately the ones through whom someone must work to bring about reforms.

Let me close on another positive point. Richardson, who believes that creative minds should continue to rise to the top, has said that creative organizations live longer than other organizations. A note very similar to this is that organizations should be able to listen effectively both within and without so that it is always very alert to new ideas and new developments from whatever source. If organizations or societies do not have this vital alertness, it will only be a matter of time until their day has passed.

A fascinating analogous hunch of Navy Captain Campbell is that creative persons may live longer. This notion suggests that creative processes might be enlivening, health-giving, and even life-lengthening processes within an individual. The creative individual who can listen and draw effectively upon available resources, both from within himself and from outside, and who can utilize these inner and outer processes effectively may be a much healthier person and may live both longer and more abundantly.

References

(1) Taylor, C. W., "Clues to Creative Teaching." A series of 10 articles in *The Instructor,* September 1963–June, 1964, usually starting on p. 5.
(2) Taylor, C. W. and F. Williams (eds.), *Instructional Media and Creativity.* New York: John Wiley & Sons, Inc., 1966.
(3) Taylor, C. W., B. Ghiselin, J. A. Wolfer, Lorraine Loy, and L. E. Bourne, Jr., "Development of a Theory of Education from Psychological and Other Basic Research Findings." (mimeographed). U. S. Office of Education Cooperative Research Project No. 621, August, 1964.
(4) Toynbee, Arnold, "On the Role of Creativity in History" and "Is America Neglecting her Creative Talents." In *Creativity Across Education,* Salt Lake City: University of Utah Press, in press.

Bibliography

Guilford, J. P., "Progress in the Discovery of Intellectual Factors." In C. W. Taylor (ed.), *Widening Horizons in Creativity.* New York: John Wiley & Sons, Inc., 1964, pp. 282–97.

Hutchinson, W. L., "Creative and Productive Thinking in the Classroom." Ph.D. diss., University of Utah, 1963.

Institute for Behavioral Research in Creativity, *Alpha Biographical Inventory,* Salt Lake City, Utah and P.O. Box 298, Greensboro, N. C.: Prediction Press, 1968.

_____*Communication and Creativity Training Exercises: Training Manual,* Salt Lake City, Utah and P. O. Box 298, Greensboro, N. C., 1968.

Taylor, C. W. (ed.) *Creativity: Progress and Potential.* New York: McGraw-Hill Book Company, 1964.

Taylor, C. W., *Climate for Creativity.* Book reporting Seventh (1966) National Research Conference on Creativity. Manuscript in preparation, 1969.

Taylor, C. W. (ed.), *Widening Horizons in Creativity.* New York: John Wiley & Sons, Inc., 1964.

Taylor, C. W., "Questioning and Creating: A Model for Curriculum Reform." *Journal of Creative Behavior, 1,* 1967, pp. 22–33.

———*Creativity Across Education.* Manuscript in preparation, University of Utah Press, 1969.

Taylor, C. W. and F. Barron (eds.), *Scientific Creativity: Its Recognition and Development.* New York: John Wiley & Sons, Inc., 1963.

Taylor, C. W., B. Ghiselin and J. A. Wolfer, "Bridging the Gap Between Basic Research and Educational Practice." *NEA Journal,* 1962, pp. 23–25.

Taylor, C. W., B. Ghiselin, and K. Yagi, "Exploratory Research on Communication Abilities and Creative Abilities." Final report submitted to the Air Force Office of Scientific Research, AF-AFOSR-144-63, Printed by the U. S. Government Printing Office, AFOSR 67-1523, April, 1967, pp. 309.

9

KARI'S HANDICAP—
THE IMPEDIMENT OF CREATIVITY

Robert E. Samples

Of course. The only way it could be explained is that snow is a cloud lying down. The ocean breathes a cloud into the air and it becomes tired as it ripples up and down across the desert. When it must rest, it will lie down on a mountain. Maybe it's making love to the mountain. Oh, if it is, I wish I were a mountain. If it stops too long, it can't leave the way it came. The mountains bleed their cloud away and it becomes soiled. But what beautiful punishment . . . it can escape out of the inside of an aspen tree to get back into the air . . . but only a little at a time. That's what it costs to be too tired. Maybe though, it could . . .

"Kari!"

Damn you! It was silent, but she thought it. Aloud, she said, "Yes, Mr. Clyde?"

"Have you solved the problem yet?"

"Oh, . . . no; I'll need more time."

The teacher's voice rang with bitterness, "You're the only one who needs more time. Have it here by 8 in the morning."

If you saw her running between classes with too many books in her arms and a little bit late, you would never notice that she was different.

Reprinted from *Saturday Review*, July 15, 1967, pp. 56–74. Copyright 1967 Saturday Review, Inc. Mr. Robert E. Samples is Director of the Environmental Studies Project, Boulder, Colorado.

When she sat in class engrossed in the patterns the window light made on the floor, she seemed commonly inattentive. But once you got to know her, you fully realized that she was different. She flushed with a kind of awareness. Kari was handicapped. But her handicap wasn't a limp or a distorted speech pattern. Her handicap was creativity.

What is creativity? Sometimes creative connection is done in a manner unique to mankind, but most often such connections bring a spark of "newness" to the connector only. In our society those who have the "duty" of determining what is creative and what is not are the critics. They are armed with peculiar kinds of subjective authority focused upon those who attempt to create. The prejudices they bring to their decision making are erudite and usually are not in the realm of the commonplace.

Teachers and other adults who must work with younger people are shadowed by the awareness of the critics' role. As a result, there is often the tendency to use the societal definitions of uniqueness when viewing the creative efforts of individual children. Few realize that both effective surprise and connecting the unconnected are *firstly* individual and *secondly* societal. A child whose perception is acute enough to see the road as a "ribbon of moonlight" cannot be punished because Alfred Noyes saw it first. Yet in many instances they are.

Teachers are instruments of society, and, in an awkward way, they are the judicial branch of society's government. The term in court called the school year is served by each child. The child is sentenced to these years of examination and indoctrination by a society bent on self-perpetuation. In this environment Kari is a misfit. Her teachers have been spawned by a society that has provided them with a host of clichés that guide their perception. They go into rooms full of thirty children with the knowledge that "each child has his own personality" and "each child is an individual" and that "the individual should respect the rights of others." In their implementing of these clichés pervasive concepts of democratic behavior and underdog worship cloud the teachers' analysis of class needs. Protectivism and conformity are built into Kari's school walls.

Kari has too many classmates. But the high numbers are only one excuse for the response of the teachers. Actually, if there were only ten students in each class, Kari would still be mistreated. The school reflects the society from which Kari comes. The school's compartmental treatment of intellectualism is a microcosm of society's patterns. Words, numbers, and activities are separated by fences labeled LANGUAGE, MATH, and GYM.

Kari tries to synthesize all the elements of her world into relevance. In doing so, *she* makes the choices—an act which gives her the plague mark of individuality. She sees an algebraic solution as symbolic poetry that rhymes in the symmetry of logic. The logic doesn't matter, but the meter she perceives does. Her teacher is disgusted by her lack of effort to please him. He makes his requirements clear and is piqued by her apparently intentional effort to ignore *his* needs.

The mathematician Jules Henri Poincaré once described the way he solved a knotty group of problems in the following manner:

> For fifteen days I strove to prove that there could not be any functions like those I have since called Fuchsian functions. I was then very ignorant; every day I seated myself at my work table, stayed an hour or two, tried a great number of combinations and reached no results. One evening, contrary to my custom, I drank black coffee and could not sleep. Ideas rose in crowds; I felt them collide until pairs interlocked, so to speak, making a stable combination. By the next morning I had established the existence of a class of Fuchsian functions.... I had only to write out the results....

This suggests something that has been known by psychologists for a long time—more than one mode of thought guides our approach to solving problems. The substantive and internally consistent mode is the "logical, clear-thinking" one that is most admired and accepted by society. More metaphoric and intuitive kinds of thought are regarded suspiciously and only a small segment of society is permitted license to perform them. Regardless of the breadth of society's approval, the capabilities for both modes exist in each of us.

In addition to these two, Lawrence Kubie cites the kind of thought whose source lies within the unconscious realm. Substantive thought is born of the conscious realm, and the intuitive is the product of the preconscious realm. Noncreative people, when solving problems and patterning their world, draw heavily upon conscious or substantive modes of thought. Creative people, on the other hand, are dependent upon their use of the preconscious or intuitive. Thoughts and behavior resulting from the interference of these two modes from the unconscious realm inhibit both logic and creativity. Thought in the unconscious realm is the kind over which the individual has no control. When this kind of thought predominates, the individual is "sick."

Schools are most dedicated to rewarding substantive thought. Thus, they are effective mirrors of society's rules, and operationally they force the position of the student toward the logical and chronological. The substantive is identified with our professional life while the intuitive dominates our personal lives. At the same time that an awareness that the leisure segment of our lives is increasing, the schools perpetrate the substantive reward patterns. What this means is that while claiming to be attendant to developing the individual to lead a better life, the schools yet serve the institutions recognized by the group. The professional and societal aspects of the role of the individual are stressed by deed and innuendo. The micro-society of the school is modeled after the industrial patterns which pervade the "real world." This means that the clichés prevail while in deed Kari and her ken are discriminated against. The teachers *say* they will serve the individual, but in action they homogenize individuals into anonymous, ineffective groups. This efficiency overwhelms effectiveness.

Kari begins to learn that society expects her, as a female, to act in an intuitive fashion. The adjectives society uses, however, are "emotional" and "irrational." She learns early that upon the male image is bestowed "logical" and "rational" expectations. The fetish of efficiency is superimposed upon the expected behavior of Kari and her classmates. The goals society has set must be reached almost ritualistically and this is what so offends this girl. She does not want to *have* to be a bright mother of two. Nor is she interested in becoming "manlike" and "rational" so that career success will be hers. Kari is just interested in being honest and free.

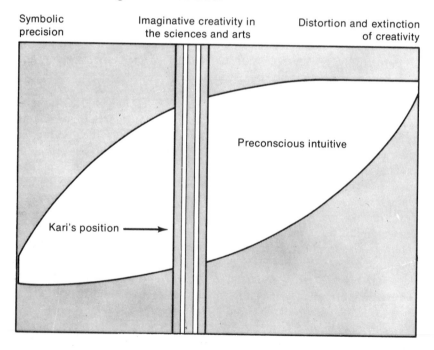

"Substantive thought is born of the conscious realm and the intuitive is the product of the preconscious realm. The capabilities for both modes exist in each of us."

When the school bells ring, Kari is required to cast an experience full of the brilliant orange of paint and the smell of linseed into a new form. This new image form is called civics. Here she learns to be "civil" by memorizing other new rules structured into a language so formalized that it brings tears to her throat as she reads them. She learns that laws are written by individuals and interpreted by groups. She learns that when she respects her own rights, the chances are she infringes on another's.

Kari obviously has begun to reject elements of the role that she has inherited. She watches fads drift like culture clouds across the scene. She sees paisley print blouses give way to ragged tennis shoes. None of these elements of controlled change apply, for they are not relevant to her. She appears strange to the conformity-cloistered society around her, for it sees her respond to herself rather than to its collective voice. She creates a guilt in the cliché-makers which they transform to resentment for their own self-preservation. They decide that she is the element of abnormality and ply her toward the norm. Her resistance is interpreted as immaturity and stubbornness that must be overcome.

She and those like her are called immoral and they are often admonished by phrases like, "These kids are getting worse every day." The difference between Kari and the voices of rebellion around her is that Kari's questions will continue. Her *why* will not be relinquished when she graduates or marries or has children. Kari is not a victim of her youth. Rather, youth, in asking similar questions and bathing in uninhibited perception, is a victim of a state of mind that is too temporary. With Kari a question is a beginning, an answer, a challenge. Kari somehow resents the giving of an answer. It makes things too pat, and its precision is immediately subject to mistrust.

Kari was the one student in the class who defended the heroine in Hawthorne's *The Scarlet Letter* for having the courage to be apart from the society. At the same time Kari damned her for her dishonesty to herself. The teacher was angry because virtue wasn't winning out in the analysis. Kari said virtue was in doing what *had* to be done, rather than "obeying like a starved rat the corridors of a maze somebody else built." The teacher was so frightened by Kari's argument that he gave her a "D" for her participation.

Kari's uniqueness is only in part due to her creativity, for most children exhibit high creative potential in their youth. Kari's main mark of difference is her courage. It requires courage to ignore the matrix defined by others. She is aware of society's rules of order as surely as she is alert to the way that $F = Ma$ in physics. Her courage is expressed in the way that she behaves. She knows that the subjectivity of society's rule, "Thou shall not," is very different from science's rule, $F = Ma$. In the first case, man's subjectivity is highly influential in guiding the interpretation, while in the second, subjectivity is far less relevant.

By knowing this, Kari has learned to trust the natural far more than the societal. Her courage is displayed by her acceptance of the responsibility that is attendant with mediation. She mediates her experience and ignores the way society claims the right to influence her conclusions. Because the schools fundamentally speak in a language of mediated clichés, they do not greatly affect Kari. She once expressed her role in society by likening herself to a tree. She claimed that the tree could not want, for a tree could use only what it needed; all else was simply irrelevant.

The creative person is able to convert substance into metaphor. Instead of a natural fact, like $F = Ma$, being a deductive end to the experience of the scientist who investigates relationship between mass and force, it is an inductive beginning. Kari weaves the substance of formalized experience into her intuition.

Her attendance to nature reflects her rejection of mediated sources of experience. Kari sees within the commonplace elements of the natural world a source of elements that are infinitely repatternable. The realm of the commonplace in the world of society is filled with already mediated devices. She is not content with the reassembling of other people's ideas or products. She instead prefers to deal with the source—nature.

In a line of poetry she once wrote, Kari claimed that "Before you can love you must know how to walk in the snow leaving no tracks." She knew the thrill of dashing chaotically through a virgin field of snow. In addition, she knew the excited fulfillment of willing abstinence. Both of these ideas were synthesized into the beautiful statement that applied to all love.

Kari is sixteen and growing up. She and her generation will soon be ours. The structured constraints of society are becoming real to these young people, and we must accept the responsibility to guarantee the nature of their course. Are they to preserve the structure or alter it? It would be foolish to claim that the structure will remain the same, so it *will* evolve. We need the Karis, all of them, but how can they be saved? The simplicity of the answer is as frightening as it is demanding: We must be more like Kari.

10

REACHING THE UNMOTIVATED

William Glasser, MD

Lack of success, more than any other one thing, contributes to nonmotivation. In an atmosphere of failure, effort and interest seep away; problems become overwhelming, and people seem to "cop out." I say "seem" because, even in alienation and withdrawal, the individual is trying to say something. What are our unmotivated youngsters in schools trying to tell us? What does nonmotivation reflect of the life they experience in school?

Everyone has a basic concept of himself, whatever that concept may be. Each of us not only has such a concept, but we are continually evaluating ourselves. This ongoing process is true of all of us. It is as though, over our heads, we have a little radar that is constantly passing back signals to us. If the signals come back continually: *The work you do is no good. You are not worth very much. I don't care much for you,* one's self-concept is bound to become a concept of failure.

When I began to work as a consultant in schools where there were large groups of unmotivated students, I realized that these were indeed the signals that are coming back to most of the boys and girls in the school. Their reaction is the same as anybody's reaction to such signals. They are upset; and they will not do anything that the

Reprinted from *The Science Teacher, 38,* March 1971, pp. 18–22. Dr. William Glasser is a psychiatrist and consultant to the Los Angeles school system. He has authored *Reality Therapy* and *Schools Without Failure.* His present residence is Los Angeles, California.

people who are giving them these signals are telling them to do. If we want something from people—not something they give to us, but something from them in terms of their attention, in terms of at least beginning to study a curriculum that we designed for them—then we must scrutinize very carefully the kind of information we feed into their self-evaluation system.

If our information is that they are not worth very much, they begin to believe they are not worth very much—unless they can find someone else who puts in information that they are worth much more than our message says.

If you ask youngsters who aren't doing well in school:

What do you believe about yourself in relationship to school? and they answer:

Well, I guess I'm not very good. I'm not very competent. I'm not doing very well, you can't expect them to be very motivated. If you tell them they are doing great, that would be phony, so you are in a bind. Ordinarily, if you want to tell people something nice about themselves, they have to do something that gives you some reason to send out this kind of positive message.

In school what we have to do is devise a way to get the students to do some work so we can give the input that they are doing something that is worthwhile. If I tell any of you, "I think you are pretty smart, pretty worthwhile, and I think you are proceeding in the right direction," there is a good chance that you will at least listen to what I have to say. This is basic to the whole procedure. This is what you must do with students. Get involved with them; help them become friendly; create some warmth and some interaction in the classroom. This is a basic minimum for getting them to listen to *you* and then, hopefully, to listen to *what* you are attempting to teach them.

If you say, *Whether we're friendly or not, learn this stuff,* youngsters won't learn. Most teachers of about my age don't really understand why this is so. Most of us can look back and see that we didn't always have teachers who were friends. We didn't always have teachers who cared about making the subject relevant. We had some pretty dull, dry teachers; but still we learned, and we didn't give the teachers a hard time while we were at it. Even when what I was told to learn didn't make much sense to me, I still gave it a try, because I thought I had to do it or because I didn't have the nerve to be obstreperous. Sometimes today, I hear principals lamenting that kids are no longer frightened. Principals today can't scare kids. I was scared into learning some things. But today's students aren't scared, and we are still unwilling to do the things that will get them to learn when they are not scared. This leaves us quite powerless.

Why aren't they scared? This has puzzled me for some years. In public schools, students are doing all kinds of disruptive things; and they are paying very little attention to teachers. Yet still we try to use the old scare tactics: *I'm going to punish you. I'll call your mother. You won't go to college. You'll fail. You'll be unsuccessful in life.* This works almost not at all in most communities today.

I believe that this being impervious to such threats relates to change. We are living through a time of cultural change. An entire generation is changing its basic social attitude toward our institutions and how they operate and toward goals for individuals and for society. Suddenly we find that institutions that have worked well for hundreds or thousands of years are no longer effective.

Many people have been explaining change. Some have said, "Our society has gone bad; our institutions are no longer working properly." But they have not explained why. *Why,* for instance, do schools no longer fit our young people? Obviously, they don't fit because so many youngsters are doing badly. But why? What has been happening? I think one very good clue comes from a Marshall McLuhan interview in the March 1969 *Playboy* magazine. In it McLuhan said that students are searching for a role not a goal. Think about that. Then think about your schools. What are schools set up to provide for our students? Our schools are set up to reinforce goals. McLuhan says students are searching for a role, not a goal. I'd like to paraphrase that, for I won't go quite that far. I'll say that students are searching for a role first, and then they are willing to search for a goal. If anything, school is destructive to role reinforcement.

Role is the person's identity, the person's feelings that "This is me, I'm a separate person—hopefully a distinctive person, a person that stands for certain things, a person that wants to be accepted." This is almost a wish to be accepted "for me, regardless of what I do." That is an overstatement, but it means not being judged solely for what one does but being accepted for one's own basic humanity. This is what I call identity.

When I was in school, and probably for most of us, our concern was in learning what we were supposed to learn, getting some security, getting a home, and so on. We thought, "I'll get this knowledge, this degree, this job, then I'll start concerning myself with who I am." First, security; then, who I am. Find your niche, earn a secure place for yourself, then work for some individuality, for some kind of human expression.

But suppose, somehow, security was already at hand. It seems to me that our present society gives this security. In a sense, youngsters feel secure when they come to school. True, many of them may be starving and don't have clothes, and their homes are chaotic. But somehow they believe that they will have something to eat, that they will ultimately have a car, a job, and the possessions they want. Even if our system hasn't given people security, it has given them a powerful illusion of security. Even in a central city, where kids are absolutely poverty-stricken, they still don't believe that they are not going to be secure. They still feel that somewhere they are going to get the Mustangs. They are going to get the sharp things. They are going to do things that secure people do. Television has fostered this illusion by hammering over the message: "You are going to have it; don't worry about it; you'll get these things somewhere," though it doesn't mention how to get the things or all the work involved. But it does get across the illusion of security.

Therefore, we are now dealing with a student who can't be frightened. He doesn't care whether he learns science or algebra or chemistry, because he feels somehow or other, it is going to be OK. It doesn't matter whether he comes from a rich home or a poor home. He feels that things are going to work out. The old scare tactics won't work because his basic aim doesn't include the old goals that we still try to make him think he won't reach if he doesn't do as we say. Young people today are seeking identity as human beings; they want to be assured that they will get this kind of acceptance.

Somehow or other in education, we must give children a positive identity reinforcement. We must make them feel that while school believes the goals are important, the school system and we as teachers also believe, *You are a human being. We care for you. We will express it to you by being friendly and being interested in you.* If we can do this, the youngster will say, *Well, I ought to begin listening to you. Maybe I ought to begin to learn some of the things that you, who are my friend and who care about me, say I should learn.*

This is a shift. In the old system, we didn't care about the human part. That was an extra. Today's youngsters want some of this extra right now.

This is easy to verify. A dialogue with a teen-aged girl might go something like this—and I've asked at least 300 the same question and gotten the same answer.

What's the most important thing to you? Really the most important?

I want to be myself. Only five words: *I want to be myself.* If you probe a little deeper, you get: *I want to be me. I want to be accepted. I want to have friends. I want to stand for something.*

And then what they say almost invariably is, *I want to be accepted for me, just for me.* If I ask, *You mean regardless of what you do?*

they'll say, *Not regardless of what I do but kind of separate from what I do.* Almost, *Accept me for me, but let's not worry about what I'm going to do. I have basic value just because I am a human being.*

If we are a society which is no longer going to worry in the traditional sense about security goals but seeks first to gain reinforcement as human beings, this calls for a vast change in our teaching.

As I have described in *Schools Without Failure,* we can use class meetings in the lower grades and discussion with students in the upper grades so that the students begin to say, *The teacher talks with us. He listens to us. He interacts with us.* In effect they are saying, *He does the things that help to reinforce me. That makes me feel worthwhile as a person.*

This is no longer optional. This is no longer what we must do only if we have spare time. I believe that this is what we must do if we are going to have any teaching. For many of you, your job is to teach science to youngsters who are relatively unmotivated, youngsters who have felt failure. Remember that in this new social need for identity, there is nothing that says it has to come out positive. We try to gain a successful identity for ourselves. We hope to get reinforcement and care from other people which confirm good feelings about ourselves. But there is another option also. The other option is that if we are not able to identify ourselves as a success, we identify ourselves as a failure. We identify ourselves as a person all right, but as a person who fails. And we behave in a way which reinforces failure. If you analyze how the students that you can't teach behave, you will find that they behave according to two patterns. One is antagonistic, anti-social; they don't care; they constantly agitate. The other way is to withdraw. These students just check out. In talking to them you are talking to the wall. You can't get through to them. Their bodies are in the class, but their minds aren't. What students are doing in both these behaviors is reinforcing their opinion of themselves, their "I am a failure" identity. They express this view actively through antagonism and passively through withdrawal. Neither of which allows any way to reach them effectively.

How do you reach an antagonistic person? Every time you reach out your hand, he only slaps it. You may sit up nights figuring out a nice lesson—something that really ought to excite and interest these youngsters, but they come in with a sour expression, *Aw! Same old thing!* It is not the same old thing, but they won't bother to look at it. They believe they are failing anyway. It seems to them that they can't do anything, so why in the world would you want to get in touch with a failure? Why would you want to sit up nights with their lessons? They can't conceive of your doing this. The job of reaching out to them is the primary job. Somehow or other, they must hear you saying: *Look, Kid, we must get acquainted—get friendly. We must make some contact with each other.* Any way that you can emphasize this is all right, but you must do it systematically—in three steps that I think will help keep the youngsters from failing and start them believing they can be successful.

Number one: We ought to stop failing kids. We ought to make it impossible for children to fail in school. Let me define failure. Failure occurs when the options are closed. That's what failure is all about.

If you are fishing 25 miles off shore, and you drop your camera overboard—that is failure. The options are all over. In 2000 feet of water, that camera is gone. There is no way you are going to get it back. That is what failure is like. All paths to success are closed.

In school, when the child takes a test and gets a low grade, and the teacher says, *That's it.* And the child says, *Gee, can I make it up? Can I do something, can I restudy it? I don't understand it.* And the teacher persists, *That's it. That's your grade. That's your place. That's every word.* That is a failure system. The grading system is one way schools practice failure. The outside world doesn't operate on a failure system nearly as much as schools do. The world operates on a fairer system—one which says that it is possible not to succeed, but usually not to have complete failure either. We must get rid of every possible way that students can identify themselves as failures in school. We can't change their homes or their roles—at least not directly, but we can change what we have control over in our own classes.

To teach science to youngsters who have been turned off by school, you will have to let them know that, *There is no failure here. We are here to learn science. I will give you credit for what you learn. If you learn a little, I'll give you credit for it. If you learn a lot, I'll give you credit for that.*

Long ago, when I entered medical school, the dean announced on the first day, "No one is going to fail." He said that the teachers were there to take care of the students; all tests would be fair and reasonable; if there were any problems they'd be straightened out. And it *was* like that for four years—four years of pure joy in school. That gave me my first inkling that all students could find school like that.

The only way to approach disadvantaged students is to say to them, *You're here to learn. We're not here to fail you. If you're up against something you don't understand, we'll explain it to you. We'll give tests—tests are important if you are going to evaluate yourself. But if you don't pass the test, take it again, take it home and study it. Work on it. Ask another kid about it. We don't care if you look at papers in this class. Trade information back and forth. Keep your books open. All we want you to do is learn.*

Teaching is not testing; it's not monitoring students. It's letting them know they can learn, and letting them know that the hardest thing to do in class is not learn. *We won't fail you.*

My philosophy of education is: *Come to school. We like you. We're interested in teaching you something, and we will give you credit for what you've learned. Come to class. We'll get involved. You'll not only get to know me, you'll get to know other kids. We'll talk to each other.*

Science is the best possible subject for this kind of teaching. No subject lends itself better than science to figuring things out and for throwing questions for inquiry and discussions back and forth.

The important thing is not to "down" anybody in these discussions. It's very critical with disadvantaged students who are used to being downed that you don't down them. Don't act judgmental in class discussions. If you ask a student something, and he gives an irrational answer—let it go. Don't pick it up immediately and say, "That's wrong." Ask another student, "What do you think of that?" Let the class kick it around. At the end of the day, if they haven't discovered the exact answer to things as you see them, let it go for another day. In science the exact answer may be somewhat doubtful anyway. Take the problem home and think about it. Ask yourself "How can I get this across? How can I develop a lesson where they begin to believe that it is possible for other ideas to be entertained?"

Even if you don't teach anything else in science, you ought to teach the fact that there is not one answer for everything. There are many ways to skin a cat. There are other ideas worth considering. Finally, the students will get the feeling that, *Here my ideas, my brains, and my application of the knowledge as I see it are worth something. It's worthwhile for me to listen to other people and for other people to listen to me.* Finally you achieve the reinforcement which convinces a person that he can succeed. Successful identity is gained through involving yourself with other people, through listening, through intellectually involving yourself, talking back and forth and arguing, but not being put down. We can change identities from failure to success through this method. Get the class involved; eliminate all of the options for failure. If you leave even one option for failure open, these failing youngsters will find it and use it. Plug all the failure options so they can't fail. *Sorry, kids, you can't fail. It's impossible, just can't do it. That's all there is to it.*

If the student says, *I won't come to class,* reply, *That's your choice. If you won't come to class, I can't teach you. But if you come here, you'll learn, and you won't fail.*

All that the student should have to do is come, at least in the beginning. Make sure he gets to school. Through this sytem of involvement and of eliminating failure, he will be motivated, because it feels good to learn things. If it didn't feel good to learn, to think, and to discuss things that are interesting and exciting and intellectually important, nobody would learn anything. In science you are especially fortunate to be teaching something you can make fairly exciting.

This brings us to the second point in feeling worthwhile. The student feels worthwhile if he can relate the material to his life. Of course, if you are teaching really bright students, really gung-ho kids, you can teach them far-out stuff, and you don't necessarily have to relate it to their lives. But the less motivated youngsters are interested in what you're saying that might possibly pertain to their lives. If what you are teaching doesn't seem to relate to their lives, they turn off very quickly. Once they turn off, it's very hard for them to turn on again. So far as possible, relate what you teach to their lives, to what they know and understand so that they can recognize that this is the kind of thing that happens to them.

For example, if you are trying to teach them the normal distribution, let them roll a pair of dice, and they will find out that there is such a thing as a normal curve. Most of them have shot enough craps to know that there is some kind of curve operating. If you are explaining how a siphon works, use the example of siphoning gas from a car if you're out of gas. You'll lose these students if you talk about siphoning a liquid from one bottle to another. They are not interested in bottles of water in a laboratory, but they are interested in siphoning in relation to cars and gasoline.

The third important point—after getting the students involved and teaching relevant material—is to get them to think. Thinking and the kind of goal-oriented education which has been going on in the schools and colleges and graduate schools for a long period of time are antagonistic to each other. We must get rid of this antagonism. We must make thinking pay off—not just occasionally, but pay off in a major way, because it's fun to think. In any situation where you are stimulated, where people get you really intellectually stimulated, and where you suddenly realize that you have thought of something new or discovered a possibility that relates to you, you will find it extremely exciting. This kind of thinking is what we have to stimulate the students to do. And that means, for one thing, no memorizing. Make it an absolute rule in your class that students don't have to memorize anything. Whatever is important enough to be memorized is important enough to be learned. Put it on the board in big letters, or on charts, or give it to the students in mimeographed notes. Tell the class, *This is some-*

*thing that ought to be learned; but for goodness sake, whenever you
need it, refer to it, and use it. It's right here.*

If you ask unmotivated youngsters to memorize something that
makes no sense to them in the first place, they'll turn off the whole
thing. You close one of the failure options if they can never get stuck,
never fail, never get stymied, because they didn't know something
that was to be committed to memory. Memorizing is not a reasonable
use of our brains anyway. Our brains aren't built to memorize things,
and we force them into all kinds of convolutions when we memorize
things.

My son has an excellent chemistry teacher who keeps important
information on the board and doesn't ask the class to memorize anything. What happens is that the students do learn a great deal by heart
—when they realize that this saves looking up what they use over
and over. People do memorize information they use every day—their
phone number, address, car license number, and the like. This is what
smart people do. They don't commit things to memory unless they
use them all the time. But don't memorize the things that are used
in science. These things can be looked up or figured out. With students,
dispel the notion that when they read a page, if they haven't got it
committed to memory, they fail. They won't commit it to memory,
anyway. Say, *We're going to use this. We're going to figure it out.
You can always open the book and look up what you need.*

After you get students involved; do relevant things; get them to thinking,
get rid of certainty, get rid of memorization; you next stop measuring
students against each other. This kind of measuring is always very
destructive. Get across the idea that, *We're interested in teaching
you. This other kid may be better or worse—we don't care-it's what
you're learning that counts.* Success breeds success; we build success
upon success. We always tend, especially with youngsters who are
behind, to go too·fast. Suppose you start in the fall with a class of
students that aren't doing as well as they should. Very carefully set
up your lesson for the first week, and then say to yourself, "I'll take
nine-tenths of it away and teach this much." However, once they
succeed they'll want a little bigger bite the next time. You can't teach
in tiny increments all along, but do start with them. As soon as the
students understand the first few lessons, give a little test that they
can all succeed on. Then compliment them and let them know what
is planned for the next day. Never start too big. I can well recall
teachers who went too fast—teachers who were going to cover the
whole text whether the class did or not. They'd turn the pages in
the book, skip forty pages, and say to go on from there. You can't
skip those forty pages and go ahead. Your job is not to get to the

end of the semester, covering the unit on A, and the unit on B, and the unit on C. Your job is to teach as much as you can to the class and then make a careful record of where they are for the next teacher. The class should succeed up to this point. You've got to keep these youngsters saying,

I can. It's important to me. Others are listening to me. The teacher cares about me. There is absolutely no way I can fail if I count. I may not do as well as the next guy. That's possible. Somebody may learn more than me, and somebody may learn less, but I can learn things in this class, and I will not fail.

This is about where we are now in our ideas about schools without failure. We have pretty well established some things that can be done in an elementary school. We are starting in secondary schools and learning how to apply these principles systematically in secondary schools. We have a few schools that believe enough in these ideas that they are going to cooperate with us to see whether together we can solve the problem of the unmotivated students. That kind of cooperation is the key to education. No one can come into your school and say, "Do it this way; it'll work." The only people who can really make it work are the faculty of the school. They can accept good ideas and give them a try. I hope you will try out these ideas in your classes, but obviously it needs more than one class. If you can get ideas like this going throughout a school so that they fit and apply to your school—that's when the real changes start. When a student walks through the door to the school he begins to feel

Here, I don't fail. Not only in science class, I don't fail any place in this school. I don't get credit for things I don't do, but they don't fail me, and I do get credit for what I do.

11

THE CULTURALLY DEPRIVED CHILD AND SCIENCE

Samuel Malkin

Educators have always had the problem of adapting the curriculum to the needs of children with special problems. Today teachers throughout the country, particularly in urban areas, are being confronted in ever-increasing numbers by the special problem of the culturally deprived or disadvantaged child. In New York City, it is estimated that 225,000 out of 573,000 elementary school children and 75,000 out of 186,000 junior high school pupils are in that category. Coupled with the disadvantaged or culturally deprived child is the non-English speaking child. About 11.5 percent of the entire elementary school population of New York City speak English haltingly or not at all (1).

What are some characteristics of these children? In working with them, one quickly becomes aware of their general lack of achievement in the basic academic skills of reading, writing, and arithmetic; their general low self-image; and their lack of interest. Then one becomes aware of their limited experiences. What we tend to take for granted in youngsters—that they are familiar with gardens, pets, automobiles, trains, bicycles, elevators, and the country—is not necessarily true for these children. Indeed, many have never strayed from their own neighborhood or block, even though they may live in a city with many places to go and things to do.

Reprinted from *Science and Children, 1,* April 1964, pp. 5–7. Dr. Samuel Malkin is supervisor of Audio-Visual Instruction, New York City Board of Education, New York, New York.

What are some of the conditions that cause cultural deprivation? Although poverty may not in itself be a cause, most culturally deprived children come from poor areas. Many come from broken homes or from families with deteriorated social standards; many come from areas where there is conflict between their own existing subculture and the standard American middle-class culture. Then, too, these areas may contain a constantly changing population with families moving in, staying awhile, and moving away again. The youngsters may have no roots, no feelings of loyalty, or no sense of responsibility to the community.

Teachers need orientation to work with these children since the children's expectations contrast sharply with the teaching and therapeutic processes which the teacher is normally trained to use. For example, these children desire authority and direction rather than training in self-direction; they desire action rather than introspection; they desire structure and organization rather than a permissive situation; they desire simple, more concrete, scientifically demonstrable explanations rather than symbolic, circuitous interpretations; and they desire informal, sympathetic, nonpatronizing relationships rather than intensive ones (3).

These desires and expectations of the disadvantaged child are positive elements upon which a functional and developmental curriculum can be built. Frank Riessman, in his book *The Culturally Deprived Child* (2), strongly advocates such an approach. His observations identify other elements which have a direct bearing on the development of curriculum for these children. These are: ability in abstract thinking, but at a slower rate than middle-class children; skill in nonverbal communication; greater achievement when tasks are motor-oriented; and greater motivation to tasks which have tangible and immediate goals.

An elementary science program for such children must be based on the positive elements of the characteristics, environment, and expectations of these children.

What Are the Features of Such a Program?

An elementary science program must be based on the pupils' environment.

Children are concerned with the world about them; the sound of bells, thunder and lightning, automobiles, airplanes, trees, birds, and their own bodies. Disadvantaged children are no exception; however, their own world may not be the same as their teacher's world. To the teacher, larva, pupa, and butterfly are part of nature; to the pupils these may be meaningless because they may never have seen these things. Skyscrapers, concrete, and alley cats are more meaningful to these children than the Grand Canyon, sedimentary rocks, and protozoa. The culturally deprived child's environment is quite restricted, and we must seek from his environment those elements familiar to him and build our program upon them.

It is also important to enlarge the pupil's environment. This suggests that he be given direct experiences through audio-visual materials. A trip to the farm or zoo where the urban slum child can see and fondle farm animals, a lesson on magnetism where he and his fellow pupils can handle many different magnets, or a film which shows him what makes night and day are all experiences which enlarge the pupil's concepts about his environment.

An Elementary Science Program Must Be Based on Real Problems

Children ask questions about their environment and want answers to their questions. Some of these questions are: How does the school bell ring? What makes the light go on? Why do we want to explore outer space? How can we keep food from spoiling? How does the weatherman forecast weather? How does a telephone work? How can my skates roll more easily? What makes a car stop? Whereas many children frequently obtain the correct answers to their questions from parents or from books, the culturally deprived youngsters generally do not. Their parents are not able to help them and they are not able or motivated to help themselves. They must rely on the school for the correct answer, or else be satisfied with misinformation or no answer. The implications are clear. The teacher must gear her program to help these children find answers to questions about their environment. Indeed, the teacher may need to help the children verbalize questions which their environment has led them to submerge. Questions, such as those listed above, could and should serve as the aims of lessons in elementary science. By basing the aims of her lessons on real problems, the teacher can capitalize on pupils' interest and compensate for the learning they should, but do not, receive at home.

Elementary Science Should Not Depend on Reading or Other Academic Skills

A major weakness of the disadvantaged child is lack of achievement in reading and other academic skills. This lack of achievement in reading probably accounts, in large measure, for lack of success in other curriculum areas which depend on reading. If an elementary science program is to be successful, then the pupils must feel that they can succeed in science. I conceive of elementary science as a truly "democratic" subject—democratic to the extent that every child can participate in, and get a feeling of, achievement and success from it. Therefore, it is important that activities be so chosen that they do not discourage children. One way to do this is to use children's language skills, other than reading, in the elementary science program. Such skills as listening, speaking, reporting, observing, and note-taking (at the pupil's level) should be encouraged.

Teachers should plan lessons which draw on pupils' experiences, and the conclusions to each lesson should be elicited from the class in the pupils' own language. Audio-visual materials should be used extensively to provide basic information and material for research. Children can use filmstrips with individual viewers just as they would use books. The formation of soil and the operation of the water cycle can be demonstrated more effectively by films than by books.

Although the basic science program should not depend on textbooks, children should have contact with many science books at their own reading level. Thus, instead of thirty books of a basic series of texts on one grade level in a class, it might be possible to have thirty books of many series at different levels. Trade books on many topics at varying reading levels should be available. In this way, children could select those books which they are able to read, and which do not frustrate them.

Elementary Science Should Reinforce Basic Academic Skills

Although this may seem contrary to what was previously stated, it is not. Elementary science can and should encourage and motivate growth in reading. As these children get a feeling of success from their science activities, they may be motivated to greater achievement. Thus, they can be encouraged to use some of the trade and textbooks that are to be found in the room. Elementary science can provide even more basic reading experiences. Labelling of specimens, models, and charts provide reading experiences, as do captions on filmstrips. In my own experience, at the end of each lesson I ask the children to tell me what they have learned from that lesson. Their own statements are written on large sheets of paper and the pupils copy these in their notebooks. Many weeks later the pupils are able to read their statements, although they may not be able to read at that level in their basal readers. They are able to read their experience charts because they are motivated to learn to read those statements which arise from their own experience. Elementary science is used to motivate these pupils.

A more formal experiment correlating science and reading is being conducted by Richard Kinney, at Public School No. 188 in Manhattan. In this experiment, reading lessons, based on the children's science experiences, are being prepared on three reading levels. The results so far have been encouraging and point to further study in this area.

Elementary Science Should Afford Children Opportunities to Handle Materials and Equipment

A fundamental concept in teaching elementary science is that all children should have an opportunity to handle materials and equipment. This is especially true for the culturally deprived child since he seems to have greater achievement when tasks are motor-oriented. Teachers, therefore, should provide every opportunity for children to participate in demonstrations and experiments. If possible, there should be enough material so that every child can use the same materials at his seat that his teacher is using at her desk. Kits of materials can be organized which contain, for example, thirty dry cells, thirty switches, thirty bells, and pieces of wire, or thirty sets of different magnets. The materials that are used should be familiar to children. Esoteric and elaborate equipment should be avoided since it may be confusing to children; and assume importance rather than the science concepts being demonstrated. Children should be given recognition for their projects by having their exhibits displayed to other pupils as well as to their parents and to the community at periodic science fairs.

Through proper adaptation of the elementary science curriculum to the needs of this large portion of our children, we may bring about an enrichment of their lives which, in turn, will benefit our entire community. We have, so far, failed to tap America's greatest resources, the creative skills and abilities of all its children. Among these disadvantaged children, there is a large reservoir of future high-level, professional, and skilled personnel, if we learn how to help them realize their potential.

Throughout the country, experimentation with curriculum development for the culturally deprived children, such as the "Higher Horizons Program" and "Mobilization for Youth" in New York City are providing insights into the techniques of teaching such children. Through implementation of our new insights, both society and the child will benefit.

References

(1) Board of Education of the City of New York, *Higher Horizons Progress Report*. January 1963.

(2) Riessman, Frank, *The Culturally Deprived Child*. New York: Harper & Row, Publishers, 1962.

(3) _____"Some Suggestions Concerning Psychotherapy with Blue Collar Patients" (mimeographed). New York: Mobilization for Youth and Department of Psychiatry, Columbia University, 1963, p. 4.

12

THE INFLUENCE OF SCIENCE IN A PROGRAM FOR EDUCABLE MENTALLY RETARDED

Norma J. Boekel
Rodger W. Bybee

"Who are the educable mentally retarded?" This is indeed a perplexing question. There is as much diversity in the answers as in the population of special education. Whether we view mental retardation as "diminished capacity for forming cell assemblies" or "arrested development below the level of formal thought" (10), classes are filled with children who are diverse in their mental operations and behavior characteristics; many almost defy description.

In educationally relevant areas, educable mentally retarded (EMR) children do differ from their normal peers. They do exhibit a rate of mental development that is slower. They do enter school with an achievement level that is low. They do exhibit an academic disparity that increases as they move into levels where abstractions replace the concreteness of early education. They are not weird little creatures with odd habits. They have the same needs as normal children, but vary in ability to fulfill them.

The trend today is to think of the educable mentally retarded as potentially *effective* rather than *defective* individuals. Many commonly held assumptions concerning the characteristics of this group have been proven to be fallacies. Coming to any area of curriculum, no two children are exactly alike in aptitude, disability, or experiential

Reprinted from a paper prepared for elementary science teachers attending a summer institute. Ms. Norma Jean Boekel is Instructor of Special Education at the Laboratory School, University of Northern Colorado, Greeley, Colorado.

background. Increasingly, special educators are cognizant that what may be described as "true" of one child may not be characteristic of the group.

Given a set of characteristics with negative overtones, adults tend to develop preconceptions that may result in social and educational rejection. Examples of how prospective teachers can be prejudiced by previous notions about the retarded are related in the following anecdotes.

Perceptions, Preconceptions, and Prophecy

SITUATION I

Setting: University of Northern Colorado, science classroom, Summer, 1971.

Two prospective teachers, in discussion, outside door of classroom.

Jane: "I've never seen any mentally retarded children. What are they really like?"

Sally: "Oh, I guess in general you could say that they have a low IQ; they lack motivation; most of them have poor social habits and don't dress very neatly; in class they don't pay attention, get frustrated and are behavior problems."

The two girls entered the classroom and observed a class of educable mentally retarded children for a few minutes. As they walked away, the first girl (Jane) turned and said, "Gee, I see what you mean!"

SITUATION II

Setting: Same. Another prospective teacher (Helen) enters the classroom.

Since we were busily engaged in activity, the woman sat quietly and watched. The boys and girls were playing a property game. On the table were a large number of plastic objects of various geometric shapes, colors, sizes and textures. The teacher asked each child to find an object with one, two, or three properties; then tell the other children about his object. After a few rounds of describing and categorizing objects, the materials were removed. Next, the children were given their aquariums to examine. There were pensive stares, and some comments, "Look, my guppies had babies!" "Where did my water go?" "Can I feed my fish?" As we asked questions of the children, they discussed answers freely and in their own style. When the lesson was over, the children put away materials and went down the hall, happily engaged in conversations. Helen asked, "When are the EMR's coming for science? I would like to observe them if you don't mind." We smiled and told her that she had been observing them for the last ten minutes.

We would like to contrast these two anecdotes. Both Jane and Helen were interested in the mentally retarded; they had never really been around them and were forming first impressions. In the first story, Jane's perceptions were formed by her friend's mixture of myth and truth. Her perceptions and future expectations were revealed when she said, "I see what you mean." However, Helen's opinions, expectations, and attitudes were quite different; further, her behavior toward these children will also be different.

A common occurrence at the University of Northern Colorado is to overhear guests and student observers express surprise that, "They look so normal!" Recently, a group of vocational level (approximately high school aged) EMR students visited a local public utility facility. After their tour, the students boarded a bus. Their teacher chatted with the manager who conducted the tour. He was indicating his amazement at how "normal" they appeared to be. He also indicated that he could pick only one who appeared to have an obvious problem. Interestingly he had chosen the student teacher!

Too often, teachers have fallen prey to fallacies about children. This has resulted in preconceptions that later become "self-fulfilling prophecies." A person reacting to a retarded individual is likely to be doing so in terms of his set of attitudes, expectations, and beliefs. These may be in contrast to what the individual is actually like. There is a growing accumulation of evidence that teachers' expectations for educable mentally retarded children influence their educational attainment in the direction of the expectation. That is, if the expectation is low, achievement is low; if expectation is high, achievement is high. The construct of expectancy is not new in sociological and psychological theories and research (1, 4, 16). The teacher's expectation is but one factor in the total environment that affects the development and adjustment of the child. Admittedly, the content and methods of school programs are important factors contributing to educational growth. However, it is our contention that the factor of teacher expectations has been underestimated to the degree that many criticisms leveled against special education are justified.

Teacher-training institutions are challenging educators to provide for individual differences in children. These "differences" are usually defined in terms of inadequacies. This is especially true in the case of EMR's. Prospective teachers, presented with behavioral descriptions of educables, tend to develop negative attitudes and low expectations for them. Reichard (15) surveyed one hundred master's degree students majoring in special education. Each student was asked to list three educational characteristics of the mentally retarded. Ninety-five percent of those characteristics had negative overtones. Those listed most frequently were:

1. Low intelligence
2. Minimal academic achievement
3. Behavior disorders
4. Lack of motivation
5. Short attention span

Certainly, preoccupation with "what's wrong with them" can nurture and even extend the exceptionality. Of greater concern should be, "How does he learn, under what circumstances and with what materials?" A more appropriate set of characteristics should include such statements as:

1. They are highly motivated by novel experiences and ideas.
2. They are attentive to experiences dealing with social reality in their perceived environment.
3. They respond to experiential learning based on real problems.
4. They are interested in their environment.
5. They should have experiences that develop and reinforce academic ability.
6. They learn best when successful in their experiences.
7. They receive and respond to concrete experiences better than abstract concepts.
8. Experience with personal meaning (or close to self) has a high motivational level.
9. They have many talents and potentials that can be developed through the educational experience.
10. They can learn best when the experience is not based on reading or other academic skills.

The important question that follows is one which asks how a teacher's expectations can become translated into behavior that will result in maximum pupil growth. Although most teachers perform the same routines in the classroom—present subject matter, question, deal with student behavior, and evaluate results—the by-product of his "teaching" is a climate in which learning either languishes or flourishes. This difference may well hinge on the teacher expectations for the children in the room.

The most successful teachers possess an optimistic outlook, with confidence in their own ability (as well as the students') to achieve the best results. Teachers must be labeled as "incompetents" if they behave toward children in a manner that fosters, aides, or complements the elements of their behavior that are making them exceptional.

With this as an introduction the following discussion will deal with science education and its influences on mentally retarded children.

Science Education and the Mentally Retarded

A minimum of research has been reported concerning science education for the mentally retarded. Recently, however, there has been some interest in this area as several curriculum groups have centered on the development of materials for the retarded. The following references are not intended to be complete descriptions of the research. They are introductions to the type of work that has been done and sources for possible reference.

McMahon (11) developed a science program for the educable mentally retarded. The children drew pictures of the world as they perceived it. Rocket ships and space travel were items of high interest. Lessons were then developed centering on the areas of interest.

Thresher (19) prepared lessons on magnetism for trainable and educable mentally retarded children. She found the unit to be encouraging, although no evaluation was mentioned.

Gitta (7) used a Montessori sensory approach for the development of recognition and observation skills in EMR's. No systematic evaluation was presented but she reported good results.

Onstead (12) compiled a science resource guide for EMR's as a doctoral dissertation. The materials included were not evaluated through classroom use.

Sweeters (18) conducted a study to determine if EMR's could learn selected science concepts through individualized, discovery-oriented instruction. He reported little difference in areas such as manipulating variables and making inferences. There were positive attitudinal changes in the experimental groups.

Bennett and Downing (2) discussed the feasibility of science education for the mentally retarded and brought information to bear on the development of a science program.

Katz (9) investigated the effectiveness of science lessons (electricity and magnetism) for (1) learning of scientific material, (2) interest, and (3) transfer of knowledge to new situations. His results indicated the science lessons were effective in the three goals mentioned.

Jehle (8) developed *A Science Program for the Educable Mentally Retarded—with Teachers Guide.* This program was tested with EMR's and produced encouraging results.

At the present time the Biological Science Curriculum Study is working on a program for the mentally retarded. Also the Allegheny County Schools in Pennsylvania are adapting *Science—A Process Approach* to the needs of the retarded child.

Teaching EMR's Science for Positive Growth

Let us proceed to the exploration of teacher strategies that positively affect the child's self-concept and educational growth. Kolstoe (10) has discussed the manner in which learning tasks should be presented to the educably mentally retarded child. They are:

1. The tasks should be uncomplicated. The new tasks should contain the fewest possible elements, and most of the elements should be familiar, so he has very few unknowns to learn.

2. The tasks should be brief. This assures that he will attend to the most important aspects of the tasks and not get lost in a sequence of interrelated events.

3. The tasks should be sequentially presented so the learner proceeds in a sequence of small steps, each on built upon previously learned tasks.

4. Each learning task should be the kind in which success is possible. One of the major problems to be overcome is that of failure-proneness. This major deterrent to learning can be effectively reduced through success experiences.

5. Overlearning must be built into the lessons. Drills in game form seem to lessen the disinterest inherent in unimaginative drill.

6. Learning tasks should be applied to objects, problems, and situations in the learner's life environment. Unless the tasks are relevant, the learner has great difficulty in seeing their possible importance.

Ours is a science-oriented society, and the development of a scientific literacy should be an educational goal. A child who has developed such an attitude has an inquiring mind, recognizes his biases, and the influence of personal prejudices. He is careful and accurate in what he does and plans before he acts. He is open to new ideas and suggestions, distinguishes between fact and opinion, and respects the judgments of experts. If we can maintain and nurture the child's natural curiosity until adult life, he will be a more alert adult with greater appreciation of the world in which he lives.

In many schools teaching science to the mentally retarded has been neglected. The reasons primarily stem from the philosophy that "science is considered too difficult." Secondarily, there is a lack of suitable science materials. As a consequence, Biological Science Curriculum Study (BSCS) has made a major commitment to the development of materials and strategies for teaching science to the retarded. Their objectives incorporate content elements and activities requiring participation of the students in operations such as observing, describing, and comparing. The BSCS staff developed a set of assumptions that would serve as criteria for curriculum design (3).

1. Most teachers of the educable mentally handicapped—EMH— need specific direction in the use of inquiry strategies in the teaching of science concepts.

2. EMH children need and can respond effectively to an activity-centered instructional approach.

3. To achieve the objectives, materials should maintain a balance between detail and motivation, for the amount of minute and abstract detail that can be learned is probably a function of the interest and motivation that can be established to deal with it.

4. The classroom environment and the materials should be uncluttered with distractors; however, a variety of perceptual modes and instructional media should be used in all efforts at communication (e.g. sight, touch, smell, etc.).

5. An activity must involve the student in ways of applying the desired behavior; transfer cannot be assumed.

6. Activities should be developed in small, discrete units that build on or reinforce a concept or skill.

7. Entry points should be concerned with concrete, tangible "things" rather than with abstract, intangible ideas or concepts.

8. Ideas must be developed without the *necessity* for reading on the part of the student.

9. Vocabulary, where possible, should involve *functional* language rather than technical terms.

10. For the EMH student to learn, the instructional approach must be slow-paced and redundant, and there must be time for participation by each student.

11. Efforts to describe the "average" EMH child are essentially futile because of variability within the population; therefore, materials and methods should allow for attention to individual differences and needs.

Teaching strategies, based on current theories about how students learn, play an important role in the development of BSCS materials. The curriculum is developed around well-defined behavioral objectives. These objectives are statements of observable behavior that students are expected to demonstrate after the lessons have been taught. Evaluation is based on these objectives in terms of student behavior.

The outcome of any educational endeavor should be only partially concerned with content. The effective teacher extends lessons far beyond content to teach problem-solving techniques and develop self-confidence in the students. Achievement of this larger, more complete educational goal is at least partially if not wholly contingent on teacher versatility.

The following discussion is based on the exploratory use of science materials and strategies for teaching young educable mentally retarded (EMR) children.

The students were elementary school level; their ages ranged from seven years to ten years. They were members of a summer class for the educable mentally retarded. As with any group, they demonstrated great variability in terms of ability and/or disability. Some were very verbal and socially outgoing. Others seemed inhibited and lacked expressive ability. They were perceived as and treated as individuals, so it is difficult to give meaning to group characteristics. However, the children were more "like" than "unlike" their normal peers.

Both authors participated in the administration of Piagetian tasks to the children. The tasks were described by Bybee (6). All children were preconcrete operational (14). As we observed and listened to the children, many other individual characteristics were revealed; for example, we gained insights relative to their persistence, articulation problems, centrism, perceptual and psychomotor abilities and/or disabilities. These observations gave us considerable data about each child and indicated direction for our science experiences. Characteristics were *not* viewed as inadequacies and could not be generalized to the total population. One reason the children could not be viewed as inadequate is that they were not compared to each other or to "normal" children. We knew about each child as a separate entity, and that is where the instruction began.

Educators such as Bruner (5) and Piaget (13) have conducted developmental research that has emphasized the importance of concrete manipulative experiences. Most of the lessons and related activities included development of elementary science concepts related to properties, materials, sorting, classification, etc. Science Curriculum Improvement Study (SCIS) materials (17) were adopted and used; however, the approach, concepts, and activities could be adopted from any curriculum project. This experience reconfirmed our belief that the teacher is more important than the materials.

As work continued with this group of EMR's the idea emerged that perhaps lessons generated in teaching these children might provide good models for all teachers. The premise behind this idea is: *teaching these children tended to magnify the problems that are minor for other children.*

Involvement in Science and the Individual

We were absolutely required to serve individual needs. The challenge presented by the "uniqueness" of each student made individualization necessary and mandatory.

We had over-all goals for the group; we could not produce specific objectives for them. There were objectives and they were specific for each child and almost instantaneous. An example may clarify this point. If the children were sorting circles, squares, triangles, and irregular shapes, the task was varied for each child according to his immediate past performance and our perceptions of his need. Thus, the objective was generated instantaneously for the child. We did not have a preconceived agenda of objectives to be reached.

The involvement portion of the equation required the teacher to establish a positive accepting and helping relationship with the children. We expected that the children would learn to the best of their ability. One cannot help but become emotional when a child finally tells a property of his fish after he had been almost nonvocal, except for intense tutoring. The children knew we were excited and optimistic about their courage and achievement. We tried to say, "I like the way you..." rather than, "That is a good way to..." when giving approval. Unfortunately, many teachers have been trained to remain objective and detached. A child's ability to succeed in life depends upon a series of personal involvements with people, and teachers are among the most important. A good way to begin this personalization is by using the first personal singular—I. "I love the way you described that!" "I think you're great!"

The successful teacher is spontaneous, enthusiastic, and unafraid to accept children as they are. The more "detached" teacher would teach Johnny about trees with pictures and discussion. The more "involved" teacher allows Johnny to climb a tree, examine the bark, and feel the wind through its branches!

Communicating in Science—
Give Them Something to Communicate

Many educators maintain there are communication problems related to teaching EMR children. It may be true that many young EMR's come to special classes with grossly inadequate sending skills; however, they may be astute receivers. Some EMR's have intact expressive skills, but display inadequate receptive ability. Often, however, we found the reverse to be true. Most teachers unintentionally communicate much more than they realize. Students are quick to pick up subtle cues, such as facial expressions, gestures, nods, and smiles. In the initial stages of our work with these children, we were often deceived by their seemingly correct responses. Actually, we were not communicating the questions; we were communicating the answer!

Concrete physical experience precedes language. We considered this when providing objects and organisms to be examined. We gave the children something about which to talk. No previous experiences were assumed. As already mentioned, part of our involvement was questioning and listening. Another dimension included that of waiting after the question had been asked. When a question was asked concerning a problem, such as properties of a tree, we waited (sometimes for ten to fifteen seconds) before we responded in any way. EMR's take time articulating thoughts; we gave them time. (Patience to do this is often difficult for teachers who find silence a heavy burden.) Often the children "lost" the questions or focus of attention. If we suspected this, we gently repeated or reminded them of the question. When the child answered, we looked him straight in the eye, and listened intently, as if nothing else mattered except his response. Communication was a two-way obligation for the teachers; the burden of understanding was ours whether we were sending or receiving.

Honesty and sincerity were the important elements in our communication with the child. We emphasized success, rewarding correct responses and behavior. However, if the child was wrong, we told him, then went back to repeat or revise the activity. Still the child knew he could succeed at the task; thus, he was not a failure. In this light we communicated success. Never did we communicate failure. With discretion we informed the student of his progress instantly and continuously.

Increasing Attention Span Through Science

"The mentally retarded have short attention spans." This is cited frequently by special educators listing characteristics of these children. The example mentioned below is one of many that occurred to melt this myth.

One of the science units included the construction of aquariums. On this day, the children examined and described fish, snails, plants, water, and sand. They discussed the materials they would need to build an aquarium and maintain the organisms. We went out to look at a pond in the school habitat and discussed the above elements in terms of what they had observed outdoors. The children were very involved for forty-five minutes with only minor personal distractions.

Several strategies enabled us to increase the attention span of these children.

1. Varying activities and changing the pace proved to be assets. We usually had enough material for two or three lessons. If one failed, we shifted and went on.

2. Occasionally we would invent reasons to go outside and look for properties and materials. The children's restlessness indicated a need for gross motor movement. A successful lesson must incorporate ways to get children out of their chairs.

3. The children's complete absorption in some activities was directly related to a personal involvement with materials they understood, and with activities at which they could succeed.

4. If some of the children displayed difficulty centering on an activity or persisting at a task, we took note and made special efforts: first, to provide activities that were intrinsically stimulating; second, to slowly increase the amount of time for interaction with materials.

5. We maintained a continuous dialog that informed them of their progress.

6. To insure enthusiasm for the next day, we concluded activities while interest was high, rather than waiting until it waned.

Observation of Their Environment

Rather than initiating our efforts with attitudes such as: "The EMR lacks curiosity," or "Retardates aren't observing," we begin by saying, "These children can be more curious" and "Given the right materials, they can learn to observe."

While they were in the science room, we provided many opportunities to make them aware of their environment. We played games that required accurate observation and precision in description. Oftentimes we would ask them to find an object with a specific property (i.e. blue, on the table in front of them); second, we would request, "I want you to find a blue object in this room and describe another property it has." These activities were, by design, started with objects or materials on or near them and later extended to objects further away from them physically and conceptually.

In addition, we used these activities to increase their ability to make comparisons and increase their realization of time-related events. "How is your garden different from yesterday?" "What will your plant be like in two days?" Through practice, recognition, and questioning relative to time, their short-term memory skills slowly improved. They learned to predict future events as well as recalling the past.

Self-Concept in Science?

Everyday the children came to science. When they came through the door, they brought many years of feedback indicating they were different, "special," and often objects of jest. Their attitudes and opinions of self came to science with them; they didn't leave them in their other classroom. Part of our teaching was to erase the failure symptoms they had and to create a success syndrome. The children were neither deluded nor demeaned. Every attempt was made to treat them without overt regard to their specialness. Little things, such as labeling of objects (Martha's objects, Bennie's aquarium, John's garden, etc.) "told" them they were trusted and we had confidence enough to let them handle the materials.

To the maximum degree possible, we provided nonverbal innuendos that "told" the students we viewed them as worthy people that could succeed at science. This positive approach resulted in a self-fulfilling prophecy. Their successes were many, some of which were related to their self-concept.

Maladaptive behavior is often the result of unfulfilled needs. The children (like all of us) have the need to be recognized by peers and significant others. Disruptive conduct is a negative behavior that produces a positive fulfillment or concept of self. There are two sets of perceptions that interact in this analysis, those of the teacher and those of the behaver. The student receives recognition and fulfillment for his action even if it is negative as perceived by the teacher.

The self-concept was one of the things to which we paid a great deal of attention. Our science activities were engineered to insure the maximum of success. Objectives varied from child to child and were in line with each child's developmental level and immediate needs. In this case the greatest lesson we taught the children was a more positive, healthy view of themselves. As the children began to reflect a brighter image, the final payoff was ours. It built our self-concepts too!

Summary

We hear protests. "But *why* teach science to the mentally retarded?" "Is the teacher's passionate interest in science enough reason to include it in the child's curriculum?" No! But we can justify it!

1. We need it as a thought process (to develop the ability to recognize relationships, etc.).
2. We must use science as an alternative to solving problems (What do students have to do to alter their environments, etc.).
3. We need science to discover ourselves as persons (parts of the body, etc.) and as humans (in interactions, etc.).

If, as teachers and science educators, we can shift from the frame of reference that views science as the transmission of facts to a view that utilizes science as a means of increasing and enhancing the growth of "special" children, then we can defend and perpetuate inquiry wherever it exists and we can develop it wherever it does not.

References

(1) Allport, G. W., "The Role of Expectancy." In H. Cantril (ed.), *Tensions That Cause Wars*. Urbana, Ill.: University of Illinois Press, 1950.

(2) Bennett, Floyd M., and Kay Downing, "Science Education for the Mentally Retarded." *Science Education, 55*, April/June 1971, pp. 155–62.

(3) Biological Science Curriculum Study, *Newsletter #43*. Biological Sciences Curriculum Study, Boulder, Colo. 1971.

(4) Bruner, J. S., "One Kind of Perception: A Reply to Professor Luchins." *Psychological Review*, 1951.

(5) _____*Toward A Theory of Instruction*. New York: W. W. Norton & Company, Inc., 1968.

(6) Bybee, Rodger and Alan McCormack, "Applying Piaget's Theory." *Science and Children, 8,* December 1970, pp. 14–19.

(7) Gitta, Lena L., "Montessori Principles Applied in a Class of Mentally Retarded Children." *Mental Retardation,* February 1967, pp. 26–29.

(8) Jehle, Daryle J., "A Science Program for the Educable Mentally Retarded—With Teacher's Guide." Master's thesis, University of Kansas, 1966.

(9) Katz, Paul J., "Science for the Educable Retardate." *Science and Children, 2,* October 1964, pp. 20–22.

(10) Kolstoe, Oliver P., *Teaching Educable Mentally Retarded Children.* New York: Holt, Rinehart & Winston, Inc., 1970.

(11) McMahon, Kenneth V., "Science Programs for the Educable Mentally Handicapped." *Exceptional Children, 21,* 1954, pp. 88–90.

(12) Onstead, Grace, "Science Resource Guide for Educable Mentally Retarded Children." Ed.D. diss., George Peabody College, 1963; Abstract No. 105, 1965.

(13) Piaget, Jean, "Development and Learning." *Journal of Research in Science Teaching,* September, 1964.

(14) ———"The Mental Development of the Child," in D. Elkind (ed.), *Six Psychological Studies by Jean Piaget,* New York: Random House, Inc., 1967.

(15) Reichard, Cary L., "Community Expectations of the Mentally Retarded." *Focus on Exceptional Children,* February, 1970.

(16) Rosenthal, R., and Jacobson, L., *Pygmalion in the Classroom.* New York: Holt, Rinehart & Winston, Inc., 1968.

(17) Science Curriculum Improvement Study, Chicago: Rand McNally & Co., 1970.

(18) Sweeters, William G., "A Study to Determine if Educable Mentally Retarded Children Can Learn Selected Science Teaching Objectives Through Individualized Discovery Oriented Instruction." Ed.D. diss., Colorado State College, 1968.

(19) Thresher, Janice, "Science Education for Mentally Retarded Children: A Rationale." *Mental Retardation, 1,* 1963.

13

LABORATORY SCIENCE FOR VISUALLY HANDICAPPED ELEMENTARY SCHOOL CHILDREN

Herbert D. Thier

The tendency of recent innovative projects to move away from a complete emphasis on textbooks and to take an active, materials-centered approach is benefitting more than just "normal" children, for many groups in special education are beginning to see the importance of applying this philosophy to their field. The visually handicapped pupil, who must deal with abstractions and rely on verbal communication at an early age, needs direct learning experiences even more than most children. He receives many verbal instructions and descriptions which he must constantly piece together into an understandable whole without visual cues. The concrete, language-building experiences on which many of the "new science" programs are based seem particularly suited to blind children.

The ASMB Project

The purpose of Adapting Science Materials for the Blind is to provide such an experience-centered instructional program in science for visually handicapped elementary school children. Cooperating agencies involved in the project are the Alameda County (California) Public

Reprinted from *New Outlook for the Blind,* June 1971, pp. 190–94. Dr. Herbert D. Thier is project director of Adapting Science Materials for the Blind and associate director of Science Curriculum Improvement Studies, University of California, Berkeley, California.

Schools, the California State School for the Blind in Berkeley, and the Lawrence Hall of Science, University of California, also in Berkeley. The project is funded by a Title III, E.S.E.A. grant from the State of California.

Analysis, Design, and Testing

Starting with the program developed by the Science Curriculum Improvement Study,[1] the project analyzes existing units and tentatively designs adaptations necessary to make the materials meaningful for visually handicapped elementary school pupils. These adapted materials are then taught in an exploratory manner by project staff members to classes at the California State School for the Blind. Based on the results of these trials, the materials are revised, written up (as teacher's guides and student manuals) and produced (in the form of equipment), and then tried out by classroom teachers working both in regular school programs (one or two visually handicapped pupils per class) and at the Frances Blend School in Los Angeles where the classes are made up entirely of visually handicapped children. As a result of these field trials, the materials are revised once more and then made available to interested teachers.

During the various exploratory and field testing phases of the program, work proceeds on the development of evaluation materials[2] that will enable the teacher to obtain information about the changes that take place in pupils in her classroom during the program. Since the program under development is based on the work of the Science Curriculum Improvement Study, the following short statement describing the work of SCIS will briefly explain the rationale and approach of the adaptation project.

SCIS Programs Are Adapted

The Science Curriculum Improvement Study is developing ungraded, sequential, physical and life science programs for the elementary school—programs which in essence turn the classroom into a laboratory. Each unit of these programs is carefully evaluated by SCIS staff as it progresses from the early exploratory stages to the published edition. The units originate as scientists' ideas for investigations that might challenge children and that illustrate key scientific concepts.

---

[1] The Science Curriculum Improvement Study is funded by the National Science Foundation and headquartered at the Lawrence Hall of Science, University of California, Berkeley.

[2] Development of evaluation material is under the direction of Dr. Marcia Linn of the project staff.

The ideas are then adapted to fit the elementary school curriculum and the resulting units are used by teachers in regular classrooms. Thus they are tested several times in elementary schools before they are published.

Theoretical Background

Central to these elementary school programs are current ideas of intellectual development. A child's elementary school years are a period of transition as he continues his exploration of the world begun in infancy, builds the abstractions with which he interprets that world, and develops confidence in his own ideas. Extensive laboratory experiences at this time will enable him to relate scientific concepts to the real world in a meaningful way. As he matures, the continued interplay of interpretations and observations will frequently compel him to revise his ideas about his environment.

The teaching strategy is for the children to explore selected science materials. They are encouraged to investigate, to discuss what they observe, and to ask questions. The SCIS teacher has two functions: to be an observer who listens to the children and notices how well they are progressing in their investigations, and to be a guide who leads the children in seeing the relationship of their findings to the key concepts of science.

Laboratory Approach

The adapted program for visually handicapped children takes a laboratory approach, stressing observation, manipulation of materials, and development of language skills to describe and explain events. Through these activities the visually handicapped child is encouraged to explore his world further and to develop confidence in his own ideas. The specially adapted and designed concrete experiences being developed by the project will give him a base from which to build the abstractions necessary for interpreting the biological and physical science aspects of his environment.

The following examples, one group of activities from the physical and the other from the biological sciences, illustrate how it is possible to adapt activities for visually handicapped children which seem totally dependent on sight.

Aquaria in a Biological Science Unit

During the SCIS first-level biological science unit, entitled *Organisms,* children are given experience with fish in order to help them further develop their knowledge and understanding of organisms.[3] Concepts like birth, death, reproduction, and habitat are introduced in relation to the children's experiences with aquaria and the fish and plants which they find in them. The first part of the unit concentrates heavily on the pupil's observation and description of fish and their properties. Ordinarily the fish, plants, snails, etc., are placed in square, one-gallon plastic containers and the children observe the motion and other behavior of the fish for themselves.

Adapted Aquarium

To enable the visually handicapped child who cannot see the fish to discover the characteristics and behavior of goldfish more directly, a special aquarium set-up was devised. A second identical plastic, one-gallon aquarium is obtained and holes are drilled in the bottom of it. The two aquaria are then placed one in the other so that the water comes up through the holes and fills the second aquarium. The fish is placed in the nested aquaria and the child is taught to tip the second, inner aquarium so that most of the water runs out and the goldfish is trapped in the small amount of water remaining at the bottom. The visually handicapped child can then place his fingers inside and feel the fish's movement, its actual shape, the action of the fins, and even the motion of the fish's gills. He can capture the fish and lift him out of the aquarium so that its size, shape, and other characteristics can be explored more effectively.

Examining Fish

Although one might expect the fish to die immediately when removed from water, only one or two fish have been lost and some have survived sessions of as long as fifteen minutes out of the water. One of the fish that died was found to have almost no scales left. On being questioned, the six-and-a-half-year-old blind boy who had been working with it explained that he had rubbed it very hard to shine up the gold so that he could see it. He no longer tries to shine his goldfish, but from further work with goldfish, he now has a much better understanding of many of the characteristics of a fish. While sighted children draw pictures of their organisms after observation, the blind child is given a piece of clay from which he can develop his own model of what fish look like.

It is also possible to place plants, snails, filamentous algae, and other organisms in the adapted aquarium so visually handicapped children can have direct experiences with them also. Based on these experiences, the visually handicapped child can not only participate in discus-

---

[3]Development of the life science adaptations is under the direction of Robert Knott of the project staff.

sions with his sighted peers about the fish, but can also internalize some of the ideas that others offer during these discussions.

Teaching the Concept of the Food Web

In integrated classes, sighted children often become interested in the adapted materials, and the activities designed for the blind child may be used to benefit the class as a whole. As an exploratory activity in teaching the concept of the food web, sighted children in the classroom observe guppies eating the water flea, *Daphnia,* in their aquaria. Although we tried repeatedly to make these tiny organisms observable to blind children, the Daphnia appear to be much too small and delicate for them to feel. A large, plastic model of the water flea was available for the blind child to manipulate, but another more concrete experience was necessary in order to get this important concept across. The goldfish was originally chosen for its size, but it has another important characteristic: it is an animal-eater and thus has the same relationship to the food web as guppies. Now the blind child's aquarium becomes a focal point for all his classmates. Small guppies, which the child can easily identify once he has had experience with the larger fish, are placed inside his aquarium. Soon afterwards, one or more of the guppies disappears. The children develop hypotheses for what might have caused this disappearance and eventually, after experimentation, are able to add goldfish to their classroom food web.

Liquid Solutions in a Physical Science Unit

Solutions are found and used by the child in all parts of his environment. Many interactions in physical science take place between solutions of various substances. As a child builds a knowledge of solutions and their properties, he extends his knowledge and understanding about matter and its conservation. In the third-level SCIS physical science unit, entitled *Subsystems and Variables,* liquid solutions are studied and the definition of a liquid solution is developed by contrasting the appearance and behavior of liquid solutions with liquid nonsolutions.

Scientific Criteria

The most useful operational criterion with which to identify liquid solutions is that they are clear (like syrup or salt water) and not cloudy or milky (like lemonade or milk). Solutions may be colored (as are coffee and apple cider), but they are clear. The cloudy appearance of a nonsolution is caused by the presence of undissolved particles or droplets that are large enough to interfere with the transmission of light through the liquid.

For sighted individuals we therefore have a two-part definition: a solution is a mixture that is clear, not cloudy. Is water a solution? Salt water? Milk? Tea? Pure water is not a mixture, hence it is neither a solution nor a nonsolution. Salt water is a clear mixture, hence it is a solution. Milk also is a mixture, but it is a nonsolution because it is not clear. Tea, a colored, clear mixture, is a solution.

Adapted Criteria

If a sighted child is given a system and asked to state whether it is a pure substance, a solution, or a nonsolution, he will first take a close look at it. If it is cloudy, he can say that the system is a nonsolution. If the system is clear, it is either a solution or a pure substance. The seriously visually handicapped child cannot visually decide whether a mixture is clear or cloudy and therefore is not able to use this ordinary method of separating mixtures from liquid solutions. The following adapted teaching program designed by the project provides the child with a nonvisual approach to determining whether or not a mixture behaves like a liquid solution.

Distinguishing Mixtures, Solutions, and Nonsolutions

First, all mixtures are separated into two groups. One group includes all those mixtures (like sand and water) where there is evidence of a residue or solid material in the liquid. This is determined by feel, the grating or other sound caused by rubbing a popsicle stick over the solid material, or the sound of the solid material hitting the sides of the container as it is shook. All mixtures which give evidence of solid material or residue are classified as nonsolutions and put aside.

The other group of mixtures includes both solutions (like salt and water) and nonsolutions (chalk and water) where the solid material is finely dispersed and cannot be directly detected by the visually handicapped child. These mixtures are filtered and all those which leave no residue on the filter paper are classified as acting like a solution. The others (like starch and water) which leave a residue in the filter paper are not solutions and are classified in the same group as the sand and water.

Limitations

The major limitation of this approach is the fact that some mixtures identified as nonsolutions by this procedure may actually contain solutions as parts (subsystems) of the mixture. For example, when you add both salt and starch to water, or more plain salt than can dissolve in that amount of water, you will, on filtering, get a residue. Each is a nonsolution even though both also contain a salt-water solution.

Overcoming Limitations

To help solve this problem, the visually handicapped children are introduced to the technique of letting what comes through the filter paper evaporate. If it is just water, little or no residue is left. If it is actually a solution, a great deal of residue remains after evaporation and so the pupils have acquired more information. This work with solutions has proven highly interesting to the visually handicapped elementary school children with whom the program has been tried in its experimental version.

These activities follow the children's earlier experiences with the properties of objects and how one finds and describes evidence of interaction between objects. Adaptations, such as using texture instead of color to differentiate between objects and the use of a small motor instead of a light bulb to indicate a complete electric circuit, have been developed and used with success.

Concurrent with the development of the program are the design of evaluation activities. The work involves developing tests specifically for visually handicapped children to determine their intellectual development, the success of the adaptations, and the effectiveness of the program as a whole.

Goals of Project

The dividends received from Adapting Science Materials for the Blind will extend beyond the blind child's greater familiarity with scientific concepts and processes. It is hoped that the children will show behavioral changes similar to those found with sighted children in the SCIS program: a reliance on evidence, confidence in their own ideas, and a variety and thoroughness in approaching problems. The project also points to new ways in which the work of innovative programs can be adapted and revised and may inspire groups working in other areas of special education.

14

SCIENCE IN A SILENT WORLD

Rodger Bybee

Bryan jumped to his feet, went to the teacher, and eagerly pulled on his pants. When the teacher looked down Bryan pointed at the clock and made a swimming or crawling motion with his arms. The teacher nodded "yes" and indicated the other six children should line up behind Bryan. The children quietly, but with a fervent enthusiasm, lined up and started down the hall to science. Upon arriving in the science room the children silently scurried around looking at the fish, rockets, snakes, mice, magnets, lizards, and other items that were about. After a couple minutes the teacher motioned that the children should be seated. Before each child was a small tray containing pieces of wood, plastic, and metal from the Science Curriculum Improvement Study unit MATERIAL OBJECTS. The teacher held up a small sign with the printed word *METAL;* then through gesture asked which of the materials on the tray was metal. The seven children quietly observed their trays, then upon discovery of their metal object held it high in the air with a broad smile that indicated they had found the correct object. The teacher smiled in return and the class continued with an inquiry of plastic and wood. The communications of these children are through their actions because they live in a silent speechless world—they are deaf.

Reprinted from *Science Activities,* 6, January 1972, pp. 25–54. Reprinted with permission of the author and publisher.

In the past, Special Education has remained rather isolated from the other realms of education. Likewise, no unique efforts have been made to develop curriculum materials or integrate these students into the mainstream of education. Recently, however, some of the artificial barriers have been eroded and materials are being developed or modified for the special education students. Also, they are being integrated into regular classes and school activities where and when possible. At the Laboratory School, University of Northern Colorado, the teaching of science to preschool deaf children was a first step toward weathering artificial educational boundries.

When first confronted with the possibility of teaching science to deaf children I was hesititant. I knew little of their handicap, needs, and special techniques used in teaching them. These were soon overcome through observation of the children, discussion with the instructor in Special Education, and finally experience. The following is a brief overview of a thirty-week project dealing with science for the deaf; it was for them—science in a silent world.

The educational needs of acoustically handicapped children are not vastly different than the needs of normal children their age. Basic to the needs of these handicapped children is language growth and development. Thus, science should be used as an instrument to develop vocabulary. In order to broaden views of the environment, materials, objects, and organisms from the natural and manmade world should be incorporated into the science program. Included with this should be opportunity for the child to explore, invent, and discover within the environment. For the deaf, like normal children, have an enthusiastic curiosity and motivation, especially in a rich learning environment. With the help of the teacher these experiences can and should operationally show the children's differences in the meaning of words. At the same time the program will help them feel better about themselves and the world they live in.

After a consideration of these needs and the primary focus of education for the deaf, Science Curriculum Improvement Study was selected as the basic curriculum from which to structure the program. SCIS has enjoyed a great deal of success in the area of language development. Likewise, the broad spectrum of students and situations in which SCIS has been used represents a universality of the materials. The materials were adapted for the young deaf child and, in particular, the method of teaching was adopted through the entire program.

The preschool class for the acoustically handicapped consisted of seven eager and excited young children: five boys and two girls. They ranged in age from four and one-half to six years. They were average or slightly above in intelligence and operated within a range of hearing loss. Three of the children had a profound hearing loss, three had severe losses, and one had a moderate hearing loss.

How do you teach deaf children? Confrontation with this problem brings one to a realization of our dependence on the spoken word for the act of teaching. For the deaf a modification of the teaching method is required, much more than a modification of the materials. I would suspect the same is true for many physically handicapped, emotionally disturbed, and mentally retarded. The visually impaired, however, require a modification in materials as well as method. Dr. Herbert D. Thier of SCIS has shown this in his work with the adaption of SCIS for the blind. Teaching the deaf does not represent a severe departure from teaching normal children. As it turns out it emphasized what is probably the best approach for both groups as far as pedogogy is concerned.

Communication was achieved through the medium of pantomime, printed words, drawings, and large work sheets. These techniques provided effective communication and subsequent physical and mental involvement on behalf of the student.

The instructional sequence was fundamentally the same as that recommended by SCIS. Exploration, invention, and discovery proved to be quite adequate for the deaf.

The *exploration* phase was introduced when the children were confronted with a number of objects relating to a concept or multiple of concepts. For example, various shapes, sizes, colors, textures, and forms of wood were shown to the children. They were then asked through the mime of gesture, "What material is this?" Their resulting puzzlement provided mental involvement with their objects. Finally, they raised their eyes and communicated through bewildered looks that they did not know which material was wood.

Invention of the concept wood immediately followed. The printed word *WOOD* was shown and associated with the multiple of pieces and forms of the material. The children continued to look, feel, smell, and even taste the wood.

After the students had grasped the concept of wood, a field trip around the school was conducted. The purpose of the field trip was to discover wooden objects in their environments. The *discovery* portion was also followed up in the classroom through sorting and grouping of wooden objects using another property, such as color, shape, or size, as criterion for the grouping.

Later simple sentences were used in the reinforcement. For example, "This object is made of _____." The child would then provide the appropriate tag for paper, metal, plastic or wood.

Finally, the student was aided with the spoken word. This was completed during their speech and language arts period. Little time was used during science for speech development. Incidentally reinforcing the words learned in science in their regular classroom was most beneficial. Speech from the deaf child can lead to an illusive impression of intelligence. In fact, speech or verbalization is the last step of concept development. However, a word can be pronounced before the concept has been mentally assimilated or accommodated. Unfortunately, teachers of normal children often use speech as a key to their understanding of concepts. For the deaf the cue is their action on tasks. Thus, the untrained observer is misled by the spoken word in both the silent world and the world of sound.

Using this approach words associated with properties, materials, ordering, and organisms were developed.

For the deaf child, there is a great need for repetition in a variety of new situations. Thus, modification of SCIS included a much slower succession of lessons and a great deal more repetition than is required for normal children. For this reason all of the lessons from MATERIAL OBJECTS and ORGANISMS were not completed in the thirty weeks. Divertissements from the regular curriculum sequence occurred often. Always, however, the concepts that had been introduced earlier were reinforced. When possible the lessons ended with the children interacting with live organisms. Frogs, snakes, turtles, salamanders, mice, and mealworms were explored by the children. From this the young boys and girls developed the crawling motion as the sign for science.

Science for the deaf aided the children in the accommodation or assimilation of concepts; second, increased their awareness of more abstract concepts because it emphasized properties, materials, and objects rather than just the name of the object. For example, a "door" is also large, smooth, brown, and wood. Third, the vocabulary of the children increased through the incorporation of words in conjunction with the involvement and activities. Thus, an operational meaning for the new words was developed.

Fortunately, we did not become enmeshed in revision and adaptation of curriculum materials. Once communication between teacher and student is overcome the lessons in MATERIAL OBJECTS do not require the student to hear. Every word in their vocabulary is known by the teacher. Initial lessons were structured around activities that could utilize vocabulary already possessed by the children. Some difficulty was encountered in trying to change a "name" and introduce the word object. This took time and patience. Property words were easily grasped. Texture words were the most difficult. If this were repeated, a tactile approach combined with a blindfold would be used. We only used a tactile approach. The names for materials and combining properties when describing materials was relatively easy for the children.

Large worksheets, similar to those in the student books, were used for sorting and grouping of materials and differentiating materials by properties. Some work was completed with liquids and gases; however, this required much greater complexities in use of vocabulary. Serial ordering was done with remarkable success.

It should be pointed out that each lesson for normal children is approximately five to seven lessons for the deaf. Further, each thirty-minute lesson had three or four different activities.

ORGANISMS was also easily adapted to the acoustically handicapped. The children had no trouble observing, describing, and growing seeds. They each had a garden. Some of the words such as *guppies*, *water snail*, and *eelgrass* were simplified to *fish*, *snail*, and *weed*. Differences in fish were observed and recorded. There was a great deal of excitement the day John, age five, became the father of several guppies. Both birth and death were experienced during the unit. The children used the sign for sleep to indicate death in the aquarium.

On several occasions the children investigated habitats around the school. To our surprise many of the concepts learned in the classroom transfered to this, the real world. The children's responses were not the result of being queried by a teacher; rather it sprang spontaneously from a need to communicate to one another. "Big fish," "green plant" provided the type of reward many teachers enjoy.

In summary, the units worked exceptionally well. Little modification of the materials is necessary. The lessons should be started at the child's level of experience and vocabulary, proceed in smaller increments, and have concepts duplicated in a variety of activities.

The results of the involvement were most satisfying for both the children and the teacher. For evaluation tasks were administered in a manner similar to the technique used by Jean Piaget. New materials were presented and the children were "asked" about the materials. The teacher then observed their actions. The task was modified and they were questioned again. The evaluator was accepting of the child's response. By the end of the project thirty-five new words were in the children's vocabulary. This represented an increase of approximately 25 percent over their projected increase in vocabulary.

Science should not be omitted from the education of the deaf. The deaf are inured to the hardships of living in a silent world. Some of these hardships are elevated for a brief time when the natural enthusiasm and curiosity for objects and organisms is cultivated into a meaningful learning experience. The Science Curriculum Improvement Study became the mediator between materials from the realm of science and the intrinsic motivation of children. The program did not negate or circumvent language development—it enhanced and enriched it. Secondarily, the children developed senses, other than hearing, as well as psychomotor skills, the capacity to observe, and the ability to describe.

The results of the project indicate the wide range, longitudinally as well as latitudinally, that SCIS materials can be used.

One of the best compliments and evaluations of the program's success was given by the children's emotions, attitudes, and feelings conveyed by actions at the conclusion of the science lesson. Perhaps the same is true for normal children.

"It's 2:20; Ronnie is late for the bus." The teacher indicated to Ronnie that it was time for him to return to the classroom, get his coat, and go to the bus. Immediately he looked down and intentionally lost eye contact with the teacher. It was as if he said, "That's OK, I am more interested in my organisms than the bus." Finally a teaching aid had to lead the unconvinced young man out of the room. Several minutes later the teacher started gathering the materials used in the lesson. Each child had a look of regret over having lost his or her aquarium and garden. With stern disappointment the children sat. Upon the sign to line up the children dispersed to all parts of the room, half feigning an interest in all the science objects they could find in their immediate environment. Finally after a short struggle the children were ready to go. On occasion one could detect a tear as they left their gardens and aquariums and terrariums. They went on in their silent world, regreting to leave, rejoicing to return. Hopefully we had translated some of their "language" into ours.

IV

Becoming a Better Elementary Science Teacher Through Understanding the Curriculum

Over the last decade there has been a revolution in the elementary science curriculum. The National Science Foundation of the federal government has spent millions of dollars to insure better curriculum materials were available for teaching elementary science. As a result, during the 60s there was a mushrooming of curriculum projects to revise, innovate, and update elementary science. Space limitations do not allow description of all funded projects in this book. The most accepted ones, however, are discussed. These are: The Conceptually Oriented Program in Elementary Science (COPES), Environmental Studies (ES), Elementary Science Study (ESS), Science Curriculum Improvement Study (SCIS), and Science—A Process Approach (SAPA). All of these emphasize the importance of having the child involved in science activities where he learns for himself. These projects vary, however, in content, sequence, and teacher strategies. It is impossible to say which project is the best. They are all good. For this reason, you should study each of them and come to know better the one you think would be the most exciting for you to teach.

To assist you in your choice the Far West Educational Laboratory has compared the various curriculum projects and has attempted to answer many questions about them. In reviewing the curriculums you should keep in mind certain questions. What do you need or want in a curriculum? An emphasis on process? or product? Well stated behavior objectives? A means to develop the affective as well as cognitive content? Freedom? or structure? You should also keep in mind that there are still many teachers using elementary science texts. What ideas and investigative approaches suggested by the curriculum projects can be adapted to texts?

15

COPES
THE NEW ELEMENTARY SCIENCE PROGRAM

J. Darrell Barnard

There are several reasons for developing a conceptually oriented program in elementary school science. For almost half a century it has been accepted that science teaching which focuses upon a relatively small number of big ideas has educational merit. This is particularly true in the science education of elementary school children and in the education of prospective elementary school teachers.

From its inception elementary school science has been much like the old 1890 bathing suit. It has covered everything but revealed little of any consequence. Collegiate programs in science education for prospective elementary school teachers have suffered from a "shotgun, broad-target" approach. One has only to examine the extensive science sections of some of the more popular textbooks on the teaching of elementary school science to verify this unrealistic breadth of superficial coverage. Something has to be done to reduce the coverage to manageable proportions and to accentuate that which is the essence of science.

The "principles of science" movement of the 1930s represented a noble effort to reduce fragmentation in elementary school science and to give it a more scientific perspective. However, the findings of such investigations as Robertson's (3) neither significantly reduced the breadth of coverage in practice nor did much to define the unifying conceptual structure of science more clearly.

Reprinted from *Science and Children, 9,* November 1971, pp. 9–11. Dr. J. Darrell Barnard is Associate Director of COPES and Professor of Science Education, New York University, New York, New York.

In 1962, the NSTA position statement on curriculum development in science (2) set the stage for a subsequent effort to define a relatively few conceptual schemes which could serve as guides for delimiting and redirecting science teaching in the schools (4). Within this context the COPES Project has undertaken the monumental task of developing a K-6 basic science curriculum.

COPES, an acronym for a Conceptually Oriented Program in Elementary Science, has been funded from its beginning in 1965 by the U.S. Office of Education. Its central purpose is to develop an understanding of matter at progressive levels of sophistication. Hopefully, such an approach will not only give teachers and pupils a clearly recognized goal but also a unified and meaningful view of science. This would be a welcome redirection from the fragmented and confused view of science that is shared by so many people today.

Five schemes make up the framework of the COPES spirally designed, conceptually constrained curriculum (1):

1. The Structural Units of the Universe

The idea that the universe is made up of structural units is a belief that has gained general acceptance by scientists as they have persisted in the search for a more satisfactory comprehension of the nature of matter, both animate and inanimate. Today scientists believe that the universe is made up of individually distinct units of matter. From a large-scale view, stars and their planets may be considered as the structural units of the universe. The individual plants and animals with which we commonly associate may be considered, at one level of organization, as the structural units of life on the earth. At a smaller level of organization the structural units of living things are cells. At yet another level of organization the structural units of the universe are crystals, molecules, and atoms. Electrons, protons, and neutrons are among the smaller units within an atom. Today scientists continue the search for even smaller and more fundamental units of matter.

2. Interaction and Change

Based upon observations conducted over the years, scientists have come to believe that the entire universe is constantly changing. They believe that this is true for stars, the earth, and all living things upon the earth. Some changes, such as geological ones, take place over extremely long periods of time. Others, such as the chemical changes in an explosion, may occur very rapidly. The scientist believes that all such changes are the results of interactions among the structural units of the universe.

3. The Conservation of Energy

One of the most basic and far-reaching beliefs of the modern scientist is that the total amount of energy in the universe remains unchanged. They believe that energy may be changed from one form to another but the total amount is conserved. In their experiments, whenever it appears that some of the energy involved in the system under observation cannot be accounted for, scientists continue to search in an effort to find the "missing energy." Belief in this idea has led to important discoveries that might not otherwise have been made.

4. The Degradation of Energy

This has to do with the direction in which energy changes. It has been observed that the natural tendency of all energy changes is in one direction, a direction that results in the ability of the energy to do less and less work. The total amount of energy is conserved; however, some of it appears in a form that makes it less usable. This energy is in the form of heat energy.

5. The Statistical View of Nature

Scientists hold to the belief that natural events ultimately cannot be predicted with certainty. They can only be predicted on a statistical basis. For example, the sex of a mother's unborn child cannot be predicted with absolute confidence. However, it can be predicted that for the population as a whole about one-half of the newborn babies will be females and the other half will be males. Experience in germinating a large number of corn seed from a selected sample of corn seed may make it possible to predict that seven out of ten of the seeds can be expected to germinate. But one cannot predict with certainty that any particular corn seed selected from the sample will or will not germinate. The statistical view of nature makes it possible to predict natural events such as radioactivity, transmission of genetic traits to successive generations, and the motion of molecules, but only when large numbers of individual events or objects are involved.

The K-6 developmental sequence for one conceptual scheme, the conservation of energy, is shown in the accompanying schematic diagram. Since the five schemes are developed concurrently, many of the subordinate concepts, as they are learned, grade by grade, contribute to an understanding of two or more conceptual schemes. For example, in the schematic on Conservation of Energy the minisequence, Heat Energy and Change of State (G), also contributes to an under-

K-6 Developmental Sequence for one conceptual scheme, the Conservation of energy.

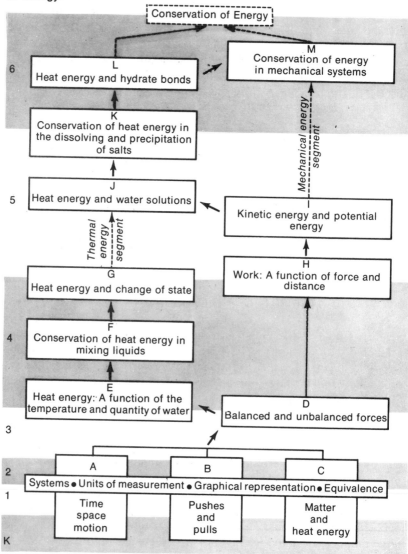

standing of Interaction and Change. The basic learning unit is called an activity. Within a grade, activities having a common goal are organized into developmental clusters called minisequences. There are several progressively arranged minisequences for each grade level.

Assessment materials, designed to maximize pupil mastery of concepts, have been prepared for each minisequence. Although COPES is a highly structured program, the minisequence components within each grade make the materials adaptable for use in a variety of ways. For example, one relatively self-contained minisequence in the fourth grade has been published as a separate teacher's guide entitled the *Water-Mix Experiments* (5). The teacher's guide for this minisequence has been used successfully in fourth, fifth, and sixth grade science classes where children have had no previous experience with COPES materials. These experiments guide the learning of children, step by step, to the concept of conservation of thermal energy in water mixes. A teacher's guide is planned for one such minisequence to be commercially published as an illustrative set of materials for each conceptual scheme. These will be released to schools before the publication and distribution of final editions of the teachers' guides for the entire curriculum. A self-contained minisequence, dealing with the statistical view of nature, is presently in the works. When it and the aforementioned materials are published, schools will be able to enrich their present elementary science programs with COPES materials ahead of the time that the entire curriculum is ready for adoption in schools.

COPES is a nonreading program in that no materials, other than worksheets and assessments, are being written for children. All materials are being published as teachers' guides. A basic tenet underlying the COPES teaching materials is that each learning activity should get children intellectually involved in ways that lead them personally to arrive at the concept. In order for this to happen children must repeatedly use such skills as analyzing, classifying, communicating, experimenting, interpreting, mathematical reasoning, measuring, observing, and predicting. The nature of the scientific enterprise is such that skills and concepts become inextricably involved in learning science. For example, very early in the program and with materials related to the Statistical View of Nature conceptual scheme, children *observe* a variety of objects in arriving at the notion that color, size, odor, texture, and the like, are properties of objects that can be used in *classifying* them in groups. Furthermore, they *analyze* their observations of a single property as it is exhibited among a group of similar objects. From this analysis they *infer* the notion of variability of the property among objects of a single population.

In later grades children record their observations in graphic and tabular form to *communicate* more clearly about the data they have collected and to facilitate analysis of it. *Measurement* is introduced early in quantifying properties such as width, length, amount, and temperature. *Experimentation* is used in the investigation of chance events such as coin tossing. *Mathematical reasoning* is involved in dealing with such concepts as distribution of properties in populations of objects, games of chance, and determining the "best value" for a quantitative property in a population. In these and many other ways the skills and concepts become inextricably involved in learning science.

The teachers' guides for Kindergarten and Grade 1 have been published in a one-volume trial edition. The teachers' guides for each successive grade level will be published in separate volumes. Although pupil worksheets and assessment materials are included in each teacher's guide, a separate package of these materials is being prepared for each grade to facilitate their reproduction.

For the most part the materials and equipment are relatively commonplace and easily obtained locally. There are no plans to prepare equipment kits. A unique design has been prepared by our staff psychologist for field testing COPES, a seven-year sequential program, in two years. Field testing will get under way early in 1972, according to current plans.

Anyone wishing to keep informed regarding the availability and price of COPES materials should write to: Director, COPES Project, New York University, 4 Washington Place, New York City 10003.

References

(1) *COPES: Conceptually Oriented Program in Elementary Science.* Supported by the United States Office of Education. New York University, March 1971, pp. 6–10.

(2) "The NSTA Position Statement on Curriculum Development in Science." *The Science Teacher,* 29, December 1962, pp. 32–35.

(3) Robertson, Martin L., "The Selection of Science Principles Suitable as Goals of Instruction in Elementary Science." *Science Education, 19,* February and April 1935, pp. 65–70.

(4) *Theory Into Action in Science Curriculum Development.* National Science Teachers Association, Washington, D. C., 1964.

(5) *Water-Mix Experiments.* American Science and Engineering, Boston, 1971.

16

ENVIRONMENTAL STUDIES:
A CURRICULUM FOR PEOPLE

Gail Griffith

"Hey man, look at that woman. She looks just like my mom. Now that's power. Let's take a picture of her."
"No, power is like that cool car or maybe those power lines over here."
"Yeh, but woman-parent power has much more power; I mean it's stronger."
"I think you're just talking about different power than I am. You'd probably say that liquor store or that church is power and I don't think so. Power means something that can do work."
"Yeh, but women, liquor, churches—they do work but it's a different kind than cars and electricity. It's more psychological and, man, that is power."

This conversation was one I overheard between two sixth graders on a street near P. S. 25 in Bedford Stuyvesant, a section of Brooklyn, New York. These students had been sent out on assignment to find something that represents "power." The assignment was one of fifty developed by the Environmental Studies project and P.S. 25 was one of more than fifty schools testing the materials across the nation. The conversation was not unique in character; it is typical of the diverse kinds of awareness that often develop in students using ES materials

Reprinted from *Science and Children*, 9, January–February 1972, pp. 18–21. Ms. Gail Griffith is a staff associate for the Environmental Studies Project, Boulder, Colorado.

as they explore such concepts as "Power Picture." Most importantly, students make such determinations by themselves in their own immediate environment, the place they live. They are concept explorers in the reality of the world that is their everyday environment.

What Is Environmental Studies (ES)?

Funded by the National Science Foundation (NSF), and sponsored by the American Geological Institute, ES is a multi-disciplinary program whose materials can be and are used from kindergarten through graduate school in science, social studies, math, art, language arts, and other disciplines. These materials currently consist of the assignment cards and ESSENCE, a teacher's "nonguide." These materials are relatively low in cost ($10.00 per set). They are designed for the teacher so that one set per classroom is all that is needed.

Each assignment card (see examples in Figure 1) consists of "the action," an ambiguous invitation to go into the immediate environment — halls, campus grounds, neighborhood — and explore some aspect of that environment. This ambiguity has an essential and characteristic outcome: it forces the student to make significant decisions about how he completes the assignment. He first decides what aspect of his environment he will explore, then he chooses the process he'll use in his explorations. Since the student is making his own decisions, the "answers" he brings back are correct because correctness depends on his personal interpretation of the assignment. This success inevitably results in growth of self-esteem and self-image, one of the fundamental objectives of ES.

The initial assignment depends on the people and environment involved. What happens after the student finishes? (Finishing time varies with the individual student, teacher, and assignment.) It sometimes simply ends with a fuller awareness of some specific aspect of the student's immediate environment, such as power, predator-prey relationships, joy, or of his own inner environment, the triggers for love and hate, for feeling good and bad.

However, in most cases, the student becomes sufficiently involved with his new-found awareness that he wants to extend it, to find out more about it. This is done by reading, by talking with others, by designing and carrying out experiments, by thinking, by using himself as a laboratory for a greater understanding of his own reactions and those of others. Such extensions are largely cognitive whereas achievement of the initial awareness and reactions to it fall into the realm of the psychomotor and the affective.

In addition to the initial assignment section on each card, there are suggestions called "more." These are possible extension activities. Many teachers use these. Others design their own or, better yet, permit students to create their own.

As you may readily guess, learning resulting from any particular assignment cannot be predicted either in terms of specific content or time required. The only thing that can be predicted is that learning *will* occur, for once the affective is served by allowing students to deal with their environment on their own terms and for their own reasons, the cognitive becomes inevitable. There is no way to stop people from learning what they want and need to know, though of course their "schools" may be the streets or what happens in afterschool hours.

For the past two years, a majority of the ES formal test population has consisted of inner city students in Los Angeles, San Francisco, Denver, Chicago, Detroit, New York City, Baltimore, Washington, D. C., and Atlanta. In addition, several thousand teachers are using the materials in suburban and rural schools, in college and university pre- and in-service teacher preparation courses. Students range from kindergarten through graduate school. Since the materials are written for teachers, they all use the same materials; the differences are not in initial involvement but in verbalization of the outcomes.

What Are the Results of Using Environmental Studies Materials?

Evaluation of results to date are formative in character, based on staff observations in pilot classrooms and feedback from teachers, administrators, and students. The chief characteristics found are desire, enthusiasm, and excitement for learning among both students and teachers. Part of the excitement, of course, is due to going outside the classroom combined with the appealing "magic" of using Polaroid cameras in some assignments. Instant photography means that the student is only ten seconds away from either success or failure, and this acts as a quick route to development of self-esteem. All camera assignments are optional, and alternatives—writing, sketching, or building—can replace the use of cameras for classes which do not have access to Polaroid cameras. A very substantial portion of the observed joy in learning is derived from the fun and joy each of us has felt when learning something on our own for our own reasons.

Much of this learning can be abstracted into ecological terms. Students become aware of and learn about relationships within the

Samples above show both sides of two of the Environmental Studies cards.

self, relationships with other people, relationships within their family, school, and the larger community beyond, relationships among things and between things and people.

In this learning, students find they need traditional academic tools: reading, communication, math. There have been numerous reports of "non-readers" requesting that they be taught how to read. One Harlem student, frustrated, watched another member of his group write a description of its findings on the blackboard, rushed next period to his reading teacher and demanded to be taught how to read. The delighted teacher was almost bewildered for he had long since given up hope for that student. Students who have shown an aversion to math are pleased when asked to go outside to find a million of something and prove it (the assignment card "Show Me A Million"). They count, measure, multiply, divide, estimate, predict, weigh, calculate volume and, then, with great authority, defend their proof for a million sand grains, tree leaves, bricks, cigarette butts, or dozens of other items. In a desire to communicate their new knowledge, students write poems, plays, essays, and advertisements, and invent graphic, artistic representations of their emotions and findings.

The key here is motivation, that inner drive *to learn something that is useful to you.* Most schools in the past have tried to rely on extrinsic stimulation hoping it would somehow engender intrinsic motivation and the inevitable resultant learning. Unfortunately, this hope was rarely fulfilled. ES, however, by its ambiguous assignments and atmosphere of trust, establishes many of the conditions necessary to intrinsic motivation. This is the philosophical base of the ES phrase mentioned earlier: "When the affective is served, the cognitive is inevitable."

During this academic year, ES will conduct its first summative evaluation effort. As the project's primary goals lie in the affective domain, an area represented by a dearth of proven evaluative tools, we have had to design our own tools and modify those of others. The use of instruments directed at cognitive outcomes are planned for the end of the current school year.

What Is the Teacher's Role in Environmental Studies?

As ES cards are designed for the teacher and not the students, the teacher's initial responsibility is to give the assignment to his students. However, many of the pilot teachers ask students to choose a card (assignment) that they want to do.

Regardless of the means used to initiate an assignment, the teacher's major role in Environmental Studies is that of facilitator. When asked, he guides students to resources, both books and people, to equipment and equipment sources. He participates in the learning rather than standing outside of it directing. Indeed, he himself sometimes does an assignment that particularly intrigues him. But, *most importantly, he does not make decisions for his students.*

Much of the success of both the facilitator role and the ES materials is due to a teacher's ability to establish an environment of trust in his classroom. Such an environment necessitates an attitude of acceptance and openness rather than one of evaluation and suspicion. Real acceptance inevitably requires risk-taking by the teacher—he trusts students to be outside without his immediate supervision, he trusts students to find out how to use equipment and then use it, he trusts students to interact with the things and people in his immediate environment. Such trust is proven and established as an environment only when he accepts the results of his trust for, of course, some students will test the teacher. But once they find the trust is real, testing halts and with it disappear "discipline problems." Trust comes from taking a risk and surviving it.

Specific teacher assistance in establishing such an environment is presented by means of the "sideways comments" that appear on each card. These are pedagogical in character. They warn of the risks and threats that may be involved so that each teacher can decide whether or not he wants to use a particular card. They offer brief suggestions as to how best to establish and maintain an open classroom environment with a particular card.

Just as ES asks teachers to trust their students, ES trusts teachers. Instead of a voluminous teachers' guide which insinuates that the teacher cannot successfully use the materials without detailed instructions, ESSENCE-ESSENSE, the ES guide, is twenty pages of words and graphics, which set forth the philosophy of ES, the psychology it is committed to, and the reactions some teachers and students have had to ES. It is not a cookbook; teachers know their students and school far better than curriculum developers (such as ES) could ever presume to, just as your students probably know their immediate environment better than you do. The essence of these materials is an atmosphere, an attitude, an invitation, and a permission slip to do and be involved in more open, more exciting, and, we believe, more humane education.

For more information, write Environmental Studies, Box 1559, Boulder, Colorado 80302.

17

PROGRAMS FOR IMPROVING SCIENCE INSTRUCTION IN THE ELEMENTARY SCHOOL: PART I, ESS*

Robert E. Rogers
Alan M. Voelker

The ERIC Center for Science Education receives numerous requests for information regarding a wide range of educational programs. One such area that is currently of major interest to teachers, teacher-trainers, school administrators, university scientists, and others interested in elementary school programs is that of science for the elementary school. Information regarding programs sponsored on the whole, or in part, by the National Science Foundation are of particular interest. In response to requests for information regarding the NSF programs, the Center has undertaken to publish a series of articles designed to answer the many questions in a more comprehensive form than would be possible through the medium of numerous individual letters.

The series of articles will present a description of three programs sponsored in part or in whole by the National Science Foundation—the Elementary Science Study (ESS), the Science Curriculum Improvement Study (SCIS), and Science—A Process Approach (AAAS).

*This paper is distributed pursuant to a contract with the Office of Education, U.S. Department of Health, Education, and Welfare. Contractors undertaking such projects under government sponsorship are encouraged to express freely their judgment in professional and technical matters. Points of view or opinions do not, therefore, necessarily represent official Office of Education position or policy.

Reprinted from *Science and Children*, 7, January–February 1970, pp. 35–43. Dr. Robert E. Rogers is a research associate at the ERIC Information Analysis Center for Science Education, Columbus, Ohio. Dr. Alan M. Voelker is an Assistant Professor of Science Education, University of Wisconsin, Madison, Wisconsin.

These three programs have been selected on the basis of the frequency of requests for information about them and the extent of the use of the materials on a national basis.

Information for writing the articles has come from three major sources:

1. Documents housed at the ERIC Center for Science Education.
2. Documents received from the projects' staffs and others who work with the project materials, and
3. Materials obtained by searching libraries and making special contacts (telephone, etc.) with a wide variety of people (workship leaders, etc.) who have worked with the projects in some capacity.

Six areas are generally covered for each of the three programs: (1) nature of the program; (2) instructional materials; (3) use of materials; (4) implementation and teacher programs; (5) evaluation; and (6) the role of the teacher.

Introduction

The last decade and a half has witnessed curriculum improvement projects in a number of subjects. Not the least among these has been in the area of science. First there were projects in secondary science: physics, biology, and chemistry. Then in the early 60's efforts of a large scale were undertaken to upgrade science instruction in the elementary school. Several projects involving scientists and educators were initiated. The Elementary Science Study (ESS) is one such project.[1]

ESS is one of the many curriculum programs under preparation at the Education Development Center (EDC) in Newton, Massachusetts. EDC, a nonprofit organization incorporating the Institute for Educational Innovation and Educational Services Incorporated, began in 1958 as a parent organization to the Physical Science Study Committee. One of EDC's largest endeavors, claiming approximately 10 percent of the total EDC budget in 1968, is the elementary science program being developed by ESS.

In 1960, ESS began on a small scale developing materials for teaching science from kindergarten through eighth grade. Since then, more than a hundred scientists and educators have been involved in the conception and design of ESS materials. These staff developers

---

[1] The sources of information for writing this article have consisted primarily of documents held at the ERIC Center for Science Education and unpublished information supplied by the ESS director and staff members. Some information has been obtained from other assorted sources. Most information came from ESS publications, articles written about ESS by staff members, and various other articles pertaining to the program.

have received considerable help from staff specialists in the design
of equipment, making of films, and producing printed materials.

Nature of ESS Program

In order to understand the nature of ESS materials, it is essential
to know how the ESS staff has gone about developing those materials.
Significantly, the materials are not based on a specific theory of how
children learn, or on the logical structure of science, or any concept
of the needs of society. This is not to say, however, that what children
do with ESS materials is psychologically unsound and scientifically
trivial. Considering the composition of the development staff (educators
and scientists) this is hardly the case. Nevertheless, ESS's approach
has been largely intuitive, rather than theoretical, particularly in the
beginning.

Of course, ESS personnel have some ideas about what constitutes
good science for children. Philip Morrison, one of the prime movers
of ESS, has provided a clue to what ESS considers important when
children and science meet: "One mandate is imperative for our style
of work: there must be personal involvement. The child must work
with his own hands, mind and heart" (20, p. 70). Indeed getting children
totally involved in working with materials is what gives direction to
the development of ESS materials. And this involvement criterion is
determined to a large extent not by theoretical assumptions about what
interests children but by how children actually respond to materials
during the developmental process. If the materials fail to turn children
on, affectively and cognitively, the idea under consideration is discarded
and others are pursued. As is readily seen, this approach to developing
instructional materials relies heavily upon feedback from teachers,
classroom observers, and administrators.

The ESS Development Process

In its final form, a phenomenon dealt with by ESS staff developers
becomes an instructional unit.[2] The development of a unit can be
thought of as progressing in stages, as described below.

1. *"Gleans" and Hunches.* A staff member has an idea that he thinks
   has potential for being developed into a unit.
2. *Early Development.* Staff members work out an opening series
   of lessons which are taught by a staff member and observed by

---

[2]The development process described here is an abbreviated version of the process
described in a communication received from ESS.

other staff members in a local (Newton, Massachusetts and vicinity) classroom. Classroom work is followed by evaluation. If the idea still seems workable, the development process proceeds to the next stage. If not workable, the idea is discarded.

3. *Advanced Development.* Local teachers try out the unit. A teacher's guide is written and prototypic equipment is perfected.

4. *Trial Teaching.* The unit is tested against a wide background of teachers and classrooms. Trial teaching feedback may lead to changes in the Teacher's Guide, equipment design, and, sometimes, content.

5. *Preparation for Commerical Release.* Feedback from trial teaching is further analyzed and on the basis of this feedback necessary changes are made in written materials and equipment. Staff members work with commercial publishers in production.

The ESS Staff is primarily concerned with developing instructional materials that are, in ESS terms, appropriate for children's science learning (8). One aspect of what is appropriate is the concrete; that is, children work with things, not ideas (2). This predilection for working with things is based partly on what motivates children to explore and partly on how children learn. Thus ESS does not teach concepts such as "living forms are orderly and complex," "matter is electrical in nature," or "energy is conserved." Rather, in the words of former ESS Director Randolph Brown:

> ... ESS finds it more profitable to help children explore the hatching and growth of tadpoles, the habits of mealworms, and the ways of lighting bulbs with batteries... ESS feels that "things" encourage children to ask great questions and find their own answers (2, p. 33).

Appropriate also means that the materials must be of such a nature that they stimulate children to raise questions, as well as being conducive to yielding answers. One of the questions that children invariably ask when they are working with the unit *Behavior of Mealworms* is "How do mealworms find food?" The children are encouraged to have the mealworm "answer" the question for them by designing some investigations that inquire about the mealworm's sense of smell, sight, and so on.

Furthermore ESS has some definite ideas about how its materials should be used in the classroom. Eleanor Duckworth has described ESS's approach in the following manner:

> There are two main characteristics which we keep in mind. One is that children use materials themselves, individually or in small groups, often raising the question themselves, answering them in

their own way, using the materials in ways the teacher had not antici-pated, and coming to their own conclusions.... The other is that we try to create situations where the children are called upon to talk to each other (8, p. 242).

David Hawkins (10), a former Director of ESS, has emphasized the importance of allowing children to "mess about" with materials in the early phase of a unit, the rationale being that preliminary free and unstructured experience (messing about) with the materials "produces the early and indispensable autonomy and diversity" that serves to give meaning and direction to children's questions and activities. This approach permits children to learn different things and to learn at different rates.

The ESS Approach and Psychology of Learning

Although no specific efforts have been made by ESS to base its approach on a particular psychology of learning, resulting materials do turn out to have a sound psychological basis, as Eleanor Duckworth, a psychologist who has worked with ESS, has observed (8). Two impor-tant aspects of ESS materials, using concrete things and children's active involvement in learning, are supported by Piaget's ideas on intellectual development (21). The notion that children should have free and unhurried periods of exploration during the early phases of learning has been stressed by Bruner (3), Hunt (14), Berlyne (1), Dewey (7), and John Holt (12). Moreover, Susan Isaacs (15), an outstanding leader in child growth and development in England, and Robert Sears (24), an American psychologist, have emphasized that children derive the greatest pleasure from those things (either animate or inanimate objects) that respond to their manipulations.

Allowing children to follow their own inclinations as they explore materials is obviously important to ESS's approach to children's learn-ing. The thinking behind this is that children learn more when they are doing what they want to do instead of what someone else wants them to do. Furthermore, such self-directed learning has more meaning for them. Hunt (14), Hull (13), Hein (11), Hawkins (10), Dewey (7), Holt (12), and Isaacs (15) have emphasized the importance of allowing children to follow their own bent as they interact with their environ-ment.[3]

---

[3]According to the *Plowden Report* (Her Majesty's Stationery Office, London, 1967), one-third of the primary schools in England happily and successfully operate from this rationale.

Motivation

While the wide variety of units developed by ESS allow all combinations of formal and informal, sequenced and unsequenced, large-group and small-group instruction, all units are designed to motivate children to explore, speculate, and try things, for as Philip Morrison and Charles Walcott have observed:

> ... a major aim of a project such as this one [ESS] is to encourage children to examine the world around them and to acquire the desire, interest, and ability to *continue* to analyze, relate, and understand it as they go through life (18, p. 49).

According to Morrison, when speaking of the work of ESS: "The complex thing we call motivation or attitude, the affective side of learning, is perhaps above all the human attribute which we hope to evoke" (19, p. 65). If these remarks are representative of the views of other ESS personnel, and the authors have no reason to believe that they are not, then one is led to conclude that above all else ESS materials are intended to motivate children to explore the world around them.

Scope and Sequence

Scope and sequence of content are factors that frequently draw considerable attention from curriculum makers. Nevertheless, ESS does not seem at all concerned about these factors, believing that there is no way of knowing whether in fact the content of science that is important now will be important in the first half of the twenty-first century, the period in which our present elementary school children are to live most of their lives (22). ESS has given two reasons for not developing a sequential science program for the elementary school. First, since learning theorists do not fully understand just which sequences of experiences lead to the kind of changes in children ESS would like to see, it would indeed be presumptuous to develop a sequential program (18). Secondly, ESS believes in any case that it is both the prerogative and responsibility of each school system to work out its own sequence with its own objective in mind (22). While ESS is willing to consult with school systems on such matters, it does not wish to dictate a certain sequential order in which its materials are to be used. This, in ESS's view, would be tantamount to making its materials a textbook or textbook series, a curriculum pitfall it wishes to avoid. Although, as has been indicated, ESS units are not designed in a way that requires that they be taught in a certain order, many schools have constructed a complete science program around them

including a locally determined sequential order in which the units are
to be taught.

Instructional Materials

As of the fall of 1969, ESS has in commercial form 50 units for use
in grades K–8. The majority of the units are concentrated in grades
four, five, and six. There are, however, at least sixteen units that
are suitable for K–3 and twelve for grades seven and eight. The variety
of units produced by ESS can be used to provide a wide range of
learning experiences. Some units are designed to develop fundamental
skills in graphing, weighing, and measuring. Other units are oriented
more toward content development; still others are concerned primarily
with developing thinking skills. Most units, in fact, provide a combination of all these experiences. The *Growing Seeds* unit, for example,
includes activities that call upon the children to graph, to measure,
and to seek ways of finding answers to their questions. At the same
time pupils learn something about the conditions favorable to germina-
tion and growth of plants, about rates of growth of different plants,
and about the structures of seeds and plants.

The basic instructional materials for a unit consist of a teacher's
guide and a pupil kit. The teacher's guide contains background information about the content of the unit, as well as suggestions for its use,
and is not written as a prescription to be followed blindly by the teacher.
Rather it respects the judgment, imagination, and individuality of the
teacher and encourages him to exercise these qualities. The pupil kit
contains all the equipment that the children will need to carry out
the ideas suggested in the teacher's guide. If encouraged to do so,
the children will find other ways to use the equipment as they explore
their own ideas.

In addition to the basic materials, worksheets, pictures, supplementary booklets, film loops, and 8mm films accompany some units.
The film loops are each three or four minutes long and are designed
to provide children with learning experiences that could not be readily
obtained directly, yet contribute to children's understanding of important phenomena related to a unit. An example of such a film loop
is one entitled the "Black Swallowtail Butterfly: Egg, Hatching, and
Larvae." It is very difficult to raise butterflies through the stages of
their life cycle in the classroom.[4] Direct observation being impractical,

---

[4]ESS staff has spent considerable time and money on this problem and has succeeded
in rearing the "carrot" butterfly, but commerical production has not been worked out.
ESS Newsletter, No. 11.

ESS developed a film in order that children can nevertheless have an "experience" with the life cycle of a butterfly.

It should be noted that ESS worksheets are not the traditional fill-in-the-blank variety. Some are designed to facilitate keeping of records and are usually based on children's observations of their own manipulations of materials. Others may be in the form of "prediction sheets" that call upon the children to make predictions on the basis of previous experiences in the unit. Frequently, these prediction problems are in the form of diagrams, as is the case with a prediction sheet in the *Batteries and Bulbs* unit. On this sheet several diagrams of wire connections between bulbs and batteries are shown and the child is asked to predict in which arrangements the bulb would light.

Some units are designed to be used by an entire class at the same time. These units frequently consist of student worksheets and film loops as well as teacher's guides and pupil kits. Such units can be accommodated in a typical classroom without major alterations of schedules or class organization. Units that fall in this category are listed below:

GASES AND "AIRS"
BATTERIES AND BULBS
MICROGARDENING
BALANCING
GROWING SEEDS
HEATING AND COOLING
ICE CUBES
PENDULUMS
BALLOONS
KITCHEN PHYSICS
COLORED SOLUTIONS
OPTICS
SLIPS AND SLIDES
SINK OR FLOAT
ROCKS AND CHARTS
SMALL THINGS

Other units are less definitive and may include only a teacher's guide which suggests activities and simple materials that are obtainable locally or are available from equipment-supply houses. Units of this type may involve the whole class or part of the class and may or may not be taught in a series of connected lessons. The teacher's guides for these units are less structured, more open-ended, and require more teacher initiative. A list of units in this category is below:

BONES
MEALWORMS
MYSTERY POWDERS

EGGS AND TADPOLES
POND WATER
MOSQUITOES
BRINE SHRIMP
STRUCTURES
WHERE IS THE MOON?
ANIMAL BOOK
LIGHT AND SHADOWS
CHANGES
MAPPING
MATCH AND MEASURE
MUSICAL INSTRUMENT RECIPE BOOK
CLAY BOATS
STARTING FROM SEEDS
LIFE OF BEANS AND PEAS
BUTTERFLIES
DAYTIME ASTRONOMY
TRACKS
PEAS AND PARTICLES
MOBILES

A third category of units is designed for individual or small group work. These units lend themselves well to meeting individual needs and interests of different children. The design of these units demand an informal and flexible classroom organization where individuals or groups of students can work at different units at the same time. Working with these units can, in an organizational sense, be thought of as project work. Units in this category are listed below:

ATTRIBUTE GAMES AND PROBLEMS
GEO BLOCKS
PATTERN BLOCKS
TANGRAMS
SAND
ANIMAL ACTIVITY
BATTERIES AND BULBS II
SPINNING TABLES
MIRROR CARDS
BALANCE BOOK
MOBILES
PRINTING PRESS
DROPS, STREAMS, AND CONTAINERS

All ESS units have gone through trial stages during the course of their development. One of the reasons for testing the materials is to determine the grade levels at which the units are most appropriate. Frequently, in trial classrooms a unit is found to work well with children in several grades. For example, *Batteries and Bulbs* has been used successfully with grades four, five, and six. The unit *Changes* has been used with children K–4. Perhaps the unstructured nature of the ESS program accounts for the appropriateness of the materials for children in different stages of intellectual development. While one child explores the materials in one direction, another child explores the same phenomenon in another direction and at a different level of understanding. Children work at their own level and pace.

From its inception one of the requisites established for ESS materials was that they should be inexpensive (8). This requisite has been met with the materials of many but not all units. For the unit *Growing Seeds,* for example, the cost of materials, including teacher's guide, for a class of thirty children comes to only $16.50. On the other hand the cost of materials, excluding films, for *Small Things* amounts to $171. It is worth noting that much of the equipment for the more expensive units can be used with other science topics. Moreover, with some effort a teacher, or school, can develop a basic supply of equipment that could be used with a number of units, and which would preclude the necessity of purchasing packaged equipment whenever a new unit is introduced to the classroom.[5] Furthermore, when ordering from the publisher, it is not necessary that one order the whole packaged kit. The components of a kit are itemized in the publisher's catalog.

It has been roughly estimated that a government-supported program, such as ESS, will cost at least three times as much to *introduce* in an elementary school as it does to introduce a traditional program that is essentially textbook centered (4). (No estimations have been made on cost comparison over the long run.) But a school or teacher need not make a commitment to the whole ESS program. If one had to be extremely cost-conscious, the less expensive, yet successful units such as *Behavior of Mealworms, Peas and Particles, Crayfish, Starting from Seeds, Mirror Cards, and Changes* could be utilized at minimal cost.

Use of Materials

According to the *Sixth Report of the International Clearinghouse on Science and Mathematics Curricular Developments* (25) over 7500 teachers and 225,000 children were using ESS materials as of January, 1968. These estimates were arrived at by using sales figures received from McGraw-Hill Book Company, the chief commercial distributor

---

[5]The Elementary Science Advisory Center at the University of Colorado in Boulder has prepared a booklet entitled *Science Equipment in the Elementary School* that may offer considerable assistance to those who wish to establish a basic supply of science equipment in their school.

of ESS materials. In a recent communication to the writers, ESS stated that approximately 40,000 teachers used ESS materials during the school year 1968–69. The ESS staff further predicts that approximately 53,000 teachers and 1,300,000 children will be using ESS materials during the school year 1969–70. All these figures were calculated from commercial sales information and from trial editions distributed by ESS. The numbers for children are calculated on the basis of twenty-five children per class.

There are a number of school systems throughout the country that use ESS materials almost exclusively for their science program. However, the largest number of schools using ESS materials use them with a few teachers who are by "disposition and inclination" attracted to the ESS approach.

ESS materials are also being used in some foreign countries. The Republic of South Korea and the province of British Columbia have adopted ESS materials and mandated their use throughout their respective elementary schools. ESS has worked with Peace Corps trainees who later adapted the materials for use in places such as Ethiopia, the Philippines, and Colombia, South America. Some of the units developed by the African Primary Science Program (an EDC project) are adapted versions of ESS units.

ESS materials are also used in preservice methods courses and inservice workshops for elementary teachers. This appears to be done for one or both of the following reasons: In the first place, course instructors and workshop leaders consider it important that elementary teachers become acquainted with some of the new elementary science projects, such as ESS. Secondly, ESS materials provide a vehicle for conveying concepts of teaching (e.g. children learn science from their own exploration of concrete materials) central to science education today.

Implementation and Teacher Programs

For a number of years ESS has held workshops for a variety of educational personnel, including teachers, supervisors, consultants, team-teaching leaders, master teachers, school administrators, and personnel from colleges and universities. The duration of these workshops varies considerably, from a day for school administrators to six weeks for college students.

A significant part of the ESS implementation program is conducting workshops at Newton to prepare participants for leadership positions in regional workshops. In this workshop program, the participants usually spend about four weeks at Newton before going out to conduct regional workshops for teachers and to assist schools within the region in the implementation process. During the summer of 1968, 32 educators attended the workshop at Newton. After the Newton workshop, these 32 implementation specialists conducted six regional workshops,[6] which involved a total of 283 teachers and administrators.

It is interesting to note that the Newton workshop included a four-day intensive sensitivity training session involving workshop staff and participants. As used in education, sensitivity training refers to a range of laboratory and workshop efforts that are designed to help teachers reconceive their role in working with children. Cultivation of the heightened awareness of children as growing, self-actualizing (fulfilling one's potentialites) individuals is the focus of such training. Sensitivity training has received much of its impetus from the work of perceptual psychologists such as Combs (6), Kelly (16), Rogers (23), and Maslow (17). It is the contention of ESS that viewing children as growing, self-actualizing individuals is consonant with its approach to children's learning science. At the end of the Newton workshop, many participants indicated that the sensitivity training had caused them to "change their procedures" during the workshop. Two of the regional teams also included sensitivity training in their area workshops.

Another important aspect of both the Newton and regional workshops is the opportunity for participants to teach with ESS materials and methods by working with small groups of children. ESS imposes two conditions of participation upon each school district that sends a teacher to the regional workshops. These conditions are: (1) the district must commit $400 to the teacher for the purpose of purchasing materials, and (2) the teacher must be released at least part time during the school year to work with teachers in his district. ESS feels that these conditions are essential in order that each school district benefit fully from the teacher's workshop experience.

During the summer of 1969, ESS conducted a second Summer Implementation Workshop involving 40 participants, who in turn conducted regional workshops.

Although ESS has directed its major thrust at inservice education, it is beginning to move more toward preservice education. It has, for example, made an arrangement with Wheelock College[7] (Boston) whereby some thirty freshmen students spend their six-week winter term half-time at ESS.

Through its workshops and preservice programs, ESS is actively involved in numerous teacher education activities. Furthermore, it is

---

[6]Regional centers were: Rochester, N.Y.; Philadelphia, Pa.; Minneapolis, Minn.; Long Island, N.Y.; Waco, Texas.

[7]Wheelock is a private college for women that is devoted entirely to the preparation of elementary school teachers.

not merely concerned with preparing teachers to teach ESS materials. It is equally concerned with the important task of informing and acquainting supportive personnel (principals, supervisors, college instructors, and so on) with the ESS materials and ESS approach to educating children.

Evaluation

ESS is first and foremost an organization that exists for the purpose of developing instructional materials. It is very much concerned with making sure that the materials developed are in fact appropriate for children's science learning and that the materials are being used as they were intended. Hence, a great deal of attention is given to the development process and to teacher programs.

ESS is, of course, concerned with evaluating children's learning. But the kinds of learning outcomes—interests, motivation, curiosity, attitudes, inquiry skills—it considers important are indeed difficult to measure. Some attempts have been made to assess the impact of ESS materials on children by tape-recording their responses to questions about provocative film loops they had just viewed. The purpose of the assessment was to see if children who had been exposed to ESS materials differed from non-exposed children (control group) in their pattern of response. The results were inconclusive.

ESS contends that while objective, quantified testing is one way to evaluate learning outcomes, the subjective impressions of teachers and administrators are also valid forms of assessment. According to ESS, the feedback gathered from teachers and administrators indicates that children who use ESS materials "like science, ask more questions, ask more perceptive questions, are more observant about things outside of school, and actively initiate projects" (22).

One of the most satisfying experiences ESS has had has been with the children involved in its Cardozo Project[8] in Washington, D. C.'s ghetto area. ESS reports that many of the Cardozo children who are "nonverbal" and generally unsuccessful in school have begun to read better and perform better in many of their school tasks (25). ESS attributes this improvement to the change in the child's view of himself; he has a healthier self-image, which gives him a greater sense of his own potential and power, not only with science but with others areas as well. If indeed this is a correct interpretation of this phenomenon, educators would do well to take a very close look at ESS materials, for a number of studies, including the Coleman Report

---

[8]See Mary Lee Sherburne, *A Peach Tree Grown on T Street,* EDC, 1967, for an informative account of the Project.

(5), have found the state of a child's self-concept to be a variable significantly related to achievement.

The Role of the Teacher

To teach ESS materials as intended demands a certain view of teaching, of the learner, and of the learning process. The teacher's role in an ESS classroom is one of consultant, guide, and catalyst. The teacher advises, listens, diagnoses, and in Hawkins' terms, acts as an external loop, doing things for the child that he cannot do for himself (9). For this reason, the teacher must see the child as having an extraordinary capacity for learning and believe that he learns best from his own activity. Teachers who already have this view of teaching, learning, and children are well suited to use ESS materials in their classroom, while others who do not share it might be persuaded to reconceive their role as teachers through sensitivity training, workshops, and reading.

Besides conceptualizing this role, the teacher needs to know how to operationalize it. He needs to see what an ESS type classroom looks like: how the teacher attends to the details of classroom management, the mechanics of distributing and storing materials, and how the teacher works with a whole class, small groups, and individual children. Participating in an ESS workshop, viewing ESS teaching films, observing existing ESS classes, reading or viewing documentation[9] of how some teachers have developed their own style in teaching ESS materials are all ways of learning how to operationalize ESS concepts of teaching.

It is very difficult for an isolated teacher to go it alone in an innovative endeavor, irrespective of his commitment to the innovation. He needs the continued philosophical and material support of his superintendent, principal, and supervisor, as well as the good will of his teaching colleagues. Real and lasting curriculum change comes only when it proceeds on a broad front and when personnel at all levels are actively committed to the same goals.

Summary Statement

ESS has so far directed its major efforts at developing instructional materials, acquainting an assortment of educational personnel with the materials, and preparing teachers to use them. ESS has not pro-

---

[9]*An Interview with Dorothy Welch* (EDC, 1969) is one such documentation.

ceeded in its development of instructional materials within the framework of a particular philosophy of education. Implicit in its approach to developing materials is a concern for the *development of the whole child*. ESS emphases—active involvement, freedom to pursue one's interests, imagination, individually—are aimed at developing self-directing, autonomous, and self-actualizing individuals. The materials include a great deal that is related to learning science concepts and developing intellectual skills. Intuitive as well as analytical thinking are cultivated. Thus, the cognitive domain is served well.

In the area of the psychomotor domain, ESS's emphasis upon children's manipulating concrete materials helps develop motor skills. But ESS's greatest strength is, perhaps, its contribution to the effective development of children. Children derive satisfaction from exploring, in their own individual ways, interesting materials, finding not only answers and solutions but also that they have the ability to learn for themselves. Perhaps, too, children who find satisfaction in exploring will in time come to value and commit themselves to it.

References

(1) Berlyne, David, "Conflict and Arousal." *Scientific American*, August 1966.

(2) Brown, Randolph, "Elementary Science Study." *Education Development Center Annual Report 1968*. Newton, Mass., 1968.

(3) Bruner, Jerome S., *Toward A Theory of Instruction*. New York: W. W. Norton & Company, 1968.

(4) Butts, David P., "The Price of Change." *Science and Children*, April 1969.

(5) Coleman, James S., et al. *Equality of Educational Opportunity*. Washington, D. C.: U.S. Government Printing Office, 1966.

(6) Combs, Arthur W., "A Perceptual View of the Adequate Personality." *Perceiving, Behaving, Becoming*. Association for Supervision and Curriculum Development Yearbook, Washington, D. C., 1962.

(7) Dewey, John, *Democracy in Education*. New York: The Macmillan Company, 1916.

(8) Duckworth, Eleanor, "The Elementary Science Study Branch of Educational Services Incorporated." *Journal of Research in Science Teaching*, September 1964.

(9) Hawkins, David., "I, Thou, It." Elementary Science Study. Newton, Mass., 1967.

(10) —— "Messing About in Science." *Science and Children*, February 1965.

(11) Hein, George E., "Children's Science is Another Culture." *Technology Review*, December 1968.

(12) Holt, John, *How Children Learn*. New York: Pitman Publishing Corporation, 1967.

(13) Hull, William. Quoted in *The Prepared Environment* by Margaret Howard Loeffler, Oklahoma City: Casady School, 1967.

(14) Hunt, J. McV., *Intelligence and Experience*. New York: The Ronald Press Co., 1961.

(15) Isaacs, Susan, *Intellectual Growth in Young Children*. New York: Shocken Books, 1966.

(16) Kelly, Earl C., "The Fully Functioning Self." *Perceiving, Behaving, Becoming*. Association for Supervision and Curriculum Development Yearbook, Washington, D. C., 1962.

(17) Maslow, Abraham H., "Some Basic Propositions of a Growth and Self-actualizing Psychology." *Perceiving, Behaving, Becoming*. Association for Supervision and Curriculum Development Yearbook, Washington, D. C., 1962.

(18) Morrison, Philip, and Charles Walcott, "Enlightened Opportunism: An Informal Account of the Elementary Science Summer Study of 1962." *Journal of Research in Science Teaching*, March 1963.

(19) Morrison, Philip, "Experimenters in the Schoolroom." *ESI Quarterly Report*, Winter-Spring 1964.

(20) —— "The Curriculum Triangle and Its Style." *ESI Quarterly Report*, Summer–Fall 1964.

(21) Piaget, Jean, "Development and Learning." *Journal of Research in Science Teaching*, September 1964.

(22) *Personal Communication from ESS*, June 23, 1969.

(23) Rogers, Carl R., "Toward Becoming a Fully Functioning Person." *Perceiving, Behaving, Becoming*. Association for Supervision and Curriculum Development Yearbook, Washington, D. C., 1962.

(24) Sears, Robert, "Process Pleasure." in *Learning About Learning*, Jerome S. Bruner (ed.), U.S. Government Printing Office, Washington, D. C., 1966.

(25) *Sixth Report of the International Clearinghouse on Science and Mathematics Curricular Developments*. Under the editorship of J. David Lockard. Science Teaching Center, University of Maryland, College Park, Md., 1968.

Bibliography

Education Development Center, "An Interview with Dorothy Welch." Newton, Mass., 1969.

Elementary Science Advisory Center, "Science Equipment in the Elementary School." University of Colorado, 1967.

Elgammal, Attia, "Elementary Science Study at Macomb County: Students' and Teachers' Reaction." Macomb Intermediate School District, Mount Clemens, Mich., 1969.

Finley, Gilbert, "The Elementary Science Study."*Elementary School Science Bulletin,* February 1963.

Hartley, Mary Lou, "Evaluation and Reflection after Attending the Elementary Science Study Summer School." *ESI Quarterly Report,* Winter–Spring 1964.

Hawkins, David, "ESI Elementary Science Activities Project." *Science Education,* February 1964.

———"Laboratory Science in Elementary Schools." *American Journal of Physics,* November 1964.

———"The Informed Vision: An Essay on Science Education." *Daedalus,* Summer 1965.

———"The Stuff from Which Questions Are Shaped." *Nature and Science* (Teacher's Edition), April 17, 1964.

Leodas, C. J., "The Elementary Science Study." *ESI Quarterly Report,* Winter–Spring 1964.

Moss, Penrod, "An Elementary Science Study Report from California." *ESI Quarterly Report,* Winter–Spring 1964.

Nichols, Benjamin, "Elementary Science Study—Two Years Later." *Journal of Research in Science Teaching,* December 1964.

Walcott, Charles, "Elementary Science Study." *Science Education News,* AAAS Miscellaneous Publication, December 1962.

Webster, David, "How To Help Children Make Mistakes." *Science and Children,* May 1964.

———"Making a Chicken Skeleton." *Nature and Science,* May 1964.

Zacharias, Jerrold R. "Learning By Teaching." *Instructor,* January 1966.

———"What's Ahead in Elementary Science." *Instructor,* January 1967.

Additional Information:
Frank Watson
Director of ESS
55 Chapel Street
Newton, Massachusetts 02160

Chief Publisher of ESS Materials:
Webster Division
McGraw-Hill Book Company
Manchester Road
Manchester, Missouri 63011

18

PROGRAMS FOR IMPROVING SCIENCE INSTRUCTION IN THE ELEMENTARY SCHOOL: PART II, SCIS*

Barbara S. Thompson
Alan M. Voelker

A few years ago when the elementary school science curriculum projects were first being funded by the National Science Foundation (NSF) and other foundations and agencies, educators adopted a "wait and see" posture in order to give the program advocates an opportunity to provide careful development and evaluation. Administrators, classroom teachers, curriculum workers, as well as college personnel are seeking various types of information for making crucial decisions regarding adoption, adaptation, or rejection.

This article is the second in a series of articles prepared by the ERIC Center for Science Education in which the authors present descriptions of elementary school science projects sponsored by NSF. The article consists of a review of the Science Curriculum Improvement Study (SCIS). The basic rationale for writing this series of articles and the procedure utilized in acquiring the information can be found in the overview of the series, *Part I, ESS* (31).

*This paper is distributed pursuant to a contract with the Office of Education, U.S. Department of Health, Education, and Welfare. Contractors undertaking such projects under government sponsorship are encouraged to express freely their judgment in professional and technical matters. Points of view or opinions do not, therefore, necessarily represent official Office of Education position or policy.

Reprinted from *Science and Children*, 7, May 1970, pp. 29–37. Dr. Barbara S. Thompson is an Instructor of Science and Mathematics Education, Ohio State University, Columbus, Ohio.

Introduction

The work of Karplus with the Elementary School Science Project, University of California (ESSP) in the late fifties raised three questions.

1. How can one create a learning experience that achieves a sure connection between the pupil's intuitive attitudes and the concepts of the modern scientific point of view?
2. How can one determine what children have learned?
3. How can one communicate with the teacher so that the teacher can in turn communicate with the pupils? (9)

It was Karplus's feeling that the only reasonable way for him to answer these questions was to try to familiarize himself with the point of view children take toward natural phenomena by actually teaching science to some elementary school classes on a regularly scheduled basis. The outcome of this experience coupled with his work with ESS and Minnemast (and other programs attempting to improve science instruction in the elementary school) served as a frame of reference for the basic SCIS work.

A succinct historical summary of the project from its conception to the present time is located in the *Clearinghouse Report*. It states:

> The Science Curriculum Improvement Study was established in the winter of 1962 by Robert Karplus, a Professor of Theoretical Physics at the University of California, Berkeley, as a result of his work with the Elementary School Science Project (ESSP) at that University. This experience had led Professor Karplus to the conclusion that science had not only to be simplified for the elementary school, but organized on a drastically different basis from the usual logical subject matter presentations to which the university scientist is accustomed (19).

Nature of the Program

The objectives of the program have been carefully articulated by Karplus and Thier to include intellectual development and scientific literacy. The belief that the concept of literacy be the principal objective of teaching science in the elementary school permeates the total program. Thier's definition of "functional scientific literacy" states: "The individual must have a conceptual structure and a means of communication that enables him to interpret the information as though he had obtained it himself" (9). This objective of scientific literacy is pursued through concrete experiences whereby children acquire the concepts and communication skills essential to its development (17). Concrete manipulation and interaction among students and teachers are important components and well developed in their laboratory approach. (See materials section.)

Another major objective is that of decision-making. It was emphasized in the 1968 *Clearinghouse Report* that:

> A second implication of scientific literacy is the development of a free and inquisitive attitude and the use of rational procedures for decision making. In the SCIS program, children learn science in an intellectually free atmosphere where their own ideas are respected, where they learn to accept or reject ideas, not on the basis of some authority, but on the basis of their own observations. Ideally, some of these experiences will carry over to other areas of life and incline the children to make decisions on a more rational basis after weighing the factors or evidence involved more objectively (19).

Psychological Bases of SCIS

Educators such as Hunt (8), Piaget (22), Bruner (4), and Almy (15), who wish to capitalize on the learning potential of children, have conducted developmental research that has illustrated the importance of concrete manipulative experiences. The SCIS designers looked closely at these findings, the child, and his elementary years in order to develop an effective program of science instruction within a framework of elementary education. The belief was:

1. The child's elementary school years are a period of transition as he continues to explore the world he began in infancy.
2. He develops confidence in his own ideas.
3. He builds abstractions with which he interprets the world.

Utilizing this rationale and drawing upon the groundwork laid by Piaget, Hunt, Bruner, and Almy, it was concluded that the elementary school years should provide:

1. A diversified program based heavily on concrete manipulative experiences (used guidelines of Piaget).
2. These experiences in a context that helps to build a conceptual framework.
3. A conceptual framework that permits them to perceive phenomena in a more meaningful way, (i.e., integrate their inferences into generalizations of greater value than the ones they would form if left to their own devices) (9).

Therefore, each lesson that has been developed fulfills one or both of two functions: to provide a new experience, and to establish or reinforce an abstract concept.

Although the cognitive aspects of the program seem to be of paramount importance, the other domains, i.e., affective and psychomotor have not been neglected (2). A possible explanation is these domains are less tangible as evidenced by Kuslan and Stone. They describe the affective domain as:

1. Attitude—a willingness to approach or avoid environmental interactions
2. Appreciation—a measure of satisfaction in interacting.
3. Interest—positively motivated and enjoys the experiences (15)

The role of the affective domain in student learning is illustrated in Figure 1. It is a continuous circular process whereby interested students become involved and if they experience feelings of success, their interest is again supported and continued via this route. The psychomotor domain encompasses the areas of physical development, neuromuscular coordination, and motor skills. The SCIS program provides numerous experiences for students to develop or improve their manipulative skills through concrete experiences.

FIGURE 1.

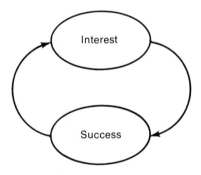

The philosophy of the SCIS program certainly reflects all three domains but the key focus for program development seems to be on the cognitive domain. However, evaluation activities are being designed in the psychomotor and affective domains.

The Learning Environment

The objectives, in conjunction with the SCIS rationale, resulted in a curriculum built around extensive laboratory experiences where the students are involved in exploring new experiences and phenomena. It is referred to as a *direct approach* to learning.

What is needed to a large extent, especially at the elementary science level is a reversal of the premise that teaching is talking and learning is listening. Very frequently, teaching is listening and observing in order to understand the capabilities of each member of the group of learners. In a textbook or other abstract based situation, this interplay between teacher and learner is impossible. Science taught through the laboratory approach, however, simulates the natural way that children acquire understanding (26).

An indirect approach to learning could be diagrammatically represented as in Figure 2 while a direct approach could be illustrated by Figure 3. The role of the SCIS teacher must evolve to a point whereby the teacher can function effectively with the type of interaction illustrated in Figure 3. Unless the teacher can function in this direct approach environment, a crucial aspect of this program becomes nonfunctional which in turn severely weakens the total program.

FIGURE 2. Traditional Diagram of Teaching/Learning

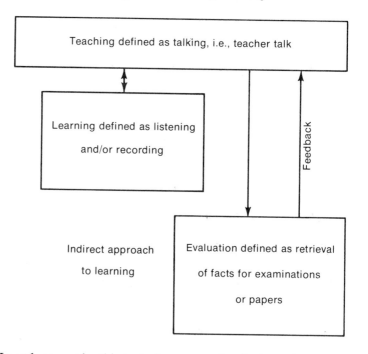

In order to make this technique operational, the "classroom" has to be designed so it becomes a laboratory in which children can have actual experiences with natural phenomena. The design and philosophy behind the SCIS materials dictates that *involvement* is of key importance. A descriptive list of levels of involvement for effective learning of science, identified by Karplus and Thier (12), has been placed in a hierarchical arrangement for the convenience of discussion. (See

FIGURE 3. (Teacher/Student Partnership)
Direct Approach to Learning—The SCIS Approach

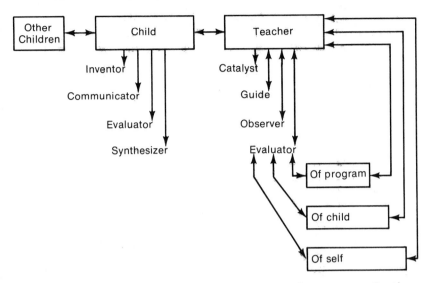

Figure 4). Each of these levels indicates an increasing amount of active student involvement with level four approaching the SCIS "ideal." It is essential in the SCIS scheme that the learning environment include the elements depicted at level four of Figure 4 and in Figure 3. They need to become operational before the full potential of this program can be realized.

Instructional Materials

All materials are carefully focused toward meeting four explicit goals: (1) Scientific Literacy, (2) Intellectual Development, (3) Rational Decision Making, and (4) To Produce Favorable Pupil Attitudes Toward Science. Hurd and Gallagher have stated:

> The subject content of SCIS is based upon science concepts chosen for their wide applicability and potential usefulness. Instruction is designed to reach pupils at their level of development and help them acquire these concepts (17).

The concepts around which the materials have been developed are representative of the "big ideas" in science, (i.e., organism, ecosystem, matter and energy; property, reference frame, system, and model). The first four are major scientific concepts while the latter are process oriented concepts.

These "big ideas" form a conceptual framework that cuts across the traditional disciplines forming a structure that illustrates the unity of the sciences (27). The lessons focus upon concepts related to the "big ideas" and provide a sequencing of experiences. Thus, a conceptual framework for a student can be built enabling the student to organize successfully subsequent science experiences as the instructional materials have been designed to reach pupils at their level of development and to provide an experience base to help to acquire a conceptual framework.

FIGURE 4. Levels of Science Involvement—SCIS		
Level	Involvement	Experiences
4	Pupil manipulates, observes, acts	Firsthand experiences
3	Teacher and/or pupil demonstration station	Vicarious experience
2	Teacher-pupil discussions	Vicarious experience
1	Reading or being told about science	Vicarious experience

Because each lesson builds upon previous classroom work, it is essential that the materials development portion of the program progress through a complex system of trial testing, evaluation, and rewriting. According to Karplus the work on one unit progresses: (9)

1. Preparation of teaching plan and design of experiments
2. Exploratory teaching in public schools by SCIS staff
3. Completion of trial materials, i.e., guide, manuals and kits
4. Classroom trial (one to two years)
5. Revisions and additional teaching by SCIS staff
6. Second classroom trial by regular teachers
7. Revisions and preliminary commercial publication
8. Classroom trial in several centers across the United States

At the conclusion of these steps, plans for a final commercial edition are put into operation.

At the present time there are four preliminary editions and four final editions with completed kits available from Rand McNally and Company;[1] i.e., Preliminary Editions—*Life Cycles, Relativity, Populations, Position and Motion.* Final Editions—*Material Objects, Organisms, Interaction and Systems, Subsystems and Variables.* Trial editions consisting of a teacher's guide and student manual can be ordered directly from SCIS. A kit is available for each unit which includes

---

[1]D. C. Heath and Company, Lexington, Mass., prepared some of the preliminary editions of SCIS materials. That contract has since been terminated.

all the necessary materials for the teacher and thirty-two students. Expendables can be purchased from Rand McNally for replacement in the kits (see list of addresses). Some of these expendables can be purchased at various local stores but for the convenience and time of the teacher, it seems advantageous to purchase these supplies as refill packages. Thus, the necessary student materials can always be complete and ready for use.

Materials are of four types:

1. Teacher's Guide This guide provides a rationale for the unit, a list of objectives, a list of necessary materials, useful suggestions from other teachers, and helpful techniques.

2. Pupil Manuals Each pupil is provided with a manual that serves as an organizational aid to assist him in keeping records. This manual is not the traditional type of workbook but specifically designed to promote organizational skills and to keep records. The utilization of these books occurs only after concrete experiences.

3. Laboratory Materials These are the materials that allow children to have firsthand concrete experiences. Kits are prepackaged so all needed equipment will be available when needed; expendable materials can be purchased in refill packages. The kits have been field tested along with the other materials in order to identify weaknesses and strengths in their use.

4. Films Motion-picture films (16-mm sound films) for all the SCIS units in Preliminary Edition are also available either on a rental basis from the Extension Center or they can be purchased through the SCIS office. Films available for use with the *Material Objects* unit are: "Observing Liquids" (Activity 18), 15 minutes; "Experimenting With Air" (Activity 29), 15 minutes; "Material Objects Overview" (5 classrooms), 14 minutes.

Other films currently available are:
Interaction: "Making Copper Chloride Solution" (Interaction Documentary), 11 minutes; "Interaction Overview" (4 classrooms), 11 minutes.
Relativity: "Relativity" (4 classrooms), 17 minutes.
Systems and Subsystems: "How Cold is Ice?", 10 minutes.
Position and Motion: "Flip Books," 12 minutes.
Organisms: "How Can We Find Out?", 9 minutes, Color.
Life Science Program: "Don't Tell Me, I'll Find Out" (representative activities from Organisms, Life Cycles and Populations), 22 minutes, Color.

Pre-Service and In-Service Films: Piaget developmental theory films by Robert Karplus and Celia B. Lavatelli. "Classification," 17 minutes; "Conservation," 28 minutes.

The units are sequential which means that activities are built upon knowledge acquired in previous lessons. The trial editions integrate the life sciences, the physical sciences, and quantitative comparisons, but the interrelationship becomes more obvious to the older students. This sequential aspect causes the development of materials to progress at a slow rate since refinement at each level is imperative for a strong program.

The trial editions currently available for purchase from the SCIS office are:

1. *Environments*
2. *Communities*
3. *Energy Sources*
4. *Periodic Motion*
5. *Models for Electric and Magnetic Interaction*
6. *Ecosystems*

The commercial editions available from Rand McNally are:

1. *Material Objects*
2. *Organisms*
3. *Interaction and Systems*
4. *Life Cycles*
5. *Subsystems and Variables*
6. *Relativity*
7. *Populations*
8. *Position and Motion*

Program Implementation

A description of the implementation process can be found in a recent *SCIS Newsletter* (Fall, 1969).

> The SCIS implementation program is designed to train science educators starting SCIS projects in their communities. Each *one* or *two* week visit is tailored to the interests and needs of the participant. Classroom visits acquaint the participant with the concepts and materials of SCIS units. Informal discussions and meetings with members of the staff allow the visitor a close look at the evolving SCIS program. Prospective participants should write Jack Fishleder. (26)

Educators who are not able to attend an implementation program prior to initiating the use of SCIS materials can obtain the names of persons in their area who can assist them. A list of these persons can be obtained by contacting Jack Fishleder, Implementation Program Leader, at the SCIS office. The SCIS office keeps an up-to-date roster of:

1. Participants in a summer leadership workshop
2. Trial Center Coordinators
3. Implementation Program participants
4. Others having a special understanding of the program

With the initiation of this service, SCIS is working toward improving its implementation program.

As Rand McNally releases the final editions, the company is planning to introduce a number of services. For those who purchase these materials the size of the school system, number of children, and number of teachers involved will determine the type of workshop their resources can provide. The proposed workshops will most likely be of three types:

1. Regional Workshop for leadership training
2. Workshop for School System Adoptions
3. Sample Kit—An orientation, training kit to assist a school in making a decision to try SCIS and to orient teachers to the SCIS program and philosophy

The Educational Products Information Exchange Institute (EPIE) has an Information Unit which is a package of materials (i.e., filmstrips, tapes, program description booklets) that was developed as an aid to use in curriculum selection and teacher training. The SCIS program is one of the six presented in this unit.

Evaluation

In curricular development one of the essential integral components is evaluation. Since this is a time-consuming, expensive task requiring specialized personnel for test development, analysis, etc., it is often the most neglected part of a program. SCIS has attempted to circumvent this problem by establishing a strong task force to pursue evaluation. This is particularly vital for this project due to its sequential nature. It would be unrealistic to expect students to advance to a new level of learning if they had not achieved the learnings and outcomes of the previous unit. A program with a sequential structure requires a large amount of evaluation time since some of the evaluation aspects may not become apparent until a student has progressed an entire school year from one grade to another. At that time a weakness may become evident which would require the modification of certain experiences in the materials used during a previous year. This type of structure also implies that schools would best start this program in kindergarten or grade one adding one more level each year over a period of 5 to 6 years. Therefore, total K–6 evaluation for this project will take longer than programs that are adopted across the K–6 span in one year.

Although the SCIS program is still less than a decade old, the quality and quantity of the studies indicate that this aspect of development has not been neglected. The information gleaned from the various studies has been classified into two categories—(1) descriptive feedback and (2) experimental.

Descriptive Feedback

This category includes studies where data have been collected through observation of and/or discussion with teachers, illustrative of what occurs in the classroom. In some instances the teacher is the observer and evaluator while at other times an outsider fulfills this role. A major function of these data has been to modify and improve existing materials.

Ness (10), Flory (10), Tresmontan (10), and Vivian (30) all collected data of these types and utilized the information either for revising instructional materials or increasing teacher sensitivity to pupils and their interaction with these materials. The first three investigators summarized their findings in an SCIS publication, *What Is Curriculum Evaluation?*

Ness (10) collected data from teachers who were using the unit *Organisms*. (Each coordinator sends a quarterly report from the SCIS Trial Centers to the headquarters office.) A variety of information was accumulated ranging from suggestions for specific unit revisions to an attempt to discover if climatic differences (e.g., Hawaii, Michigan, New York) affected the behavior of organisms in the classroom. Resulting information was used for revision purposes and preparing of an *Organisms Feedback* booklet to help teachers acquire information concerning students' understanding of the material. Student responses were used by the classroom teachers as an aid in planning future lessons. Positive comments about this device, as well as student feedback, indicated a satisfactory level of concept understanding.

Ness discovered that teachers are an invaluable source of critical analysis of materials; and may have been a major resource in this project. By having them collect information for the project staff, they are able to help themselves too.

Flory (10) in an observational study of twenty-eight classrooms discovered that a large percentage of the time was being spent at the discussion level which is in contradiction to the SCIS philosophy.

The major outcome of the study seems to be that teachers need to have inservice training when working with a program of this type.

Tresmontan (10) conducted an exploratory study and SCIS in an attempt to determine the needs of teachers as well as pupils and identify ways that SCIS could provide beneficial services for them. The investigator conducted observational studies, biweekly sensitivity training sessions, and interviews. An attempt was made to change teacher attitudes and behaviors by helping them understand their roles in relation to the SCIS program. This study points up that content background is necessary, and it could best be provided by an inservice program in conjunction with the adopted program. Also it seems that once teachers accept the confidence of the people with whom they are working, they are open to talking and are very interested in the improvement of instruction. They accept and use constructive criticism when they are respected as knowledgeable persons.

A final study submitted by Vivian (30) describes a checklist evaluation scheme for SCIS materials. This checklist provides a vehicle for classroom teachers to focus their attention on some of the cognitive and affective behavioral outcomes of the SCIS program. Vivian's study again points out that teachers are very responsible persons, are an extremely valuable resource, and are far more perceptive than some people believe, provided they are involved in the planning and decision-making processes.

Experimental

In this area specifically constructed measurement devices are employed to determine whether the SCIS goals or objectives are being met; i.e., resultant learning outcomes. A definition of "desirable behavior" is determined prior to constructing or administering a test.

A series of doctoral dissertations by Bruce (3), Moon (20), Neuman (21), and Kondo (13) fit the research category. Bruce (3) taped a non-SCIS science lesson of fifteen teachers prior to participation in a three-week SCIS workshop and all the participants (thirty-three teachers) SCIS lessons on returning to their classrooms. An analysis of the tapes indicated that higher level questions, requiring more thinking, were asked after the workshop and the initiation of an SCIS program.

Moon (20) did a comparative study between sixteen teachers who taught in a conventional program and sixteen who were teaching an SCIS program after all completed a three-week SCIS workshop. The SCIS teachers used a greater number of higher level questions which was also supported by the Bruce (3) study.

An investigation by Kondo (13) focused on an analysis of the relationship between questioning behavior of the teacher and different types of SCIS lessons, (i.e., *Invention and Discovery)* from four lessons found in the unit *Material Objects*. The results indicated that the way the lesson is approached (e.g., teacher demonstration, children handling materials), has a greater influence on the type of question the teacher asks than the type of lesson.

Neuman (21) attempted to measure intellectual growth of first-grade children utilizing the *Material Objects* unit. He found that the group of SCIS girls scored significantly higher on a post test. Various comparisons were made within the SCIS groups as well as with first graders in a conventional program.

Besides these studies, Wilson (32), Rowe (24), Codispoti (26), and Gilbert (26), have also researched in the area of questioning and verbal behavior. Wilson (32), using SCIS materials as a vehicle, discovered that the SCIS teachers used a significantly higher level of questioning than the non-SCIS teachers. His findings support those completed by the other researchers.

Rowe (10) describes a study conducted with eight SCIS and eight non-SCIS second graders. After they examined two different systems, (i.e., aquarium and an SCIS whirlybird), through observations, the examiner disagreed with all statements made by these students. Six of the SCIS students argued their point of view but only one from the non-SCIS group even attempted a second experiment to support his argument.

In an inner-city school study Rowe (10) found that the children demonstrated a verbal deficiency that posed problems for the development of conceptual skills, (e.g., missing final sounds makes comparisons impossible, great*er*, larg*er*, etc.). Her study showed that after sampling numbers of sentences spoken during SCIS science, language arts, and math that the most spontaneous language and the most subject relevant talk occurred in the SCIS science lessons; the science talk exceeded language arts by 200 percent. No comparison was made with other types of science classes.

After reviewing the preceding studies the indications are that the SCIS approach to teaching science seems to have an effect on students' behavior, what they do, how open they are in discussing things, and the kind of responses they give. It appears the teachers become more flexible and make changes in their teaching behavior, (e.g., questioning).

Other aspects of teacher behavior have been investigated by researchers at the Far West Laboratory for Educational Research and Development in Berkeley, California (16), the Magnolia Elementary Schools in cooperation with Southern State College (6), Haan (16), and Fischler (7). Each of these investigators has selected a different area for analysis, but all provide information in the area of teacher behavior.

The initial research conducted by the Far West Laboratory (16) was considered exploratory in nature. SCIS and non-SCIS first-grade teachers were observed using their own teaching styles. Those students whose teachers employed teaching styles that were in accord with the SCIS style descriptions demonstrated improved performance in a variety of SCIS tasks. Perhaps more consideration needs to be given to the induction as well as the maintenance of SCIS teachers.

When should inservice work occur? The Magnolia Elementary Schools in conjunction with Southern State College in Arkansas (6) conducted an NSF Cooperative College-School Science workshop which provided an initial three-week workshop as well as seminars and conferences throughout the year. When the teachers were provided with supportive assistance throughout the year, they emerged confident that they had done a good job and had positive feelings about their efforts. It appears that in-service work should not come in large segments, but initial introductions should be followed by continuous and regular contacts.

Fischler (7) at Nova University used SCIS materials as a vehicle for teacher preparation. It appears that inherent in SCIS is embodied a philosophy of teacher behavior which is useful in preparing teachers to be self-critical and self-analytical of their behavior. The SCIS lessons along with video-tape equipment facilitated this investigation.

Haan (16) has a belief that the SCIS program may have some effect on self-concepts and self-determination. She is doing research in this area. A study of children working with the *Material Objects* unit lends support to this hypothesis.

Currently there are many studies in areas related to concept development, the SCIS program is no exception. Siegelman and Karplus (10), Thier (29), Allen (1), Stafford (28), and Raven (23) have all been exploring concept development with the SCIS materials although they have approached it from a variety of directions.

Siegelman and Karplus (10) utilized the information from their study to make revision decisions about the unit *Relativity*. Out of the five unit objectives it was found that only partial attainment was made in three. Data collected helped to initiate the necessary revisions.

Thier (29) investigated first graders' understanding of the concept matter using the *Material Objects* unit. When a lack of understanding was identified as being significant, this portion was submitted to SCIS for revision; conversely, aspects that were effective were recommended for retention.

Allen (1) found that middle-class students do not develop any better classification skills as a result of working with the classification skills and activities in SCIS than they would as a result of their general experiencial background and; therefore, it may not be contributing to the total program.

Stafford's (28) research focused on the question of accelerating concept skills in the area of conservation. The experimental group showed greater growth[2] in each of the six areas tested (i.e., conservation of number, length, liquid amount, solid amount, weight, and area). Stafford is presently involved in an evaluation of the SCIS *Material Objects* unit at the kindergarten level.

Raven (23) used SCIS as a vehicle to investigate concept development. The purpose of the study was to determine the developmental sequence necessary for the understanding of momentum. The results supported Piaget's findings that children understand concepts about matter before they understand concepts about speed. SCIS supported this research in an attempt to assist them in determining sequencing of certain concepts because what may be logical sequencing for the discipline may be inconsistent with the psychological development of the learner.

In the book, *A New Look at Elementary School Science* (9) the authors indicate that additional research is continually being pursued. Karplus and Thier describe in detail two examples of evaluation studies as an illustration of the work that precedes publication of student materials. For example, the following information they obtained from their research caused revisions to be made:

1. SCIS students who have completed the unit *Relativity* have a greater understanding of relative motion than non-SCIS students.
2. There was little difference between groups on either configuration or the spatial perceptives test.
3. The *Solutions* unit helped to develop mastery of experimental techniques and an understanding of concentration.
4. Children need experience with the repeated use of measure, displacement, and deformation of objects in the *Variation and Measurement* unit.
5. In *Variation and Measurement* the lessons on diameter, perimeter, and area need to be clearer.

Studies of this nature are time-consuming for the curriculum staff, but the outcomes indicate revisions that lead to stronger, more effective materials which are more apt to meet the intended objectives of the program. All of the work done in the area of evaluation should eventually be reflected in stronger programs.

Role of the Teacher

The units are structured in such a way that children are to have (1) first-hand experiences, (2) a laboratory setting, and (3) be able to explore

---

[2]There is no indication that the control group dealt directly with these concepts.

natural phenomena in small groups or individually, depending upon the activity. The developers believe that the teacher should provide substantial guidance and help with discussion. Thus, the development of erroneous ideas is circumvented. The teacher should then provide opportunities for children to extend their learnings by applying those concepts with which they were working in a new context. The materials are structured in such a way that the teacher is provided with equipment and suggestions for the extension of these concepts. It is imperative with a program such as SCIS that the teachers assume a role of guide instead of the more conventional information giver. This aspect of teacher behavior becomes of prime importance if the program is to be successful.

Summary

The SCIS project's staff is attempting to produce materials that *are effective* in meeting the objectives of elementary science education. These outcomes have been identified by Hurd and Gallagher:

1. An understanding of science principles
2. Skills for acquiring knowledge
3. Favorable attitudes toward science

In making SCIS program selection decisions, it is important to see if the instructional package effectively helps students obtain these outcomes. The SCIS program is time consuming since it takes more time than elementary school teachers have traditionally spent on science, but it is a different kind of experience where the teacher is a guide and the children pursue their learnings. Also, this program is more expensive than simply purchasing a single text for each child since kits of equipment accompany the materials.[3] This aspect does save teacher preparation time as well as insure that the appropriate materials are available for each lesson.

Selection decisions need to be made on the basis of compatibility with local plans keeping in mind whether or not it will be effective for local needs. This review has oriented the reader to the SCIS program and has provided a review of the literature and research currently available. Although this program is of recent origin there is substantial information available, which, along with the objectives for elementary science education, should provide a basis for wise decision making.

---

[3] The David Butts article. *The Price of Change* (5) published in *Science and Children* is helpful when considering current costs of programs. (The reader should note that there may be some fluctuation in prices since this article was prepared.)

Addresses

Science Curriculum Improvement Study
Lawrence Hall of Science
University of California
Berkeley, California 94720

School Department
Rand McNally and Company
P. O. Box 7600
Chicago, Illinois 60680

Educational Products Information Exchange Institute
386 Park Avenue South
New York, New York 10016

References

(1) Allen, Leslie Robert, "An Examination of the Classificatory Ability of Children Who Have Been Exposed to One of the 'New' Elementary Science Programs." Ph.D. diss., University of California, 1967.

(2) Bloom, Benjamin S., et al., *Taxonomy of Educational Objectives.* New York: David McKay Company, 1967.

(3) Bruce, Larry Rhea, "A Determination of the Relationships Among SCIS Teachers' Personality Traits, Attitude Toward Teacher-Pupil Relationship, Understanding of Science Process Skills and Question Types." (M)* 1969.

(4) Bruner, Jerome S., *Toward A Theory of Instruction.* New York: W. W. Norton & Company, 1968.

(5) Butts, David, "The Price of Change." *Science and Children,* April 1969.

(6) *Final Report on SCIS Activities for the 1968–69 School Year at the Magnolia Public Schools.* Magnolia, Ark., 1969.

(7) Fischler, Abraham S., "Change in Classroom Behavior Resulting from an In-Service Program Utilizing Television." *School Science and Mathematics,* April 1967.

(8) Hunt, J. McV., *Intelligence and Experience.* New York: The Ronald Press Co., 1961.

(9) Karplus, Robert, and Herbert D. Thier, *A New Look at Elementary School Science.* Chicago: Rand McNally & Co., 1967.

(10) Karplus, Robert, *What is Curriculum Evaluation?* Science Curriculum Improvement Study, Berkeley, Calif., 1968.

*(M) denotes University Microfilms, Ann Arbor, Mich.

(11) Karplus, Robert, Cynthia Ann Powell, and Herbert D. Thier, "A Concept of Matter for the First Grade." *Journal of Research in Science Teaching,* December 1963.

(12) Karplus, Robert, and Herbert D. Thier, "Science Teaching is Becoming Literate." *Education Age,* January–February 1966.

(13) Kondo, Allan K., "The Questioning Behavior of Teachers in the Science Curriculum Improvement Study Teaching." Paper presented at the NARST Meeting, Pasadena, Calif., February 1969.

(14) Kuslan, Louis I., and A. Harris Stone, *Readings on Teaching Children Science.* Belmont, Calif., Wadsworth Publishing Company, Inc., 1969.

(15) _____*Teaching Children Science: An Inquiry Approach.* Belmont, Calif., Wadsworth Publishing Company, Inc., 1968.

(16) Haan, Norma, *An Exploratory Investigation of the Effect of an Initial Experience With SCIS's Material Objects Unit on First-Grade Children and Their Teachers.* Far West Laboratory for Educational Research and Development, Berkeley, Calif., 1968.

(17) Hurd, Paul DeHart, and James Joseph Gallagher, *New Directions in Elementary Science Teaching.* Belmont, Calif., Wadsworth Publishing Company, Inc., 1968.

(18) Lerner, Marjorie, and Edward Victor, *Readings in Science Education for the Elementary School.* New York: The Macmillan Company, 1967.

(19) Lockard, J. David (ed.), *Sixth Report of the International Clearinghouse on Science and Mathematics Curricular Development.* University of Maryland and AAAS, College Park, Md., 1968.

(20) Moon, Thomas Charles, "A Study of Verbal Behavior Patterns in Primary Grade Classrooms During Science Activities." Ph. D. diss., Michigan State University, 1969.

(21) Neuman, Donald B., "The Influence of Selected Science Experiences on the Attainment of Concrete Operations by First Grade Children." Paper read before 42nd meeting of the National Association for Research in Science Teaching, Pasadena, Calif., February 1969.

(22) Piaget, Jean, "Development and Learning." *Journal of Research in Science Teaching,* September 1964.

(23) Raven, Ronald J., "The Development of the Concept of Momentum in Primary School Children." *Journal of Research in Science Teaching,* 5, 1967.

(24) Rowe, Mary Budd, "Science, Silence, and Sanctions." *Science and Children,* March 1969.

(25) Sanders, Norris M., *Classroom Questions.* New York: Harper & Row, Publishers, 1966.

(26) Science Curriculum Improvement Study, *Newsletter,* Nos. 1–18. Science Curriculum Improvement Study, Lawrence Hall of Science, University of California, Berkeley, Calif.

(27) Showalter, Victor, "Unified Science, An Alternative to Tradition." *The Science Teacher,* February 1964.

(28) Stafford, Don. "The Influence of the Science Curriculum Improvement Study First-Grade Program on the Attainment of the Conservations." Ph. D. diss., 1969.

(29) Thier, Herbert D., "A Look at a First Grader's Understanding of Matter." *Journal of Research in Science Teaching,* March 1965.

(30) Vivian, V. Eugene, "An Evaluation Scheme for Elementary Science." Glassboro State College. Paper read before the National Science Teachers Association, Dallas, Tex., 1969.

(31) Voelker, Alan, and Robert Rogers, "Programs for Improving Science Instruction." *Science and Children,* January–February 1970.

(32) Wilson, John H., "Differences Between Inquiry-Discovery and the Traditional Approaches to Teaching Science in the Elementary Schools." Ph.D. diss., University of Oklahoma, 1968.

19

SCIENCE—A PROCESS APPROACH
Purposes—Accomplishments—Expectations

Robert M. Gagné

The development of an elementary science curriculum called *Science—A Process Approach* is now approaching completion. This curriculum, for children in kindergarten and grades one through six, has been developed by the Commission on Science Education of the American Association for the Advancement of Science. The six-year effort has been financially supported by the National Science Foundation, and has involved the enthusiastic participation of more than a hundred scientists and educators, representing a wide spectrum of backgrounds, interests, and specialized knowledge.

Initial plans for the design of this new curriculum were formulated in two conferences held in the summer of 1962. On the basis of these conferences, the Commission on Science Education outlined a projected elementary science program which would emphasize the laboratory method of instruction and would focus upon ways of developing basic skills in the processes of science. The processes include observing, classifying, measuring, predicting, and other skills needed for scientific investigations. The annual cycle of activities, which was repeated each year, 1963–68, followed this sequence: (1) planning for development, during winter and spring; (2) a "summer writing conference" of scientists and teachers; (3) a fall period of revision, editing, and

Reprinted from a paper that was prepared for the AAAS Commission on Science Education by Dr. Robert M. Gagné with the assistance of members of the Summer Writing Team, University of Maryland, 1967. AAAS Miscellaneous Publication 67–12.

publication of experimental materials; (4) a simultaneous activity, beginning in the fall and extending to the next summer, of trying out the newly developed materials in a group of participating schools in various parts of the country.

Since 1964, a *Newsletter* describing important events and outcomes of this developmental cycle has been published (see References: 1–10). A summary of the program's history is given in the *Newsletter*, Volume 3, No. 2 (1967). Additional accounts of early events are given by Mayor (19) and by Livermore (15, 16).

Characteristics of the Program

Science—A Process Approach shares certain purposes and characteristics with other modern science curricula. Like them, it is designed to present instruction which is intellectually stimulating and scientifically authentic. Like other programs, it is based upon the belief that an understanding of the scientific approach to gaining knowledge of man's world has a fundamental importance as a part of the general education of any child.

The program also has characteristics which make it different from other curricula in elementary science. The noteworthy and distinctive features of *Science—A Process Approach* may be summarized as follows:

1. Instructional materials are contained in booklets written for, and used by, the teacher. Accompanying kits of materials are designed for use by teacher and children. Except for certain data sheets in the later grades, there are no printed materials addressed to the pupil. What the teacher does is to organize and set up science problem situations designed for participation by the children.

2. The topics covered in the exercises sample widely from the various fields of science. The exercises are ordered in sequences of instruction to provide a developmental progression of increasing competence in the processes of science.

3. Each exercise is designed to achieve some clearly stated objectives. These are phrased in terms of the kinds of pupil behavior which can be observed as outcomes of learning upon completion of the exercise.

4. The coverage of fields of science is broad. Mathematics topics are included, to be used when needed as preparation for other science activities. Some of the exercises draw from the social

and behavioral sciences. Most involve principles in physics, biology, and chemistry, with a lesser representation of earth sciences and astronomy.

5. What is to be learned by the children is an accumulative and continually increasing degree of understanding of, and capability in, the processes of science. Progress begins in the kindergarten with observation and description of object properties and motion, and advances through the sixth grade to the design and conduct of scientific experiments on a variety of topics.

6. Methods for evaluating pupils' achievement and progress are an integral part of the instructional program. The exercises contain tests of pupil achievement reflecting the objectives of the exercises and providing means of assessing outcomes. In addition, separate measures have been developed for use in determining pupil attainments in process skills prior to instruction.

7. A *Commentary for Teachers* (9) and a *Guide for Inservice Instruction* (2) include essential general information on the science principles and processes involved in the program, and a set of exercises providing opportunities for teachers to practice relevant instructional techniques.

The Meaning of Process

There are a number of ways of conceiving of the meaning of "process" as exemplified in *Science—A Process Approach*. First, perhaps, it should be mentioned that an emphasis on process implies a corresponding deemphasis on specific science "content." Of course, the content is there—the children examine and make explorations of solid objects, liquids, gases, plants, animals, rocks, and even moon photographs. But, with some few notable exceptions, they are not asked to learn and remember particular facts or principles about these objects and phenomena. Rather, they are expected to learn such things as how to observe solid objects and their motions, how to classify liquids, how to infer internal mechanisms in plants, how to make and verify hypotheses about animal behavior, and how to perform experiments on the actions of gases. For example, in an exercise on the movement of liquids in materials (Part E), the children learn to design and carry out experiments on the relation between kinds of materials and rate of movement of liquids within them, including the control and manipulation of relevant variables; but they are not required to learn particular facts about the rate of liquid movement in blotting paper, fabrics, sand, clay, or other materials employed in the exercise. Such facts may be incidentally learned, and may be useful to the child, but the primary objective is one of learning to carry out the process of controlling variables in an experiment.

A second meaning of process, referred to by Gagné (12), centers upon the idea that what is taught to children should resemble what scientists do—the "processes" that they carry out in their own scientific activities. Scientists do observe, and classify, and measure, and infer, and make hypotheses, and perform experiments. How have they come to be able to do these things? Presumably, they have learned to do them, over a period of many years, by practicing doing them. If scientists have learned to gain information in these ways, surely the elementary forms of what they do can begin to be learned in the early grades. This line of reasoning does not imply the purpose of making everyone a scientist. Instead, it puts forward the idea that understanding science depends upon being able to look upon and deal with the world in the ways that the scientist does.

The third and perhaps most widely important meaning of process introduces the consideration of human intellectual development. From this point of view, processes are in a broad sense "ways of processing information." Such processing grows more complex as the individual develops from early childhood onward. The individual capabilities that are developed may reasonably be called "intellectual skills," a phrase which many would prefer to the term "processes."

When one considers processes as intellectual skills, certain general characteristics become apparent. One of the most important is the degree of generalizability one can expect in human capabilities of this sort. The typical development of intellectual skills, as Piaget's work (11) amply reminds us, is from the very concrete and specific to the increasingly abstract and general. Highly general intellectual skills are typically formed over a period of years, and are thought to depend upon the accumulated effects of learning a considerable variety of relatively concrete principles. Accordingly, the skills which _Science—A Process Approach_ is designed to establish begin in highly specific and concrete forms, and increasing generality of these skills is systematically provided for by a planned progression of exercises. Evidence shows that these skills do generalize to a variety of new situations (_Newsletter, 3:_ No. 3, 1967; (5), 2nd Report, 1968). The instructional program of _Science—A Process Approach_ attempts to deal realistically with the development of intellectual skills, in the sense that the goals to be achieved by any single exercise are modest. In a longer-term sense, substantial and general intellectual development is expected to result from the cumulative effects of an orderly progression of learning activities.

Processes and Intellectual Development

There is, then, a progressive intellectual development within each process category. As this development proceeds, it comes to be increasingly interrelated with corresponding development of other processes; inferring, for example, partakes of prior development of skills in observing, classifying, and measuring. The interrelated nature of the development is explicitly recognized in the kinds of activities undertaken in grades four through six, sometimes referred to as "integrated processes," including controlling variables, defining operationally, formulating hypotheses, interpreting data, and as an ultimate form of such integration, experimenting.

A brief description of the expected sequence of development in both basic and integrated process categories is as follows. More complete descriptions of these processes are contained in the *Commentary for Teachers* (9).

Observing

Beginning with identifying objects and object-properties, this sequence proceeds to the identification of changes in various physical systems, the making of controlled observations, and the ordering of a series of observations.

Classifying

Development begins with simple classifications of various physical and biological systems and progresses through multi-stage classifications, their coding and tabulation.

Using Numbers

This sequence begins with identifying sets and their members, and progresses through ordering, counting, adding, multiplying, dividing, finding averages, using decimals, and powers of ten. Exercises in number-using are introduced before they are needed to support exercises in the other processes.

Measuring

Beginning with the identification and ordering of lengths, development in this process proceeds with the demonstration of rules for measurement of length, area, volume, weight, temperature, force, speed, and a number of derived measures applicable to specific physical and biological systems.

Using Space-Time Relationships

This sequence begins with the identification of shapes, movement, and direction. It continues with the learning of rules applicable to straight and curved paths, directions at an angle, changes in position, and determinations of linear and angular speeds.

Communicating

Development in this category begins with bar graph descriptions of simple phenomena, and proceeds through describing a variety of physical objects and systems, and the changes in them, to the construction of graphs and diagrams for observed results of experiments.

Predicting

For this process, the developmental sequence progresses from interpolation and extrapolation in graphically presented data to the formulation of methods for testing predictions.

Inferring

Initially, the idea is developed that inferences differ from observations. As development proceeds, inferences are constructed for observations of physical and biological phenomena, and situations are constructed to test inferences drawn from hypotheses.

Defining Operationally

Beginning with the distinction between definitions which are operational and those which are not, this developmental sequence proceeds to the point where the child constructs operational definitions in problems that are new to him.

Formulating Hypotheses

At the start of this sequence, the child distinguishes hypotheses from inferences, observations, and predictions. Development is continued to the stage of constructing hypotheses and demonstrating tests of hypotheses.

Interpreting Data

This sequence begins with descriptions of graphic data and inferences based upon them, and progresses to constructing equations to represent data, relating data to statements of hypotheses, and making generalizations supported by experimental findings.

Controlling Variables

The developmental sequence for this "integrated" process begins with identification of manipulated and responding (independent and dependent) variables in a description or demonstration of an experiment. Development proceeds to the level at which the student, being given a problem, inference, or hypothesis, actually conducts an experiment, identifying the variables, and describing how variables are controlled.

Experimenting

This is the capstone of the "integrated" processes. It is developed through a continuation of the sequence for controlling variables, and includes the interpretation of accounts of scientific experiments, as well as the activities of stating problems, constructing hypotheses, and carrying out experimental procedures.

Description of Intellectual Development

Descriptions of these sequences of intellectual development serve a number of purposes in the execution of the educational program embodied in *Science—A Process Approach*. These descriptions are contained in behavioral hierarchies, which bear a derivative relation to the learning hierarchies described by Gagné (13) for smaller portions of various curricula. Charts depicting the hierarchies for all of the processes have recently been published (Process Hierarchy Chart, Basic, 1967; Integrated, 1969), and an explanation of them is also given in booklets introducing each Part, entitled *Description of the Program*.

The behavioral hierarchies constitute the "skeleton" of *Science—A Process Approach* and the rationale for selecting and ordering the sequence of exercises. Thus the behavioral hierarchies orient the teacher to the purposes of the program, or of any portion of it. The teacher may examine the progression of behavioral development depicted in these hierarchies, and derive from them a view of where teaching starts and where it is expected to go. In addition, they show the interrelationships between any one exercise and others which precede or follow it, including those primarily devoted to other processes. To aid the teacher in maintaining this viewpoint towards the progressive development of processes, there is included in each exercise a section showing the relevant preceding steps and subsequent steps in the behavioral hierarchy. This section is, in actuality, simply a small portion of the entire hierarchy, providing the teacher with a rather specific view of what has gone before and what is coming next. The interpretation of such diagrams is expected to be: (1) here are the prerequisites for the present exercise; (2) here is what the child is expected to learn in this exercise; and (3) this is what the exercise will prepare him to undertake in later learning.

The second major use of the behavioral hierarchies is as guides to the assessment of student achievement and program evaluation [*Newsletter, 3:* 3, 1967; Walbesser, 1963]. Initial evaluation of the student, to determine whether or not he has achieved the objectives of each exercise, is carried out by performance tests based upon the objectives stated in the exercises themselves. Such tests, however, are designed to be consistent with the behavioral hierarchies, so that in each case what is being measured is a new achievement, and not something that has already been achieved as a result of some earlier exercise.

In addition, provision must be made to measure achievement in a sense other than as the immediate effects of instruction; in fact, in a developmental sense. The basis for such measurement is again the developmental sequence of the behavioral hierarchy, represented in a test which attempts to assess how far a pupil has progressed in each process (10). Finally, the hierarchies also guide the development of measures of achievement which are "terminal" to the program, insofar as they help to define what the minimum set of behaviors may be for children who have participated in the program for a period of years.

Purposes of the Program

The major characteristics of *Science—A Process Approach* which have been described surely serve in large part to convey what the program is all about. Some additional understanding of the approach, however, may be gained from an account of the purposes which have guided the effort. An important statement of these purposes was prepared at an early stage of development by a committee of the Commission on Science Education (9). In addition, several papers dealing with the goals of various aspects of the development were prepared at different points along the way and are collected together under the title *The Psychological Bases of Science—A Process Approach* (1).

General Education

From the outset, it has been a guiding purpose to develop a curriculum which could become part of the general education of every child. The goal has not been to produce students of science who have a large amount of highly specialized knowledge. Rather, the aim is for every child to acquire the basic knowledge and point of view which provide him with a highly generalized method of gaining an understanding of himself and the world in which he lives.

Preparation for Systematic Study of Scientific Disciplines

Another important guiding purpose has been to provide the student in the elementary grades with some highly generalizable intellectual skills, and some knowledge of scientific procedures for gaining new knowledge, which can serve as a springboard for later study of any of the sciences. There are some very basic ideas, it is believed, which are important to the understanding of systematic science, and which cannot be readily identified as portions of the traditional elementary curriculum. It is these ideas that are intended to be represented as the "processes" of the new science curriculum.

Generalizability of Knowledge

A related aim is that of providing the child with the kind of knowledge that is generalizable to new situations. In part, this is accomplished by the use of a variety of content. In part, it is attempted by asking the child to practice making generalizations from one field of science to another. Controlling variables in an experiment on rusting of iron may be followed by an exercise that poses a problem of controlling variables in plant growth.

Level of Achievement

Certainly, the program aims for a level of achievement in understanding science and making scientific investigations which has not heretofore been attained by elementary school students. The purpose is to give these children capabilities for thinking and acting in the realm of science which go far beyond what has previously been customary. It is hoped that such capabilities may be applied in all their pursuits, not solely to the further study of scientific subjects.

Intellectual Challenge

The materials of the program were prepared with the aim of presenting children with intellectual challenges. Pupils are required to remember few "facts," and those few will most probably be retained without effort. However, they are frequently asked to think, to use reasoning, and to invent methods and explanations. This is considered to be an important part of what is meant by learning to use science "processes."

Pupil Interest

The well-known principle of proceeding in instruction from the familiar to the unfamiliar is used throughout the program. The attempt is made to appeal to initial pupil interest, and to maintain it as new problems are introduced. Thus one important goal of instruction is to bring about a broadening of pupil interest in the many fields of science. It is hoped that the child will come to recognize many new problems, previously unknown to him, which can be viewed scientifically; and that over the course of the program he will develop a lasting interest in science, whether or not he chooses it for a life work.

Achievement Motivation

Besides the motivation of curiosity and intellectual challenge, the program intends to make use of achievement motivation. Comments from teachers and the measured achievements of children during the tryout period have been used as bases for revisions and adjustments in the exercises designed to accomplish this purpose. The exercises are aimed at *all* children, not solely the bright ones. The objectives are intended to be not too difficult for the vast majority of children to achieve. When they are achieved, this accomplishment will, it is hoped, reward the child and thus contribute to the maintenance of his interest in further exploration of science and its processes.

Accomplishments

The goals of *Science—A Process Approach*, although moderately ambitious, appear to be attainable. What evidences are there, at the present time, that progress is being made toward these goals? What accomplishments can be described?

A Systematic Course of Study

The instructional materials of *Science—A Process Approach* (Parts A-C, 1967; Parts D and E, 1966; Parts F and G, 1970) provide the basic evidence that a systematic course of study in the processes of science has been developed. Successive exercises in each process build upon earlier exercises in a progressive sequence, while at the same time variations in subject matter are deliberately introduced.

Empirical findings concerning the existence of ordered relationships among the exercises, in the sense that successful completion of one contributes to the learning involved in a subsequent one, have been described in reports of the results of pupil testing [*Newsletter, 3:* 3, 1967; (5)]. Additional findings have been obtained, and are to be reported, by administering an individual test of performance in the various processes (10) to groups of children who have participated in the program for one or more years. In general, with some notable exceptions, it has been shown that achievement of lower levels of development in each process increases the probability of attaining subsequent steps in these intellectual skills. As for the exceptions, these have led to a re-examination of the exercises and the sequencing of developmental steps; and in many instances the latter have been reordered as reflected in the Basic Process Hierarchy Chart (4, 1967).

Continued Revision for Improvement

From the outset the materials of *Science—A Process Approach* have been subjected to periodic improvement based upon information collected during tryouts in fifteen school systems located in various parts of the country. Reports from teachers have provided systematic information on the ease of teaching, technical difficulties, degree of pupil enthusiasm, appraisals of pupil understanding, and related matters. Measures of competence administered to children upon the completion of each exercise have yielded data on the proportion of children achieving each of the defined objectives of the exercise. The target has been to have 90 percent of the children achieve 90 percent of the objectives. Each revision of the exercises, in four successive years for each part, has been based upon these findings regarding pupil achievement and teacher reception; and each revision has approached more closely the stated goals of the program. Comprehensive accounts of the information yielded by these two sources of data have been reported (5).

Broad Coverage of Science

The booklets of *Science—A Process Approach* exhibit the varied coverage of the fields of science which reflect the aims of the program. The distribution of content in relation to acepted categories of science is approximately as follows: Physical Science, 40 percent; Life Science, 25 percent, Mathematics, 18 percent; Earth Science, 10 percent; Social and Behavioral Science, 7 percent. An account of content coverage in biology has been described by Kurtz (14). Livermore (17) has made an analysis of the content in the field of chemistry, and Mayor (19) has given a description of the mathematics content.

Available Teacher Performances

Another notable accomplishment of the program has been its concerted approach to the problem of orienting and educating teachers of elementary science. The need for materials for the education of teachers was recognized early, and much effort has been devoted to the preparation of a course and accompanying materials for the teacher who is preparing to teach the program. Emphasis is given in teacher education to the science processes and their relation to human intellectual development, in addition to helping teachers acquire the competencies included in *Science—A Process Approach* for application in the classroom. The *Commentary for Teachers* (9) is actually much more than a commentary, for it contains carefully prepared self-instructional lessons relevant to each of the processes. The materials have been tried out and evaluated in several teacher workshops; and their latest form reflects revisions based upon systematic information collected within these sessions. The AAAS-Xerox edition also includes notes on the historical development and psychological bases of the program.

Still another product of development is a guide intended for the leaders of sessions for teacher education, reflecting the science processes, their psychological bases, and the variety of science activities and teaching strategies to which they lead. The *Guide For Inservice Instruction* (2) incorporates brief instructional films, self-instructional booklets, and tests for diagnosis and evaluation of teacher learning.

Student Achievements

Reports of results on program evaluation [(5); *Newsletter, 3:* 3, 1967] generally provide much favorable evidence regarding student achievements. For example, it has been found that immediate achievement measures indicate 90 percent of the children to have acquired at least 70 percent of the desired competencies for 97 of 102 exercises in Parts A through D. Further, 90 percent of the children reached the 80 percent level of achievement for all but fourteen of these exercises. When children who had participated in the program for one year were compared with children at the same grade level who had participated for three years, differences favoring the latter group ranged from 2 to 20 percent. When achievements of a group of children from a low socioeconomic background were compared with those of medium and high levels of family income, it was found that although the former group completed fewer exercises, their success on the completed exercises was as high as that of the other children.

Other evidences of the effects of the program have yet to be gathered. More information will be sought on the lasting effects of this program. Answers are needed to such questions as what children know and what they are able to accomplish at the end of the fourth grade, the fifth, and the sixth, after having completed several years of *Science—A Process Approach*. In addition, it is hoped that evidence can be obtained of increased pupil interest in science, as well as an increased degree of the children's positive valuation of scientific activities after participation in the program over a period of several years.

Expectations

What will a "graduate" of *Science—A Process Approach* be like? What will he know? What will he be able to do? These questions, of course, cannot be answered at the present time with any great degree of assurance. The evidence of what these children are like will have to come, after a period of years, from evidence of what they can accomplish in grades subsequent to the sixth. Perhaps also it will come from evidence of how they behave toward science in even later periods of their lives.

The following descriptions of what may be expected of a child who has completed the program are speculative, although stated in concrete terms. They represent goals which have given implicit guidance to the development of *Science—A Process Approach*. While the full attainment of these goals is greatly to be desired, even partial attainment would surely be viewed as a substantial indication of the program's effectiveness.

1. He will tend to apply a scientific mode of thought to a wide range of problems, including social ones, distinguishing facts from conjectures and inferences, and identifying the procedures required to obtain verification of hypotheses and suggested solutions.

2. He will be able to acquire an understanding of the structure of those particular scientific disciplines he pursues in junior and senior high school more rapidly and with less difficulty than is the case with students today.

3. In a printed account of a scientific experiment, using terms that are understood or defined, he will be able to identify the question being investigated; the variables manipulated, controlled, and measured; the hypothesis being tested; how such a test relates to the results obtained; and the conclusions which can legitimately be drawn.

4. In an oral account of a scientific experiment, given by a scientist using terms intended for laymen, he will be able to identify those elements of scientific procedure and findings mentioned in 3.

5. In an incomplete account of a scientific experiment, such as might appear in a newspaper, he will be able to infer, where necessary, the question being investigated and the elements of scientific procedure described in 3.

6. Given a problem amenable to scientific investigation, and within his understanding as to factual content, he will be able to design (and under certain conditions, carry out) one or more experiments to test hypotheses relevant to the problem.

7. He will show his appreciation of, and interest in, scientific activities by choices made in reading, entertainment, and other kinds of leisure-time pursuits.

To those who have developed the program, these predictions seem not unreasonable. They are things that should happen. If and when they do, the truly important outcomes of *Science—A Process Approach* will be known.

References

(1) AAS Commission on Science Education, *The Psychological Bases of Science—A Process Approach*. Washington, D.C., 1965.

(2) _____*Guide for Inservice Instruction and Response Sheets*. Washington, D.C., 1967.

(3) _____*Science—A Process Approach*, Parts A-G. New York: Xerox Corporation, 1967, 1968, 1970.

(4) _____*Science—A Process Approach*, Hierarchy Charts. New York: Xerox Corporation, 1967, 1969.

(5) _____*An Evaluation Model and Its Application*. 2nd report. Washington, D.C., 1968.

(6) _____*Process Measure for Teachers*. Washington, D.C., 1969.

(7) _____*Supplement to the Guide for Inservice Instruction*. Washington, D.C., 1969.

(8) _____*How to Plan for Science—A Process Approach*. Washington, D.C., 1970.

(9) _____*Science—A Process Approach*, Commentary for Teachers. New York: Xerox Corporation, 1970.

(10) _____*Science Process Instrument*. Experimental edition. Washington, D.C., 1970.

(11) Flavell, J.H., *The Developmental Psychology of Jean Piaget*. Princeton, N.J.: D. Van Nostrand Company, Inc., 1963.

(12) Gagné, Robert M., "Elementary Science: A New Scheme of Instruction." *Science, 151*, 1966, pp. 49–53.

(13) _____"Learning Hierarchies." *Educational Psychologist, 6*, 1968, pp. 1–9.

(14) Kurtz, Edwin B., Jr., "Biology in Science—A Process Approach." *American Biology Teacher, 29*, March 1967, pp. 192–96.

(15) Livermore, Arthur H., "Science—A Process Approach." *Science and Children*, May 1964, pp. 24–25.

(16) _____"The Process Approach of the AAAS Commission on Science Education." *Journal of Research in Science Teaching, 2,* 1964, pp. 271–82.

(17) _____"AAAS Commission on Science Education Elementary Science Program." *Journal of Chemical Education, 43,* 1966, pp. 270–72.

(18) Mayor, John R., "AAAS Commission on Science Education." *Science Education News,* December 1962, pp. 1–4.

(19) _____"Science and Mathematics in the Elementary School." *The Arithmetic Teacher, 14,* 1967, pp. 629–35.

Bibliography

Gagné, Robert M. "Why the "Process" Approach for a Modern Curriculum." *The EPIE Forum,* April–May 1968.

_____*The Conditions of Learning.* New York: Holt, Rinehart, & Winston, Inc., 1970, ch. 7.

Kessen, William, "Statement of Purposes and Objectives of Science Education in School." *Journal of Research in Science Teaching, 2,* 1964, pp. 3–6.

Kolb, John R., "Effects of Relating Mathematics to Science Instruction on the Acquisition of Quantitative Science Behaviors." *Journal of Research in Science Teaching, 5,* 1968, pp. 174–82.

Livermore, Arthur H., "Curriculum Research in Science." *Journal of Experimental Education, 37,* 1968, pp. 49–55.

Livermore, Arthur H. and John R. Mayor, "Curriculum Change in Other Sciences." *Geotimes, 13,* March 1968, pp. 21–25.

Mayor, John R., "Science and Mathematics: 1970s—A Decade of Change." *The Arithmetic Teacher, 17,* April 1970, pp. 293–97.

Mayor, John R. and Arthur H. Livermore, "A Process Approach to Elementary School Science." *School Science and Mathematics, 69,* May, pp. 411–16.

Walbesser, H. H., "Science Curriculum Evaluation: Observations on a Position." *The Science Teacher, 33,* February 1966, pp. 34–39.

Walbesser, H. H. and Heather L. Carter, "Some Methodological Considerations of Curriculum Evaluation Research." *Education Leadership, 26,* October 1968, pp. 53–64.

_____"Acquisition of Elementary Science Behavior by Children of Disadvantaged Families." *Educational Leadership, 25,* May 1968, pp. 741–48.

_____"The Effect on Test Results of Changes in Task and Responses Format Required by Altering the Test Administration From an Individual to a Group Form." *Journal of Research in Science Teaching, 7,* 1970, pp. 1–8.

20

GUIDE TO THE SELECTION OF AN
ELEMENTARY SCIENCE CURRICULUM

C. L. Hutchins

The Guide to the Selection of an Elementary Science Curriculum is intended to promote discussion of issues involved in reviewing new science programs. Each section of the Guide follows this format: It introduces a key question facing those making curriculum decisions, briefly discusses some of the controversial aspects of the question, and then directs the readers' attention to each program's position on the issue in question. In order to specify these positions, the Far West Laboratory staff has made judgments extending beyond the kind of reporting found elsewhere in the Information Unit. The judgments do not reflect any endorsement or agreement by program developers, consultants to the Laboratory, or the United States Office of Education.

Process versus Content?

To the question, "What shall we teach and to what end?" many people answer that a major goal of science education should be the learning of scientific processes, that is, of the diverse procedures involved in

Reprinted from *Elementary Science Information Unit,* Berkeley, The Far West Laboratory for Educational Research and Development, 1970. The Elementary Science Information Unit is a multi-media kit designed to assist elementary school decision makers in selecting from among six leading new elementary science programs. The kit contains reports on each of these programs, film strips showing them in action, and other materials. Further information can be obtained from the Far West Laboratory. Dr. C. L. Hutchins is associate director of the Far West Laboratory for Educational Research and Development, Berkeley, California.

obtaining and applying knowledge. Examples of processes range from such general behaviors as "inquiring," "questioning," exploring," "observing," and "communicating," to more specific behaviors, such as "measuring," "hypothesis building," and "controlling variables." It is argued that processes—the scientists' tools—more accurately reflect the nature of science than the products of scientific investigation; the process approach insures that learning will continue when formal education is completed.

Rather than discussing "process versus content" then, the question is, "How should a process-oriented approach to content be accomplished?" It is this question that focuses on most of the variations among the programs presented in this Information Unit.

If you want a program that focuses on the processes and skills of scientific investigation, see Science—A Process Approach. The program is organized around specific processes and skills to be learned; evaluation is judged in terms of the attainment of process skills. Concepts and facts are necessary parts of the Science—A Process Approach curriculum, but are *not* its focus. They do not control the sequencing of objectives of the units directly.

If you want an approach that identifies a single process— inquiry—as the essential scientific process, examine IDP. Individual units are drawn from specific physical science subjects, but all focus on the process of developing and testing theories about how and why things behave as they do.

If you want a program that focuses on basic concepts more than on identifying the processes to be learned, examine COPES and SCIS. These programs reflect the belief that concepts are abstractions explaining a large number of phenomena and should be the organizers for studying and understanding how a scientist operates.

If you want a program that tries to combine the teaching of processes and concepts of science and math, examine MINNEMAST.

If you want a program that focuses on things in the environment —objects and phenomena, such as bones and shadows—and lets questions about causes and effects and ways to obtain answers flow from non-directed exploration, review ESS. Although the program doesn't systematically develop a process approach, the developers believe it can be used in this way if so desired.

Should You Build Your Own Curriculum or Adopt One That Is Already Well Developed?

Do you want to "do your own thing"?

Would you be able to use a program that has already been worked out?

These are difficult questions to answer. Most school personnel probably would prefer to build a unique curriculum to match specific backgrounds and learning characteristics of the children in their schools. Such an effort, however, requires much time, money, and talent, if it is to be done well. If the resources are not available, can you then rely on a program developer to present you with a "complete" curriculum that specifies goals, defines the terms under which success is to be measured, and prescribes the teaching techniques to be used? There is no single solution that will work best in all situations. Only you can decide how well any particular program fits the goals you would identify, if time and resources permitted you to develop your own program.

If you want a program that should not *be adopted piecemeal, see SCIENCE—A PROCESS APPROACH and MINNEMAST. (However, MINNEMAST is K–3 only.)*

If you want a program that probably *should not be broken up or adopted piecemeal, see COPES and SCIS.*

If you want a program that could be considered a complete package for use in one upper elementary grade, see IDP. IDP is, however, more frequently used as a source of independent lessons introduced into an ongoing program.

If you want a program that could be used as a complete curriculum if you work out your own objectives and sequence the units, see ESS. ESS is more frequently used, however, as a source of independent units to be introduced into an ongoing program.

How Do You Define Goals and Objectives?

There is considerable disagreement among educators today about the answer to this question. One view frequently expressed is that learning objectives should be defined as precisely as possible. Ideally, they should be defined in behavioral terms that indicate what student performance an observer should expect to see in order to measure success under given conditions. Another point of view holds that current methods for measuring behavioral or performance objectives are inadequate. Proponents of this viewpoint argue that the inadequacies are particularly apparent when trying to define mastery of complex scientific processes like hypothesis-building, or when trying to complete measurement within the limits of a single year. The programs reviewed in the Information Unit reflect the differences of opinion.

If you are not inclined toward behaviorally defined outcomes, consider ESS, IDP, SCIS, MINNEMAST, and COPES. Of these five, however, MINNEMAST and SCIS are the easiest to translate into performance terms if you are willing to spend the time.

How Important Is the Sequencing of Individual Lessons or Units in the Programs?[1]

This question involves two issues: first, the degree to which the program developers have conditioned success in one unit upon success in a preceding one; and, second, the degree of flexibility allowed the teacher in resequencing units. In other words, if learning in one lesson depends on having completed a previous one, the teacher is restricted in determining the order of lessons. If you want maximum flexibility for the teacher, you would be ill-advised to select a program whose sequencing pattern is rigid. If you hope to increase student learning by using a sequenced program, you will have to forego a certain amount of teacher freedom.

If you want a program that specifies the sequencing of individual lessons closely, see SCIENCE—A PROCESS APPROACH and COPES.

If you want a program that specifies sequencing but acknowledges the occasional need to resequence lessons to suit individual needs or preferences, see SCIS and MINNEMAST.

If you want a program that recommends an order for presenting units but does not require that it be retained if another order is preferred, see IDP.

If you want a program that specifies no order for using units other than indicating they are appropriate for primary or intermediate levels, see ESS.

What Is the Instructional Strategy of the Programs?

All of the programs presented in the Information Unit suggest procedures for teaching individual units—ways to introduce and conduct the lessons, and ways of defining success. Generally speaking, the procedures identify an approach that might be called "Inquiry." In other words, the role of the teacher is relatively nondirective and the students are encouraged to explore, explain, and transfer learning on their own. One of the key features of the inquiry approach as represented in all the programs is that students are required to work directly with the materials of science.

The programs vary, however, in how closely the teacher should follow the suggested instructional method and how uniform the approach must be for all lessons. Some developers make "suggestions" but urge the teacher to develop his own approach. Others prescribe

---

[1]Sequencing also influences how easily a program can be adapted to an existing program. For a discussion of this consideration see the section, "Can the programs be coordinated with existing programs or texts?"

one methodology for all lessons. Still others recommend one or two procedures to achieve the desired result but urge the use of any method, so long as the over-all objectives of the lesson are achieved.

Some schools have made multiple adoptions to permit teachers to use the strategy that best fits their individual needs.

In none of the programs is the instructional strategy so rigorously prescribed that the teaching situation is completely structured. All of the programs require the contributions of creative teachers.

If you want a program that specifies a single strategy of instruction for most of the units, examine SCIS and IDP.

If you want a program that indicates different instructional procedures for different units and encourages the teacher to devise his own method if he is dissatisfied with the one suggested, see SCIENCE—A PROCESS APPROACH, ESS, MINNEMAST, and COPES.

SCIENCE—A PROCESS APPROACH qualifies the instructional options by insisting that whatever procedure is selected, the outcome must be consistent with the behavioral objectives set for the unit.

Can the Programs Be Coordinated with Existing Programs or Texts?

In areas where state-adopted texts or curriculum guides dictate what programs schools may use, and in schools that have accumulated many science kits and other materials, supplementary materials that can be coordinated with existing programs may be desired. The danger in such piecemeal adoption is greatest with comprehensive programs that are intended to stand alone. This is particularly true of programs in which the units are tightly sequenced.

If you want to incorporate new materials into an ongoing program, see ESS and IDP. Most of the units in ESS and IDP can be used independently of all the others.

If you want programs that are so sequenced that units probably should not be used independently, see SCIS, SCIENCE—A PROCESS APPROACH, COPES, and MINNEMAST.

How Much Background in Science Should Teachers Have to Use the Programs Effectively?

Although it always seems safe to assume that a strong science background is better than a weak one, the developers of most of the programs in the Information Unit indicate that success with their programs does not depend upon above-average science knowledge. One, however, suggests the use of a science specialist in the upper grades.

If you want a program that tries to supply most of the information that might be required by the teachers, see SCIS, SCIENCE—A PROCESS APPROACH, and MINNEMAST.

If you want a program that provides considerable information but may require more than is provided, see IDP. In IDP, students develop theories to explain what they are puzzled by and the teacher is expected to field questions that may not be answered in teacher or student manuals and materials.

If you want a program that encourages questioning, that may not provide enough information to cover some situations, and that urges the teacher to "learn along with the students," see ESS. It should also be noted that because ESS provides no comprehensive outline for sequencing materials or for setting objectives, a teacher with a strong science background probably will be at an advantage.

If you want a program that provides or assumes that the average teacher has an adequate background in order to teach the K–2 materials but clearly requires a specially trained science teacher for the 3–6 materials, see COPES.

If you want a program that requires a minimum of science background, see SCIENCE—A PROCESS APPROACH, SCIS, or ESS.

Should Provisions for Individualizing Be Required?

With twenty-five to thirty students in a room, the problems of accommodating previous experience, background, and differences in style and rate of learning are complex. Programs are now being developed that try to provide for some of these variations. It will be several years, however, before they are ready for widespread use. Even the newest of the science programs do not yet make explicit provisions for individualizing. No program recommends procedures for bringing a student that fails to meet group standards for a lesson or unit up to the expected level while, at the same time, permitting his classmates to advance.

If you want a science program that explicitly provides for individual instruction, none of the programs described in the Information Unit will satisfy you. However, if you have teachers with the training and resources to adapt a program for individual instruction, then there is no reason why any of the programs could not be used.

If you want a program that does not explicitly control individual learning but, because of its emphasis on open-endedness, permits a student to participate in a lesson to the extent of his ability, see ESS. The ESS developers suggest that more than one unit at a time could be used in the same class.

V

Becoming a Better Elementary Science Teacher Through Understanding the Facilitation of Learning

The teacher, child, and curriculum have been investigated. The learning environment, however, is not composed of separate components but is an interaction between all. Teachers design the environment to help facilitate learning. In the process of facilitation, teachers are becoming increasingly aware of the need to interact totally with the child and develop him maximally as a person. Historically, education emphasized developing the cognitive part of a person. Teachers today are still concerned with this, but also strive to give attention to the affective domain as well. Affectivity involves emotions, feelings, attitudes, beliefs, and values of the individual.

Carl Rogers believes interpersonal relations facilitate learning as long as trust, realness, empathy, and positive regard are the keystones of the human interaction. Rogers questions how well teachers have traditionally demonstrated these behaviors; further, he suggests a new role for teachers as facilitators of learning. What do you think the teacher's behavior should be? What evidence is there that good interpersonal relations are more effective than other types of experiences?

Helen Heffernan discusses variations in concept development. Imagine the following children: a poor white, a middle-class Black, a Spanish-speaking migrant, and a white upper-class child. Each has a different life space, life style, and perhaps life time. They are all in our schools to learn science. How reasonable is it to treat them all the same? What is the most effective way to teach each of these groups of children concepts? How are affectivity and concept development related to a teacher's objectives? Ronald Anderson presents ways of developing objectives for elementary science in behavioral terms. He shows how teachers can write good cognitive and affective objectives. These should specifically define behaviors, conditions, and acceptable performances in order for education to progress at a more accountable level. If this is done, evaluation becomes easier since test items can be correlated with the behavioral objectives.

The affective realm is introduced by Robert Samples. Different types of values—their manifestations in individuals and their influences in the classroom—are outlined. Other articles in this section suggest techniques elementary teachers can use to clarify values relative to science. For example, by asking value-oriented questions, teachers help children deal with values, so they come to rely on and understand their own values. How will you help to instill value awareness in your science teaching?

The last article in this section summarizes elementary science research, providing several suggestions for improving instruction.

21

FORGET YOU ARE A TEACHER: CARL ROGERS TELLS WHY

Carl R. Rogers

Not long ago, a teacher asked me, "What changes would you like to see in elementary education?" I answered the question as best as I could at the time, but it stayed with me. Suppose I had a magic wand that could produce only one change in our educational systems. What would that change be?

I finally decided that my imaginary wand would with one sweep cause every teacher at every level to forget that he is a teacher. You would all develop a complete amnesia for the teaching skills you have painstakingly acquired over the years. You would find that you were absolutely unable to teach.

Instead, you would find yourself holding the attitudes and possessed of the skills of a *facilitator of learning*. Why would I be so cruel as to rob teachers of their precious skills? It is because I feel that our educational institutions are in a desperate state; and that unless our schools can become exciting, fun-filled centers of learning, they are quite possibly doomed.

You may be thinking that "facilitator of learning" is just a fancy name for a teacher and that nothing at all would be changed. If so, you are mistaken. There is *no* resemblance between the traditional

"Forget You Are A Teacher: Carl Rogers Tells Why," reprinted from *Instructor*, August/September 1971, The Instructor Publications, Inc., used by permission. Dr. Carl R. Rogers is resident fellow of the Center for the Studies of the Person, La Jolla, California.

function of teaching and the function of the facilitator of learning.

The traditional teacher—the *good* traditional teacher—asks himself questions of this sort: "What do I think would be good for a student to learn at his particular age and level of competence? How can I plan a proper curriculum for him? How can I motivate him to learn this curriculum? How can I instruct him in such a way that he will gain the knowledge which he should have? How can I best examine him to see whether he has actually gained this knowledge?"

On the other hand, the facilitator of learning asks questions such as these, not of himself but of his *students*: "What do you want to learn? What things puzzle you? What are you curious about? What issues concern you? What problems do you wish you could solve?" When he has the answers to these questions, he asks himself, "Now how can I help him find the resources—the people, the experiences, the learning facilities, the books, the knowledge in myself—which will help him learn in ways that will provide answers to the things that concern him, the things he is eager to learn?"

The attitudes of the teacher and the facilitator are also at opposite poles. Traditional teaching, no matter how disguised, is based essentially on the mug-and-jug theory. The teacher asks himself: "How can I make the mug hold still while I fill it from the jug with these facts which the curriculum planners and I regard as valuable?" The attitude of the facilitator has almost entirely to do with climate: "How can I create a psychological climate in which the child will feel free to be curious, will feel free to make mistakes, will feel free to learn from his environment, from fellow students, from me, from experience? How can I help him recapture the excitement of learning which was his in infancy?"

Once this process of facilitation of wanted learning was underway, a school would become for the child *"my* school." He would feel that he was a living, vital part of a very satisfying process. Astonished adults would begin to hear children say, "I can't wait to get to school today." "For the first time in my life I'm finding out about the things *I* want to know." "Hey, drop that brick! Don't you break the windows in *my* school!"

Beautifully, the same phrases would be used by the retarded child, the gifted child, the ghetto child, the underprivileged child. This is because every student would be working on the problems of real concern and interest to him, at the level at which he could grasp the problem and find a useful solution. He would have a continuing experience of success.

Some educators believe that such individualized learning is completely impractical because it would involve an enormous increase in the number of teachers. Nothing could be further from the truth. For one thing, when a child is eager to learn, he follows up his own leads and engages in a great deal of independent study on his own. There is also a great saving of the teacher's time because problems of discipline or "control" drop tremendously. Finally, the freedom of interaction which grows out of the climate I have so briefly described makes it possible to use a great untapped resource—the ability of one child to help another in his learning. For John to hear, "John, Ralph is having trouble carrying out the long division which he needs to solve his problem. I wonder if you could help him?" is a marvelous experience for both John and Ralph. It is even more marvelous for the two boys to work together, helping each other learn, without being asked! John *really* learns long division when he tries to help another learner understand it. Ralph can accept the help and learn because he is not shown up as being stupid, either in public or on a report card.

Barbara Shiel tells of her exciting, challenging experiences when, almost desperate with a difficult sixth grade, she took the risk of trying—with many uncertainties, setbacks, and difficulties—to become a facilitator of learning rather than a teacher. It is such a human, exciting account that I made it the first chapter of my book, *Freedom to Learn* (1). One of the results which most surprised Miss Shiel was that she had *more* time to spend with each child, not less, when she set each child free to learn.

I cannot stress too strongly how much I wish that someone could wave that magic wand and change teaching to facilitation. I deeply believe that traditional teaching is an almost completely futile, wasteful, overrated function in today's changing world. It is successful mostly in giving children who can't grasp the material a sense of failure. It also succeeds in persuading students to drop out, when they realize that the material taught is almost completely irrelevant to their lives. No one should ever be trying to learn something for which he sees no relevance. No child should ever experience the sense of failure imposed by our grading system, by criticism and ridicule from teachers and others, by rejection when he is slow to comprehend. The sense of failure he experiences when he tries something he wants to achieve that is actually too difficult for him is a healthy one which drives him to further learning. It is very different from a person-imposed failure, which must devalue him as a person.

The most basic of the attitudes that are essential to the facilitation of learning is realness or genuineness in the teacher's relationship with his students. You must take the risk of stepping out from behind your teacher role and becoming a person to your students.

Another outstanding attitude of those who facilitate learning is what I call "prizing" the learner—his feelings, his opinions, his person. It is an acceptance of the other as a person of worth, a basic belief that the other person is fundamentally trustworthy.

A third element is empathic understanding—the ability to understand the way the process of education and learning seems to the student. It is not "I understand what is wrong with you"; it's an attitude that causes the learner to think, "He understands how I feel!"

The methods for you to use in building freedom into your classroom must grow out of direct interaction with your students, and be suited to your own style. What you do *not* do is to set lesson tasks, assign reading, or lecture or expound (unless students ask you to). You do not require examinations or take sole responsibility for grades; you do not evaluate or criticize unless it is requested.

The sort of thing you can do is to draw out from your students their real problems relevant to the course at hand, thus tapping the child's intrinsic motivation. You can provide resources, making them easily available, both practically and psychologically. You can use such techniques as inquiry, simulation games, programmed instruction. You may find student contracts useful to give security and responsibility within an atmosphere of freedom. You will look for ways in which children can express their feelings, work through their own problems, become involved in evaluation of their own learning. You even trust the student's own feelings about himself enough not to force freedom upon him. However, as the child slowly begins to develop his own value system and becomes less threatened by responsibility, he will be able to accept and use freedom to a greater and greater degree.

Gratifyingly, more and more people are joining me in feeling the urgency of the situation, and a growing number of schools are deeply involved in making educational freedom work. Teachers are forgetting to be teachers; and, in setting their students free to learn, are finding that they have also set themselves free. We have the theories, the methods, and the skills to radically change our whole educational system, and perhaps to rescue our civilization. *Do we have the courage?*

Reference

(1) Rogers, Carl R., *Freedom to Learn*. Columbus, Ohio: Charles E. Merrill Publishing Company, 1969.

22

CONCEPT DEVELOPMENT IN SCIENCE*

Helen Heffernan

To anyone who has had a lifelong interest in the place of science in the education of young children, the developments of recent years have been a source of much gratification. We are much farther ahead than we were ten years ago.

"Farther ahead" means a number of things. Children are more involved in the processes of science. Children are having more firsthand experiences, greater opportunity to conduct explorations of scientific phenomena, and more opportunity to do critical thinking.

Also, teachers are participating in inservice education programs specifically directed toward the maturity level of the children they teach. Teachers and children have access to more ample material. Much effort is being directed to curriculum planning. School districts are developing laboratory centers for teachers.

As science education moves forward on so many fronts, critical needs command renewed attention. Much must be done to lessen the lag between what is now known about science teaching and classroom practice. As cases in point, how rapidly can we provide the focus, freedom, and responsive environment essential to J. Richard Such-

*This article is based on a speech originally presented at the luncheon meeting of NSTA and the Council for Elementary Science International during the 1966 NSTA Annual Convention in New York City.

Reprinted from *Science and Children, 4,* September 1966, pp. 25–26. Dr. Helen Heffernan was formerly chief of the Bureau of Elementary Education, State Department of Education, Sacramento, California.

man's[1] inquiry program? Dr. Suchman has made a significant contribution to learning in his demonstration that a child must confront a discrepancy in events which cannot be explained by the theories with which he is operating.

Another significant forward thrust has been given by Ben Strasser (3) of the staff of the Los Angeles County School Superintendent who has focused his interest on the teacher's self examination of his own teaching behavior. Mr. Strasser is concerned about what it is that learners do when they inquire and what are the behaviors a teacher exhibits which stimulate learners to perceive, to inquire, to discover, and to experiment. Mr. Strasser views teaching as a truly dynamic process. To achieve education of the quality he envisions requires conditions of reasonable class size and opportunity for inservice education. Observation of learners, their actions and interactions, interpreting such data, making diagnoses in terms of the learner, the situation and the goals and resultant change in teacher behavior in terms of the diagnoses made will not happen in overcrowded classrooms with harassed teachers and inadequate facilities.

A third most promising line of thinking and research is being carried on at the University of Arizona, by Alphoretta Fish (1). She indicates another level to which inquiry can be taken. In her model, inquiry shifts from the level on which alternative methods of science inquiry are focal, to the level on which decisions about which methods to select are focal. Her purpose is to guide pupils to make the decisions about the method to use in their science inquiry, experience the consequences of their decisions, and assess the consequences by inquiring into the science inquiry methods which produced the consequence. Dr. Fish is aiming at five goals in her research:

1. Expanding meanings by expanding relations instituted,
2. Analyzing the questions children ask and the methods they use for inquiring in science,
3. Evaluating their questions and methods-building criteria,
4. Reconstructing the questions and the methods of their science inquiry, and finally
5. Evaluating and reconstructing their criteria.

These three sophisticated studies point toward the development of the rational powers of the learner. All aim toward learners becoming more independent; learners dealing with problems of significance to them; learners able to perceive discrepancies and invent theories which

[1]Suchman, J. Richard, Acting Director, Division of Elementary and Secondary Research, Office of Education, U.S. Department of Health, Education, and Welfare, Washington, D.C.

satisfy their explanations; learners able to draw and test their inferences; and finally learners with wide experience with a variety of phenomena.

Concept Development

The psychologist tells us that "a concept is a generalization about related data." The philosophers say that "a concept is a mental image of a thing formed by generalization from particulars." We know that a concept is arrived at through various kinds of *perceptions*.

To illustrate: Looking out into your garden, you *perceive* some colorful, fluttering, strutting, chirping, flying objects. Some time in your past experience, someone has helped you to attach *verbal symbols* to these objects and you proceed to recall: robin, blue jay, woodpecker, dove, finch, English sparrow. Each of these is a *percept*, an impression gained solely by the use of the senses. When you *generalize* from these percepts and say "birds" you have arrived at a concept.

But for few, if any, is the concept of "bird" ever complete. The exception might be an ornithologist with a global range of study in the field of his specialization. He would come nearest to perceiving all facets of the concept.

Your concept of "bird" will change over the years with the addition of new percepts. You may travel to Africa and for the first time make contact with a bird that cannot fly—the ostrich. This may mean you will correct your previous concept if your experience had led you to generalize "that all birds fly"

This illustration, beginning with what seemed a relatively simple concept, could take us far—to South America for a glimpse of the scarlet ibis, to New Guinea to see the bird of paradise, to Europe to see the great white stork, to Australia to see the amazing plumage which gave the lyre-bird its name. Your expanding concept of "bird" might lead you to learn about the pattern and variety of bird structures, their nesting habits, birds' eggs, feeding habits, migrations, their evolution probably from reptillian ancestors, extinct birds and much, much more.

By elaborating on the concept "bird" we have a good illustration of the vast number of related experiences that contribute to expanding knowledge and an increasingly more accurate concept about one familiar object in our global environment. Sensations, recalled percepts or memories, mental images of things not actually present to the senses at the moment all enter into the complex process called concept building.

We discuss this process because it is essentially the process of education. Concepts develop out of related perceptual experiences and as a result of the child's reorganization of his experiences to solve a problem or to express himself creatively.

The teacher who is aware of the way concepts are developed will seek continuously to provide children with a wide variety of sensory experiences. Children learn first through perceptions; their sensory equipment provides the means through which they observe their world. Not solely through vision, on which education has relied far too much, but on all the senses—through hearing, smelling, tasting, and through handling and manipulating objects.

The teacher at any level of the elementary school enters the life of a child at a point in a continuum in the process of concept development. All children at every stage of development have been acquiring concepts. They have been perceiving the world around them, and attempting to relate to it. They have modified, corrected, or enlarged their concepts through each relevant experience.

Sometimes we forget that when a child is born he knows nothing about the world, people, his relation to that world, what to do, and how to make it yield what he must have to satisfy his basic human needs. All he will ever know he must learn. What he learns will depend upon his experiences, because experience is the basis of all learning. A child can learn to know and do *only what he has access to through experience.*

Every human being has a life-space, an area of the world with which he comes into contact. What this life-space contains, the people in it, what they do, how they act, how they feel, how they speak is the culture the child internalizes. Only as his life-space is expanded by family trips; by experiences his home, school, and community provide for him; the motion pictures or television programs he sees; his opportunity for personal exploration of his community; or by talking and reading can he acquire knowledge beyond his immediate life-space. And he will interpret whatever he hears or reads about beyond his life-space in terms of the word meanings, concepts, and attitudes learned in it.

Nothing is more important to the teacher than to understand the essential relationship between the child's life-space and what the child himself knows, does, says, thinks, feels, and understands. Let us not expect all children of the same age to know more or less the same things, have the same interests, think and feel in the same way, and associate the same meaning with words. Children's life-spaces and the ways in which people within their life-spaces act, think, feel, and believe are dramatically varied, with the result that children vary widely in their concepts, attitudes, ways of acting, language patterns, and skills.

We see concepts as providing the material for children's thinking. They develop slowly from percepts, mental images, and need verbal symbols attached to them to make them manageable by a child. We see children arriving at, expanding, and correcting concepts by an inductive process.

The nursery school is not too early to begin to develop concepts leading to basic understandings of the structure of science (2). To understand about

1. Variety and pattern in living and nonliving things
2. Continuity and change and that continual change occurs with living and nonliving things
3. Interaction and interdependence that occurs among living organisms and nonliving things
4. Evolutionary development where changes have occurred over a long period of time and continue to occur among living and nonliving things.

Gerald Craig has said, "The question of how much of the content of science is taught is not of nearly so great importance as is the question of *what* is taught, *how* it is taught, and the *purpose* for which it is taught."

The Head Start program, begun in the summer of 1965, has offered young preschool children an enriched program of educational experiences. Fortunately, for their science education, these babes cannot read. Their educative experiences, therefore, do not need to be restricted by the limitations imposed by their mastery of printed symbols. They learn directly from the realities of their environment and follow the discovery-exploration-experimental approach to learning which educators generally extol.

Neither children nor teachers in the Head Start program are expected to know about science, but science learning goes on as children observe and talk about the behavior of frogs, or ducks, or chickens, or guinea pigs, or tortoises, or guppies, or any of the animals encountered on study trips.

As Dr. Craig points out, our success in helping young children to understand their scientific environment does not depend primarily upon specific *content* selected. The content is limitless and can be explored to any depth the interest of children take them. No teacher could possibly know all the facts of science but she can know the sources of data and the process by which needed information can be secured.

With young children the real success comes as a result of the skills of the teacher in arranging an environment that

1. Opens up new experiences about weather, seasons, temperature, variety in plants and animals
2. Impels children to observe carefully and to formulate significant questions
3. Encourages them to discover for themselves
4. Leads them to gain new *ideas* and *feelings*
5. Excites them to express their ideas and feeling in words, in construction, in painting, in modeling, in dramatic play, in rhythmic expression.

Where there is zest, meaning, and depth in the science experiences the skills of the language arts and mathematics fall into their proper relations. Education has in the past focused inordinately on the *skills* of learning. We need an about-face and a focus on all the wonderful *content* which makes this a world of wonders.

Well-Designed Materials

Well-designed curriculum materials are needed for use by teachers who are not and can not become specialists in science. Such curriculum should be organized in terms of a sequence of science experiences appropriate for three, four, and five year olds. Each experience should be clearly presented as a separate unit showing the materials needed to carry on appropriate activities in which children may engage, types of questions designed to result in concept formation and thinking and variations in the opportunities for learning related to the major purpose of the experience.

For example, suppose the activity proposed were gardening, the materials suggested would include short shovels, hand rakes, hoes, watering pot, and seeds, such as carrot, radish, sweet pea. The suggestion to the teacher might include use with the children of *Carrot Seed* by Ruth Kraus and *Up Above and Down Below* by Irma Webber. The teacher's questions during the activity would concern preparation of soil, depth to plant seeds, putting in seeds, watering. Later the children would return to the garden for weeding, watering, and talk about the growth of their plants. The unit might suggest other experiences such as: growing plants indoors and exposing them to various amounts of sunshine, giving plants varying amounts of water. Each child might have a piece of sponge in which grass seeds are grown; they might grow plants from bulbs and cuttings according to the season.

In addition to the preparation of explicit curriculum material for use by teachers, well-qualified science educators are needed to work in programs set up for training assistants to work with young children in nursery school and in child-care or child-development programs.

In this new expansion of educational experience to the very young, are to be found unparalleled opportunities for research in selection of curriculum content and use of scientific processes in teaching. My hypothesis here is that if we based a preschool program on significant firsthand science experiences so children had faith in their own observations and conclusions based on experience we would then have a far more meaningful and much less bookish science program through the elementary school. In an effort to answer the demand for a standard or pattern of effective science courses in the elementary school, over twenty or more groups of scientists and educators are experimenting with new elementary science curriculum programs.

Presently, many of the individual units produced by these groups are excellent, but they represent unorganized fragments of the broad scope upon which a program having continuity depends. Therefore, for the future, professional organizations are challenged to set up task forces to coordinate current promising efforts and expand science education experimentation to the end that science education throughout the nation achieves horizontal coherence and vertical continuity. The challenges at this moment lie chiefly in an intensive study of science education and in providing present teachers with the time and leadership essential to measure up to the changing, emerging, dynamic, creative world of which they are a part.

References

(1) Fish, Alphoretta. Ph.D. diss., University of Maryland, 1965.
(2) *Science Curriculum Development in the Elementary School.* Sacramento, Calif.: California State Department of Education, 1964, pp. 12–13.
(3) Strasser, Ben, "A Conceptual Model of Instruction Evolves as a Way to Study Interaction Processes," Parts I and II. *Curriculum Exchange,* 8, February and March 1966. Los Angeles County Superintendent of Schools Office, Los Angeles, Calif.

23

FORMULATING OBJECTIVES FOR ELEMENTARY SCIENCE

Ronald D. Anderson

BEHAVIORAL OBJECTIVE FOR THIS ARTICLE—Using reference materials such as elementary school science curriculum guides and textbooks, teachers should be able to write one or more objectives for each science lesson that they teach which have the following characteristics:

1. They are behavioral.
2. They give the conditions under which the behavior is expected.
3. They give the minimum acceptable level of performance.
4. They include all the desired outcomes of instruction.

The Key to Good Evaluation

The objectives of an instructional program and the program's evaluation are intimately related. Without well-stated objectives there is no basis for making any judgment as to whether or not the program has achieved the desired goals (objectives). Before examining evaluation practices and procedures, it is first necessary for us, as teachers, to be sure we have a set of objectives which is an adequate basis for our evaluation.

Reprinted from "Evaluation in Elementary School Science, Part I." *Science and Children*, 5, September 1967, pp. 20–27. Dr. Ronald D. Anderson is an Associate Professor of Science Education at the University of Colorado, Boulder, Colorado.

In this first of a series of two articles on evaluation, attention will be centered on the formulation of such objectives.

Stated objectives for elementary school science, as well as other parts of the curriculum, are found in abundance in textbooks, curriculum guides, and courses of study. In most cases, however, they are so general and vague that they are of little help to the classroom teacher either in determining what he will do in teaching science to his children at 10:25 a.m. Tuesday, or in evaluating the success of his efforts. For example, a frequently identified objective in science is that children should develop problem-solving skills. Although it is agreed that this is a worthwhile and important objective of science instruction, it is so general and vague that it is of little worth to a teacher in determining specifically what he will do with the children. Also this vagueness makes it almost impossible to determine at the end of a unit whether or not the objective has been achieved. In sharp contrast to the above-mentioned objective is this specific one concerning observation and classification: Each child will be able to separate a group of twelve different leaves into four groups according to their size and shape.

At this point some readers are probably asking, "Why be so specific?" The answer is simple. Unless an objective is stated precisely, it is not clear what steps should be taken to achieve the objective. Some teachers teach science only because it is part of the school program or because it has always been taught in their school. They have not stopped to consider carefully *why* science is taught. Whereas, the reasons why science is part of the curriculum determine what aspects of science will be emphasized, what approach will be used, and what objectives will be realized. Without clearly defined reasons, which in turn determine the objectives, teachers have no basis for deciding the questions of "what aspects" and "how." A broad objective such as "to develop problem-solving ability" may be a good starting point but it must be broken down into a more detailed description before decisions are made about "what aspects" and "how" for classroom use. In the grouping of leaves activity, the broad objective has not been rejected, only stated in much greater detail, i.e., classifying objects is part of solving some problems.

Basically, science is included in the curriculum because it is such a large and influential part of our culture. Of course, science is much more than a body of knowledge about the material universe. To understand science, one must understand the process of science (the means of investigation by which the body of knowledge is acquired) as well as the products of science (the body of knowledge that results from the investigations). Since a basic objective is for children to understand science, our specific objectives for each unit or day should reflect this basic and far-reaching objective. The precise objectives that are formulated for each class period should reflect the fact that a basic and overriding objective is that children will acquire an understanding of both the products and processes of the scientific enterprise.

Make Provision for all Objectives

A basic consideration in preparing objectives is that provision must be made for instruction in and evaluation of all the important desired outcomes of science instruction. The stated objectives which serve as the basis for instruction and evaluation should reflect all of the desired outcomes. A brief look at a classification of educational objectives might be useful in determining if the objectives are limited and unimaginative. Such a classification is Bloom's *Taxonomy of Educational Objectives* (1). In this scheme, all objectives have been classified into one of three "domains"—*cognitive, affective,* and *psychomotor.* The objectives which are generally given most attention by the teacher of elementary science fall within the cognitive domain, which includes the recognition and recall of information and also the development of various intellectual abilities. Many of the objectives which are included in textbooks and curriculum guides, but to which teachers less often direct their teaching, are part of the affective domain. These pertain to the development of attitudes, values, interest, and appreciation. Physical, manipulative, and motor abilities are part of the psychomotor domain.

Since the cognitive domain receives most attention, it will be examined here in greater detail. A look at the various levels of this domain will give some insight into the level of sophistication of objectives.

The first and lowest level in the cognitive domain is the *knowledge* level. It includes the recall of specifics (e.g. ice is a form of water), structures (e.g. the skeletal structure of vertebrates), or scientific processes (e.g. a control is an important part of an experiment). The knowledge level emphasizes that which would be described as remembering. Of course, the examples given here could be understood at a deeper level. They are classified at this level if it is only a matter of being able to remember the information rather than a deeper understanding such as being able to apply it to a new situation or synthesizing several items of knowledge. These deeper understandings are dealt with in other levels of this classification system. The entire taxonomy is a hierarchy in which each lower level of understanding is necessary before understanding at the next higher level is possible.

The second level is *comprehension* which includes translation from one form to another. Examples would be drawing a graph of daily temperature changes from a list of temperatures recorded over a period of days or weeks, or explaining verbally what is meant by a statement which is expressed in mathematical symbols.

Application, which is the third level, requires the ability to apply abstract ideas in a concrete situation. Examples would be the ability to use a knowledge of the relationship between heat and the expansion and contraction of liquids to explain how a thermometer works, use a knowledge of classification to classify a group of seashells according to size, shape, or color, or use a knowledge of electric circuits to cause a light bulb to light using a cell, bulb, and pieces of wire.

Analysis, the fourth level, involves breaking down an idea into its various parts and determining the relationship between the parts. Determining which statements about an experiment are facts and which are hypotheses, or determining which factors led to an unexpected conclusion of any experiment would be examples.

Synthesis, the fifth level, includes taking parts and putting them together to form a whole such as skill in expressing verbally or in writing the results of an experiment using an appropriate organization of ideas. Other examples would be formulating a hypothesis to explain why some animals are less active in the daytime than at night or why water poured on a fire will often put out the fire.

Evaluation, the highest of the six levels in the cognitive domain, includes making judgments. An example is the ability to state the fallacies in an analysis of an experiment. Another example is the ability to evaluate popular beliefs about health.

The reason for looking at this classification of objectives is to gain some insight into the sophistication of the objectives we actually are endeavoring to reach in our teaching. Is teaching aimed at the remembering of facts and ideas or are children expected to be able to apply these facts and ideas? Do some children arrive at junior high school without having been challenged to analyze, synthesize, or evaluate ideas? Do the children gain a greater interest in science or a better appreciation of its place in society? If this classification of objectives has caused the readers to think critically about the objectives of their science program, it has served the purpose for which it was included here.

Objectives Should Be Behavioral

So far, it has been pointed out that objectives should be specific, in keeping with the area of study at hand, and not be limited to the knowledge level. In addition, objectives should be stated in a manner that permits a judgment about the attainment of the objectives. To make this possible, objectives should be stated in terms of the behaviors which will be exhibited by the children. Objectives stated in this form are often spoken of as behavioral objectives or performance objectives. Behavioral objectives have been talked about for years, but recently they have received renewed and closer attention. For example, *Preparing Instructional Objectives*, a small book by Mager (2), is devoted entirely to the "how" of writing good behavioral objectives. *Science—A Process Approach* (3), the experimental elementary science program sponsored by the American Association for the Advancement of Science, has behavioral objectives set up for each lesson in the program. In addition to providing a basis for the teacher's efforts in aiding student learning, the behavioral objectives provide the basis for the extensive evaluation which is being conducted by the sponsors of the program.

In order to understand what is meant by a behavioral objective, let us look at some of the basic ideas presented by Mager. First of all, an appropriate objective is *not* a description of what the lesson is about, but is a statement of what the learner will be able to *DO* at the end of the learning activity. For example, "a study of the kinds of materials that are attracted by magnets" is a description of what is to be included in a certain science lesson. It is not an objective. In contrast, although in some ways incomplete, the following is an objective: "At the conclusion of this lesson the children will be able to state what kinds of materials are attracted by magnets." It describes what the children will be able to do. Thus, the first step in formulating good behavioral objectives is deciding what the child should be *DOING* when the instruction has been successful.

A key to writing good objectives is the verb which describes what the child will be able to do. Some are vague and open to many interpretations. Others have clarity and convey a definite meaning. Consider carefully the [accompanying] chart of examples from Mager (2, p. 11) . . .

Words Open to Many Interpretations	Words Open to Fewer Interpretations
to know	to write
to understand	to recite
to *really* understand	to identify
to appreciate	to differentiate
to fully appreciate	to solve
to grasp the significance of	to construct
to enjoy	to list
to believe	to compare
to have faith in	to contrast

There is nothing wrong with teaching children to "understand" and "enjoy," but clear communication of ideas requires that objectives be stated in terms of what they will be *DOING* that indicates they "understand" or "enjoy." How else will teachers know if children are "understanding" or "enjoying"?

After determining what behaviors are the object of instruction, a second major question can be considered: Under what conditions will these behaviors be observed? The answer to the question will progress one step further toward a precisely stated performance objective. Consider this objective: At the end of this lesson, the child should be able to identify constellations in the night sky. Does it state the conditions under which the objective is to be reached?

It does not indicate whether the child is expected to make the identification with or without the aid of a star chart or other references. It does not state whether the student is given a list of the names and asked to assign these names to the appropriate constellation or whether the student is expected to produce the names from memory. Therefore, the objective should be restated.

A third major question that should be considered in formulating performance objectives is "How well is the child expected to perform?" or "What is the minimum acceptable level of performance?" Look again at the objective above on identifying constellations in the night sky. Is the objective stated in such a way that this kind of question is answered? It does not tell *how many* constellations the child is expected to identify. Also, in the case of some objectives, it may be desirable to indicate *how long* the child has to attain the objective.

Now the objective concerning identification of constellations can be restated in a more precise form: At the end of this lesson the child should be able to identify at least five constellations when given a star chart as a guide. This objective answers the three basic questions: What is the behavior? What are the conditions? and What is the minimum acceptable level of performance?

Can Objectives Be Made Behavioral?

Readers are no doubt asking "Can all of our objectives be stated in behavioral form with the conditions and minimum level of performance clearly indicated?" It may not always be easy. For example, a common objective of science education is the development of interest in science. It must be asked what behaviors on the part of the child will indicate that this interest is present. Would behaviors such as reading books on science, visiting a local science museum, or building a simple telescope for observing the stars and planets be indicators of this interest? Difficulties may be encountered in giving the *conditions* and *minimum level* of performance for such an objective, but the objectives can be framed in terms that will allow teachers to make judgments on the basis of student performance. A teacher's objective might be: the child will pursue his interest in astronomy by such means as, reading library books on astronomy, visiting the local museum, and making night-sky observations.

As another example, there is certainly a place in the elementary school science curriculum for free exploration on the part of children, such as "playing around" with magnets in an undirected fashion or observing mealworms for an extended period of time without definite directions concerning what they should observe. Such activities often lead to the posing of interesting questions and interesting hypotheses that might answer the questions as well as creating means of testing hypotheses. Objectives for such activities should reflect *why* the children are being encouraged in this direction. Objectives might be: by the end of the class the child will have posed two or more questions concerning magnets, or by the end of the class the child will have posed two or more hypotheses as possible answers to questions concerning the behavior of mealworms, or the child will design an experiment for testing a hypothesis concerning the behavior of mealworms. Here again, there may be some difficulties stating conditions and minimum levels, but the children's behavior can be used as the referent in determining if the activity was worthwhile. It must be granted that educators cannot always state their objectives as precisely as they would like, but they can certainly do better than they often have done in the past.

Objectives are dynamic not static. They are based on more than the structure of the subject and thus they change as a result of experience with children in the classroom. The teacher may find that an object is not realistic in view of the level of maturity of the children or a classroom experience may suggest a different objective which is more profitable to pursue than the one originally stated. It is necessary to begin by carefully specifying objectives, but to be flexible enough to alter them as experience indicates. Careful stating of objectives provides an aid to the clear thinking and planning which must continue throughout the duration of the science instruction.

This article has been concerned with the formulation of objectives for the elementary school science curriculum. After they are formulated, the next step is to teach to attain these objectives. That is the job of the reader. The next article in this series will deal with using meaningful objectives as a basis for evaluating the success of the teaching [see this volume, pp. 244–50].

References

(1) Bloom, Benjamin S. (ed.), *Taxonomy of Educational Objectives, The Classfication of Education Goals, Handbook I: Cognitive Domain.* New York: David McKay Company, Inc., 1956.

(2) Mager, Robert F., *Preparing Instructional Objectives.* Palo Alto, Calif.: Fearon Publishers, 1962.

(3) *Science—A Process Approach.* Washington, D.C.: American Association for the Advancement of Science, 1966.

24

HAS THE OBJECTIVE
BEEN ATTAINED?

Ronald D. Anderson

BEHAVIORAL OBJECTIVE FOR THIS ARTICLE—Using reference materials such as elementary school science curriculum guides and textbooks, teachers should be able to write one or more objectives for each science lesson that they teach which have the following characteristics:
1. They are behavioral.
2. They give the conditions under which the behavior is expected.
3. They give the minimum acceptable level of performance.
4. They include all the desired outcomes of instruction.

In Part I of this two-part article (*S&C*, September 1967, page 20) [see this volume, pp. 236–43], guidelines were given for formulating specific behavioral objectives (See box). In the first article attention also was called to the importance of formulating specific performance objectives for each day on which science is taught. Broad general objectives are important to give general guidelines, but if they are to serve as an adequate basis for planning either teaching or evaluation, they must be translated into specific objectives for each day. In fact, if specific objectives for the day are formed, a great deal of the planning for the teaching and evaluation already has been done. The evaluation, in particular, is aided by stating as part of an objective, the conditions

Reprinted from "Evaluation in Elementary School Science, Part II." *Science and Children*, 5, October 1967, pp. 33–36.

under which the behavior is expected and the minimum acceptable level of performance.

Reasons for Evaluation

The most important reason for conducting careful evaluation of the science program is to locate learning difficulties that individual children are encountering and aid them in overcoming these difficulties. To accomplish this purpose, the evaluation must be a continuous activity that is done each day and not put aside until the end of a unit when a formal evaluation is made. It may be difficult in a large classroom, but the teacher must continually attempt to determine what obstacles, if any, each child is encountering.

A second important reason for careful evaluation is to enable the teacher to change and alter her teaching practices and procedures in the manner that will best improve the learning situation. The idea that appeared promising before trying it in the classroom may, in practice, be a complete failure in terms of the objective it was expected to accomplish. Or possibly the objective itself is unreasonable when viewed with respect to the classroom experience. An evaluation at the end of the unit should show if the promising idea "fizzled." Here again, the continuous day-to-day evaluation of the teaching techniques is important so that revisions can take place.

A third reason for evaluation is as a base for reporting a child's progress to his parents and other members of the school staff who work with him. Usually this is referred to as grading, although the report may include more than just a grade. Grading or reporting of student progress is a matter of importance but is not our major concern. Even though it is one of the reasons for evaluation in elementary school science, the focus of this article is on the evaluation itself.

Types of Evaluation

It might be helpful to discuss two types of evaluation which can be referred to as informal and formal. Formal evaluation refers to paper-and-pencil tests, or other devices such as individual tasks which are administered uniformly to all the children in the class. This type of evaluation will be discussed in detail in the following sections. Much of a teacher's evaluation is more informal and is based upon her observations while the usual classroom activities are underway. The responses that children make to the teacher's questions and the questions that children ask are noted by the perceptive teacher. In addition to verbal statements and questions, the actions of children as they work with equipment provide important information for informal evaluation.

It is important that the teacher's informal evaluation be centered on those behaviors which are her objectives and that she not be unduly influenced by unrelated behaviors of the children. If one of the objectives for the day's work is that children be able to formulate hypotheses concerning a particular phenomenon, such as the breaking of rocks during freezing weather, the teacher should be listening for statements that indicate that a hypothesis has been suggested. The central objective is for the children to develop their ability to formulate hypotheses. The behavior that is indicative of this should be of major concern to the teacher rather than verbal fluency or discussion of the breaking of rocks in freezing weather which is unrelated to hypotheses concerning the phenomenon.

Informal evaluation of the type described above is dependent upon a certain type of teaching. The teacher who does not have much student involvement (for example, the discussion of thought-provoking questions), often is not in a position to observe student behaviors which are indicative of whether or not an objective has been reached. This indicates clearly the close "tie-in" between objectives, teaching, and evaluation. Ample evidence is available to show that student involvement is important for science teaching, particularly for objectives related to the processes of science. This student involvement also is important for the informal evaluation in which a teacher evaluates on the basis of what students *DO* on a day-to-day basis. What is good teaching practice also is generally advantageous for evaluation.

Cover All Objectives

The more formal evaluations such as paper-and-pencil tests should be planned carefully to insure that all objectives are given proper attention and that the measurement planned actually does measure the stated objectives. The first step, specifying the objectives, was discussed in the first article. It is well to remember, however, that teaching is a very dynamic and flexible activity, and as a result of interaction with the children, the objectives may have been altered or given a different emphasis. Now that preparations are being made for the evaluation, it is time to consider again exactly what goals *have* been sought.

The next step is to weight the various objectives according to the relative emphasis given to them during the teaching. For example, if two days were spent on the measurement of temperature and one day on formulating hypotheses concerning the change of state of water from one form to the other, the former should receive twice as much emphasis in the evaluation. If it is a paper-and-pencil test, the number of items or questions should be in proportion to the time spent on the objectives which they are designed to measure.

A crucial step is the selection of the evaluation technique which will be used to measure the various objectives. The technique used is dependent upon the nature of the objective. Many teachers use a particular type, e.g. an objective paper-and-pencil test, regardless of their objectives. Sometimes a particular evaluation technique is appropriate; many times it is not. This teacher then asks herself, "What are some items that are related to the topics that have been considered?" There are at least two things wrong with this approach. First, the achievement of the objective at hand may not be measurable with this technique. Second, just because the test items chosen are on the same topic as the objectives, does not insure that the items actually measure the students' achievement of the specific objectives.

The first type of error is shown by the following example. One of the objectives for a unit is that children should be able to classify a group of leaves into three groups on the bases of color, size, or shape. Paper-and-pencil items are probably not the most appropriate means of evaluating whether or not this objective has been achieved. In this case, each child could be given a group of leaves and asked to classify them. It may be possible to devise paper-and-pencil items using pictures that test such an ability, but a teacher is more likely to devise a means of measuring the stated objectives by the above technique than by objective test items which she devises.

The second type of error is shown by a teacher's evaluation of the following objective: Given data showing the daily fluctuations in temperature over a two-week period, the child should be able to construct a graph which shows the relationship between time and temperature. In this case the teacher constructed this true-false item which referred to a graph of time versus temperature: The graph above shows the relationship between time and temperature. This item was on the same topic as the objective, yet it was not a measure of the students' achievement of the objective. The item required that the student be able to determine what had been plotted on the graph, but the objective stated that the child should be able to construct a graph. In this case, it would have been more appropriate to give the student some data and ask him to construct a graph.

Variety of Formal Evaluation Techniques

Two main types of formal evaluation techniques have been referred to thus far—paper-and-pencil tests and the systematic use of situations in which individual children are presented a situation which includes the use of material objects. The latter type is used very extensively in the evaluation program of *Science—A Process Approach* (2). Each child is individually presented with a standard situation and given specific directions for indicating his responses on a check sheet. Some of their items and the objectives they were designed to access will serve as good examples of this evaluation technique.

One of the objectives for a lesson on color in Book One is that the child should be able to "identify the following colors by sight: yellow, orange, red, purple, blue, and green" (2, Book One, p.1). A competency measure designed to assess the achievement of this objective has the following directions:

> Show the child each of three blocks—a yellow (1), a red (2), and a blue (3) one, and say to the child, WHAT IS THE COLOR OF THIS BLOCK? Repeat for all three blocks. One check should be given in the acceptable column for each correct name (2, Competency Measures, Parts One and Two, p. 11).

In Book Four is a lesson on communicating entitled "Describing an Experiment." The objectives of this lesson are:

> The child should be able to describe any one of the following portions of an experiment which he has just observed or conducted:
> 1. The question to be answered.
> 2. The method or approach used
> 3. The apparatus and procedures used
> 4. The results obtained, as observed
> 5. The answer to the original question (2, Book Four, p. 95)

The competency measure designed to assess the achievement of this objective is as follows:

> Tell the child: I AM GOING TO EXPERIMENT TO SEE WHAT HAPPENS TO A PENCIL FLOATING IN WATER WHEN SALT IS ADDED TO THE WATER. I WANT YOU TO WATCH ME CAREFULLY SO THAT YOU WILL BE ABLE TO DESCRIBE WHAT I DID. Fill the test tube with water and place a pencil in the tube. Place the test tube next to a ruler and record the reading either at the bottom or the top of the pencil. Pour salt (two tablespoons) into the test tube and record the reading again. (Change in level will be about one half centimeter.) Ask the child: WRITE DOWN OR TELL ME IN WORDS ALL THAT YOU CAN ABOUT THIS EXPERIMENT. Give him one check for each of the following steps that he includes:
> 1. Question to be answered
> 2. Proposed method or approach
> 3. Apparatus and procedures required
> 4. Results obtained, as observed
> 5. Answer to the original question (2, Competency Measures, Parts Three and Four, p. 85)

Note some characteristics of these examples. In contrast to informal evaluation, this is a carefully defined standard situation which is the same for each child. There is a close correlation between the stated objectives and the items used for evaluation. It is apparent that the evaluation items were designed specifically to measure the corresponding stated objective. Also, these items are not dependent upon either the child's reading or writing ability. In both cases the child does not read anything. In the second example the child may write his answer but only if he prefers this method to telling the teacher his answer.

An obvious difficulty with this type of evaluation is the time required to administer the assessment to each child in the class individually. On the other hand, its freedom from dependence on writing and reading ability gives it an advantage over paper-and-pencil tests. The reading difficulty of paper-and-pencil tests is a major problem when employing them at the elementary school level. Both varieties of assessment devices have their advantages and disadvantages. In choosing between them the basic question should be, "What can I use that will determine if my objective has been attained?" As a result, an assessment of the student's achievement over a fairly long period of time will probably include some of both types.

The situation evaluation technique, with some modifications, can be used with groups of children rather than individuals. When used with groups, the children generally are required to give their responses on paper rather than verbally. This is a useful form of evaluation in that it combines the flexibility of the situation technique with the efficiency of paper-and-pencil tests. Because of these dual advantages, some teachers find this technique to be the most useful of all the evaluation techniques which they employ.

The higher the grade level, the more paper-and-pencil tests are likely to be employed. This is understandable, since as the child's reading and writing abilities increase, the better able he is to respond to this kind of examination. At present it is the most widely used type of evaluation for elementary school science. Since science is being tested, every effort should be made to reduce the influence of the child's reading ability upon his score. This influence is greater than most teachers realize. One helpful procedure is to project the test on a screen with an overhead projector and read each item to the children as they respond to the questions on their own copy of the test. With the modern equipment which many schools have today it is relatively easy to make an overhead projector transparency of any printed material.

The construction of good essay, matching, true-false, completion or multiple choice items is not a simple matter. An adequate discussion of this topic would require far more space than is available here. For helpful information on the construction of good items, the reader is referred to one of the many good books in this area such as those written by Stanley (3) or Ebel (1). If the reader is not thoroughly familiar with the principles of constructing good test items, he should spend time studying the relevant chapter or chapters of such a book.

In summary, the key to good evaluation is carefully defining objectives and then devising a means of determining if the objectives have been achieved through informal and formal evaluation.

References

(1) Ebel, Robert L., *Measuring Educational Achievement*. Englewood Cliffs, N. J.: Prentice-Hall, Inc., 1965.

(2) *Science—A Process Approach*. Washington, D. C.: Amerian Association for the Advancement of Science, 1965 and 1966.

(3) Stanley, Julian C., *Measurement in Today's Schools*, 4th ed. Englewood Cliffs, N. J.: Prentice-Hall, Inc., 1964.

25

THINGS YOU HAVE ALWAYS WANTED TO KNOW ABOUT VALUES— BUT WERE AFRAID TO ASK

Robert Samples

"The value structure of the teacher cannot be divorced from what goes on in the classroom."

If I express one of the values by which I live to you, I am stating a prejudice. All values are prejudice postures. When dealing with value education it is common among educators today to talk about the psychology of the cognitive and affective domains. In a widely accepted way there is a tendency to utilize the psychology of the cognitive domain to relate to specific kinds of intellectualized learning. This has been championed by Piaget, Bruner, Gagné, and a variety of others who have strongly influenced American education. The affective domain is far hazier although many of the tenets of the research in cognitive psychology are now being applied to the affective. Generally, most educators tend to think of the affective as the domain of values, of feelings, and of all of those ambivalent qualities Bruner, in the mid-fifties, reflected upon in a book called *Essays for the Left Hand.*

Much of the research and interpretation of the cognitive and affective domain seems to cast the cognitive as the hard, able-to-be-researched, easier-to-translate kind of educational content. The affective, on the other hand, has appeared to be more elusive. When getting into the realm of feelings, values, and emotions even the hard core researchers trained in the more behavioristic theories find it very difficult to keep their values, feelings, and emotions out of research.

Reprinted from *Colorado Journal of Educational Research, 11,* Fall 1971, pp. 12–17.

In a strange way I see what is going on in research of the affective domain to be something like the Heisenberg principle in physics. The position and velocity of an electron cannot be defined simultaneously because in determining the position or velocity of the object it changes its position or velocity. Once the position is changed the velocity cannot be determined. What I think we are dealing with in the arena of the affective will defy an application of the research strategies that are consistent with cognitive models.

In 1964 in the *Journal of Abnormal and Social Psychology,* Carl Rogers wrote an article entitled, "Toward A Modern Approach to Values, The Valuing Process in the Mature Person." In this article Rogers dealt with three kinds of values. He talked about *operative values, conceived values* and *objective values.* The operative values generally turn out to be those values that just allow us to function in a day-to-day existence. They tend to be the result of a sense of concern for personal preferences and attitudes as opposed to a great deal of concern for others. The conceived values generally turn out to be the values an individual develops after some degree of intellectual involvement and has codified so they can be communicated to others. In addition, I feel there is a compulsion on the part of the individual to communicate these values. These can turn out to be generalization but they are almost always focused on someone else's relationship to the individual possessing them. The objective values are more global value postures that would represent well-thought-out social consensus positions regarding particular group value preferences. In general, it would appear the objective values would be ones which tend to have certain universal acceptance within a culture and would have a specificity more closely allied to that culture.

My earlier application of the word prejudice to the categories of value structures can now be understood in a different light. In the first category of values, the operative ones, I feel the function of the individual is to exercise certain extremely personal preferential prejudices in expressing the values he considers to be operative. Many of these are based on experience and have a great deal to do with personal pain or pleasure. That these tend to have little connection with broader based value structures does not make them any less a prejudice posture. For example, that I like long hair on girls or the smell of lilacs has little to do with larger or more inclusive categories of values. However, if I were asked to list a characteristic of girls I liked the most, or to cite my favorite flower, I might well express the two values just cited. Ordinarily, neither of these have the capacity to be turned into "isms", such as "long-hairism" and "lilacism". To do so would be to elevate them to a posture that would require other people to be assessed by my standards. All of the values I possess

.

in this first category are generally capricious, have had to do with personal experiences and are deeply ingrained in an extremely personal prejudice field of my own. My personal behavior usually betrays these to people in my presence.

Before moving on to the other categories it would be well to acknowledge I am using prejudice in a broader sense than the term is ordinarily used. The purpose for this use should be obvious. Prejudice is a negatively loaded word. For a very long time we as educators have been choosing very polite researchable terms to deal with human interaction and human existence. The politeness of our choices very often kept real issues at arm's length and the result has been that we have never dealt with fundamentally important issues. When dealing with curriculum and teaching strategies in the last ten years, much of the effort of educators has been to verify the results of research done in the cognitive domain. A frighteningly small percentage of the effort expended has been to deal directly with the children, their feelings, growth, and development. I know dozens of educators, in all parts of the country who, when upon entering a classroom, look furtively around to find some behavior that verifies a premise that they learned in graduate school. *Prejudice is the word I want to use.*

Conceived values are more generalized and more generalizable. They tend to be the result of direct human experience with other human beings and other characteristically human activities. An example Carl Rogers uses has to do with honesty. Dishonest responses to another person's attempt to communicate often lead to frustration, hurt feelings, anxieties, and a variety of other human ills. Because this tends to create a rather negative situation, a value that Rogers cites that could well be an outgrowth of this is "honesty is the best policy." Generally, this middle ground of values tends to relate to the sort of interaction we have with other human beings within a social context. The generalizations often can be codified into statements. These then are carried along as a rule of conduct, so to speak, that tends to affect the way we interact with other people. There is a certain management quality in this category of values that is absent in the first. Since the conception of these values tend to have involved other human beings, they very definitely take them into consideration. As a result there is a stabilizing influence to these values. The result is they have a generalizability that can be applied to more than one person. They tend to make sense to more than one person and as a result they can begin to influence the behavior of groups of people toward each other.

Fairness emerges as one of the important characteristics of this category. From the concept of fairness can grow seeds of competition. In a sense, attempts to carry out values in this category lead to a kind of interpersonal competitiveness within the realm of values. If

I believe, for instance, honesty is the best policy then I may well try to be more honest than other people. My prejudice towards this concept may make me competitively hard to deal with. Whereas it is very difficult for me to compete with other people on the basis of my preference for lilacs it is very easy for me to compete with other people on the basis of my preference for honesty or politeness or any other characteristic of this category.

Rogers' objective values are ones that generally tend to result from consensus positions of large numbers of people. These values are societally voted upon so to speak. Although there is no overt attempt to engage everyone in a society to put these values together, usually certain selected spokesmen, sages, philosophers, and politicians, tend to cite which of the values provide the greatest guarantee for survival for that particular society. Currently we have found ourselves in an ecological value argument that varies depending upon the expert. The crisis is imminent enough that we are alerted to the notion we are facing ecological chaos if certain things are not done.

Values in the third category are usually those values that appear in textbooks, in films, and other elements of the media intended to transmit the cultural heritage. These are the values with which the predominant number of social scientists are infatuated. They have made a scholarly profession out of their concern for these particular values.

In value education, as it is currently talked about by most people, these objective values are the ones which tend to dominate the thinking of people involved in the enterprise. The second category, the category of conceived values, is currently appearing in textbooks that have to do with problems between people and interpersonal relationships. Generally, these appear as stories which contain some value crisis between two textbook people. The students in the classroom are supposed to attempt to resolve the value conflict and come to a conclusion and thus have a greater awareness of their own value postures. Almost nothing is currently being done in classrooms for the first category of operative values, except teachers often tend to create the mandate that their own set of operational values be substituted for the ones the children brought with them.

Herein lies the deepest condemnation of any posture that currently exists in value education. The operative values are the values we live by. These are the ones through which we testify to other people on an extremely subtle level the nature of the prejudice field that has resulted in the value posture possessed by each of us as individual human beings. In the area of conceived values, the management values, we find value education in the schools, churches, homes, and other places being a suite of incredibly manipulative practices. For the convenience of management of groups of people, ground rules of behavior are developed to exercise the maximum amount of control with the minimum amount of risk. In the third category, values are disseminated in God-given flag-wrapped, survival-stamped packages. So grand and glorious are these very little of an individual's value system gets involved with them when approving or disapproving of them.

My prejudice for long-haired girls and lilacs is much closer to me than my prejudice for the notion that "honesty is the best policy," and incredibly closer to me than my prejudice for the protection of the bald eagle because he is the national bird. The values that are always closest to me are the ones that are fundamentally operative. As I have matured and grown in a profession and in the kinds of experiences I have had, I find very often values that once were in the conceptual area have become operative for me, but seldom for the reasons codified in the value statements as stated. Also, I have found values in the objective category have become operative for me but never for the reasons stated. In using the example of the bald eagle, it is not a great deal of concern for men that bald eagles are our national symbol and thus should be protected. My concern is that here is a living thing that is essentially part of a world I have experienced and have come to love and it has suffered from the vagaries of man. My value posture then would be to defend the protection extended to this bird on the basis of the fact *I simply like this bird.*

The internalization of the responsibility for assessing values tends to provide people in value education with another quandary. Rokeach, in his book *The Open and Closed Mind,* paints a vivid portrait of the way different people tend to respond to values and prejudice postures depending upon whether they have what he called an open mind or a closed mind. The categories of values cited by Rogers exist in both open and closed-minded people. However, one of the tendencies for close-minded people is to make *all* their values in *all* categories into veritable commandments.

This a compulsion that tends to be an effort to externalize the sources of decision making and of propriety. An open-minded person generally does quite the opposite. The open-minded person tends to internalize the sense of responsibility and propriety for the decisions he makes. As a result, there is far less of a tendency to worry about objective values *as they exist.* Instead, the person will tend to internalize the nature of the value decision and for all practical purposes moves it back through the categories so it becomes an operative value.

Because the focus of these value postures is so intangible there is a frightening challenge to those who are going to be involved in value education. The somewhat humorous and yet paranoiac demands upon educators, called "assessment and accountability," comes at the very moment in time when there is a growing realization that *value education is vital.* The enterprise faces the high risk of being conceived in a hostile womb. The majority of people who are supporting value education as a virtue *are doing so under the pretext of making value instruction a new content, a new indoctrination ground by which contemporary conceptual and objective values can be transmitted to young people.* In a sense, values have simply become the new content in just the same way some of physics became a new content with the advent of the PSSC. If this is done then accountability techniques will provide no problem because the values will have been turned into facts and these will be transmitted to the students through a variety of clever tactics. Accountability in value education will be easy because all that need be assessed are the facts. Simple stimulus-response recall will suffice.

The only problem with this whole argument is it has absolutely nothing to do with value education. The most frightening aspect of the value-as-content prejudice is it is consistent with prevailing evaluative procedures. If on the other hand values are to be included in the educational experience of young people, they can be treated in a very different way. There can be an approach to values by which the students would be encouraged to expose their own value structures in all three levels in a *non-evaluative* field. In such a non-evaluative environment students can honestly question each other, interact with adults, and induce an evolution in their own value postures without memorizing or role playing lists of conceptual and objective values. My particular prejudice is in such an environment the students would generally tend toward a more open value posture. A result of all of this would be a more accepting and more tolerant group of people.

Gordon Allport pointed out in *The Nature of Prejudices* that under the pressure of prejudice the resulting frustration tends to elicit a group of easily identifiable kinds of behavior in people who are being subjected to prejudice. The following is a list of these characteristics: Denial of membership in their own group; withdrawal and passivity; clowning; rebellion; competitiveness; enhanced striving; stealing; strengthening of in-group ties; slyness; obsessive concern and suspicion. If these are characteristic behaviors exhibited by people who are being subjected to prejudices, then educators must look upon this list with a great deal of chagrin, *because generally it typifies behavior viewed in most classroom situations.* My feeling the reason this kind of behavior exists is because most classrooms are highly prejudicial environments. The nature of the prejudice is usually determined by the teacher. The value structure of the teacher cannot be divorced from what goes on in the classroom. I was taught while in teacher training to spend a great deal of time divorcing myself from exhibiting my feelings and expressing emotions in the classroom. This resulted in a situation in which the children were responding to teachers as having no values and being unemotional and the result was this seemed to the kids to be a generally inhumane condition. The result was we, fortunately, lost this tendency in a hurry. Surprisingly enough there are many schools of education which are still preparing teachers to perform in classrooms fundamentally as robots. To guarantee this, the educational psychology courses the teachers take often convey the notion Skinnerian behaviorism and its pigeon pecking solutions to educational learning is the last word. I know of very few educational psychology courses that have anything to do with education. Most of them are research resumés that seldom even name people like Allport, Rogers, Perls, and Maslow.

Beyond the prejudices the teachers receive in their training while going through graduate school and undergraduate training, teachers, like all other human beings, are a hot bed of prejudices of their own making. Because we have come from a society in which the operative prejudices and operative values are considered to be fundamentally evil, we find the values of conceptual or management postures are highly rewarding. In addition the over-all societal values, perhaps more appropriately called cliché values, are the ones the teachers are led to believe have the greatest amount of virtue. The result is that when a teacher comes into a classroom, he often tries to divorce himself from the value posture that represents him as an individual person and attempts to role play the appropriate management and the societal values in the name of "value education." This would probably work if it weren't for the fact that the kids are too turned on in the 1970s to be fooled by it. The hypocrisy of the teacher's posture tends to negate any validity in communicating values in a positive sense.

Work O. J. Harvey has done at the University of Colorado related to the core personality postures of teachers has demonstrated some surprising results. Harvey has devised a series of assessment strategies that allow trained psychological observers to watch teachers and determine from the nature of the values they expose, and the way they expose them, what the teacher's probable core personality is. On the basis of his inventive categories, Harvey found a great deal of correlation between certain kinds of behavior and the characteristics of the personality cores. The observers for this task were rather highly trained and carefully screened to be able to objectify their observations. In work done later, Harvey found, much to his delight and surprise, that when the particular traits were put in the vocabulary of the students, the students were as accurate in commenting about the teacher's core personality as were the trained psychological observers. Thus values are transparent to everyone but the person transmitting them.

To summarize the basic points of this paper I would say the first assumption is that values are prejudices. Regardless of the category of the value, whether operative, conceptual, or objective, *the retention* _of that particular value is the responsibility of the person who possesses it._ That I have been force-fed a particular value does not remove me from facing the responsibility that _I am the one who is fundamentally retaining it._ Since operative values are incredibly subtle and highly personal, it is impossible for anyone in his everyday involvement with others not to expose these particular values. As a result there are hundreds of things we do each day that tend to expose our value posture to other human beings. This exposure expresses many of our prejudices. They are read and interpreted by other people who come within our presence. In classrooms, as well as in everyday life, if we were to take the posture that treated values as prejudices and accepted the responsibility for keeping them it would be easier to relate to other people as human beings. _Individualized instruction must assume individualized value schemes._ I feel only through preparing teachers and supporting them in the recognition of this particular posture will value education ever become a reality in our schools. In attempting to communicate these ideas to teachers by working through the basis of _prejudice_ as opposed to the hierarchies of the affective or cognitive domains, I have sensed a greater amount of communication.

Whereas cognitive education was the shibboleth of the 60's, I fear that value education can become the banner slogan for the 70's. To be consistent with the terminology of this article the cognitive domain was the prejudice of the 60's, the affective domain will probably be the prejudice of the 70's. A spin-off aspect of the prejudice of the cognitive researchers is many of the research characteristics consistent with study in the cognitive doman are currently being applied to the affective. I fear this will have a diluting influence. _Research models can be incredible filters of relevant information in exactly the same way evaluation is an incredible filter of reality._ The demand for accountability can be one of the most devastating influences in education in current times. Generally, the only people who are infatuated with accountability are legislators and the educational technicians whose whole professional and personal posture resides in measurement. I sometimes feel the research community provides the greatest lobby for confinement in education practice. But this is a prejudice I feel only when I sense the constriction imposed upon educational progress by demands for accountability. I do not feel measurement or accountability are inherently bad, but until we move steadily toward a view of the human condition more like the view held by Carl Rogers and Abraham Maslow and less like E. L. Thorndike and B. F. Skinner—then I will continue to be suspicious of some educators' faith in measurement as opposed to a faith in man. In closing I would add _love is a positive prejudice._

26

VALUE CLARIFICATION FROM SCIENCE TEACHING

J. Bruce Shattuck

Immediately after the launching of Sputnik I in October of 1957, the field of science education was filled with revision tremors. Unfortunately, desirable changes in our schools seem only to occur when a threat to the national security seems imminent.

Most of the changes in science education took the form of a dual attempt. There was first an increase in the quantity of subject matter taught. This was followed by an attempt to reestablish the grade level in which various topics would be covered. An all too common educational process then occurred—we took what was formerly taught within the domain of the senior high schools, added more "depth," and handed the package to the junior high schools. The junior high schools then repeated the same skillful process and handed their package to the elementary schools, and so on.

The results, at least from a superficial point of view, were positive. Students were doing more science and more experiments. There were all kinds of funds available to purchase equipment. Children now knew the distance and diameter of Venus. Teachers were improving their skills by enrolling in courses such as quantum mechanics and igneous petrology.

At this time it might be appropriate to take more than a cursory glance at some of the "positive" results.

Reprinted from *Science and Children*, 8, April 1971, pp. 16–18. Dr. J. Bruce Shattuck was associated with Michigan State University, East Lansing, Michigan, at the time this article was published.

Students *were* doing more science. At least they were doing more reading in science. They were reading about science and not doing it. This is analogous to attempting to teach a person to ski by having him read the best books rather than trying the slopes. Experientially, a science program that centers around textbooks offers little.

The second positive result was that there were more experiments being conducted in the classrooms. The teacher would stand in front of the room and state an hypothesis that had previously been proven several times, thus nullifying the possibility of it actually being an hypothesis. Then proceeding with steps 1–5 in numerical order so as not to violate the scientific method, the teacher would finish with the "correct" or "proven" result.

Consider the classical experiment of the candle being extinguished beneath an inverted container. This was intended to "prove" there was no oxygen remaining in the container. Recently this writer and several colleagues had occasion to observe a similar experiment—with the addition of two white mice. After the candle was extinguished the mice were still active. This would lead one to draw two possible conclusions. Either the candle suffocated due to a lack of oxygen or white mice can hold their breaths for extended periods of time.

The process of "experimenting" generally consumes a class period of fifty minutes. On occasion, however, with interruptions from the students in the back row who cannot see the experiment anyway, an hour might be necessary. To call pre-solved activities "experiments" is a misnomer. "Lab drills" would be a more realistic appraisal.

Currently there are numerous curriculum projects and study groups devoted to the improvement of science education in the schools. Most of them attempt to place content in a newer perspective, favoring the processes of scientific exploration.

It is this writer's contention that curriculum projects and study groups are still not enough. The most important component is still missing, perhaps now more than ever before. We strive to improve curricula, equipment, scope and sequence, grade placement, and objectives. Rarely do we attempt to improve in terms of people. In a sense we have succeeded in dehumanizing the stuff of scientific information. There is an urgent need to make subject matter relevant, and relevancy means that the subject matter should attempt to illuminate a student's value structure.

How this can be accomplished might be illustrated by placing scientific questions and information into three categories or levels.

Fact Level

What is the earth's diameter?

At what temperature on a Fahrenheit scale will water boil?

Name the stages of development of the butterfly larva.

The above are examples of questions composed of facts and specifics. Most of their answers are difficult to remember, are rarely interesting to students, and are of little use in attempting to enlighten the student's values. Their encyclopedic nature renders them practically useless in transferring to other areas of learning.

Concept or Generalization Level

What causes the movements of air currents?

Apply the principle of Newton's action–reaction theory to a swimmer diving into a pool.

How are igneous, sedimentary, and metamorphic rocks formed?

Concept or generalization questions are considered to be strong and indicative of good teaching. They serve as a means of coalescing facts and specifics into a unified whole. Most teaching is constructed around a set of the most significant concepts related to the topic under consideration. An inherent weakness of concept type questions occurs when one assumes verbalization implies understanding. The strengths of concept or generalization questions far outweigh any weaknesses, but in this writer's view they are still limited.

Values Level

I will not attempt to entirely dismiss teaching at the fact and concept level. What is needed is a newer perspective on both. Regardless of how skillful teaching is conducted at the fact and concept level, science instruction will usually be limited to mere information giving. Science educators need to penetrate into the third level, that of teaching for value clarification. For example, you could ask:

What kind of person do you suppose would make a good scientist?

Have you ever wanted to invent something that would benefit mankind in some way?

Have you ever wanted to try an experiment but decided not to because you thought it might make you look silly? Can you think of any inventors who people thought had strange, unworkable ideas, at least at first?

If you were in complete charge of how our atomic resources were used, how would you use them?

What are some of the things we need to assume for your experiment to work out that way?

What are some of the good things that resulted from the development of . . . (add almost any invention or discovery).

What are some of the alternate ways you can choose to gather data? Which of these do you use?

When do you think a person can predict the results of an experiment with reasonable accuracy?

Can you think of any way a person might be able to tell the difference between scientific evidence and mere hearsay or guesswork?

Can you think of anything in history that people once believed in but have since changed their minds?

Can you give me some examples of scientific beliefs that people are in disagreement over today?

Try to think of any animals that have certain territories that they closely guard. Do you have any such territories?

Do you think enough emphasis is being placed upon the prevention of air pollution? Have you ever done anything about it?

How do you feel about using laboratory animals in such a way that might be unnecessarily cruel and injurious to them? Is this a personal preference or do you think that most people should feel the same way?

Have you ever done anything in your science classes that made you feel particularly satisfied or pleased?

If you could choose what to study in your science classes, what would be your first three choices?

How do you feel when the weatherman forecasts a sunny day and it rains? How do you think the weatherman feels?

The absence of *why*-centered questions is conspicuous. This does not suggest that questions of this nature should be eliminated. However, due to their usual assumption that the student is aware of a causal relationship, *why*-oriented questions are generally not considered to be of a value clarifying nature.

Questions utilizing value clarification have a heavy component of "you" in them. These kinds of questions attempt to lead the student towards a greater awareness of his own thoughts and feelings. He can see how his life is related to the subject matter under consideration, and this helps facilitate his learning. On occasion the student is asked to examine alternatives and consider their consequences; possibly there are elements of pride in his choices.

Often the teacher's dialogue with students consists of inculcating, indoctrinating, or moralizing. Utilization of value clarifying questions helps the student rely upon his own abilities to consider questions. Rather than appealing to authority for information he now has another channel of a more self-directed nature.[1]

---

[1]For a more complete treatment of the value theory that underpins this and several related articles, see *Values and Teaching* by Louis E. Raths, Merrill Harmin, and Sidney B. Simon. Columbus, Ohio: Charles E. Merril Publishing Company, 1966.

27

AN ANALYSIS OF RESEARCH
Related to Instructional Procedures
in Elementary School Science

Gregor A. Ramsey
Robert W. Howe

There is little doubt that science has a place in the elementary school. This position has become more firmly established in recent years; however, what that place is seems not at all clear from the research studies which have been undertaken and are reviewed in this article. If science were removed from the elementary school curriculum, it is difficult to know what would be lost because there is a lack of adequate and appropriate research which examines the actual outcomes of science instruction. Instructional procedures selected for study by researchers seem to be chosen on the basis of whim or tradition rather than from a firmly established proposition that if a certain procedure is used then definite, specifiable, and desirable outcomes will be the end result.

The authors found it necessary, while reviewing the available research literature, to sketch a working model of the complete instructional process. It was then possible to match any given research study to that part of the model being investigated, and also relate its relevance to the total instructional picture. The reviewers are aware that this practice may impose a model on a researcher to which he may not

Reprinted from *Science and Children*, 6, April 1969, pp. 25–33. At the time the article was published Dr. Gregor A. Ramsey was an information analyst, ERIC Information Analysis Center for Science Education, Columbus, Ohio. Dr. Robert H. Howe is Acting Director, ERIC Information Analysis Center, Columbus, Ohio.

subscribe. However, very few researchers established clearly which part of the instructional process they were attempting to investigate.

The fact that there seemed to be no common model among researchers as to what constitutes instruction made it difficult for the authors to draw together a number of studies and make common generalizations regarding them. Also, there was some confusion over terminology used by investigators to describe the instructional process, and there seems to be an urgent need for a common set of terms to describe both the instructional procedure and the expected outcomes of the instructional sequence. More basically perhaps, what is required is a viable instructional theory which can act as a common springboard for research; however, until this is achieved, a common set of terms based on a functional model of instruction would help greatly in bringing order to the field of educational research.

Science is taught in the elementary school presumably because it is expected to bring about pupil growth in the cognitive, affective, and psychomotor domains of knowledge—a growth not as easily achieved through another content area. Evidence of such growth can only be observed through desirable changes in pupil behavior—so before embarking on any instructional sequence, it should be possible to define what behavior changes to expect, and after the sequence, be able to measure if they occur. Any learning experience will provide unexpected and unmeasurable (at least for the present) changes in behavior; however, this is not sufficient reason to neglect all attempts at measuring expected pupil growth. Only rarely did the authors review studies which paid close attention to the dual problems of devising a procedure to produce certain specified outcomes, and then measuring to see whether the outcomes have been attained.

The working model of the instructional process against which the research studies were reviewed is shown in the accompanying chart. This chart is provided for the reader not because it is complete, nor even completely accurate, but because it was useful to the reviewers for pinpointing those aspects of instruction being researched, and helped them in deciding quickly whether the researcher had accounted for all the variables which could influence instruction and its outcomes.

The boxes on the left represent three important inputs which help decide which instructional procedure should be used. The instructional materials and media available, the characteristics of the pupils to be taught, and the personalities and other traits of the teachers are relatively constant factors in any given instructional situation. The two major variables are the possible instructional means and the expected outcomes. For example, if an outcome like creativity is desired, then it is unlikely that a conventional class—teacher-didactic situation—will

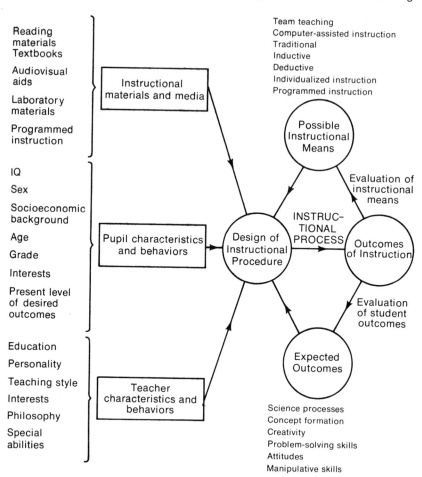

Reading
materials
Textbooks

Audiovisual
aids

Laboratory
materials

Programmed
instruction

Instructional
materials and media

Team teaching
Computer-assisted instruction
Traditional
Inductive
Deductive
Individualized instruction
Programmed instruction

Possible
Instructional
Means

IQ

Sex

Socioeconomic
background

Age

Grade

Interests

Present level
of desired
outcomes

Pupil characteristics
and behaviors

Design of
Instructional
Procedure

INSTRUC-
TIONAL
PROCESS

Evaluation of
instructional
means

Outcomes
of Instruction

Evaluation
of student
outcomes

Education

Personality

Teaching style

Interests

Philosophy

Special
abilities

Teacher
characteristics and
behaviors

Expected
Outcomes

Science processes
Concept formation
Creativity
Problem-solving skills
Attitudes
Manipulative skills

A Model of an Instructional Sequence[1]

produce the greatest gains. So, if expected outcomes are defined, they help determine the instructional procedure to be used within the constraints imposed by the characteristics and behaviors of both the teachers and pupils, and the instructional materials and media available.

Once an instructional procedure has been established and used to teach children, then certain outcomes are attained. These outcomes

---

[1]At the end of any instructional sequence, the inputs, e.g., student or teacher characteristics and behaviors have been changed by the sequence and this will have to be taken into account when planning the next.

are evaluated, usually by some form of testing, against the outcomes expected when the procedure was designed. How closely the outcomes attained match the outcomes expected will give some indication of what changes are needed in the instructional procedure chosen.

In reviewing the research, the model was used in the following way: There are four major sets of variables which may affect the outcomes of instruction—the instructional materials and media used, pupil characteristics and behaviors, teacher characteristics and behaviors, and the instructional means chosen. To know whether a particular instructional means (e.g., a problem-solving method) does produce the change in behavior indicating the desired outcome, then all the other factors must be held constant or allowed for in the research design before one can be reasonably certain that it was the instruction and not some other variable which produced the change. Any one of the components of each of the four areas could be investigated in this way. If, in a comparative study, one wanted to investigate the effect of pupil socioeconomic background on the outcomes of a particular instructional sequence, then all *other* student characteristics must be controlled, the teachers should have essentially the same characteristics and philosophies, and the materials used must be identical in all classes taught the method.

This complex arrangement of variables which can develop may help the elementary school teacher understand some of the problems of research in this area. In fairness, it must be pointed out that most researchers coped very well with all the variables. Randomization of pupil populations is a much more effective way of controlling student characteristics than identifying matched pairs, and was used in many studies. Major objections to many of the designs were in terms of teacher characteristics not being fully controlled, and the instructional sequence not used for a long enough time in many cases for marked gains to be noted. No doubt these weaknesses are partly due to the problem that much of the research reviewed was done for doctoral dissertation purposes, where the rush to ''get finished'' was a contributing factor.

The reviewers found it necessary to place arbitrary limits on the studies reviewed so that the field could be contained in manageable form. In general, only studies reported after 1960 were examined, and from these only those studies which attempted some objective evaluation of the outcomes of an instructional sequence are discussed in detail in this article. Likewise, studies which were designed to test various aspects of learning theory, although they may have used a novel instructional procedure to do this, were ignored. Learning theory forms an important basis for designing an instructional procedure, but it has only an indirect effect on classroom teaching.

A number of classification systems could have been chosen in terms of the model to systematize the widely divergent research studies encountered. Four variables seemed to stand out, namely: the instructional procedure used, the outcomes evaluated, the subject matter taught, and the grade level of instruction. In practice only the first two remained relevant. The choice of subject matter in most cases seemed quite arbitrary, and when grade level was considered, more than 95 percent of the studies involved grades 4–6 and the bulk of this attention was directed at grade 6.

The studies are reviewed in terms of whether they focused on the instructional procedure, e.g., inductive or deductive, individualized instruction, programmed instruction, or whether the studies focused on outcomes, e.g., development of concepts, attitudes, problem-solving skills, creativity, or understanding content. It was surprising to find the outcome category "development of psychomotor skills" void, since it might be expected that this would be an important area to be developed in elementary school science. No information was obtained concerning what manipulative skills in science can be developed in elementary school children, nor whether a hierarchy of such skills can be identified. This area requires much more basic research.

A number of "status" studies were identified. School systems were surveyed for procedures used, e.g., Snoble (113) and Swan (120), or wider surveys of national practices were made, e.g., those by McCloskey (79), Moorehead (83), Smith and Cooper (111), Blackwood (13), Stokes (116), and Melis (81).

These status studies are in a sense reviews themselves and provide sound statements of the position in the areas mentioned. They are not discussed further in this article, but are cited as useful sources for the interested reader.

Only one study was identified which attempted evaluation of one of the newer course improvement projects in elementary science. This study was undertaken by Walbesser et al. (126) and the American Association for the Advancement of Science in their comprehensive study of *Science—A Process Approach.* An evaluation model was posed which described expected learner behaviors and established what might be accepted as evidence of learner accomplishment. Evaluation in these terms allows for objective comparisons of courses, gives objective evidence that learning has occurred, and makes independent replication of the findings possible.

The behavioral objectives of each instructional sequence were clearly identified, and they were evaluated by determining the percentage of pupils acquiring a certain standard percentage of specified behaviors, and comparing this to an established level of expectation. From this information, feedback to improve the instructional sequence was constantly available. For example, an arbitrary 90/90 (90 percent of students acquire 90 percent of the prescribed behaviors) was chosen as the standard. If the standard attained by pupils were lower than this, then modifications were made to the instructional sequence.

Specific findings of the evaluation were too varied and far reaching to be described in a review of this nature; however, it is the model provided by the evaluation, rather than the results which are important. Much has been said and written about the efficacy of stating objectives in behavioral terms. This study gives concrete evidence that this is so.

Comparative Studies: Traditional versus Nontraditional

In this section are reviewed those studies which compared outcomes obtained when the same body of content is taught by two methods. A "conventional" or "traditional" method was the usual standard of comparison, although what researchers meant by these terms was not always clear. Methods investigated included "inductive," "directed self-discovery," a "field method," "democratic," and "problem solving." It was in this area of comparison studies that the reviewers had the most concern regarding the research design. It is extremely difficult in such circumstances to control all the variables which may affect instruction. A study by Brudzynski (16) illustrates this point. He compared an inductive method where pupils learned concepts by "directed self-discovery" in a pupil-centered atmosphere to a "lecture-demonstration" teacher-centered one. The "inductive" method favored above-average students while the "lecture-demonstration" method favored average and below average students in the fifth-and sixth-grade population studied. These differences need not be ascribed to the particular instructional method. Teacher expectation may have been far more important. The less-able students may not be "expected" by the teacher, perhaps subconsciously, to perform as well in a self-directed situation. He may act in the classroom accordingly and this subconscious expectation could affect the outcomes of the students more than the instructional procedure used.

Anklam (5) identified the teachers who liked to use "democratic" instructional methods and those who preferred a more "autocratic" approach. No significant differences in achievement motivation existed between the groups of pupils taught in each of these environments. This finding points clearly to the importance of teacher characteristics and behaviors to the whole instructional procedure, and the danger of imposing a particular procedure upon teachers who do not have the personal characteristics to teach it. In this study, the teachers investigated had adopted a style of teaching which suited them. Even though the simplicity of the democratic-autocratic dichotomy may be doubted, the study did show that teachers performing within a frame of reference which they have built for themselves motivated students equally. What is needed is research into determining instructional procedures which suit different personality types, rather than research directed to finding one procedure "best" for all teachers.

Other studies where no significant differences were found between methods used included Gerne (51) who compared a traditional textbook method with a method utilizing a specially designed board to teach electricity and magnetism, and one by Bennett (10) who compared a field method with a classroom method for teaching ecology. Smith (110) compared a lecture-demonstration style of teaching carried out in a classroom to teaching in a planetarium for presenting a lesson on astronomy concepts to sixth-grade pupils. Children in the classroom achieved significantly higher than those taught in the planetarium. These studies suggest that the use of any visual aid or direct experience will not necessarily of itself produce significant outcome gains in children.

Carpenter (24) used fourth-grade pupils to compare a "textbook recitation method" with a "problem method." In effect, the textbook method included no demonstrations while the problem method was based on classroom demonstration and experimentation. Achievement of content gains were strongly in favor of the problem-solving method for teaching units on "magnetism" and "adaption of animals." This finding was even more definite for the slower learners—who were, in general, poor readers.

Pershern (91) investigated student achievement outcomes obtained by integrating industrial-arts activities with science instruction in grades 4, 5, 6. He used electricity and machines as his content vehicles and found significant gains in favor of integration for the electricity unit, but no significant differences for the machines unit. Integration seems to add an important dimension to instruction, and may prove a useful approach for further research.

It is difficult to generalize from comparison studies; however, it seems that pupil activity and pupil-performed experiments are important prerequisites to the effective learning of science concepts. Instructional procedures where the responsibility for the conceptual leap is placed upon the child, as in problem solving and inductive methods, do seem to bring about more significant achievement gains than do those methods where the teacher or the text material provides the concept. It appears that for these inductive methods to be fully effective, the teacher must have a certain teaching philosophy and a certain set of personal characteristics.

Audiovisual Aids

The bulk of the research in this area involved the use of television and movie film in the classroom. How these aids can best be used in an instructional situation, what their effect is on student achievement and attitudes, and how they can improve classroom instruction are all questions to which research has been directed. Much of the research was of the "direct-comparison" type where control of all variables is extremely difficult. Conclusions based on such studies should be viewed with some caution.

Bickel (12), Decker (36), and Skinner (109) investigated changes in attitude, achievement, and interest in children following television instruction. Bickel (12) found no significant differences in the learning outcomes of his fourth-, fifth-, and sixth-grade pupils taught science by closed-circuit television incorporating a "talk-back" facility and teacher follow-up, when compared with students taught science without the aid of television.

Skinner (109) compared two television presentations for two separate groups of fifth graders. In one presentation a problem was identified, and many questions were posed which were not answered in the lesson. In this way, it was hoped that pupils' curiosity and interest in science would be aroused. The other presentation included the same materials, but used a direct expository teaching style with very few questions. Teacher follow-up of these lessons was either a modified inquiry session where the teacher answered only pupils' questions or a typical discussion session with teacher and pupils participating fully. Skinner found that pupils who experienced the television presentation with unanswered questions, regardless of teacher follow-up, achieved significantly higher than pupils who viewed "explanation" on television.

Decker (36), like Skinner, also worked with fifth graders and followed a somewhat similar procedure. He prepared two sets of ten half-hour television programs using the same materials for each. One set stressed providing information, concepts, and generalizations while the other stressed the posing of problems. No significant differences in pupil achievement were detected, so Decker concluded that the problem-solving method was as effective as the information-giving method in teaching natural science.

These conflicting results of Skinner and Decker, where one finds a significant difference in one and no significant difference in the other, point clearly to the difficulties associated with these direct-comparison type studies. They oversimplify the learning process and do not take into account how individual student needs, interests, and abilities interact with instruction. An instructional method which may be in tune with the profile of characteristics of one group of students in the class may be out of tune with another, so any gains obtained with one group will be offset by the losses in the other, and no significant differences are detected. Research on instructional procedures must be increasingly multi-dimensional, since no one method of instruction can be considered "best" for all students.

Bornhorst and Hosford (15) investigated television instruction at the third-grade level by comparing the achievement of a group of television-taught pupils with a group who had only classroom instruction. The television group achieved significantly higher results on tests than the control group, and it was felt that the "wonder-box" where children placed questions arising from the television lessons for future discussion was an important factor.

Allison (3) investigated the influence of three methods of using motivational films[2] on the attitudes of fourth-, fifth-, and sixth-grade students toward science, scientists, and scientific careers. He adapted the Allen attitude inventory[3] for use with these elementary school children. Allison concluded that the films did change the attitudes of the students favorably toward science, scientists, and scientific careers, and that these changes in attitude were not related to mental ability, science achievement scores, sex, science training, or the economic status of parents. This study suggests that film sequences can be devised which will effectively bring about a desired attitude change. More research in this area is needed particularly in the development and evaluation of material.

Novak (87) describes the development and use of audiotape programmed instruction for teaching first- and third-grade elementary science. Cartridge tape recorders and projectors with simple "on-off" switches were used. Some of the problems associated with setting up such a program included vocabulary difficulty, pace of audio instruction, difficulty of task to be performed, density of information to be presented, inadequacies of filmloops, and unexpected distractions. Four to eight revisions of each program sequence were necessary to be sure that students could proceed with very few apparent difficulties.

Evaluation of the program was highly experimental. Individual interview using loop films, display materials, and appropriate question-

---

[2]"Horizons of Science." Films produced by Educational Testing Service, Princeton, N.J.
[3]Allen, Hugh Jr., "Attitudes of Certain High School Seniors Toward Science and Scientific Careers." Teachers College, Columbia University, New York, 1960.

ing was found too time consuming. Pencil-and-paper tests using drawings, administered orally to the whole class, were then tried. Also, several suggestions as to future possible avenues of evaluation were developed along with other ways the materials may be used. The study leaves little doubt that audiotutorial instruction is feasible in grades one, two, and three, and should be looked on as a useful way to individualize instruction.

Programmed Instruction

The role of programmed instruction in the elementary school has had some attention from researchers. This is understandable since such programs encourage individual student work, and free the teacher from direct instruction to perform other tasks.

Hedges and MacDougall (61) investigated the effectiveness of teaching fourth-grade science using programmed science materials and laboratory experiences. The study had three phases. In phase one, the purpose was to establish the possibility of programmed instruction as a teaching method. This was done by observing students using the materials, and determining student and teacher attitudes. The information was used to revise and rewrite the programs as part of phase two of the study. The final report on the evaluative phase (phase three) has not yet come to the reviewers' attention; however, the intention was to compare innovative ways of using the materials with a more traditional approach under the headings: achievement, interest, problem-solving ability, ability to generalize, and retention. This three-phase method of determining feasibility, defining materials and methods, and evaluating student and teacher outcomes outlines a promising sequence for the development of instructional procedures.

Blank (14) investigated developing inquiry skills through programmed-instruction techniques. The programs trained children to ask questions about the relative dimensions of problems before attempting to solve them. He found that the children given inquiry training asked significantly more questions (as well as a lower proportion of irrelevant ones) on oral and written criterion tests than did students in control groups. This improvement in inquiry skills was not at the expense of other achievement criteria, so it was found possible to introduce inquiry training without affecting progress in regular course work.

Dutton (41) investigated pupil achievement using programmed materials on heat, light, and sound with fourth graders. He found that children did proceed at different rates and that they could perform simple science experiments with little teacher supervision. Pupils using the programmed materials learned concepts more efficiently than did those in classes taught in a conventional way.

Crabtree (30) studied the relationships between score, time, I.Q., and reading level for fourth-grade students by structuring programmed science materials in different ways. Linear programs seemed preferable to branched versions since the same amount of material was learned in less time. Other findings were of the "no significant difference" type, although there was some evidence that multiple choice type response requires a higher reading ability than other response forms.

Taylor (122) investigated the effect of pupil behavior and characteristics and teacher attitudes on achievement when programmed science materials are used at the fourth-grade level. Teacher attitudes, combinations of pupil and teacher attitudes, pupil intelligence, interest, and initial knowledge of science, along with other selected personality and performance factors all contribute significantly to pupil final achievement. The study indicates that any given set of programmed science materials cannot meet the needs of all the students at any given grade level.

Individualized Instruction

Instruction may be classified as individualized if experiences are specifically designed for each individual child, taking into account such factors as background, knowledge and experience, reading level, interests, and intelligence. There have been several attempts at individualizing which have tried to allow for the individual needs of children in the instructional design.

Baum (8) prepared materials to test the feasibility of individualizing science experiences for fifth-grade pupils. He devised a series of pretests of skills and knowledge so that pupils deficiencies could be identified. Each pupil was then assigned a kit specially designed to help him acquire the skill or competency shown to be deficient on the tests. This method was found suitable for helping pupils achieve curricular goals in the area of science. Evaluation was carried out by observing pupil reactions to this instruction, and though the evaluation was subjective, the strengths of the program in terms of desired outcomes clearly emerged.

O'Toole (89) compared an individualized method with a teacher-centered approach in the teaching of science to fifth graders. He found no significant differences between his groups in achievement, problem-solving ability, or science interest. The teacher-centered program stressing problem solving as a major objective was more effective in developing the ability to identify valid conclusions while the individualized program was more effective in developing the ability to recognize hypotheses and problems.

It is likely that group methods of instruction will develop some outcomes more effectively than individualized methods, while other outcomes will develop more effectively in an individualized situation. This study was the only one which attempted to identify what some of these outcome differences might be.

Schiller (102) used activity booklets and data sheets to individualize instruction for sixth-grade pupils. The materials were designed to give children an opportunity to complete some science experiments and other activities which were in addition to the formal instructional program. Much of the evaluation was subjective, but students were eager to participate in the activities and seemed to gain from them.

Other attempts at individualizing instruction were undertaken by LaCava (69) who used the tape recorder as an aid in individualizing, Carter (25) who developed a science experience center, and Lipson (74) who developed an individualized program by coordinating audio-tapes to simple science kits. These studies, in general, support the contention that individualizing instruction is possible and educationally desirable at the elementary level. To date, however, evaluation has been highly subjective.

A more rigorous evaluation of an individualized program was undertaken by Gleason (54). He measured pupil growth in areas of general science knowledge, liking for science, and learning to generalize. Although he found no specific advantages in favor of individualized self-study activity in science, pupils learned as much content by themselves as they did when taught by a teacher.

An important project related to individualizing instruction is the Oakleaf Project for Individually Prescribed Instruction discussed by Lindvall and Bolvin (72). Here, the Oakleaf Elementary School is used as a laboratory for testing the feasibility of individualizing instruction, developing suitable programs, and evaluating the effects of such instruction.

Ability Grouping—Socioeconomic Status of Students

Three studies investigated the effects of socioeconomic status on achievement in elementary school science. Some of the findings have clear implications for instruction.

Rowland (98) compared the science achievement of sixth-grade pupils of high socioeconomic status with those of generally low status. He found that given equal intelligence and equal science background experiences, higher socioeconomic status pupils show greater science achievement than do lower groups, and these differences carry over to all the various types of science achievement measured. He found that it is of great importance that lower socioeconomic status pupils have opportunities to manipulate and study simple science materials, and this should precede experience with more complex types of commerical science aids. Also these students should engage in concrete science experiences before being expected to learn from reading or discussing science material.

Wagner (124) compared the responses of economically advantaged and disadvantaged sixth-grade pupils to science demonstrations. Pupil responses to the demonstrations were obtained by getting them to either write about, tell about, or construct pictorially, using predesigned plastic templates, suitable applications of the demonstrations. Advantaged pupils were significantly superior in written and oral responses, but no differences were detected in the construction responses. This finding suggests that disadvantaged pupils understand and can communicate their understandings of science concepts when placed in situations requiring limited language response.

Becker (9) investigated the achievement of gifted sixth-grade students when segregated from, partly segregated from, or homogeneously mixed with students of lower ability. No significant differences were detected between the groups, and no special advantages accrued when gifted children were placed in special groups. Unfortunately, the description of the design of the study did not mention some important aspects, one of which was the length of time students were placed in these various arrangements. This time factor is likely to be highly significant in such a study.

These studies point to the great importance which must be placed on student characteristics in the design of instructional procedures. Selecting one factor, e.g., ability, from the whole range of factors which influence learning, and then separating instructional groups on the basis of it, is unlikely to significantly improve student outcomes. The factor involved in determining the outcomes of instruction are much more subtle than this.

Use of Reading Materials

Little research was detected on investigating ways reading materials may be used in an instructional situation. Some very interesting studies, however, were identified.

Fryback (48) evaluated some elementary science curriculum materials which had been written to accommodate five different reading levels in a fifth-grade class. Other variables in the design included whether the students performed experiments or not, and the extent of class discussion. He found that the provision for different reading ability levels and class discussion did not show any significant influence on achievement. Only when pupils worked experiments were significant achievement gains noted. The provision of different reading levels and class discussion may have a motivational effect for later work and may affect other outcomes, but these data indicate that the provision of experiments to be performed individually by pupils is important.

Bennett and Clodfelter (11) investigated student learning of earth-science concepts when the science unit was integrated within the reading program of second-grade children. For the integration, a "word-analysis" approach was used. In this method, the child was given a basic list of words to be used in the new resource unit on earth science, and then introduced to their meanings before presentation of the unit. The "word-analysis" group showed greater achievement gains than the control groups where the science was taught in the traditional way. The study demonstrated that certain earth-science concepts can be learned at the second-grade level.

Williams (128) rewrote sixth-grade science materials to a third-grade level of readability, and used them with his sixth-grade pupils. Gains in reading speed and comprehension seemed to occur when the materials were used, but the duration of the study was far too short for differences in learning outcomes to be evaluated.

Research in the area of the use of reading materials is indeed thin. More and more textbooks and other materials directed to the elementary pupil are coming onto the market, yet the role of reading materials in science instruction has had little recent evaluation.

Critical Thinking

Over the period of review, only one study was identified which investigated the development of critical thinking in children. Mason (78), in a two-year study, developed materials for teaching critical thinking in grades K–6. The first year was devoted to developing materials and providing inservice seminars for the teachers who would eventually teach the course. Basic assumptions were that children should have planned experiences in science rather than incidental ones, they should have direct experience with both content and methods of science, and that experiences can be identified to give students direct training in the acquisition of scientific skills and attitudes. Evaluation of the course was subjective for grades K–3 because of the lack of suitable instruments; but, in grades 4–6 significant gains in critical thinking were made over the period of a year. The materials were particularly effective at the fifth-grade level where maximum gains were made.

It seems quite clear that instructional sequences can be devised which will develop pupils' powers of critical thinking. Only by evaluating the outcomes of the experiences can the effectiveness of these materials be assessed. There is a lack of activity in this area, particularly in grades K–3.

Process: Inquiry in Science

Much emphasis has been placed on the development of science process skills and the use of inquiry methods to develop certain cognitive abilities by the new elementary science course improvement projects. Less research has been reported in this area than might have been expected if one judges from the significant sums of money spent on developing these programs.

Raun (95) investigated the interaction between curriculum variables and selected classroom-student characteristics using the AAAS *Science—A Process Approach* materials. He was interested in the changes in cognitive and affective behavior brought about by children using some of the strategies of science. Some of the factors investigated included problem solving, perceptual closure, verbal fluency, ideation fluency, tested intelligence, achievement, and attitudes toward science and scientists. The strategies of inquiry selected for performance evaluation after five months instruction were classifying, observing, using number relations, and recognizing space-time relations. He found limited evidence of significant grade differences between behaviors and performance in the strategies of inquiry in science, and that there was no consistent pattern of behavioral change among grades. In fact, on many of the factors investigated, grades 5 and 6 showed regressive tendencies which support the argument that there is rather slow development of science process skills beyond grade 5.

Price (93) investigated whether students who had manipulated objects and materials to gather empirical data in an elementary classroom would transfer this manipulative process behavior to a test situation outside the classroom. It was found that children rarely sought data by overt manipulative processes in the test situations, even though verbal responses to them indicated high motivational interest. Also gifted children showed no greater tendency to empirically gather data to solve problems than students in the normal range of intelligence.

Scott and Sigel (107) used grades 4–6 to investigate the effects of inquiry training in physical science on creativity and cognitive style. Pupils receiving inquiry training learned science concepts as well or better than children in conventional classes, and no significant differences were found between boys and girls. Cognitive styles did seem to be influenced by the inquiry process, and some differences in the developmental trends of cognitive styles of boys compared to girls were apparent.

More studies like the above are needed if instructional procedures are to be developed which meet the individual needs of students at each stage in their development. Inquiry methods and methods designed to have children working with the processes of science are likely to produce different outcomes than conventional procedures. These new procedures are becoming more carefully controlled, and with the development of more sensitive evaluative instruments, a clearer idea of what these differences may be is starting to emerge. Increased research on ways the new materials may be used and the outcomes obtained seems essential.

Problem Solving

A number of studies investigated problem solving in elementary children. Dyrli (42), Gunnels (55), and Harris (59) all made some analysis of the problem-solving behavior of children at various grade levels. Only Schippers (103) extended what is known about problem solving into a suggested instructional sequence.

Dyrli (42) wished to discover whether instruction had any effect on the length of transition period from the stage of concrete operations to more formal patterns of thought in the Piagetian developmental sequence. Gunnels (55) also investigated cognitive development based on the Piagetian stages of intuitive, concrete, and formal thought. He used an interview technique to study the development of logical judgments in science of successful and unsuccessful problem solvers in grades 4–9. In general, the Piagetian order of development was confirmed that successful problem solvers operate at a higher level of operational thought than do unsuccessful problem solvers; however, even though a child is at a given chronological age, this does not guarantee a definite level of thought process skills.

Harris (59) used sixth graders and investigated the usefulness of pupil drawings in developing a problem-solving approach to learning science concepts. He identified two kinds of problem-solving behavior: verificational and insightful, but his study concentrated on the verificational aspects which seem most often encountered in school. He made an intensive individual analysis of the problem-solving processes of eighteen children. Some of his findings are pertinent to the development of instructional procedures. He found that children do not use consistent patterns of thinking in different problem situations, and that the confidence of the child in his ability to solve problems is an important factor in his success. Also instruction in science, which includes drawing of concepts in a tangible form by the learner, was not significantly related to growth in the ability of the learner to use these concepts in problem-solving situations. A particularly significant finding relating to the evaluation of an instructional sequence was that pencil-and-paper tests did not provide an adequate means for evaluating problem-solving processes in individual children.

Schippers (103) designed materials and a procedure to teach sixth graders a problem-solving instructional method using a multireference activity base. Three steps in the instructional process were identified: first, establish the background situation; second, understand the problem; and third, work out a solution. Supervision and the use of illustrative lessons were found important if inexperienced teachers were to use the method effectively. Evaluation of student outcomes was largely subjective.

Creativity

Only two studies were identified which made an attempt to develop materials and procedures for encouraging creativity and creative thinking in students.

DeRoche (37) used creative exercises with sixth-grade pupils to see if these produced any gains in creative thinking and achievement not seen in classes doing more traditional work. The experimental group had creative exercises in 26 space science lessons and four "brainstorming" sessions, while control classes either had 30 space science lessons without the exercises or no space science instruction at all. The *Minnesota Tests of Creative Thinking* and specially prepared content achievement tests were used to evaluate outcomes. For high intelligence students, the experimental method was significantly superior to the control in developing creative factors like verbal fluency, flexibility, originality, and elaboration. This trend was less marked for average and low ability students. No significant differences on the achievement tests were found between the "creative" group and the "traditional" group taught space science.

Tating (121) studied ways of developing creative thinking in elementary school science. Creative thinking was defined operationally as divergent and original thinking measured in terms of questions asked and hypotheses given. More divergent responses were obtained with the trained groups than with the control, but the number of divergent responses decreased if pupils were given instructions to be original. Tating "primed" creative thinking by getting pupils to write down as many questions as they could about a particular demonstration, which, if given a "yes-no" answer by the teacher, would help the child understand why a given event occurred. Another method of priming used was to get students to write down a number of words in response to a given word.

Although the asking of questions could be primed, the development of hypotheses was not as responsive to training. The formulation of hypotheses in science is a highly complicated mental process, and the formation of an original hypothesis probably requires more time than is needed to think of questions.

The evidence is mounting that creative exercises can be designed to increase creative responses in children without any losses in content achievement. Teachers are constantly being urged to teach science creatively, and more research needs to be done to estimate the effectiveness of various forms of instruction.

Concept Development

Many of the studies in this area were concerned with concept development as part of research into learning theory, rather than evaluating different instructional procedures for their efficiency in developing concepts.

Voelker (123) gives an example of pertinent research on the development of concepts within the field of science education. He compared two instructional methods for teaching the concepts of physical and chemical change in grades 2–6. Using essentially similar lesson procedures and materials in both cases, he found that formulation and statement by the teacher of the generalization to be learned was not superior to a procedure in which the pupil individually formulated the generalization concerning physical and chemical change. An interesting sidelight of the study was that although sixth-grade pupils were significantly better verbalizers of the concepts, if the criterion of understanding was simply to classify observed phenomena, no significant differences could be detected among grades 2–6. In this study, where teaching method and materials were carefully controlled, there did not seem to be any significant advantages of an "inductive-discovery" approach over a "deductive" one on the outcomes selected. Unfortunately, the concept of physical and chemical change appeared rather difficult except for pupils in grade 6.

Salstrom (100) compared concepts learned by sixth grade pupils in two types of guided discovery lessons. The same experimental lessons were presented as a science game to each of his groups. Following this, one group had an oral inquiry session while the other received a battery of cards which on one side had printed questions a pupil might ask in an inquiry session and on the other, the answers to those questions were printed. In the card group, each pupil could draw only cards that would yield information needed to solve the problem. They were then ordered by the pupil to give a solution to the problem posed in the lesson. The card treatment group showed greater gains in concept development than the oral inquiry group, supporting the contention that more guidance than can be given each pupil in an oral inquiry session helps concept development.

Three studies were directed at finding the relationship between the child's level of maturity and the understanding of a particular concept. Carey (21) investigated the particle nature of matter in grades 2–5, Haddad (56) investigated the concept of relativity in grades 4–8, and Helgeson (62) investigated the concept of force. Maturity studies like these are extremely useful in helping course developers decide the level to which a particular concept may be unfolded with pupils at a particular stage in development. The studies suggested that there was almost as much variation in maturity within a grade level as there was between grade levels. These data question the grouping of children by grades if the aim is to provide a group of children at the same stage of mental development.

Kolb (66) investigated integrating mathematics and science instruction with fifth-grade pupils to determine if such integration would facilitate the acquisition of quantitative science behaviors. He used *Science—A Process Approach* materials and found that such integration with mathematics did significantly increase achievement. Integration seems a promising way to reduce the time spent in developing concepts which have elements common to both mathematics and science, and this aspect should be pursued further.

Ziegler (132) investigated the use of mechanical models in teaching theoretical concepts regarding the particle nature of matter to pupils in grades 2–6. They found that children who had not previously learned to use such a model could learn to do so with suitable instruction, and those who had some knowledge of such models improved their ability to use them. These concrete experiences with mechanical models helped pupils form theoretical concepts to explain expansion, contraction, change of phase, and mixtures by the time they completed grade 4.

Studies like this and those of Carey (21), Haddad (56), Voelker (123), and Helgeson (62) should be extended into other concept areas so that a more complete picture of the concepts which may be developed at any given level may emerge. From this, suitable instructional procedures using mechanical models and other devices can be developed. Until this is done, courses of instruction in elementary schools will be based on subjective opinion and feeling about what can be accomplished at any given grade level or stage of development, rather than on a soundly researched experimental base.

Summary and Conclusions

Reviewing the available research into the outcomes of instruction in elementary science has revealed a number of areas where little in the way of a planned attack on the problems has been initiated. Such areas include the development of psychomotor skills, critical thinking skills, creativity, and work in the affective domain on the development of attitudes toward science and scientists. Only in the field of understanding concepts can one see steady progress being made.

The tentative nature of the findings of much educational research and the massive qualifications which surround any generalizations made by researchers often appear confusing to the classroom teacher. The feeling is sometimes expressed that research "has nothing to say to the classroom teacher." In light of this, the reviewers have decided to outline a number of tentative conclusions which seem to emerge from the research reviewed. They are stated without qualification so that they may be readily grasped by teachers. The purists may assume that they are surrounded by the usual modifiers demanded by the idiosyncrasies of educational research.

1. *Instructional procedures, whether in the classroom or in the research situation, should be based on some clearly defined model of what constitutes the instructional process.* The major criteria for such a model should be that it is useful in helping understand the components of instruction and that the instruction develops desired behavior changes in pupils.

2. *For teachers skilled in handling them, problem-solving or inductive methods or instructional procedures designed to improve creativity can bring about gains in outcome areas which are greater than if more traditional approaches are used.* This is not achieved at the expense of knowledge of content.

3. *Audiovisual aids and reading materials should be carefully integrated into the instructional sequence for a definite instructional purpose, otherwise little effect on achievement outcomes will be noted.*

4. *Pupil activity and pupil performed experiments are important prerequisites for the effective learning of science concepts.* This seems true for all levels of ability.

5. *Instructional procedures can be devised to bring about specific outcomes, provided these outcomes are clearly defined.* Both problem-solving skills and creativity can be developed.

6. *Individualized instruction is a satisfactory alternative to total class instruction.* Even very young children can work alone on preplanned experiences using quite sophisticated aids with minimal teacher help.

7. *Elementary children càn learn by using programmed-instruction materials.* Outcomes from these are enhanced if they are integrated with laboratory experiences.

8. *Each child should have the opportunity to develop science concepts and process skills in both individual and group situations.* The outcomes of one kind of instruction will complement rather than parallel the other.

9. *Verbalization of a concept is the last step in a child's understanding of it.* He can demonstrate aspects of his understanding in concrete situations long before he can verbalize them.

10. *Any given class in elementary school is likely to contain children who are in at least two stages of cognitive development—that of concrete operations and formal thought.* These two groups require quite different instructional strategies.

11. *Ability grouping has little effect on the achievement of high ability students.* Other student characteristics are just as significant as intelligence in the learning process.

12. *Educationally disadvantaged students can communicate their understanding of science concepts if the response mode is by a means other than language; e.g., pictorial representation.*

13. *Integration of mathematics and science saves time.* Where common concepts are being developed, achievement in both areas seems to be enhanced.

14. *Educationally disadvantaged children need even greater recourse to simple materials and individual experiments if they are to develop the desired science concepts to the level of other children.*

15. *Teachers should decide on instructional procedures which suit their own personal characteristics and philosophy.* Modification of firmly established patterns of teaching can only occur if there is a corresponding modification of personal characteristics and behaviors.

These conclusions are given in this way so that the classroom teacher may be encouraged to try something new or do something different and the educational researcher to assemble evidence either to support or reject them. If both these aims are met, then this review may have sparked some improvement both in classroom instruction per se, and in its enigmatic research.

References

(1) Ainslie, D. S., "Simple Equipment and Procedures in Elementary Laboratories." *The Physics Teacher*. September 1967.

(2) Allen, L. R., "An Examination of the Classificatory Ability of Children Who Have Been Exposed to One of the 'New' Elementary Science Programs." (M)[4] 1967.

(3) Allison, R. W., "The Effect of Three Methods of Treating Motivational Films Upon the Attitudes of Fourth-, Fifth-, and Sixth-Grade Students Toward Science, Scientists, and Scientific Careers." Pennsylvania State University, 1967.

(4) Anderson, R. D., "Children's Ability to Formulate Mental Models to Explain Natural Phenomena." *Journal of Research in Science Teaching*, December 1965.

(5) Anklam, P. A., "A Study of the Relationship between Two Divergent Instructional Methods and Achievement Motivation of Elementary School Children." (M) 1962.

(6) Barker, D., "Primary School Science—An Attempt to Investigate the Effects of the Informal Use of a Discovery Table on the Scientific Knowledge of Primary School Children." *Educational Research*, February 1965.

(7) Barrett, R. E., "Field Trip Tips." *Science and Children*, October 1965.

(8) Baum, E. A., "Report of the Individualization of the Teaching of Selected Science Skills and Knowledges in an Elementary School Classroom with Materials Prepared by the Teacher." (M) 1965.

(9) Becker, L. J., "An Analysis of the Science and Mathematics Achievement of Gifted Sixth-Grade Children Enrolled in Segregated Classes." (M) 1963.

(10) Bennett, L. M., "A Study of the Comparison of Two Instructional Methods, the Experimental-Field Method and the Traditional Classroom Method. Involving Science Content in Ecology for the Seventh Grade." *Science Education*, December 1965.

(11) Bennett, L. M. and C. Clodfelter, "A Study of the Integration of an Earth Science Unit Within the Reading Program of a Second Grade

---

[4](M) denotes University Microfilms, Ann Arbor, Mich.

by Utilizing the Word Analysis Approach." *School Science and Mathematics,* November 1966.

(12) Bickel, R. F., "A Study of the Effect of Television Instruction on the Science Achievement and Attitudes of Children in Grades 4, 5, and 6." (M) 1964.

(13) Blackwood, P. E., "Science Teaching in the Elementary School: A Survey of Practices." *Journal of Research in Science Teaching,* September 1965.

(14) Blank, S. S., "Inquiry Training Through Programed Instruction." (M) 1963.

(15) Bornhorst, B. A., and P. M. Hosford, "Basing Instruction in Science on Children's Questions: Using a Wonder Box in the Third Grade." *Science Education,* March 1960.

(16) Brudzynski, A. J., "A Comparative Study of Two Methods for Teaching Electricity and Magnetism with Fifth- and Sixth-Grade Children." (M) 1966.

(17) Brusini, J. A., "An Experimental Study of the Development of Science Continua Concepts in Upper Elementary and Junior High School Children." (M) 1966.

(18) Buell, R. R., "Inquiry Training in the School's Science Laboratories." *School Science and Mathematics,* April 1965.

(19) Butts, D. P., "The Degree to which Children Conceptualize from Science Experiences." *Journal of Research in Science Teaching,* June 1962.

(20) _____"The Relationship Between Classroom Experiences and Certain Student Characteristics." University of Texas, February 1967.

(21) Carey, R. L., "Relationship Between Levels of Maturity and Levels of Understanding of Selected Concepts of the Particle Nature of Matter." (M) 1967.

(22) Carlson, J. S., "Effects of Instruction on the Concepts of Conservation of Substance." *Science Education,* March 1967.

(23) Carpenter, F., "Toward a Systematic Construction of a Classroom Taxonomy." *Science Education,* April 1965.

(24) Carpenter, R., "A Reading Method and an Activity Method in Elementary Science Instruction." *Science Education,* April 1963.

(25) Carter, N., "Science Experience Center." *Science and Children,* February 1967.

(26) Caruthers, B., Sr., "Teacher Preparation and Experience Related to Achievement of Fifth-Grade Pupils in Science." (M) 1967.

(27) Chinnis, R. J., "The Development of Physical Science Principles in Elementary-School Science Textbooks." (M) 1962.

(28) Cobun, T. C., "The Relative Effectiveness of Three Levels of Pictorial Presentation of Biological Subject Matter on the Associative Learning of Nomenclature by Sixth-Grade Students." (M) 1961.

(29) Cox, L. T., "Working with Science in the Kindergarten." *Science Education,* March 1963.

(30) Crabtree, J. F., "A Study of the Relationships Between 'Score,' 'Time,' 'IQ,' and 'Reading level' for Fourth-Grade Students Using Programed Science Materials." *Science Education,* April 1967.

(31) Crabtree, C. A., "Effects of Structuring on Productiveness in Children's Thinking: Study of Second-Grade Dramatic Play Patterns Centered on Harbor and Airport Activities under Two Types of Teacher Structuring." (M) 1962.

(32) Cunningham, R., "Implementing Nongraded Advancement with Laboratory Activities as a Vehicle—An Experiment in Elementary School Science." *School Science and Mathematics,* February 1967.

(33) Cunningham, J. D., "On Curiosity and Science Education." *School Science and Mathematics,* December 1966.

(34) Dart, F. E., and P. L. Pradham, "Cross-Cultural Teaching of Science." *Science,* February 1967.

(35) Davis, J. E., Jr., "Ice Calorimetry in the Upper Elementary Grades." *Science and Children,* December 1966.

(36) Decker, M. G., "The Differential Effects Upon the Learning of the Natural Sciences by Fifth Graders of Two Modes of Teaching over Television and in the Classroom." (M) 1965.

(37) DeRoche, E. F., "A Study of the Effectiveness of Selected Creative Exercises on Creative Thinking and the Mastery of a Unit in Elementary Science." (M) 1966.

(38) Dietmeier, H. J., "The Effect of Integration of Science Teaching by Television on the Development of Scientific Reasoning in the Fifth-Grade Student." (M) 1962.

(39) Downing, C. E., "A Statistical Examination of the Relationship Among Elementary Science Achievement Gains, Interest Level Changes, and Time Allotment for Instructional Purposes." (M) 1963.

(40) Drenchko, E. K., "The Comparative Effectiveness of Two Methods of Teaching Grade School Science." (M) 1966.

(41) Dutton, S. S., "An Experimental Study in the Programing of Science Instruction for the Fourth Grade." (M) 1963.

(42) Dyrli, O. E., "An Investigation into the Development of Combinational Mechanisms Characteristic of Formal Reasoning, through Experimental Problem Situations with Sixth-Grade Students." (M) 1967.

(43) Eccles, P. J., "Research Reports—Teacher Behavior and Knowledge of Subject Matter in Sixth-Grade Science." *Journal of Research in Science Teaching,* December 1965.

(44) Elashhab, G. A., "A Model for the Development of Science Curricula in the Preparatory and Secondary Schools of the United Arab Republic." (M) 1966.

(45) Englemann, S. and J. J. Gallagher, "A Study of How a Child Learns Concepts about Characteristics of Liquid Materials." EDRS, National Cash Register Company, 1966.

(46) Fischler, A. S., "Science, Process, The Learner—A Synthesis." *Science Education*, December 1965.

(47) Fish, A. S., and B. Goldmark. "Inquiry Method—Three Interpretations." *The Science Teacher*, February 1966.

(48) Fryback, W. H., "Evaluation of Multi-Level Reading Materials, Intra-Class Discussion Techniques and Student Experimentations on Achievement in Fifth-Grade Elementary Science." (M) 1965.

(49) Garone, J. E., "Acquiring Knowledge and Attaining Understanding of Children's Scientific Concept Development." *Science Education*, March 1960.

(50) Gehrman, J. L., "A Study of the Impact of Authoritative Communication of Expected Achievement in Elementary School Science." (M) 1965.

(51) Gerne, T. A., Jr., "A Comparative Study of Two Types of Science Teaching on the Competence of Sixth-Grade Students to Understand Selected Topics in Electricity and Magnetism." (M) 1967.

(52) Glaser, R., "Concept Learning and Concept Teaching." University of Pittsburgh, Learning Research and Development Center, 1967.

(53) ———— "The Design of Instruction." National Society for the Study of Education *Yearbook,* 1966.

(54) Gleason, W. P., "An Examination of Some Effects of Pupil Self-Instruction Methods Compared with the Effects of Teacher-Led Classes in Elementary Science of Fifth-Grade Pupils." (M) 1965.

(55) Gunnels, F. G., "A Study of the Development in Logical Judgments in Science of Successful and Unsuccessful Problem Solvers in Grades Four Through Nine." (M) 1967.

(56) Haddad, W. D., "Relationship Between Mental Maturity and the Level of Understanding of Concepts of Relatively in Grades 4-8." (M) 1968.

(57) Harris, W., and V. Lee, "Mental Age and Science Concepts—A Pilot Study." *Journal of Research in Science Teaching,* December 1966.

(58) Harris, W., "A Technique for Grade Placement in Elementary Science." *Journal of Research in Science Teaching,* March 1964.

(59) Harris, W. N., "An Analysis of Problem-Solving Behavior in Sixth-Grade Children, and of the Usefulness of Drawings by the Pupil in Learning Science Concepts." (M) 1962.

(60) Haugerud, A. R., "The Development of a Conceptual Framework for the Construction of a Multi-Media Learning Laboratory and its Utilization for Elementary School Science." (M) 1966.

(61) Hedges, W. D., and M. A. MacDougall, "Teaching Fourth-Grade Science by Means of Programed Science Materials with Laboratory Experiences." *Science Education*, February 1964.

(62) Helgeson, S. L., "An Investigation into the Relationships between Concepts of Force Attained and Maturity as Indicated by Grade Levels." (M) 1967.

(63) Hinmon, D. E., "Problem Solving." *Science and Children,* April 1966.

(64) Johnson, M. L., "A Determination of Aerospace Principles Desirable for Inclusion in Fifth- or Sixth-Grade Science Programs." (M) 1966.

(65) Karplus, R., "Science Curriculum Improvement Study." *Journal of Research in Science Teaching,* December 1964.

(66) Kolb, J. R., "Effects of Relating Mathematics to Science Instruction on the Acquisition of Quantitative Science Behaviors." *Journal of Research in Science Teaching,* 1968.

(67) Korey, R. A., "Contributions of Planetariums to Elementary Education." (M) 1963.

(68) Kraft, M. E., "A Study of Information and Vocabulary Achievement from the Teaching of Natural Science by Television in the Fifth Grade." (M) 1961.

(69) LaCava, G., "An Experiment Via Tape." *Science and Children,* October 1965.

(70) Languis, M. and L. L. Stull, "Science Problems—Vehicles to Develop Measurement Principles." *Science Education,* February 1966.

(71) Lansdown, B., and T. S. Dietz, "Free Versus Guided Experimentation." *Science Education,* April 1965.

(72) Lindvall, C. M. and J. D. Bolvin, "Individually Prescribed Instruction—The Oakleaf Project." University of Pittsburgh, Learning Research and Development Center, February 1966.

(73) Lipson, J. I., "Light Test—Comparison Between Elementary School Children and College Freshman." University of Pittsburgh, Learning Research and Development Center, February 1966.

(74) _____ "An Individualized Science Laboratory." *Science and Children,* December 1966.

(75) Livermore, A. H., "The Process Approach of the AAAS Commission on Science Education." *Journal of Research in Science Teaching,* December 1964.

(76) Lowery, L. F., "An Experimental Investigation into the Attitudes of Fifth-Grade Students Toward Science." *School Science and Mathematics,* June 1967.

(77) Los Angeles City Schools, "The Art of Questioning in Science—Summary and Implications." 1967.

(78) Mason, J. M., "The Direct Teaching of Critical Thinking in Grades Four Through Six." *Journal of Research in Science Teaching,* December 1963.

(79) McCloskey, J., "The Development of the Role of Science in General Education for Elementary and Secondary Schools." (M) 1963.

(80) McKeon, J. E., "A Process Lesson in Density." *Science and Children,* December 1966.

(81) Melis, L. H., "The Nature and Extent of Reading Instruction in Science and Social Studies in the Intermediate Grades of Selected School Districts." (M) 1964.

(82) Mermelstein, E., E. Carr, D. Mills, and J. Schwartz, "The Effects of Various Training Techniques on the Acquisition of the Concept of Conservation of Substance." U.S. Department of Health, Education, and Welfare, February 1967.

(83) Moorehead, W. D., "The Status of Elementary School Science and How it is Taught." (M) 1965.

(84) Nasca, D., "Effect of Varied Presentations of Laboratory Exercises within Programed Materials on Specific Intellectual Factors of Science Problem-Solving Behavior." *Science Education,* December 1966.

(85) Neal, L. A., "Techniques for Developing Methods of Scientific Inquiry in Children in Grades One Through Six." *Science Education,* October 1961.

(86) New York State Department of Education. "Tips and Techniques in Elementary Science." Bureau of Elementary Curriculum Development. 1966.

(87) Novak, J. D., "Development and Use of Audio-Tape Programmed Instruction for Elementary Science." Purdue University, February 1967.

(88) O'Toole, R. J., "A Review of Attempts to Individualize Elementary School Science." *School Science and Mathematics,* May 1968.

(89) _____ "A Study to Determine Whether Fifth-Grade Children Can Learn Certain Selected Problem-Solving Abilities Through Individualized Instruction (Research Study Number 1)." (M) 1966.

(90) Perkins, W. D., "The Field Study as a Technique in Elementary School Science." *Science Education,* December 1963.

(91) Pershern, F. R., "The Effect of Industrial Arts Activities on Science Achievements and Pupil Attitudes in the Upper Elementary Grades." (M) 1967.

(92) Pollach, S., "Individual Differences in the Development of Certain Science Concepts." (M) 1963.

(93) Price, L., "An Investigation of the Transfer of an Elementary Science Process." (M) 1968.

(94) Ramsey, I. L., and S. L. Wiandt, "Individualizing Elementary School Science." *School Science and Mathematics,* May 1967.

(95) Raun, C. E., "The Interaction Between Curriculum Variables and Selected Classroom Student Characteristics." (M) 1967.

(96) Reese, W. F., "A Comparison of Interest Level and Problem-Solving Accuracy Generated by Single Concept Inductive and Deductive Science Films (Research Study Number 1)" (M) 1966.

(97) Riessman, F. "Education of the Culturally Deprived Child." *The Science Teacher*, November 1965.

(98) Rowland, G. W., "A Study of the Relationship Between Socio-Economic Status and Elementary School Science Achievement." (M) 1965.

(99) St. John, C., "Can Science Education be Scientific? Notes Toward a Viable Theory of Science Teaching," *Journal of Research in Science Teaching*, December, 1966.

(100) Salstrom, D., "A Comparison of Conceptualization in Two Types of Guided Discovery Science Lesson." (M) 1966.

(101) Sands, T., R. E. Rumery, and R. C. Youngs, "Concept Development Materials for Gifted Elementary Pupils—Final Report of Field Testing." Illinois State University, 1966.

(102) Schiller, L. "A Study of the Effect of Individualized Activities on Understanding in Elementary School Science." (M) 1964.

(103) Schippers, J. V. "An Investigation of the Problem Method of Instruction in Sixth-Grade Science Classes." (M) 1962.

(104) Scott, L., "An Experiment in Teaching Basic Science in the Elementary School." *Science Education*, March 1962.

(105) Scott, N. C., Jr. "Science Concept Achievement and Cognitive Functions." *Journal of Research in Science Teaching*, December 1964.

(106) _____ "The Strategy of Inquiry and Styles of Categorization." *Journal of Research in Science Teaching*, September 1966.

(107) Scott, N. C., Jr., and I. E. Sigel, "Effects of Inquiry Training in Physical Science on Creativity and Cognitive Styles of Elementary School Children." U.S. Office of Education, Cooperative Research Branch, 1965.

(108) Shulz, R. W., "The Role of Cognitive Organizers in the Facilitation of Concept Learning in Elementary School Science." (M) 1966.

(109) Skinner, R. Jr., "An Experimental Study of the Effects of Different Combinations of Television Presentations and Classroom Teacher Follow-up on the Achievement and Interest in Science of Fifth Graders." (M) 1966.

(110) Smith, B. A., "An Experimental Comparison of Two Techniques (Planetarium Lecture-Demonstration and Classroom Lecture-Demonstration) of Teaching Selected Astronomical Concepts to Sixth-Grade Students." (M) 1966.

(111) Smith, D. M. and B. Cooper, "A Study of the Use of Various Techniques in Teaching Science in the Elementary School." *School Science and Mathematics*, June 1967.

(112) Smith, R. F., "An Analysis and Classification of Children's Explanations of Natural Phenomena." (M) 1963.

(113) Snoble, J. J. "Status and Trends of Elementary School Science in Iowa Public Schools, 1963-1966." (M) 1967.

(114) Stapp, W. B. "Developing a Conservation Education Program for the Ann Arbor Public School System, and Integrating It into the Existing Curriclum (K-12)." (M) 1963.

(115) Stauss, N. G., "An Investigation into the Relationship between Concept Attainment and Level of Maturity." (M) 1967.

(116) Stokes, W. W., "An Analysis and Evaluation of Current Efforts to Improve the Curriculum by Emphasis on Disciplinary Structure and Learning by Discovery." (M) 1963.

(117) Stone, R. M., "A Comparison of the Patterns of Criteria Which Elementary and Secondary School Teachers Use in Judging the Relative Effectiveness of Selected Learning Experiences in Elementary Science." (M) 1963.

(118) Suchman, J. R., "Idea Book—Inquiry Development Program in Physical Science." Chicago: Science Research Associates, Inc., 1966.

(119) _____ "Inquiry Training: Building Skills for Autonomous Discovery." *Merrill-Palmer Quarterly,* 1961.

(120) Swan, M. D. "Science Achievement as it Relates to Science Curricula and Programs at the Sixth-Grade Level in Montana Public Schools." *Journal of Research in Science Teaching,* June 1966.

(121) Tating, M. T., "Priming Creative Thinking in Elementary School Science." (M) 1965.

(122) Taylor, A. L., "The Influence of Teacher Attitudes on Pupil Achievement with Programed Science Materials." *Journal of Research in Science Teaching,* March 1960.

(123) Voelker, A. M., "The Relative Effectiveness of Two Methods of Instruction in Teaching the Classificational Concepts of Physical and Chemical Change to Elementary School Children." (M) 1967.

(124) Wagner, B. A., "The Responses of Economically Advantaged and Economically Disadvantaged Sixth-Grade Pupils to Science Demonstrations." (M) 1967.

(125) Walbesser, H. H., "Science Curriculum Evaluation—Observations on a Position." *The Science Teacher,* February 1966.

(126) Walbesser, H. H., et. al., "Science—A Process Approach, An Evaluation Model and Its Application—Second Report." American Association for the Advancement of Science, AAAS Miscellaneous Publication 68–4, 1968.

(127) Washton, N. S., "Teaching Science for Creativity." *Science Education,* February 1966.

(128) Williams, D. L., "The Effect of Rewritten Science Textbook Materials on the Reading Ability of Sixth-Grade Pupils." (M) 1964.

(129) Wilson, J. H., "Differences Between the Inquiry-Discovery and the Traditional Approaches to Teaching Science in Elementary Schools." (M) 1967.

(130) Wolinsky, G. F., "Science Education and the Severely Handicapped Child." *Science Education,* October 1965.

(131) Zafforoni, J., "A Study of Pupil-Teacher Interaction in Planning Science Experiences." *Science Education,* March 1963.

(132) Ziegler R. E., "The Relative Effectiveness of the Use of Static and Dynamic Mechanical Models in Teaching Elementary School Children the Theoretical Concept—The Particle Nature of Matter." (M) 1967.

VI

Becoming a Better Elementary Science Teacher Through Understanding The Role of Listening, Learning, and Questioning

Through listening we learn; for both teachers and children there is a time for listening and a time for questioning. Unfortunately both groups often confuse these roles. Teachers usually love to talk, often spending up to three-quarters of class time doing it while children sit passively listening. Often experienced teachers attempt to reduce their dominance of class time by asking exciting questions and encouraging children to discuss. However, as Dr. Stone states in his article, many of these questions leave much to be desired and, in fact, are not truly questions. Dr. Rowe's article indicates, furthermore, that when it is time to listen after a question, most teachers wait less than a second for the child to respond and then they listen selectively.

Questioning and listening, we feel, are basic to good science teaching. Questioning is a common technique having relevance to all areas of the curriculum. How can the quality of questions be improved? Why do you think teachers do not wait after a question has been asked? How can most teachers obtain a fluency and flexibility of questioning techniques? What can you do to change your behavior to insure you question and listen well?

Involved in any social interaction are questioning and listening skills. Listening enhances the interpersonal relationship. How many friends do you have that seldom listen to you? When teachers truly listen, they learn a great deal about children's attitudes, problems, under-standing, needs, and intelligence. Listening provides a direct evalua-tion by the greatest evaluation instrument known, the human mind. Furthermore, intelligently composed questions help gain insights into the talent potential, intellectual development, and psychological adjustment of the individual.

The articles in this section should help change your behavior so you become a better elementary science teacher—one who knows the value of applying good listening and questioning techniques.

28

SCIENCE, SILENCE, AND SANCTIONS

Mary Budd Rowe

When you ask a child a question, how long do you *think* you wait for an answer before you either repeat the question, ask him another question, or call on another child? If you are like many experienced teachers, you allow an *average of one second* for a child to start an answer. After a child makes a response, you apparently are still in a hurry because you generally wait slightly less than a second to repeat what he said or to rephrase it or ask another question.

In inservice training classes for experienced teachers, we have been studying such questioning-teaching techniques to discover which techniques are most effective for teaching science when utilizing some of the national experimental science programs for the elementary school, e.g., Science Curriculum Improvement Study (SCIS), Science—A Process Approach (AAAS), Elementary Science Study (ESS). We have found that when teachers change certain verbal patterns, students change their verbal patterns too. We began to experiment to test the effect of the following factors on the verbal behavior of children.

1. Increasing the period of time that a teacher waits for students to construct a response to a question.

Reprinted from *Science and Children*, 6, March 1969, pp. 11–13. Dr. Mary Budd Rowe is Associate Professor of Natural Science, Teachers College, Columbia University, New York.

2. Increasing the period of time that a teacher waits before replying to a student move.
3. Decreasing the pattern of reward and punishment delivered to students.

"Wait-Time"

While a fast pace in questioning may be suited for instruction in some subjects, it presents some special problems for teachers who are trying to conduct inquiry-oriented science lessons. In most of the new science programs that actually give children access to materials and information, ideas that develop come largely from what children do with the materials. In any collection of objects there may be more than one possible arrangement, more than one kind of experiment, more than one kind of result. The basic notion that underlies all new science programs is the belief that in inquiry the information or relevant cues lie hidden in the materials and not in the head of the teacher. Since that is the case, children need to monitor their materials more carefully than they monitor the teacher's face. Ideas can be modified or even discarded if the evidence requires. No particular point of view in the class is more sacred than another. What counts is what happens in the system of materials. Authority rests with the idea that "works." That point of view means you and the children need time to think and to evaluate. One second may not be long enough.

What happens in science if you increase the time you wait before you ask another question or call on another child? And what happens if you increase the amount of time you wait to speak *after* a child speaks? It turns out that all kinds of surprising and sometimes puzzling things result.

If you can prolong your average "wait-time" to five seconds, or preferably longer, the length of student responses increases. When wait-time is very short, students tend to give very short answers or they are more prone to say, "I don't know." In addition, their answers often come with a question mark in the tone, as if to say, "Is that what you want?" But if you increase the wait-time, especially the period after a child has made a response, you are more likely to get whole sentences, and the confidence as expressed by tone is higher. Another bonus that results from increased wait-times is the appearance of speculative thinking (e.g., "It might be the water," . . . "but it could be too many plants") and the use of arguments based on evidence.

If the wait-time is prolonged an average of five seconds or more, young children shift from teacher-centered show-and-tell kinds of behavior to child-child comparing of differences. Why this happens is not clear. It may be that longer wait-time allows children to trust the materials so that they shift from the teacher's face to the objects they are studying.

It is the teacher who gets the most practice asking questions in the classroom. Children rarely ask questions in class even when they have materials in front of them, yet we know they are usually curious. As you increase the wait-time, the number of questions children ask and the number of experiments they need to answer the questions multiply.

Suppose you do learn to control wait-time, what are the advantages? First, by increasing the wait-time, you buy for yourself an opportunity to hear and to think. As an example, examine a learning experience with a teaching machine. Suppose the machine begins to instruct a student by showing him some objects and saying, "Tell me how these are arranged. What does the arrangement look like?" The student might answer, "A xylophone." Now if the machine is programmed to expect the student to say "steps," there is a problem. The machine either goes on with whatever is next in its program or it cycles back and asks the question again and again until the student gives the "right" answer. Teachers often behave the same way. When the wait-times are very short, teachers exhibit little flexibility in the responses they allow. Contests for control of the metaphors (e.g., steps versus xylophone) are common, and the teacher usually prevails. A machine could do as well. Errors of this kind become less frequent as wait-time increases.

Second, wait-time can change your expectations about what some children can do. Teachers who have learned to use silence report that children who do not ordinarily say much start talking and usually have exciting ideas. In one inservice experiment, each of fifty teachers taught science to two first-grade children. The teachers knew the children had been grouped in combinations of two high verbal children, or two low verbal children, or one high and one low verbal child. At the end of the lesson, each teacher tried to decide which combination she had. To the delight of everyone in the experiment, the teachers usually misjudged the combination. Most often they classified low verbal youngsters as high verbal. The interaction of children with materials plus the protracted silences of the teachers apparently "turned on" children who usually "tuned out." When these teachers returned to their classrooms and experimented with wait-times, they reported that children who did not ordinarily contribute began to take a more active part in doing and talking about science.

Expectations teachers hold for children can have a deadly effect in terms of opportunities in which children get to practice speculative thinking. For example, on request, twelve inservice teachers each identified their five best and five poorest students. After sampling the teachers' wait-times in three lessons each of science and mathematics, it was found that the twelve teachers waited *significantly less time* in both subjects for poor students to reply to questions. That is, students rated as slow or less apt by teachers had to try to answer questions more rapidly than students rated as bright or fast. This result apparently surprised the teachers. As one of them said, "I guess we just don't expect an answer, so we go on to someone else." This group of twelve teachers then began to experiment deliberately with increasing wait-times for poorer students. Response by "slow" students increased, gradually at first, and then rapidly.

Questioning behavior also varies with wait-time. As wait-time increases, teachers begin to show much more variability in the kinds of questions they ask. Students get more opportunity to respond to thought rather than straight memory questions. When the pacing is fast, teachers often ask and answer their own questions. ("What color was it? It was green, wasn't it?") For some reason when teachers gain control of wait-time, questioning becomes less barrage-like and more flexible in form.

Rewards and Punishments

There is another factor besides silence that seems to have something to do with how children learn science and whether or not they learn to trust evidence as a basis for making judgments.

Usually, teachers use sanctions (positive and negative rewards) in the classroom somewhat indiscriminately. Sometimes teachers seem to be rewarding effort because they commend answers or work which is incorrect. At other times they reward correct responses. In fact, sanctions constitute as much as one quarter of teacher talk in many classrooms. Since evaluative comments constitute such a large part of teacher talk, it is useful to know how they influence science instruction.

Modern science programs for the elementary school seek to develop self-confidence in children by allowing them to work out their ideas in experiments. Children find out how good their ideas are by the results. When predictions no longer work or when new information makes a point of view untenable, then pupils are free to change their views. The point is that the authority for changing comes from the results of their experiments rather than from the teacher.

It appears that when teachers measurably reduce the amount of overt verbal rewarding they do, children seem to demand less of their time for showing what happens. Instead they do more comparing and arguing which leads to more experiments. When silence on the part of the teacher increases, and/or when sanctions decrease, the incidence of speculative thought on the part of the children increases. It is doubtful whether children can distinguish when they are being rewarded for effort and when for appropriate responses. When rewards are high, children tend to stop experimenting sooner than when the number of rewards is relatively lower. There is some reason to suspect that when children work on a complex task, rewards given by the teacher may interfere with logical thought processes. When children start attending to the reward rather than to the task, the incidence of error or the necessity to repeat steps increases.

Try It Yourself

Tape record a science lesson as you would normally teach it. Listen to what children say and how they say it. Now teach another lesson, but this time experiment with the wait-times or the rewards, but not both at once. If you try to change both factors at once, you will find it more difficult to discover the effect each has by itself. Find out whether the following statements are supported by your experiments.

1. Very short wait-times combined with high teacher rewards produce short student responses, high likelihood of inflected answers reflecting low student confidence, virtually no child-child exchanges of ideas, and a high incidence of answers unsupported by evidence.
2. Long wait-times (not less than five seconds) combined with low teacher rewards produce longer responses, more confidence, more exchanges between children, and more speculation supported by evidence.

The children may be inquiring about natural phenomena, but inquiry into teaching is the business of the professional teacher. Run your experiments on silence and sanctions in science enough times to be sure of how the factors act in your class. Let me know what kind of results you get.

29

THE ART OF QUESTIONING OR:
HOW YOU ASK MAKES A DIFFERENCE

A. H. Stone

The business of Inquiry, and its corollaries of thought and intellectual development, are instinctively tied to the nature of questioning and the design of questions. Questions, answers, inquiry and thought processes in general, are essentially attitudinal. Throughout the history of thought we find the role of attitudes playing a major part in how questions are formulated, what questions are suitable for asking, and how answers are expressed and accepted. An example of how questions are attitudinally asked and answered is evident in an old story of a conversation between two friends.

John said, "Harry, I want you to buy a ticket to her concert.

Harry was a man who knew how to answer a question without answering a question. His *exact* response to the question has been lost for eternity, but to be sure it was one of the following responses:

"*You* want me to buy a ticket to her concert?"
"You *want* me to buy a ticket to her concert?"
"You want *me* to buy a ticket to her concert?"
"You want me *to buy* a ticket to her concert?"
"You want me to buy *a* ticket to her concert?"
"You want me to buy a *ticket* to her concert?"

Reprinted from a paper presented at the 1971 Northeast Regional Conference of the National Science Teachers Association, Hartford, Connecticut, October 7–9, 1971. Dr. A. Harris Stone is Professor of Science Education, Southern Connecticut State College, New Haven, Conn.

"You want me to buy a ticket *to* her concert?"
"You want me to buy a ticket to *her* concert?"
"You want me to buy a ticket to her *concert*?"

What would Harry have meant if he used anyone of these responses to John's question? The words themselves do not convey Harry's meaning. It is his emphasis and his inflection in each of the nine possible responses which gives meaning to the listener. This example points out two major elements of questioning—the words and the emphasis placed on the words. Anyone who is familiar with the daily performance of the art of teaching must know the significance of questions and their use. It is with questions that we introduce listeners to ideas—particularly when we want them to actively participate in ideas on a cognitive or intellectual level. Often the questioner does not expect a verbal response when a question is asked. In that regard, questions are really not questions, but more statements which request the listener to "think about" a particular notion. Evidence of this kind of questioning is most prevalent when the questioner allows zero amount of response time. And, to be sure, response time is an integral part of questioning. We have all experienced the teacher who asks a question and immediately proceeds to give an answer. To wit, the questioner never intended the question as a question—at least not in the sense that the question was to be answered by the listener. We have also experienced the questioner who waits for a response but who is unwilling to accept any response which is not the specific one the questioner had carefully hidden in his mind. Again, the question is not really a question. It is more in the nature of a stimulus–response mechanism, and particularly one where a preconceived response is the only one which is suitable. So we can see several cases in which questions are used in ways other than those which could be described as *intellectually honest questioning techniques*.

Let us turn from these rather obvious comments about questioning techniques to some considerations of the nature of questions and how they are used in teaching. Consider the case of the Astronomy Professor who addressed his freshman class with the following:

"What is the position of Mars today according to the Ephemeris?" (The Ephemeris, for those readers who do not regularly look up the position of Mars, is the nickname for the *American Ephemeris and Nautical Almanac*).

I have it on good authority that when this question is asked of most college students, their response is instantly underwhelming. There is an obvious lack of enthusiasm and a distinct unrush in the direction of the Ephemeris. But the question can be phrased differently if one is aware of the inherent interest of a given group of students. Professor

Mike Zeilik presents the "question" in this way.[1] *If you can find today's position of Mars by using the Ephemeris, I can show you how to cast your horoscope.* In his paper, "Astrology—The Space Age Science?", Professor Zeilik approaches the study of geocentricity in the universe by looking at its relationship to astrology—"Since a horoscope depends purely on the geocentric aspects of the heavens, it is not necessary to know any celestial mechanics to cast one, but simply some idea of the geocentric motions of the celestial bodies" (3, p. 3).

Professor Zeilik capitalizes on the inherent interest of students when he proposes a direction of study for them. It is clear that Zeilik has asked a question when he *states* "If you can find today's position of Mars by using the Ephemeris I can show you how to cast your horoscope." But his statement is just that, a statement—it is not a question. Yet, this non-question questioning technique is reported by Zeilik to create a near-stampede of students toward the Ephemeris. Apparently everyone wants to answer the question that has not quite been asked. Here we have a fine example of a teacher who knows full well that teaching is a performing art, and an art that must be executed with more concern for the internal motivation of students than for the nature of the academic content of what is being taught.

Looking at the world of questioning from a broader prospective, let us now turn a moment to some of the ramifications of questioning. One of the oldest sources of information available to English speaking people is the Oxford English Dictionary. The word *question* and its various derivatives appear in the O.E.D. quite frequently, with more than fifteen entries. Almost all of these entries deal with words such as inquiry, investigation, discussion, controversy, decision, consideration, discourse, and interrogation. Words of this nature easily lead us to consider the thinking processes employed by men in their continual effort to know more about themselves and their environment. Each of these words, moreover, implies conflict of thoughts, at least within oneself. From the teacher's point of view, however, these words must involve more than the questioner. Uniquely, in the field of education, the questionee is one who should be able to respond to the questioner with limited personal risk. In many professions, as in the field of law, for example, the questionee is often asked to respond to questions in such a way that his own personal well-being may be affected. Clearly, this should not be the case among teachers and students. Thus, we come to the topic of the attitudes of questioners and questionees. We have all experienced that malevolent teacher whose questions are designed to be unanswerable or embarrassing. This teacher's attitude

---

[1]Personal communication with Professor Mike Zeilik of Southern Connecticut State College, New Haven, 06515.

is clear and we need spend no further time in what might be called the negative history of education. Rather, let us look at the benevolent teacher whose question can be characterized as being searching, provocative, helpful, intriguing, and demanding. Anyone of us in the position of questionee would far prefer the latter teacher than the former. It is the benevolent teacher's questioning which often has been responsible for new insights, self-development, and intellectual advance in students. It is also this teacher who is likely to be the instigator of academic and intellectual freedom. The environment called the open classroom, for example, is probably most successful in the hands of an *accomplished "questioner"*, than in the grips of the classically rigorous interrogator *or* the laizzez-faire structureless teacher.

Let us further consider the attitudes and techniques of the benevolent teacher who is successful in the business of questioning. Surely the matters of timing and pacing are of prime concern. If a question is honestly provocative to a learner it is unreasonable to expect the learner to have an immediate response. It follows then, that to ask a meaningful question demands that a period of time be allowed to elapse *before the questioner seeks a response*. What has happened in the learner's head during the time elapsed between question and answer cannot be known, but it can be estimated. If the question has been truly provocative and stimulating then certain processes are likely to have occurred in the learner's head. First, the learner may have categorized a great deal of information which he initially deemed appropriate and fitting to the nature of the question. This may have been followed by a rapid analysis of the information in which certain of it was retained and some disregarded. Perhaps most important of all, the questionee has probably made value judgments based on his own manipulation of his information. Finally we have the response of the questionee—a response that is certainly based on the individual's best thought *at the moment*. Thus it is a response which carries for the student a large and obvious risk. The risk is the *verbalization* of his "information analysis/value judgement/best thinking/at-the-moment." The student must *make public,* at least to his teacher and perhaps to an entire class, his best efforts. He is revealing his thoughts for all to see. If the teacher shoots down this response or dismisses it out of hand, then the most common response that most students have is understandable. Having an answer rejected by a teacher is to experience personal rejection. And personal rejection does not encourage the questionee to answer more questions in the future. It is only through the teacher's honest attempt to understand an answer that the questionee will have an opportunity to further think and further modify a response. This process is *in fact* the learning process which evolves from the questioning technique.

There are many ways in which teachers can reinforce this process of learning. One of the most effective ways, and perhaps one of the most difficult because it is attitudinal, concerns a technique in which the teacher assumes the position of having *no knowledge* of an answer. As questioneers give their response, the teacher's role becomes one of a colleague who is as interested in finding a valid answer as is the student. The teacher in this role is apt to question a response with some content or process objection. But this teacher never rejects an answer out of hand. Seldom does he give a correct or valid response when students are unable to do so. This teacher is never guilty of the objection to teaching raised by Piaget.

> To comprehend is essentially to invent or to reinvent, and every time that one teacher too quickly an outcome of reflection, one hinders the child from discovering it or from inventing it by himself (1).

Piaget's comment has great impact particularly if you have ever had the experience of receiving the answer to a question you were interested in solving *before* you wanted that answer.

Finally let us look at the function of questions that function to titillate the philosophic self. Barry Stevens in *Don't Push The River* asks this question of herself.

> Why do we use a capital for *I*, and lower case *m* for me? It's not a question to be answered, but asking it feels good, like opening up something that had been closed before—and no teacher telling me, "That's the way it *is*, so learn it, and stop disrupting the class (2, p. 30).

Miss Stevens' message is clear to every teacher who cares about learners.

References

(1) Piaget, Jean, Address given at the University of Pennsylvania, Philadelphia, Pa., January 22, 1966.

(2) Stevens, Barry, *Don't Push the River*. Real People Press, 1970.

(3) Zeilik, Mike, "Astrology—The Space Age Science?" Prepublication print, 1971. Available from author on request.

30

STRATEGY FOR LEARNING*

Hilda Taba

From the educational tumult of the past decade, certain trends and patterns are now emerging that promise much more interesting teaching for all of us and more enthusiastic learning by our students. For example, research in education is shifting from laboratory to actual classroom situations. New concepts of learning processes offer clues to better understanding of how people learn. We can even begin to think of "strategies" of learning. Teaching, too, is developing strategies—to fit the newer concepts of learning. There is much here that is of special interest for teachers of science in the elementary grades.

An important effect of the shift to classroom-based research is the new perception of the idea of the unlimited potentiality of human learning—including the learning of those whose abilities we currently do not rate too high. The notion of a fixed IQ is being questioned, and the idea of a "functioning IQ" is developing. While no one pretends to know what the upper limit of human potentiality is, there seems to be a fairly widespread agreement that it is much higher than we have known how to realize. Gardner Murphy's book *Freeing Intelligence Through Teaching* (1) offers excellent reading on this subject.

---

*This Article is based on a speech originally presented at the luncheon meeting of NSTA and the Council of Elementary Science International during the 1965 Annual Convention in Denver, Colorado.

Reprinted from *Science and Children, 3,* September 1965, pp. 21–24. Dr. Hilda Taba is deceased. She was Professor of Education at San Francisco State College, San Francisco, Calif.

From observations of what happens in classrooms in which both the curriculum and teaching concentrate on developing the use of thinking-cognitive powers, I believe that in twelve years of schooling we could achieve a level of maturity about four years beyond what we now attain. This would be especially true if our techniques of studying learning were refined to include some factors that we do not study now because they seem statistically insignificant. Some of these could well be the "trigger" factors that set off processes which could reorganize the entire approach of an individual to learning. By studying the effects of these factors, we may be able to determine more precisely the effect of certain strategies of teaching. For example, how does a certain strategy affect the learning of individuals who have certain abilities, certain types of social-cultural background, or certain motivational patterns? Such knowledge would be invaluable at all grade levels. We need to be alert to findings in this area and to contribute to such research whenever possible.

Recent studies are also revolutionizing the concept of readiness to learn by shifting attention from what readiness individuals *have* to how to *build* readiness—certainly an area of special interest to teachers in the elementary grades. In the first flush of enthusiasm about readiness studies, the findings that children can learn more and earlier have been translated into programs of acceleration. Eventually, it is hoped, these ideas will be translated into creating more potent learning in depth, rather than merely a more rapid covering of the same ground.

Perhaps the most interesting and productive consequence of the new studies of the teaching-learning processes has been the restoration of a balance between content and process as ingredients of learning. In the past, too much time has been spent on conflict between these two areas. Recent emphasis on analyzing the structure of content clarifies the function of the different levels of content in curriculum, in teaching, and in learning. We are analyzing more clearly the processes of learning.

Today, we can identify more precisely the four targets of learning: knowledge, thinking, attitudes, and skills. We need to recognize that only the objective of knowledge can be implemented through organizing curriculum content. The other three depend upon process or the kind of learning experiences that are made available to children. For example, an objective such as thinking has remained in the realm of "pray and hope," because almost anything from daydreaming to inventing the concept of relativity could be, and has been, classified as thinking. This lack of analysis of what constitutes thinking has naturally resulted in uneconomical and ineffective teaching and learning of "thinking." It was too easy to assume that thinking is an automatic by-product of mastering "a subject matter" or of a "natural ability for it." True enough, a small percentage of children did learn some things on their own. Now that all kinds of children remain in school longer, we have an obligation to help all children learn to think.

Because of an inadequate behavioral analysis of thinking as an objective and ingredient of learning, we have relied on accumulating descriptive knowledge in order to enable learners to "think with it" later. Our curriculum in many areas, and especially so in the social studies, has been extremely descriptive. It has called for the same level of thinking, no matter what shifts have been made in content at successive grade levels. These shifts in content have not always been accompanied by systematically escalating the opportunities (or demands) to apply more complex and abstract modes of thinking.

We need to develop categories of the processes of thinking which can be learned and taught. The study of thinking in elementary school children attempts to do this (3). It deals with three cognitive tasks: (1) concept formation, or the organizing of specific information into conceptual systems; (2) interpretation of data, or the inductive process of developing generalizations and inferences from specific data; and (3) the application of principles and facts, or the deductive process of using knowledge to explain unfamiliar phenomena, to predict, and to hypothesize. These are learnable and teachable targets, because each represents a cluster of skills that can be identified and taught. They are surely especially pertinent to the teaching of science in the elementary grades. In fact, the science teacher should feel particular responsibility for developing these skills. Let us look briefly at each of these targets.

Concept formation involves essentially a way of putting unorganized information into some kind of mental filing system by grouping together an array of dissimilar objects or events on the basis of some common property that they possess, such as grouping together climate, weather, altitude, and topography, because all represent some elements of climate.

Interpretation of data is essentially a process of evolving generalizations from an analysis of concrete data. This is an inductive way of processing data and making inferences from the data. It involves the ability to go beyond that which is directly given and to arrive at a larger meaning, such as putting together the data on species of animals in a particular area and the data on water and vegetation in the same areas and inferring that generally certain species of animals are found in certain types of environments.

Application of principles and facts to new situations involves a deductive sequence. It starts when either a problem or a set of conditions is presented and hypothesizing regarding the possible solutions

Concept Formation

Overt activity	Covert mental operation	Eliciting question
1. Enumeration and listing	Differentiation	What did you see? Hear? Note?
2. Grouping	Identifying common properties, abstracting	What belongs together? On what criterion?
3. Labeling, categorizing	Determining the hierarchical order of items; super-and sub-ordination	How would you call these groups? What belongs under what?

Interpretation of Data

Overt activity	Covert mental operation	Eliciting question
1. Identifying points	Differentiation	What did you note? See? Find?
2. Explaining items of identified information	Relating points to each other Determining cause-and-effect relationships	Why did so-and-so happen?
3. Making inferences	Going beyond what is given Finding implications, extrapolating	What does this mean? What picture does it create in your mind? What would you conclude?

Application of Principles

Overt activity	Covert mental operation	Eliciting question
1. Predicting consequences Explaining unfamiliar phenomena Hyphothesizing	Analyzing the nature of the problem or situation Retrieving relevant knowledge	What would happen if . . .?
2. Explaining, supporting the predictions and hypotheses	Determining the causal links leading to prediction or hypothesis	Why do you think this would happen?
3. Verifying the prediction or hypothesis	Using logical principles or factual knowledge to determine necessary and sufficient conditions	What would it take for so-and-so to be true or probably true?

or consequences is required, such as asking students who have studied nomadic life in a desert to hypothesize what changes would occur in the way of life in the desert if water became available. It also involves a support of verification of these hypotheses and predictions by the application of relevant factual knowledge or generalizations, such as that the presence of water makes possible the growing of crops and, therefore, also a form of settled life and growth of cities.

Each of these cognitive tasks involves several levels of overt activity and of covert mental operations. Therefore, there must also be corresponding teaching strategies which elicit these processes. The three levels of the three dimensions of the teaching-learning process are shown in the chart.

Some Principles For Strategies of Learning

Several theoretical principles underlie the identification of these skills and especially the formulation of teaching strategies for helping students master them.

1. *Learning is a transactional process.* An individual organizes whatever he receives by way of information, from whatever source, according to his current conceptual system. This system may be faulty, partial, productive, or unproductive. For example, in his inquiry training, Suchman shows a filmed "episode" in which what appears to be a plain metal blade is put over a flame (2). The blade bends downward. The students tend to interpret this phenomenon in terms of the concept that metal softens with heat and therefore bends downward. They are, therefore, baffled when the same blade bends upward when it is turned over and inserted into the flame again.

Or, the third graders who see in a film a girl in a jungle village putting the coins she received from the sale of carved figures into a pot and then burying it in the floor of the hut may interpret this act as "keeping the money safe from baby sitters," because this is part of their concept of reasons for keeping money safe, inappropriate as it is to the jungle situation. In a sense, then, an individual "remakes," or reorganizes, reality according to his conceptual scheme. The information does something to the individual, and the individual does something to the information.

To aid students acquire increasingly more productive conceptual systems for organizing information, we need to devise learning-teaching strategies designed to help them learn to organize knowledge and not just present them with organized knowledge. One important aspect of these strategies is to stress the asking of questions instead of the giving of answers. The types of questions the teacher asks determine what students can or will be allowed to do.

2. *The learning of cognitive skills is a developmental process.* Each cognitive task involves a series of hierarchical skills that represent sequential steps in mastering the task. Each preceding step is a pre-

requisite to mastering the next one, and each successive step should capitalize on what preceded. The development of cognitive skills is not instantaneous learning. Each subsequent step requires the use of more complex and more sophisticated operations than did the preceding step. The success with each subsequent step depends on the mastery of the cognitive operations involved in the preceding one.

The concepts themselves are hierarchical in the sense of representing different degrees of complexity, abstractness, and generality. This introduces still another developmental sequence: that of combining concepts of a lower order into those of a higher order.

In an ideal over-all sequence, one would rotate tasks which require assimilating new information into an already established conceptual organization with tasks that require a reorganization and stretching of that scheme.

3. *Maturation of learning requires escalation both of content and of cognitive processes.* The planning of learning experiences to promote thinking of this type requires planning on two tracks. One is the sequence and escalation of the basic concepts, ideas, and the required information. The other is the sequence and the escalation of the processes by which information is organized and used. These need to progress together; the neglect of either may prevent or hinder the development of autonomous thinking. Sequences must be planned for both content and mental operations. If not, the pacing of learning is likely to be faulty in the sense that either more or less is required than is possible for the student. The result in the first case is the loss of the autonomy of student thinking, because the student must revert to passive absorption. In the second case the students are bored because the performance required represents repetition of concepts and skills which are already mastered.

Strategies of Teaching

What strategies of teaching should the teacher apply for this type of learning? First, the teacher needs to construct for himself two sets of cognitive maps by which to guide the process of learning: (1) the map of the content topics, of the dimensions of the topics, and of the basic ideas and concepts that the study of these topics is to produce, and (2) of the nature of intellectual skills involved and of the ways in which these skills are mastered.

Second, teachers need to change their role from the customary answer-giving to question-asking. Cognitive operations are stimulated only as the students are required to *search* for answers and to invent and discover the processes by which to deal with the tasks proposed by the questions.

Third, such a concept of learning introduces a different approach to handling content topics. The direct emphasis is not on "covering" a quantity of specific content but on sampling judiciously the specific instances which are valid examples of certain basic ideas and concepts. These instances must then be explored in sufficient detail to make it possible for students to "discover" the basic idea, generalization, or a concept. A teaching strategy which leads to mastery of powerful inductive generalizations and the necessary application of the corresponding skills is teaching for transfer, because transfer can occur only through the mediation of generalizations.

If these cognitive processes are learned in an interactive process, such as classroom discussion, students have a new source of learning new modes of thinking. In an interactive classroom, students are aided in extending their models for thought processes by "taking off from each others' shoulders," so to speak.

Finally, teachers need to understand and to accept the fact that it takes both time and practice to acquire new skills in thinking. This is especially true when preceding instruction has cultivated habits which are inconsistent with the processes required in thinking.

However, the results in our study of thinking suggest that, given adequate teaching strategy and a curriculum design which facilitates the stepwise development of concepts and ideas, even a student who is considered a "slow learner" will learn to master the higher levels of cognitive skills. All students make great strides both in the mastery of essential knowledge and in the mature use of reasoning power which is considerably beyond the level usually attained. At first the pacing will be slow for all because of the additional task of learning cognitive skills. Later the progress in both content mastery and thinking is cumulatively accelerated.

References

(1) Murphy, Gardner, *Freeing Intelligence Through Teaching*. New York: Harper and Brothers, 1961.

(2) Suchman, J. R., *The Elementary School Training in Scientific Inquiry*. Illinois Studies in Inquiry Training, Title VII, Project No. 216, U. S. Office of Education, Washington, D. C., 1962.

(3) Taba, Hilda, S. Levine, and F. F. Elzey, *Thinking in Elementary School Children*. Cooperative Research Project No. 1574, U. S. Office of Education, Washington, D.C., 1964.

VII

Becoming a Better Elementary Science Teacher Through Understanding Creativity, Discovery, and Inquiry

When educators speak of discovery and inquiry what exactly do they mean? Are they methods of teaching or are they individual mental processes? This section is designed to introduce several different views of discovery and inquiry. It is neither our intent to pit one author's views against another nor to indicate that one is right while others are wrong. They are provided to give different points of view and allow the reader to develop his own teaching style. A discovery approach does provide personal meaning for the student.

We have also attempted to incorporate examples of actual teaching behavior. This should answer, at least in part, the ever-present question "How is this done in the classroom?" While some of the authors represent specific curriculum projects, many of their ideas are universal. That is, they could be incorporated regardless of the classroom, materials, or text. We have found this to be true even if a textbook series is used.

Becoming a better elementary science teacher involves growth in the effective use of discovery and inquiry teaching. We would like to add that it is not a curriculum, method, or technique that provides an enjoyable teaching experience. When you combine all the components discussed in this book and internalize them so your behavior begins to change, then you are on the way to excellence in elementary science teaching.

31

PSYCHOLOGICAL CONTROVERSIES
IN THE TEACHING OF
SCIENCE AND MATHEMATICS*

Lee S. Shulman

The popular press has discovered the discovery method of teaching. It is by now, for example, an annual ritual for the Education section of *TIME* magazine to sound a peal of praise for learning by discovery (e.g., *TIME*, December 8, 1967 [7]). *TIME's* hosannas for discovery are by no means unique, reflecting as they do the educational establishment's general tendency to make good things seem better than they are. Since even the soundest of methods can be brought to premature mortality through an overdose of unremitting praise, it becomes periodically necessary even for advocates of discovery, such as I, to temper enthusiasm with considered judgment.

The learning by discovery controversy is a complex issue which can easily be oversimplified. A recent volume has dealt with many aspects of the issue in great detail (8). The controversy seems to center essentially about the question of how much and what kind of guidance ought to be provided to students in the learning situation. Those favoring learning by discovery advocate the teaching of broad principles and problem-solving through minimal teacher guidance and maximal opportunity for exploration and trial-and-error on the part of the student.

---

*Invited paper to the American Association for the Advancement of Science, Division Q (Education), New York City. December 1967.

Reprinted from *The Science Teacher, 35,* September 1968, pp. 34–90. Dr. Lee S. Shulman is Professor of Educational Psychology and Medical Education, Michigan State University, East Lansing, Mich.

Those preferring guided learning emphasize the importance of carefully sequencing instructional experiences through maximum guidance and stress the importance of basic associations or facts in the service of the eventual mastering of principles and problem solving.

Needless to say, there is considerable ambiguity over the use of the term *discovery*. One man's discovery approach can easily be confused with another's guided learning curriculum if the unwary observer is not alerted to the preferred labels ahead of time. For this reason I have decided to contrast the two positions by carefully examining the work of two men, each of whom is considered a leader of one of these general schools of thought.

Professor Jerome S. Bruner of Harvard University is undoubtedly the single person most closely identified with the learning-by-discovery position. His book, *The Process of Education* (1), captured the spirit of discovery in the new mathematics and science curricula and communicated it effectively to professionals and laymen. His thinking will be examined as representative of the advocates of discovery learning.

Professor Robert M. Gagné of the University of California is a major force in the guided learning approach. His analysis of *The Conditions of Learning* (3) is one of the finest contemporary statements of the principles of guided learning and instruction.

I recognize the potential danger inherent in any explicit attempt to polarize the positions of two eminent scholars. My purpose is to clarify the dimensions of a complex problem, not to consign Bruner and Gagné to irrevocable extremes. Their published writings are employed merely to characterize two possible positions on the role of discovery in learning, which each has expressed eloquently at some time in the recent past.

In this paper I will first discuss the manner in which Bruner and Gagné, respectively, describe the teaching of some particular topic. Using these two examples as starting points, we will then compare their positions with respect to instructional objectives, instructional styles, readiness for learning, and transfer of training. We will then examine the implications of this controversy for the process of instruction in science and mathematics and the conduct of research relevant to that process.

Instructional Example: Discovery Learning

In a number of his papers, Jerome Bruner uses an instructional example from mathematics that derives from his collaboration with the mathematics educator, Z.P. Dienes (2).

A class is composed of eight-year-old children who are there to learn some mathematics. In one of the instructional units, children are first introduced to three kinds of flat pieces of wood or "flats." The first one, they are told, is to be called either the "unknown square" or "X square." The second flat, which is rectangular, is called "1 X" or just X, since it is X long on one side and 1 long on the other. The third flat is a small square which is 1 by 1, and is called 1.

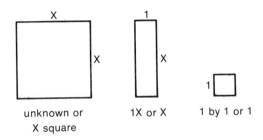

unknown or   1X or X   1 by 1 or 1
X square

After allowing the children many opportunities simply to play with these materials and to get a feel for them, Bruner gives the children a problem. He asks them, "Can you make larger squares than this X square by using as many of these flats as you want?" This is not a difficult task for most children and they readily make another square such as the one illustrated below.

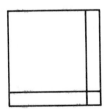

Bruner then asks them if they can describe what they have done. They might reply, "We have one square X, with two X's and a 1." He then asks them to keep a record of what they have done. He may even suggest a notational system to use. The symbol $X^{\square}$ could represent the square X, and a + for "and." Thus, the pieces used could be described as $X^{\square} + 2X + 1$.

Another way to describe their new square, he points out, is simply to describe each side. With an X and a 1 on each side, the side can be described as X + 1 and the square as (X + 1) (X + 1) after some work with parentheses. Since these are two basic ways of describing the same square, they can be written in this way: $X^{\square} + 2X + 1 =$

(X + 1) (X + 1). This description, of course, far oversimplifies the procedures used.

The children continue making squares and generating the notation for them. (See next diagram.)

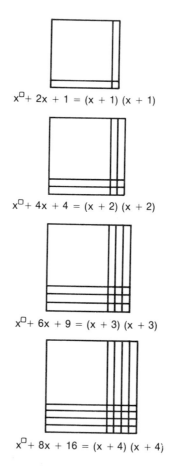

$x^{\Box}$+ 2x + 1 = (x + 1) (x + 1)

$x^{\Box}$+ 4x + 4 = (x + 2) (x + 2)

$x^{\Box}$+ 6x + 9 = (x + 3) (x + 3)

$x^{\Box}$+ 8x + 16 = (x + 4) (x + 4)

At some point Bruner hypothesizes that they will begin to discern a pattern. While the X's are progressing at the rate of 2, 4, 6, 8, the ones are going 1, 4, 9, 16, and on the right side of the equation the pattern is 1, 2, 3, 4. Provocative or leading questions are often used Socratically to elicit this discovery. Burner maintains that, even if the children are initially unable to break the code, they will sense that there is a pattern and try to discover it. Burner then illustrates how the pupils transfer what they have learned to working with a balance beam. The youngsters are ostensibly learning not only something about quadratic equations, but more important, something about the discovery of mathematical regularities.

The general learning process described by Bruner occurs in the following manner: First, the child finds regularities in his manipulation of the materials that correspond with intuitive regularities he has already come to understand. Notice that what the child does for Bruner is to find some sort of match between what he is doing in the outside world and some models or templates that he already has in his mind. For Bruner, it is rarely something *outside* the learner that is discovered. Instead the discovery involves an internal reorganization of previously known ideas in order to establish a better fit between those ideas and the regularities of an encounter to which the learner has had to accommodate.

This is precisely the philosophy of education we associate with Socrates. Remember the lovely dialogue of the *Meno* by Plato, in which the young slave boy is brought to an understanding of what is involved in doubling the area of a square. Socrates maintains throughout this dialogue that he is not teaching the boy anything new; he is simply helping the boy reorganize and bring to the fore what he has always known.

Bruner almost always begins with a focus on the production and manipulation of materials. He describes the child as moving through three levels of representation. The first level is the *enactive level,* where the child manipulates materials directly. He then progresses to the *ikonic level,* where he deals with mental images of objects but does not manipulate them directly. Finally he moves to the *symbolic level,* where he is strictly manipulating symbols and no longer mental images of objects. This sequence is an outgrowth of the developmental work of Jean Piaget. The synthesis of these concepts of manipulation of actual materials as part of a developmental model and the Socratic notion of learning as internal reorganization into a learning-by-discovery approach is the unique contribution of Jerome Bruner.

The Process of Education was written in 1959, after most mathematics innovations that use discovery as a core had already begun. It is an error to say that Bruner initiated the learning-by-discovery approach. It is far more accurate to say that, more than any one man, he managed to capture its spirit, provide it with a theoretical foundation, and disseminate it. Bruner is not the discoverer of discovery; he is its prophet.

Instructional Example: Guided Learning

Robert Gagné takes a very different approach to instruction. He begins with a task analysis of the instructional objectives. He always asks the question, "What is it you want the learner to be able to do?" This *capability*, he insists, must be stated *specifically* and *behaviorally.*

By capability, he means the ability to perform certain specific functions under specified conditions. A capability could be the ability to solve a number series. It might be the ability to solve some problems in nonmetric geometry.

This capability can be conceived of as a terminal behavior and placed at the top of what will eventually be a complex pyramid. After analyzing the task, Gagné asks, "What would you need to know in order to do that?" Let us say that one could not complete the task unless he could first perform prerequisite tasks *a* and *b*. So a pyramid begins.

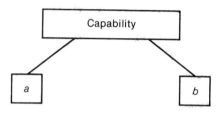

But in order to perform task *a*, one must be able to perform tasks *c* and *d* and for task *b*, one must know *e*, *f*, and *g*.

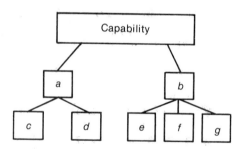

So one builds a very complex pyramid of prerequisites to prerequisites to the objective which is the desired capability.

Gagné has developed a model for discussing the different levels of such a hierarchy. If the final capability desired is a *problem-solving* capability, the learner first must know certain *principles*. But to understand those principles, he must know specific *concepts*, and prerequisite to these are particular *simple associations* or *facts* discriminated from each other in a distinctive manner. He continues the analysis until he ends up with the fundamental building blocks of learning—classically or operantly, conditioned responses.

Gagné, upon completing the whole map of prerequisites, would administer pretests to determine which have already been mastered. Upon completing the diagnostic testing, the resulting pattern identifies precisely what must be taught. This model is particularly conducive to subsequent programming of materials and programmed instruction. When prerequisites are established, a very tight teaching program or package develops.

Earlier, we discussed the influences on Bruner. What influenced Gagné? This approach to teaching comes essentially from a combination of the neobehaviorist psychological tradition and the task analysis model that dominates the fields of military and industrial training. It was precisely this kind of task analysis that contributed to successful programs of pilot training in World War II. Gagné was trained in the neobehaviorist tradition and spent the major portion of his early career as an Air Force psychologist.

Nature of Objectives

The positions of Bruner and Gagné take very different points of view with respect to the objectives of education. This is one of the major reasons why most attempts at evaluating the relative effectiveness of these two approaches have come to naught. They really cannot agree on the same set of objectives. Any attempt to ask which is better—Michigan State's football team or the Chicago White Sox—will never succeed. The criteria for success are different, and it would be absurd to have them both on the same field competing against each other.

For Gagné, or the programmed-instruction position which can be derived from him, the objectives of instruction are capabilities. They are behavioral products that can be specified in operational terms. Subsequently they can be task-analyzed; then they can be taught. Gagné would subscribe to the position that psychology has been successful in suggesting ways of teaching only when objectives have been made operationally clear. When objectives are not clearly stated, the psychologist can be of little assistance. He insists on objectives clearly stated in behavioral terms. They are the cornerstones of his position.

For Bruner, the emphasis is quite different. The emphasis is not on the *products* of learning but on the *processes*. One paragraph from *Toward a Theory of Instruction* captures the spirit of educational objectives for Bruner. After discussing the mathematics example previously mentioned, he concludes,

> Finally, a theory of instruction seeks to take account of the fact that a curriculum reflects not only the nature of knowledge itself—the specific capabilities—but also the nature of the knower and of the knowledge-getting process. It is the enterprise par excellence where the line between the subject matter and the method grows necessarily

indistinct. A body of knowledge, enshrined in a university faculty, and embodied in a series of authoritative volumes is the result of much prior intellectual activity. To instruct someone in these disciplines is not a matter of getting him to commit the results to mind; rather, it is to teach him to participate in the process that makes possible the establishment of knowledge. We teach a subject, not to produce little living libraries from that subject, but rather to get a student to think mathematically for himself, to consider matters as a historian does, *to take part in the process of knowledge-getting. Knowing is a process, not a product.* [2, p. 72] (Italics mine)

Speaking to the same issue, Gagné's position is clearly different.

Obviously, strategies are important for problem solving, regardless of the content of the problem. The suggestion from some writings is that they are of overriding importance as a goal of education. After all, should not formal instruction in the schools have the aim of teaching the student "how to think"? If strategies were deliberately taught, would not this produce people who could then bring to bear superior problem-solving capabilities to any new situation? Although no one would disagree with the aims expressed, it is exceedingly doubtful that they can be brought about by teaching students "strategies" or "styles" of thinking. Even   these could be taught (and it is possible that they could), they would not provide the individual with the basic firmament of thought, which is subject-matter knowledge. Knowing a set of strategies is not all that is required for thinking; it is not even a substantial part of what is needed. *To be an effective problem solver, the individual must somehow have acquired masses of structurally organized knowledge. Such knowledge is made up of content principles, not heuristic ones.* [3, p. 170] (Italics mine)

While for Bruner "knowing is a process, not a product," for Gagné, "knowledge is made up of content principles, not heuristic ones." Thus, though both espouse the acquisition of knowledge as the major objective of education, their definitions of *knowledge* and *knowing* are so disparate that the educational objectives sought by each scarcely overlap. The philosophical and psychological sources of these differences will be discussed later in this paper. For the moment, let it be noted that when two conflicting approaches seek such contrasting objectives, the conduct of comparative educational studies becomes extremely difficult.[1]

---

[1]Gagné has modified his own position somewhat since 1965. He would now tend to agree, more or less, with Bruner on the importance of processes or strategies as objectives of education. He has not, however, changed his position regarding the role of sequence in instruction, the nature of readiness, or any of the remaining topics in this paper (5). The point of view concerning specific behavioral products as objectives is still espoused by many educational theorists and Gagné's earlier arguments are thus still relevant as reflections of that position.

Instructional Styles

Implicit in this contrast is a difference in what is meant by the very words *learning by discovery*. For Gagné, *learning* is the goal. How a behavior or capability is learned is a function of the task. It may be by discovery, by guided teaching, by practice, by drill, or by review. The focus is on *learning* and discovery is but one way to learn something. For Bruner, it is learning *by discovery*. The method of learning is the significant aspect.

For Gagné, in an instructional program the child is carefully guided. He may work with programmed materials or a programmed teacher (one who follows quite explicitly a step-by-step guide). The child may be quite active. He is not necessarily passive; he is doing things, he is working exercises, he is solving problems. But the sequence is determined entirely by the program. (Here the term "program" is used in a broad sense, not necessarily simply a series of frames.)

For Bruner much less system or order is necessary for the package, although such order is not precluded. In general Bruner insists on the child manipulating materials and dealing with incongruities or contrasts. He will always try to build potential or emergent incongruities into the materials. Robert Davis calls this operation "torpedoing" when it is initiated by the teacher. He teaches a child something until he is certain the child knows it. Then he provides him with a whopper of a counterexample. This is what Bruner does constantly—providing contrasts and incongruities in order to get the child, because of his discomfort, to try to resolve this disequilibrium by making some discovery (cognitive restructuring). This discovery can take the form of a new synthesis or a new distinction. Piaget, too, maintains that cognitive development is a process of successive disequilibria and equilibria. The child, confronted by a new situation, gets out of balance and must accommodate to achieve a new balance by modifying the previous cognitive structure.

Thus, for Gagné, instruction is a smoothly guided tour up a carefully constructed hierarchy of objectives; for Bruner, instruction is a roller-coaster ride of successive disequilibria and equilibria until the desired cognitive state is reached or discovered.

Readiness

The guided learning point of view, represented by Gagné, maintains that readiness is essentially a function of the presence or absence of prerequisite learning.

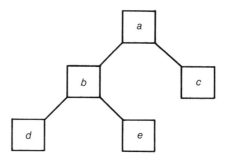

When the child is capable of *d* and *e* above, he is by definition ready to learn *b*. Until then he is not ready. Gagné is not concerned with genetically developmental considerations. If the child at age five does not have the concept of the conservation of liquid volume, it is not because of an unfolding in his mind; he just has not had the necessary prior experiences. Ensure that he has acquired the prerequisite behaviors, and he will be able to conserve (4).

For Piaget (and Bruner) the child is a developing organism, passing through cognitive stages that are biologically determined. These stages are more or less age-related, although in different cultures certain stages may come earlier than others. To identify whether the child is ready to learn a particular concept or principle, one analyzes the structure of that to be taught and compares it with what is already known about the cognitive structure of the child at that age. If they are consonant, it can be taught; if they are dissonant, it cannot.

Given this characterization of the two positions on readiness, to which one would you attribute the following statement? ''. . . any subject can be taught effectively in some intellectually honest form to any child at any stage of development.'' While it sounds like Gagné, you recognize that it isn't—it's Bruner! [2, p. 33] And in this same chapter he includes an extensive discussion of Piaget's position. Essentially he is attempting to translate Piaget's theories into a psychology of instruction.

Many are puzzled by this stand, including Piaget. In a recent paper delivered in the United States, he admitted that he did not understand how Bruner could make such a statement in the light of Piaget's experiments. If Bruner meant the statement literally; i.e., *any* child can learn *any*thing, then it just is not true! There are always things a child cannot learn, especially not in an intellectually honest way. If he means it homiletically, i.e., we can take almost anything and somehow resay it, reconstruct it, restructure it so it now has a parallel at the child's level of cognitive functioning, then it may be a truism.

I believe that what Bruner is saying, and it is neither trivial nor absurd, is that our older conceptions of readiness have tended to apply Piagetian theory in the same way as some have for generations applied Rousseau's. The old thesis was, "There is the child—he is a developing organism, with invariant order, invariant schedule. Here, too, is the subject matter, equally hallowed by time and unchanging. We take the subject matter as our starting point, watch the child develop, and feed it in at appropriate times as he reaches readiness." Let's face it; that has been our general conception of readiness. We gave reading readiness tests and hesitated to teach the pupil reading until he was "ready." The notion is quite new that the reading readiness tests tell not when to begin teaching the child, but rather what has to be done to get him more ready. We used to just wait until he got ready. What Bruner is suggesting is that we must modify our conception of readiness so that it includes not only the child but the subject matter. Subject matter, too, goes through stages of readiness. The same subject matter can be represented at a manipulative or enactive level, at an ikonic level, and finally at a symbolic or formal level. The resulting model is Bruner's concept of a spiral curriculum.

Piaget himself seems quite dubious over the attempts to accelerate cognitive development that are reflected in many modern math and science curricula. On a recent trip to the United States, Piaget commented,

> ... we know that it takes nine to twelve months before babies develop the notion that an object is still there even when a screen is placed in front of it. Now kittens go through the same stages as children, all the same sub-stages, but they do it in three months—so they're six months ahead of babies. Is this an advantage or isn't it? We can certainly see our answer in one sense. The kitten is not going to go much further. The child has taken longer, but he is capable of going further, so it seems to me that the nine months probably were not for nothing.
>
> It's probably possible to accelerate, but maximal acceleration is not desirable. There seems to be an optimal time. What this optimal time is will surely depend upon each individual and on the subject matter. We still need a great deal of research to know what the optimal time would be. [6, p. 82]

The question that has not been answered, and which Piaget whimsically calls the "American question," is the empirical experimental question: To what extent it is possible through a Gagnéan approach to accelerate what Piaget maintains is the invariant clockwork of the order? Studies being conducted in Scandinavia by Smedslund and in this country by Irving Sigel, Egon Mermelstein, and others are attempting to identify the degree to which such processes as the principle of conservation of volume can be accelerated. If I had to make a broad generalization, I would have to conclude that at this point, in general, the score for those who say you cannot accelerate is somewhat higher than the score for those who say that you can. But the question is far from resolved; we need many more inventive attempts to accelerate cognitive development than we have had thus far. There remains the question of whether such attempts at experimental acceleration are strictly of interest for psychological theory, or have important pedagogical implications as well—a question we do not have space to examine here.

Sequence of the Curriculum

The implications for the sequence of the curriculum growing from these two positions are quite different. For Gagné, the highest level of learning is problem solving; lower levels involve facts, concepts, principles, etc. Clearly, for Gagné, the appropriate sequence in learning is, in terms of the diagram below, from the bottom up. One begins with simple prerequisites and works up, pyramid fashion, to the complex capability sought.

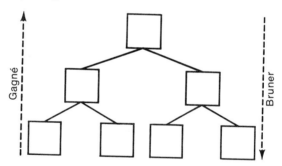

For Bruner, the same diagram may be appropriate, but the direction of the arrow would be changed. He has a pupil begin with *problem solving*. This process is analogous to teaching someone to swim by throwing him into deep water. The theory is that he will learn the fundamentals because he needs them. The analogy is not totally misbegotten. In some of the extreme discovery approaches we lose a lot of pupils by mathematical or scientific drowning. As one goes to the extreme of this position, he runs the risk of some drownings. For Gagné, the sequence is from the simple to the complex; for Bruner one starts with the complex and plans to learn the simple components in the context of working with complex.

It is unclear whether Bruner subscribes to his position because of his concept of the nature of learning or for strictly motivational reasons. Children may be motivated more quickly when given a problem they cannot solve, than they are when given some little things to learn on the promise that if they learn these well, three weeks from now they will be able to solve an exciting problem. Yet, Bruner clearly maintains that learning things in this fashion also improves the transferability of what is learned. It is to a consideration of the issue of transfer of training that we now turn.

Transfer of Training

To examine the psychologies of learning of these two positions in any kind of comprehensive form would require greater attention than can be devoted here, but we shall consider one concept—that of transfer of training. This is probably the central concept, or should be, in any educationally relevant psychology of learning.

Gagné considers himself a conservative on matters of transfer. He states that "transfer occurs because of the occurrence of specific identical (or highly similar) elements within developmental sequences" [4, p. 20]. To the extent that an element which has been learned, be it association, concept, or principle, can be directly employed in a new situation, transfer will occur. If the new context requires a behavior substantially different from the specific capability mastered earlier, there will be no transfer.

Bruner, on the other hand, subscribes to the broadest theories of transfer of training. Bruner believes that we can have massive transfer from one learning situation to another. Broad transfer of training occurs when one can identify in the structures of subject matters basic, fundamentally simple concepts or principles which, if learned well, can be transferred both to other subject matters within that discipline and to other disciplines as well. He gives examples such as the concept of conservation or balance. Is it not possible to teach balance of trade in economics in such a way that when ecological balance is considered, pupils see the parallel? This could then be extended to balance of power in political science, or to balancing equations.

Even more important, for Bruner, is the broad transferability of the knowledge-getting processes—strategies, heuristics, and the like— a transfer whose viability leaves Gagné with deep feelings of doubt. This is the question of whether learning by discovery leads to the ability *to* discover, that is, the development of broad inquiry competencies in students.

What does the evidence from empirical studies of this issue seem to demonstrate? The findings are not all that consistent. I would generalize them by saying that most often guided learning or expository sequences seem to be superior methods for achieving immediate learning. With regard to long-term retention, the results seem equivocal, with neither approach consistently better. Discovery learning approaches appear to be superior when the criterion of transfer of principles to new situations is employed (9). Notably absent are studies which deal with the question of whether general techniques, strategies, and heuristics of discovery can be learned—by discovery or in any other manner—which will transfer across grossly different kinds of tasks.

Why is transfer of training superior in the discovery situation when the learning of principles is involved? There are two kinds of transfer—positive transfer and negative transfer. We call something positive transfer when mastery of task X facilitates mastery of task Y. Negative transfer occurs when mastery of task X inhibits mastery of task Y. Positive transfer is a familiar notion for us. Negative transfer can be exemplified by a piece of advice baseball coaches often give their players. They tell them not to play golf during the baseball season because the baseball swing and the golf swing involve totally different muscles and body movements. Becoming a better golf swinger interfers with the baseball swing. In psychological terms there is negative transfer between golf and baseball.

What is needed for positive transfer is to minimize all possible interference. In transfer of training, there are some ways in which the tasks transferred to are like the ones learned first, but in other ways they are different. So transfer always involves striking a balance between these conflicting potentials for both positive and negative transfer. In discovery methods, learners may transfer more easily because they learn *the immediate things less well.* They may thus learn the broad strokes of a principle, which is the aspect most critical for remote transfer, while not learning well the detailed application of that specific principle, which could interfere somewhat with successful remote transfer.

If this formulation is correct, we are never going to find a method that will both allow for tremendous specific learning of products and broad transfer, because we are dealing in a closed system in which one must make a choice. To the extent that initial learning is well done, transfer is restricted. The instructor may have to decide which is more important—an immediate specific product or broad transfer—and choose his subsequent teaching method on the basis of that decision. This is a pessimistic view, and I hope that future studies might find it flawed.

Synthesis or Selection

Need we eternally code these as two alternatives—discovery versus expository teaching—or can we, without being heretical, manage to keep both of these in our methodological repertories as mathematics and science educators?

John Dewey was always very suspicious whenever he approached a controversy between two strongly stated positions, each of which insisted that the other was totally in error. The classic example of this is in his monograph *Experience and Education,* in which he examines the controversy of traditional versus progressive education. Dewey teaches us that whenever we confront this kind of controversy, we must look for the possibility that each position is massively buttressed by a brilliant half-truth from which is extrapolated the whole cloth of an educational philosophy. That is, too often a good idea wears thin as its advocates insist that it be applied outside its appropriate domain.

As educators, we find it extremely important to identify the conditions under which each of these theories can be applied most fruitfully. First, one must examine the nature of the objectives. More than half of this controversy can be resolved not at the level of which is the better psychology, but at the level of evaluative philosophical judgments. Given one set of goals, clearly the position Gagné advocates presently has more evidence in its favor; given another set of goals, there is no question but that Bruner's position is preferable to Gagné's.

But there are other questions. The age and personality of the learner must be taken into account. All things being equal, there are some kinds of children who cannot tolerate the ambiguity of a discovery experience. We all know this; some of us prefer to hear lectures that are well organized so that we can take notes in a systematic manner. Others of us like nothing better than a free-flowing bull session; and each of us is convinced that we learn more in our preferred mode than the others learn in theirs. Individual differences in learning styles are major determinants of the kinds of approaches that work best with different children.

Yet this is something we have in general not taken into consideration at all in planning curricula—and for very good reasons. As yet, we do not have any really valid ways of measuring these styles. Once we do, we will have a powerful diagnostic tool. Subject matter, objectives, characteristics of children, and characteristics of the teacher are all involved in this educational decision. Some teachers are no more likely to conduct a discovery learning sequence than they are to go frugging at a local nightclub.

There appear to be middle routes as well. In many of the experimental studies of discovery learning, an experimental treatment labeled *guided discovery* is used. In guided discovery, the subjects are carefully directed down a particular path along which they are called upon to discover regularities and solutions on their own. They are provided with cues in a carefully programmed manner, but the actual statement of the principle or problem solution is left up to them. Many of the well-planned Socratic dialogues of our fine teachers are forms of guided discovery. The teacher carefully leads the pupils into a series of traps from which they must now rescue themselves.

In the published studies, guided discovery treatments generally have done quite well both at the level of immediate learning and later transfer. Perhaps this approach allows us to put the Bruner roller-coaster of discovery on the well-laid track of a Gagné hierarchy.

Thus, the earlier question of which is better, learning by discovery or guided learning, now can be restated in more functional and pragmatic terms. Under what conditions are each of these instructional approaches, some sequence or combination of the two, of some synthesis of them, most likely to be appropriate? The answers to such questions ought to grow out of quite comprehensive principles of human learning. Where are we to find such principles?

Theories of Learning and the Science and Mathematics Curriculum

There is a growing psychology of learning that is finally becoming meaningful to curriculum construction and educational practice. Children are being studied as often as rats, and classrooms as often as mazes. Research with lower animals has been extremely useful in identifying some principles of learning that are so basic, so fundamental, so universal that they apply to any fairly well-organized blob of protoplasm. But there is a diminishing return in this approach insofar as transfer to educational practice is concerned. Today, a developing, empirically based psychology of learning for *homo sapiens* offers tremendous promise. But it can never be immediately translatable into a psychology of the teaching of mathematics or science. Mathematics and science educators must not make the mistake that the reading people have made and continue to make. The reason that the psychology of the teaching of reading has made such meager progress in the last twenty-five years is that the reading people have insisted on being borrowers. Something new happens in linguistics and within three years a linguistic reading series is off the press. It is an attempt to bootleg an idea from one field and put it directly into another without the necessary intervening steps of empirical testing and research.

Mathematics and science education are in grave danger of making that same error, especially with the work of Piaget and Bruner. What is needed now are well-developed empirically based psychologies of mathematics and science learning. Surely they will grow out of what is already known about the psychology of learning in general, but they must necessarily depend upon people like yourselves, your students, and your colleagues who are interested in mathematics and science conducting empirical studies of how certain specific concepts are learned under certain specific conditions with certain specific kinds of pupils. If anything is true about the field of mathematics and science education today, it is that rarely have any disciplines been so rich in theory and brilliant ideas. But we must seriously consider the admonition of Ivan Pavlov, the great Russian psychologist, who is said to have told his students the following:

> Ideas and theories are like the wings of birds; they allow man to soar and to climb to the heavens. But facts are like the atmosphere against which those wings must beat, and without which the soaring bird will surely plummet back to earth.

References

(1) Bruner, Jerome S., *The Process of Education*. Cambridge, Mass.: Harvard University Press, 1960.

(2) ——— *Toward a Theory of Instruction*. Cambridge, Mass.: Belknap Press, 1966.

(3) Gagné, Robert M., *The Conditions of Learning*. New York: Holt, Rinehart & Winston, 1965.

(4) ——— "Contributions of Learning to Human Development." Address of the Vice-President, Section I (Psychology), American Association for the Advancement of Science, Washington, D.C., December 1966.

(5) ——— Personal communication. May 1968.

(6) Jennings, Frank G., "Jean Piaget: Notes on Learning." *Saturday Review*, May 20, 1967, p. 82.

(7) "Pain & Progress in Discovery." *Time*, December 8, 1967, pp. 110 ff.

(8) Shulman, Lee S. and Evan R. Keislar (eds.), *Learning by Discovery: A Critical Appraisal*. Chicago: Rand-McNally, 1966.

(9) Worthen, Blaine R., "Discovery and Expository Task Presentation in Elementary Mathematics." *Journal of Educational Psychology Monograph Supplement, 59,* February 1968.

32

MESSING ABOUT IN SCIENCE

David Hawkins*

"Nice? It's the *only* thing," said the Water Rat solemnly, as he leant forward for his stroke. "Believe me, my young friend, there is *nothing*—absolutely nothing—half so much worth doing as simply messing about in boats. Simply messing," he went on dreamily, "messing—about—in—boats—messing—"

Kenneth Grahame,
The Wind in the Willows

As a college teacher, I have long suspected that my students' difficulties with the intellectual process comes not from the complexity of college work itself, but mainly from their home background and the first years of their formal education. A student who cannot seem to understand the workings of the Ptolemaic astronomy, for example, turns out to have no evident acquaintance with the simple and "obvious" relativity of motion, or the simple geometrical relations of light and shadow. Sometimes for these students a style of laboratory work which might be called "Kindergarten Revisited" has dramatically liberated their intellectual powers. Turn on your heel with your head back until you *see* the ceiling—turn the other way—and don't fall over!

In the past two years, working in the Elementary Science Study, I have had the experience, marvelous for a naive college teacher,

*The author of this article was the Director of the Elementary School Science Study of Educational Services, Inc., Watertown, Massachusetts from January 1962 to September 1964.

Reprinted from *Science and Children, 2,* February 1965, pp. 5–9. Dr. David Hawkins is Professor of Philosophy, University of Colorado, Boulder, Colo.

of studying young children's learning in science. I am now convinced that my earlier suspicions were correct. In writing about these convictions, I must acknowledge the strong influence on me by other staff members in the Study. We came together from a variety of backgrounds —college, high school, and elementary school teachers—and with a variety of dispositions toward science and toward teaching. In the course of trial teaching and of inventing new curricular materials, our shop talks brought us toward some consensus but we still had disagreements.[1] The outline of ideas I wish to present here is my own, therefore, and not that of the group which has so much influenced my thinking. The formulation I want to make is only a beginning. Even if it is right, it leaves many questions unanswered, and therefore much room for further disagreement. In so complex a matter as education, this is as it should be. What I am going to say applies, I believe, to all aspects of elementary education. However, let me stick to science teaching.

My outline is divided into three patterns or phases of school work in science. These phases are different from each other in the relations they induce between children, materials of study, and teachers. Another way of putting it is that they differ in the way they make a classroom look and sound. My claim is that good science teaching moves from one phase to the other in a pattern which, though it will not follow mechanical rules or ever be twice the same, will evolve according to simple principles. There is no necessary order among these phases, and for this reason, I avoid calling them I, II, and III, and use instead some mnemonic signs which have, perhaps a certain suggestiveness: ○ , △, and □ .

○ *Phase*. There is a time, much greater in amount than commonly allowed, which should be devoted to free and unguided exploratory work (call it play if you wish; I call it work). Children are given materials and equipment—*things*—and are allowed to construct, test, probe, and experiment without superimposed questions or instructions. I call this ○ phase "Messing About," honoring the philosophy of the Water Rat, who absentmindedly ran his boat into the bank, picked himself up and went on without interrupting the joyous train of thought:

> —about in boats—or *with* boats . . . In or out of 'em, it doesn't matter. Nothing seems really to matter, that's the charm of it. Whether you get away, or whether you don't; whether you arrive at your destination or whether you reach somewhere else, or whether you never get anywhere at all, you're always busy, and you never do anything in particular; and when you've done it there's always some-

---

[1] I would also like to acknowledge the assistance of Frances Hawkins, who has long practiced in preschool what I now wish to generalize over the entire elementary range.

thing else to do, and you can do it if you like, but you'd much better not.

In some jargon, this kind of situation is called "unstructured," which is misleading; some doubters call it chaotic, which it need never be. "Unstructured" is misleading because there is always a kind of structure to *what* is presented in a class, as there was to the world of boats and the river, with its rushes and weeds and mud that smelled like plumcake. Structure in this sense is of the utmost importance, depending on the children, the teacher, and the backgrounds of all concerned.

Let me cite an example from my own recent experiences. Simple frames, each designed to support two or three weights on strings, were handed out one morning in a fifth-grade class. There was one such frame for each pair of children. In two earlier trial classes, we had introduced the same equipment with a much more "structured" beginning, demonstrating the striking phenomenon of coupled pendula and raising questions about it before the laboratory work was allowed to begin. If there was guidance this time, however, it came only from the apparatus—a pendulum is to swing! In starting this way I, for one, naively assumed that a couple of hours of "Messing About" would suffice. After two hours, instead, we allowed two more and, in the end, a stretch of several weeks. In all this time, there was little or no evidence of boredom or confusion. Most of the questions we might have planned for came up unscheduled.

Why did we permit this length of time? First, because in our previous classes we had noticed that things went well when we veered toward "Messing About" and not as well when we held too tight a rein on what we wanted the children to do. It was clear that these children had had insufficient acquaintance with the sheer phenomena of pendulum motion and needed to build an apperceptive background, against which a more analytical sort of knowledge could take form and make sense. Second, we allowed things to develop this way because we decided we were getting a new kind of feedback from the children and were eager to see where and by what paths their interests would evolve and carry them. We were rewarded with a higher level of involvement and a much greater diversity of experiments. Our role was only to move from spot to spot, being helpful but never consciously prompting or directing. In spite of—because of!—this lack of direction, these fifth-graders became very familiar with pendula. They varied the conditions of motion in many ways, exploring differences of length and amplitude, using different sorts of bobs, bobs in clusters, and strings, etc. And have *you* tried the underwater pendulum? They did! There were many sorts of discoveries made, but we let them slip by without much adult resonance, beyond our spontaneous and manifest enjoyment of the phenomena. So discoveries were made, noted, lost, and made again. I think this is why the slightly pontifical phrase "discovery method" bothers me. When learning is at the most fundamental level, as it is here, with all the abstractions of Newtonian mechanics just around the corner, don't rush! When the mind is evolving the abstractions which will lead to physical comprehension, all of us must cross the line between ignorance and insight many times before we truly understand. Little facts, "discoveries" without the growth of insight, are *not* what we should seek to harvest. Such facts are only seedlings and should sometimes be let alone to grow into. . . .

I have illustrated the phase of "Messing About" with a constrained and inherently very elegant topic from physics. In other fields, the pattern will be different in detail, but the essential justification is the same. "Messing About" with what can be found in pond water looks much more like the Water Rat's own chosen field of study. Here, the implicit structure is that of nature in a very different mood from what is manifest in the austerities of things like pendular motion or planet orbits. And here, the need for sheer acquaintance with the variety of things and phenomena is more obvious. before one can embark on any of the roads toward the big generalizations or the big open question of biology. Regardless of differences, there is a generic justification of "Messing About" that I would like, briefly, to touch upon.

Preschool Influences

This phase is important, above all, because it carries over into school that which is the source of most of what children have already learned, the roots of their moral, intellectual, and esthetic development. If education were defined, for the moment, to include everything that children have learned since birth, everything that has come to them from living in the natural and the human world, then by any sensible measure what has come before age five or six would outweigh all the rest. When we narrow the scope of education to what goes on in schools, we throw out the method of that early and spectacular progress at our peril. We know that five-year-olds are very unequal in their mastery of this or that. We also know that their histories are responsible for most of this inequality, utterly masking the congenital differences except in special cases. This is the immediate fact confronting us as educators in a society committed, morally and now by sheer economic necessity, to universal education.

To continue the cultivation of earlier ways of learning, therefore; to find *in school* the good beginnings, the liberating involvements that will make the kindergarten seem a garden to the child and not a dry and frightening desert, this is a need that requires much emphasis on the style of work I have called ○, or "Messing About." Nor does the garden in this sense end with a child's first school year, or his tenth, as though one could then put away childish things. As time goes on, through a good mixture of this with other phases of work, "Messing About" evolves with the child and thus changes its quality. It becomes a way of working that is no longer childish, though it remains always childlike, the kind of self-disciplined probing and exploring that is the essence of creativity.

The variety of the learning—and of inhibition against learning—that children bring from home when school begins is great, even within the limited range of a common culture with common economic background (or, for that matter, within a single family). Admitting this, then if you cast your mind over the whole range of abilities and backgrounds that children bring to kindergarten, you see the folly of standardized and formalized beginnings. We are profoundly ignorant about the subtleties of learning but one principle ought to be asserted dogmatically: That there must be provided some continuity in the content, direction, and style of learning. Good schools begin with what children have *in fact* mastered, probe next to see what *in fact* they are learning, continue with what *in fact* sustains their involvement.

△ *Phase.* When children are led along a common path, there are always the advanced ones and always the stragglers. Generalized over the years of school routine, this lends apparent support to the still widespread belief in some fixed, inherent levels of "ability," and to the curious notions of "under-" and "over-achievement." Now, if you introduce a topic with a good deal of "Messing About," the variance does not decrease, it increases. From a conventional point of view, this means the situation gets worse, not better. But I say it gets better, not worse. If after such a beginning you pull in the reins and "get down to business," some children have happened to go your way already, and you will believe that you are leading these successfully. Others will have begun, however, to travel along quite different paths, and you have to tug hard to get them back on to yours. Through the eyes of these children you will see yourself as a dragger, not a leader. We saw this clearly in the pendulum class I referred to; the pendulum being a thing which seems deceptively simple but which raises many questions in no particular necessary order. So the path which each child chooses is his best path.

The result is obvious, but it took me time to see it. If you once let children evolve their own learning along paths of their choosing, you then must see it through and *maintain* the individuality of their work. You cannot begin that way and then say, in effect, "That was only a teaser," thus using your adult authority to devalue what the children themselves, in the meantime, have found most valuable. So if "Messing About" is to be followed by, or evolve into, a stage where work is more externally guided and disciplined, there must be at hand what I call "Multiply Programmed" material; material that contains written and pictorial guidance of some sort for the student, but which is designed for the greatest possible variety of topics, ordering of topics, etc., so that for almost any given way into a subject that a child may evolve on his own, there is material available which he will recognize as helping him farther along that very way. Heroic teachers have sometimes done this on their own, but it is obviously one of the places where designers of curriculum materials can be of enormous help, designing those materials with a rich variety of choices for teacher and child, and freeing the teacher from the role of "leader-dragger" along a single preconceived path, giving the teacher encouragement and real logistical help in diversifying the activities of a group. Such material includes good equipment, but above all, it suggests many beginnings, paths from the familiar into the unknown. We did not have this kind of material ready for the pendulum class I spoke about earlier, and still do not have it. I intend to work at it and hope others will.

It was a special day in the history of that pendulum class that brought home to me what was needed. My teaching partner was away (I had been the observer, she the teacher). To shift gears for what I saw as a more organized phase of our work, I announced that for a change we were all going to do the same experiment. I said it firmly and the children were, of course, obliging. Yet, I saw the immediate loss of interest in part of the class as soon as my experiment was proposed. It was designed to raise questions about the *length* of a pendulum, when the bob is multiple or odd-shaped. Some had come upon the germ of that question; others had had no reason to. As a college teacher I have tricks, and they worked here as well, so the class went well, in spite of the unequal readiness to look at "length." We hit common ground with rough blackboard pictures, many pendula shown hanging from a common support, differeng in length and in the shape and size of bobs. Which ones will "swing together"? Because their eyes were full of real pendula, I think, they would *see* those blackboard pictures swinging! A colloquium evolved which harvested the crop of insights that had been sowed and cultivated in previous weeks. I was left with a hollow feeling, nevertheless. It went well where, and only where, the class found common ground. Whereas in "Messing About" all things had gone uniformly well. In staff discussion afterward, it became clear that we had skipped an essential phase of our work, the one I am now calling △ phase, or Multiply Programmed.

There is a common opinion, floating about, that a rich diversity of classroom work is possible only when a teacher has small classes. "Maybe *you* can do that; but you ought to try it in my class of forty-three!" I want to be the last person to belittle the importance of small classes. But in this particular case, the statement ought to be made that in a large class one cannot afford *not* to diversify children's work —or rather *not* to allow children to diversify, as they inevitably will, if given the chance. So-called "ability grouping" is a popular answer today, but it is no answer at all to the real questions of motivation. Groups which are lumped as equivalent with respect to the usual measures are just as diverse in their tastes and spontaneous interests as unstratified groups! The complaint that in heterogeneous classes the bright ones are likely to be bored because things go too slow for them ought to be met with another question: Does that mean that the slower students are *not* bored? When children have no autonomy in learning everyone is likely to be bored. In such situations the over-worked teachers have to be "leader-draggers" always, playing the role of Fate in the old Roman proverb: "The Fates lead the willing; the unwilling they drag."

A Good Beginning

"Messing About" produces the early and indispensible autonomy and diversity. It is good—indispensible—for the opening game but not for the long middle game, where guidance is needed; needed to lead the willing! To illustrate once more from my example of the pendulum, I want to produce a thick set of cards—illustrated cards in a central file, or single sheets in plastic envelopes—to cover the following topics among others:

1. Relations of amplitude and period
2. Relations of period and weight of bob
3. How long is a pendulum (odd-shaped bobs)?
4. Coupled pendula, compound pendula
5. The decay of the motion (and the idea of half-life)
6. String pendula and stick pendula—comparisons
7. Underwater pendula
8. Arms and legs as pendula (dogs, people, and elephants)
9. Pendula of other kinds—springs, etc.
10. Bobs that drop sand for patterns and graphs.
11. Pendulum clocks
12. Historical materials, with bibliography
13. Cards relating to filmloops available, in class or library

14. Cross-index cards to other topics, such as falling bodies, inclined planes. etc.
15.-75. Blank cards to be filled in by classes and teachers for others.

This is only an illustration; each area of elementary science will have its own style of Multiply Programmed materials, of course, the ways of organizing these materials will depend on the subject. There should always be those blank cards, outnumbering the rest.

Careful!

There is one final warning. Such a file is properly a kind of programming—but it is not the base of rote or merely verbal learning, taking a child little step by little step through the adult maze. Each item is simple, pictorial, and it guides by suggesting further explorations, not by replacing them. The cards are only there to relieve the teacher from a heroic task. And they are only there because there are apparatus, film, library, and raw materials from which to improvise.

☐ *Phase.* In the class discussion I referred to, about the meaning of *length* applied to a pendulum, I was reverting back to the college-teacher habit of lecturing; I said it went very well in spite of the lack of Multiply Programmed background, one that would have taken more of the class through more of the basic pendulum topics. It was not, of course, a lecture in the formal sense. It was question-and-answer, with discussion between children as well. But still, I was guiding it and fishing for the good ideas that were ready to be born, and I was telling a few stories, for example, about Galileo. Others could do it better. I was a visitor, and am still only an amateur. I was successful then only because of the long build-up of latent insight, the kind of insight that the Water Rat had stored up from long afternoons of "Messing About" in boats. It was more than he could ever have been told, but it gave him much to tell. This is not all there is to learning, of course; but it is the magical part, and the part most often killed in school. The language is not yet that of the textbook, but with it even a dull-looking textbook can come alive. One boy thinks the length of a pendulum should be measured from the top to what he calls "the center of gravity." If they have not done a lot of work with balance materials, this phase is for most children only the handle of an empty pitcher, or a handle without a pitcher at all. So I did not insist on the term. Incidentally, it is not quite correct physics anyway, as those will discover who work with the stick pendulum. Although different children had specialized differently in the way they worked with pendula, there were common elements, increasing with time, which would sustain a serious and extended class discussion. It is this pattern of discussion I want to emphasize by calling it a separate, □ phase. It includes lecturing, formal or informal. In the above situation, we were all quite ready for a short talk about Galileo, and ready to ponder the question whether there was any relation between the way unequal weights fall together and the way they swing together when hanging on strings of the same length. Here we were approaching a question—a rather deep one, not to be disposed of in fifteen minutes—of theory, going from the concrete perceptual to the abstract conceptual. I do not believe that such questions will come alive either through the early "Messing About" or through the Multiply Programmed work with guiding questions and instructions. I think they come primarily with discussion, argument, the full colloquium of children and teacher. Theorizing in a creative sense needs the content of experience and the logic of experimentation to support it. But these do not automatically lead to conscious abstract thought. Theory is square! □

We of the Elementary Science Study are probably identified in the minds of those acquainted with our work (and sometimes perhaps in our own minds) with the advocacy of laboratory work and a free, fairly ○ style of laboratory work at that. This may be right and justified by the fact that prevailing styles of science teaching are □ most of the time, much too much of the time. But what we criticize for being too much and too early, we must work to re-admit in its proper place.

I have put ○, △, and □ in that order, but I do not advocate any rigid order; such phases may be mixed in many ways and ordered in many ways. Out of the colloquium comes new "Messing About." Halfway along a programmed path, new phenomena are accidentally observed. In an earlier, more structured class, two girls were trying obediently to reproduce some phenomena of coupled pendula I had demonstrated. I heard one say, "Ours isn't working right." Of course, pendula never misbehave; it is not in their nature; they always do what comes naturally, and in this case, they were executing a curious dance of energy transference, promptly christened the "twist." It was a new phenomenon, which I had not seen before, nor had several physicists to whom, in my delight, I later showed it. Needless to say, this led to a good deal of "Messing About," right then and there.

What I have been concerned to say is only that there are, as I see it, three major phases of good science teaching; that no teaching is likely to be optimal which does not mix all three; and that the one most neglected is that which made the Water Rat go dreamy with joy when he talked about it. At a time when the pressures of prestige education are likely to push children to work like hungry laboratory rats in a maze, it is good to remember that their wild, watery cousin, reminiscing about the joys of life, uttered a profound truth about education.

33

CREATIVITY, CHILDREN, AND ELEMENTARY SCIENCE

Rodger W. Bybee

The number one specific recommendation of the 1970 White House Conference on Children was: to provide opportunities for every child to learn creatively, to grow creatively, and to live creatively. This is to be accomplished by a reordering of national priorities. Creativity is now educational priority for the decade 1970–1980.

Traditionally our classrooms have only emphasized talents closely aligned with the academic. Yet the worlds of work, home, and recreation require other talents such as creativity, ability to plan on a short-and long-range scale, ability to forecast, communicate, make decisions and the all important talent—the ability to interact socially.

Science education responded to the priorities of curriculum development in the last decade. We have become leaders in the area of teaching by inquiry and recognizing the child's cognitive development. Finally the acceptance of affective education is emerging in the literature and curriculum materials. The new response will include the individual teacher's creative behavior, as well as teaching for creativity with an emphasis on process and product. With this the foundation has been established for a wider, more complete view of creativity. This product is then a particular special kind of human being, a creative person. The distinction is between creativity in terms of the ability to produce and the creative being. One *does* something, the second *is* something. This is high level abstraction but one worth considering.

Reprinted from *Science and Children, 9,* March 1972, pp. 22–26.

Education is in an era characterized by words such as *individualization, relevancy,* and *accountability.* One output from this consciousness toward education will be the realization that education, as a profession, has generally maintained a monopoly that has been historically insensitive to the demands and needs of its clients. Recognition of creativity and other talents will allow a new consciousness to evolve in the elementary classroom. This new consciousness is part of the continuing evolution that originated with the transfer of knowledge and then moved to curriculum materials utilizing inquiry and discovery as a means to convey facts. Now our society, and subsequently education, is moving in a direction described by Charles Reich in *The Greening of America.* We are now involved with a consciousness generally concerned with needs of the individual. The new focus is on the inquiry and discovery of self. By recognizing creativity and other high level talents beyond cognition and memory and combining these with the affective realm science educators will develop a consciousness that is functional and approaching the needs of the whole child.

What types of needs do students have? The noted Third Force psychologist, Abraham Maslow, studied the healthiest people, psychologically, that he could find in our culture. They are self-actualized people. He describes self-actualization in the following way:

> ... the full use and exploitation of talents, capacities, potentialities, etc. Such people seem to be fulfilling themselves and to be doing, reminding us of Nietzsche's exhortation, "Become what thou art." They are people who have developed or are developing to the full stature of which they are capable. These potentialities may be either idiosyncratic or species wide (2, p. 150).

At present education does not approach the needs of the whole person's talents, capacities and potential as described by Maslow. Creative potential is one area of concern, for it is too often lost as children grow to adults. As Maslow continued his studies of self-actualized people, creativity emerged as a universal characteristic of these individuals. There were no exceptions to this rule (2, p. 170). These people were courageous, spontaneous, open, and were willing to make mistakes as they pursued their creative endeavors.

Creativity is the ability to view the familiar in a unique way, to make transformation, to see a multiple of things in a single object, and to synthesize isolated schemes in new and original ways. The process or product is useful to either self or society.

All children are creative. They are continuously exploring their environment, curious about the unknown and involved with discovering their world. Slowly creativity wanes or waxes as the child encounters the adult world. This adult world is, in part, the teacher in the classroom.

Often the freshness, simplicity, and spontaneity of a child's creativity is lost as he learns the fear of ridicule, the threat of individuality and the judgments by others. Thus, as the teacher looks for creativity in children it may seem that some are mute; they are not, they are simply creatively silent. When discovered, creativity can be expressed in a variety of different ways: some eloquently, some articulate, some haltingly and some humorously. These are all individual differences. These differences also can be expressed in other talents such as planning, forecasting, decision making, and communicating. Education in the past has generally emphasized the rate of personal progress through material. The emphasis on expression in realms other than the academic for the elementary teacher approaches a true recognition of individual differences.

The creative person is characterized as an individual with a longitude or fluency of ideas, a wide latitude or flexibility of ideas, and finally the potential for original ideas. They have a high tolerance for ambiguity, wide interests, the ability to control perceptions and often give the outward appearance of complexity. Courage against the influences of other's spontaneity or personal freedom as well as self confidence and self respect are components of the creative. Further, "Creative people... are dependent upon their use of the preconscious or intuitive" (3, p. 57). This implies the individual engaged in the creative process can forget the conscious self and appeal to the preconscious for an outpouring of ideas.

The creative process can be metaphorically compared to a volcano. Creative ideas and patterns originate intrinsically in the chamber of the preconscious. The initial desire, puzzlement, or need is motivated from within. Just as a volcano prepares for the eventual eruption, the creative person prepares himself by searching and seeking material, manipulating and finally incubating the problem. Magma seeks a channel of least resistance and prepares itself for release through eruption. The results of the eruption can be either constructive or destructive; they build up the earth's surface and often cause damage and hardship to property and people. As creativity is liberated in the classroom the teacher has an option that man does not have over natural processes. He can control or channel the creative output into positive constructive directions. This positive release is nurtured in part by a feeling of freedom within self and an understanding that a responsive environment exists in the conscious world. A repressive environment can vent the release in a destructive direction. There may be slight rumblings and minor tremors before the volcano erupts; the individual has a feeling or intimation the solution is near. Finally illumination, understanding, and resolution emerge from the materials used in preparation. A restructuring of the material has occurred and a new pattern is formed. The magma is now lava and is readily visible as it flows to the surface.

The process that built the tension has been freed and it spewed forth in the product, ready for verification. Often the ensuing eruption distorts and the magma becomes obsidian, ash, tuff or basalt. Still the basic components are in evidence. They are on the surface in a position for examination or possible service after the violence of the volcanic eruption. The creative potential has been released; eruptions can occur from quiescent volcanoes; the capacity for creativity always exists in children; it is sometimes dormant or latent.

Science curricula focus on problem solving, inquiry, discovery, and invention. These are all related to creativity and differentiated in the following ways. One clear distinction that is often overlooked is the level at which these processes occur. They are contributions to personal growth or to cultural growth. In the science classroom inquiry, discovery, and problem solving can also be viewed as a process that occurs within children or as teaching methods. I will discuss these on the personal level for this is the level where they are of greatest value to children. All originate with a need or problem that arises intrinsically or is imposed extrinsically. The immediate exploration, search, or quest for a solution to this problem is *inquiry*. In *discovery* the search results in the revelation of an existing product. *Invention* on the other hand does not have a perceived existing solution. A historian gathers clues in the present and discovers an event that existed in the past or an elementary child is involved with materials that will aid his discovery of a science concept. The artist takes clay and invents a new form or young children use simple materials to invent a new toy. A further example should clarify the distinction between invention and discovery. In the SCIS unit *Interaction and Systems* children investigate pulley systems. One strategy the teacher may use is to provide an example where handles and propellers are visible and the actual pulley system is covered. The teacher turns the handle, the system interacts and the propeller turns. The children are then given materials to construct a pulley system. They are encouraged to *inquire* until they *discover* the relationships of pulley, shafts, rubber bands, etc. that produced the results they observed earlier. There was an existing solution to the problem; it was up to them to find it or learn of its existence. To extend the activity the teacher can have the boys and girls use the same materials and think of or *invent* a new relationship of pulleys, shafts, and rubber bands. They may use large or small pulleys, cross the rubber band, or combine systems with other children. They then invent a new relationship, the solution for which did not exist priorly. In both cases they were involved with problem solving and inquiry. In one example they used convergent thinking to find the existing solution; in the latter they used divergent thinking to originate new ideas. Convergent and divergent thinking are components of the creative processes. Think of the pulley investigation. In one case the children used their thinking to converge and discover while in the second case they diverged and invented. Bringing ideas or information together and solving a specific problem or generating a unique outcome is convergent thinking. Convergent thinking is similar to bringing an object into focus on the stage of a microscope. However, starting with a focal point and producing a multiple of new ideas is divergent production. As you move the optics of the microscope up, the object of original focus becomes blurred while the area in view becomes larger. Creativity is the encompassing process by which the individual comes to the solution. You can demonstrate degrees of creativity within the inquiry processes as well as in the product. Fluency, flexibility, originality or insight are the variables of the exploration. These are individual processes, not methods of teaching. Teachers are in a position to establish atmospheres that encourage these individual operations.

The elementary science teacher is the architect that can design an environment to facilitate creativity. First and foremost is to openly value creative expression. Such an environment would also include a threat-free, nonevaluative, nonjudgmental, and listening climate. Students should perceive the teacher as a person with curiosity and the ability to solve problems creatively. Teachers and students should learn to accept multiple and diverse responses while avoiding "killer phrases." Enthusiasm and involvement are also essential for the teacher. This enthusiasm is contagious and soon the students will become active participants.

The following are questions, activities, methods, and techniques to aid the elementary science teacher in fostering creativity and other talents. I have included activities for the teacher as well as the students. The areas emphasized in the remainder of the article will deal with the convergent and divergent production of ideas, questioning, planning, forecasting, decision making, and communicating. Start the whole class on some *warm-up* exercises. After that small group and individual work can proceed. A progression or cycle of work in large groups, small groups, and individually is ideal. As the children start their activity of brainstorming remind them—*all ideas are accepted;* this will support and sustain the flowing of ideas. Evaluation and ridicule will reduce or stop the flow. The activities outlined are generally in order of increasing complexity. After warming up, different activities can be selected by either the students or the teacher.

Warming Up

Try the following warm-up activities: *What objects can you see in the room? Think of all the words you can that start with the letter R*—red, run, rough... (you continue). *Think of all the objects you can that are blue*. Other activities include: property words, material words, and science words, animals, cars, and names of people.

All the Uses for

Start this activity with simple objects you have placed on the children's desks. Later move to the larger more complex objects. *Have them think of all the uses for*—a pin, magnet, plastic bag, toothpick, pencil, old string, ball, brick or pop bottle, paper clip, bottle caps, old beer cans, tin can, old gum under desks. An interesting twist to this activity is to find something that is polluting and find a new use for the object, one that is productive for man and nature.

What if You Were

Walt Whitman has written:

> There was a child went forth every day,
> And the first object he look'd upon, that object he became,
> And that object became part of him for the day or a certain part
> of the day,
> Or for many years or stretching cycles of years ... (4, pp. 69–70)

Walt Whitman has captured one of the exciting aspects of childhood, the ability to imagine and fantasize, to use the common in unusual ways, and displace oneself into another person or world. Children use personal analogy naturally; with a little encouragement they will do it in the science classroom.

What if you were

a flower blooming	an atmosphere being polluted
a rock weathering	a zero
a thunderstorm	a ray of light
a kite flying	a molecule that decided to change
a meteor falling	the temperature
an atom	a molecule causing pressure in the
air that was polluted	classroom
	a polluted stream

Construct a Word, Sentence, or Paragraph

How many words can you discover using the following letters? A F F E C T I V E. How about—A C T, F A C T, F I V E... you continue. Try the following with the students:

TALENT   ELEMENTARY   ECOLOGY
ENTILS   CTEVIFAF   ESRADNUTD GNIN
NNEEPOSS   NSEICEC   RAETHC
ALVEUS   URESIDCOY   AEETNMGRONECU

Try something a little harder. Using the following letters form a phrase, clause or sentence. For example, ESS=Every Student Succeeds, SAPA=Students Appreciate Process Approach, SCIS=Sensitive Concerned Interested Students. Now you try some: NSTA=? CESI=? NARST=? AAAS=? Use the following as starters in your class:

S I F   T S R A D   T T B E W O
B A B   C I A I G   M T A T S T
T D I C   A S S H F   T A T I A A H

Try to write a paragraph using the following words. You may add verbs, prepositions and articles.

People   Pollution   Peace
Place   Population   Pedagogy
Product   Prejudice   Process

To generate lists of words brainstorm words that start with a particular letter, fall into a particular topic area, or are associated with a group experience. These can then be incorporated into a paragraph. Examples for children include:

FOOD   ORGANISM   SCIENCE   FIELD TRIP
FAMILY   HOME   EXPERIMENT   FREEDOM
FUN   HABITAT   PROBLEM   FUN

Using Comparisons

The ability to think in terms of metaphors, similies, and analogies is certainly one of the keys to the chamber of creativity. When the use of comparison is combined with a fluency and flexibility of thought the creative process will almost inevitably produce a quantity *as well as* quality products. Earlier I compared the creative process to a volcanic eruption. In that case the metaphor was carried through an entire paragraph. In a shorter example used above comparisons were metaphorically likened to keys that could release creativity. Before you try comparisons with the students you should do some on your own. Try these: Students are sometimes like magnets... Yes, they are different shapes and different sizes, some repel... you continue. On the other hand some students are telephones... some days the line is busy, you often get a wrong number and occasionally you receive a pleasant and unexpected call from someone... Can you think of any more? For your science class:

The earth is like a space ship because...
Bees are like ants because...
Sometimes I feel like _____ because...
Some weather is like _____ because...
  but other times it seems more like _____
Molecules are like cars in a city because...
Growing up is a walk in the woods because...
Science is like _____ because...
I am like science because...
Time is a river because...
Feelings are like clouds because...
I see myself in science as...
Experiments are cars because...
Erosion is _____ because...
Animals are like plants because...
Pollution is like _____ because...
  but sometimes it is more like _____

Using a Feeling

Children, like adults, have many feelings. When they can be used to the teacher's advantage the learning experience is increased and permanent because of the total involvement.

One day I decided it was time to feed the snake his monthly mouse. Quite unintentionally I placed a mouse in the snake's cage just before the children arrived. Immediately they were attracted to the cage and the ensuing drama. As the snake pursued the hapless mouse, their interest, enthusiasm, and emotions heightened. Finally the mouse was removed due to the children's request. Still, however, I was left with a group of excited fifth graders. I decided to use their feelings to my advantage. We warmed up and then listed all the words we could think of that *we felt* as we watched the mouse in the cage. We then turned to the feelings the *mouse* might have had and finally the *snake*. In each category the children had easily listed about sixty to seventy words. The children then used these banks of words to write three paragraphs, each in first person but each from a different point of view: me, the mouse, and the snake. Their papers were a pleasure to read.

How about brainstorming all the words for feelings experienced when:

a science investigation is successful
a science test is given
you discover something for yourself
you see a butterfly
you have a good day in science

you finally find the solution to a science problem
you fire a model rocket
you teacher reads an exciting science story
you find something for science class
you have an interesting object for show and tell in science

It is obviously best to wait until the children have just experienced the feelings. Focus on experiences that are immediate, have personal meaning, and are in general successful or good.

What Would Happen if

Children can create some very interesting science fiction stories. Let them work in groups using the techniques of brainstorming to produce the story outline. Each group can contribute to a class story or the groups can produce their own science fiction story. For example, *list all the things you can think of that would occur if the sun's energy were reduced by one-half.* Would the water cycle be the same? What about the atmosphere and the temperature? Each of these areas could then be brainstormed in turn to produce more ideas about water, climate, weather, and temperature. By the time the groups have finished brainstorming each subdivision under the main heading there should be a number of ideas that can be pulled together for a paragraph and these combined into an interesting story.

Accurate forecasting in changed situations is based on an understanding of the processes existing at present. Understanding the present is a key to understanding future changes. This is true for the themes of the stories.

Some interesting themes for their stories are given below:

Gravitational force is doubled.
The earth stopped rotating on its axis.
The atmosphere was *completely* polluted.
The earth did not have a magnetic field.
Energy and matter could be created and destroyed.
Continents drifted at a rate of five meters per year.

What Questions Would You Ask if

Very seldom, if ever, do we emphasize the talent of questioning. Yet this is very important for teachers and children. As teachers we should constantly evaluate the questions we ask children. It should be obvious by now that much of the child's creativity can be released through the proper questions.

Arthur Carin has written, "The heart of teaching–learning science by discovery is in questions properly asked and answers to them properly used" (1, p. 13). The main emphasis of this statement is directed toward teacher questioning. A further extension of this quote is in the ability of the child to develop skill in asking questions. Teachers emphasizing creativity can operationally develop questioning talent in children.

The object of this activity is to have the students generate a question or questions for objects they are studying. For example, *What one question would you ask a rock in order to obtain the maximum amount of information possible?* In this case a convergent question by the teacher produces a more divergent question by the student. *What are all the questions you would ask a person from another planet?* A more divergent question from the teacher often produces lists of convergent questions by children. If the teacher prepares beforehand, many times the children's questions can be answered. The following are interesting objects for questioning:

A MOON ROCK
A MINERAL
A WATER DROP
A LEAF
A FOSSIL
A METEORITE
A MOLECULE

What the World Needs is

This is a group activity utilizing the technique of hitchhiking on an idea. Have the students sit in a circle with you as a facilitator. If possible small groups are best. The facilitator starts the idea and passes it to the next person who in turn adds to the idea and passes it on to the next. This continues around the circle with each individual adding something, or they can pass for the round. For example, *What the world needs is*—a hard boiled egg slicer—(continued)—Yes, it could be electric—(continued)—and chrome plated—(continued) and so on around the group. Potential topics include:

A POLLUTION SOLUTION	A NEW SCIENCE TOY
ANOTHER CONTAINER	ANOTHER SCIENCE GAME
A NEW MEANS OF	A T.V. PROGRAM ABOUT
TRANSPORTATION	SCIENCE
SOMETHING TO REPLACE	AN EFFICIENT WAY TO
POP CANS	DISPOSE OF WASTE

A NEW MACHINE   A NEW SCIENCE TROPHY
TO _____   FOR _____

The talents of questioning, forecasting, wise decision making, communicating, and planning can be included in the following manner. Once a topic is chosen the facilitator has the option of changing the focus of the round. Statements such as the following will change the focus:

MAJOR TOPIC: A SOLUTION TO POLLUTION

These questions should have been asked ten years ago... (questioning)
If this doesn't change, we can forecast... (forecasting)
These decisions should have been made... (decision making)
Plans to overcome this include... (planning)
These ideas could be communicated to the public by... (communicating)

Each round could focus on a different talent. Surprisingly, the children often generate some exciting ideas. Very often new individuals emerge as leaders in the different talent areas.

These activities are only starters. With these the teacher can start afternoon showers of creative activity, which in turn grow to short-term weather, and finally the classroom will have a climate of creativity. There are many more activities the elementary science teacher can use to teach for creativity and other talents. There are references listed in the bibliography that will aid the teacher interested in creativity.

Education in any elementary classroom can be thought of as a process located somewhere along a continuum between static and dynamic. As long as cognition and memory are of primary concern education is functioning toward the static end of the continuum. As education moves across the continuum from static to dynamic it parallels an education dealing with isolated bits of a child's potential to a holistic approach to children.

References

(1) Carin, Arthur, "Techniques for Developing Discovery Questioning Skills." *Science and Children, 7,* April 1970, p. 13.

(2) Maslow, Abraham, *Motivation and Personality.* New York: Harper & Row, Publishers, Inc., 1970.

(3) Samples, Robert E., "Kari's Handicap—The Impediment of Creativity." *Saturday Review*, July 15, 1967, p. 57.

(4) Whitman, Walt, *Leaves of Grass–Poems of Walt Whitman*. Lawrence Clark Powell (comp.), New York: Thomas Y. Crowell Company, 1964.

Bibliography

Gordon, William J. J., *Synectics*. New York: Harper & Row, Publishers, Inc., 1961.

"Making It Strange," *Synectics*. New York: Harper & Row, Publishers, Inc., 1968.

Piltz, Albert and Robert Sund, *Creative Teaching of Science in the Elementary School*. Boston: Allyn & Bacon, Inc., 1968.

Samples, Robert E., "Nature and Creativity." *Science and Children*, 7, November 1969, pp. 9–10.

Taylor, Calvin W., "Finding the Creative." *The Science Teacher*, 6, December 1961, p. 13.

_____, "Clue to Creative Teaching." Ten articles in *The Instructor*, September 1963–June, 1964.

_____, "Learning and Creativity with Special Emphasis on Science." National Science Teachers Association Publication, 1967.

"You and Creativity," *Kaiser Aluminum News, 25:* 3, 1968.

34

DISCOVERY OR INVENTION?*

J. Myron Atkin
Robert Karplus

More recently, the discussion of the role of discovery in teaching has intensified. Many authors have stressed the great educational benefits to be derived if pupils discover concepts for themselves (2). Other authors have warned that discovery teaching is so time consuming and inefficient that it should not, in general, replace expository teaching (1).

There is a way in which autonomous recognition of relationships by the pupils; i.e., "discovery" can and should be combined with expository introduction of concepts in an efficient program. This will produce understanding rather than rote verbalization. The approach can be described more clearly, if a historical example[1] is given of how a particular scientific concept is developed.

*NOTE: The experiments in this article were carried out by the authors at the Berkwood School, Berkeley, California, through the cooperation of the Director, Betty Halpern. Financial support for the project was provided by the National Science Foundation, Washington, D.C.

[1]The historical development and its analysis in this illustration have been greatly oversimplified. For a fuller and more profound discussion see: Thomas Kuhn, "The Nature of Scientific Revolutions." University of Chicago Press, Chicago, Illinois. (In process.)

Reprinted from *The Science Teacher, 25,* September 1962, pp. 45–51. Dr. J. Myron Atkin is Dean of the School of Education, University of Illinois, Urbana, Ill. Dr. Robert Karplus is Director of the Science Curriculum Improvement Study, Berkeley, Calif.

In ancient times the sun and the planets were observed by man. These observations gave rise to various conceptual interpretations. There were the mythological interpretations, the interpretation as "celestial matter" with certain properties, and eventually the modern interpretation of planets orbiting around the sun. With the help of each of these concepts, man could attempt to understand other phenomena beside the ones that had led him to suggest the interpretation originally. These attempts, if successful, led to a reinforcement and refinement of the concept; if they failed, they revealed limits of the usefulness of the concept or even stimulated a search for a new concept. Of the three interpretations we have mentioned, the final and currently accepted one has turned out to be much more powerful than its predecessors.

In the development of a concept, it is useful to distinguish the original introduction of a new concept, which can be called invention, from the subsequent verification or extension of the concept's usefulness, which can be called discovery. Of course, this distinction is not completely clear-cut, because the inventor must recognize that the new concept is applicable to the phenomena he is trying to interpret; otherwise he would discard the invention immediately. Return therefore to the example for determining how the distinction can be applied. Assume that the deities, the celestial matter, and the solar system were inventions. In the mythological framework, one could then discover that the deities intervened in human affairs in certain ways and refine one's idea of the characteristics of the gods. In the framework based on the existence of celestial matter, one could discover that celestial objects move in cycles and epicycles. Finally, in the framework of the solar system, one could discover additional planets.

Undoubtedly, an invention is not complete and static, but it is the germ of a concept that is developed to greater significance by the subsequent discoveries. When an invention is made, its full significance is not evident. Still, the concept must be introduced and the invention must be made, if it is to grow in meaning.

Applying this distinction between discovery and invention to science teaching, acknowledge the fact that the pupil has experience both before he enters school and also outside the school environment during the school years. He therefore makes observations all the time, and he invents concepts that interpret the observations as well. He also makes discoveries that enable him to refine his concepts. Most of the discoveries and inventions reveal a type of natural philosophy—a "common-sense" orientation popular in the culture at a given point in history.

Yet, the objective of the science program is to teach children to look at natural phenomena from the distinctive vantage point of modern science. And in the mid-twentieth century, this vantage point differs from the culturally prevalent view. In a small way the situation is analogous to that of a Copernican teacher instructing his students that the sun is at the center of the solar system while almost everyone else in the society *knows* that the earth is at the center of the universe.

In general, no results are evident if a teaching program is based on the expectation that children can invent the modern scientific concepts, because their spontaneously invented concepts, some of which even exist at the time the child enters school, present too much of a block. After all, concepts were developed to interpret their experience; why should they change these concepts on their own? Indeed, it does not seem crucial to teach the children to invent concepts, because they can and do invent concepts readily. The educational problem, rather, is to teach the children to carry out their creative thinking with some intellectual discipline. And the development and refinement of modern scientific concepts in the light of observations would seem to be one excellent vehicle for achieving this goal.

If the children are not able to *invent* the modern scientific concepts, it is necessary for the teacher to *introduce* the modern scientific concepts. During this introduction, the teacher must make clear which previous observations of the children can be interpreted (or perhaps reinterpreted) by using a concept. Further, he must follow the introduction with opportunities for the children to discover that new observations can also be interpreted by using a concept. This type of discovery is made possible by the availability of a concept to the children, because their perception is oriented by the teacher's formulation of the new idea. This type of discovery can be extremely valuable to solidify learning and motivate the children; it is essential, if a concept is to be used with increasing refinement and precision. Categorically, the teacher must not present the concept in a complete, definitive, and authoritarian way, for concepts are never final.

As an example of this teaching approach, a thirty-minute lesson will be described in which second graders discovered the usefulness of the magnetic field concept after the teacher had invented it for them. In thirteen previous sessions, a class of fifteen pupils had discussed the selection of systems by the specification of the objects in the system, and the existence of interactions among the objects, and had been introduced to the notion of the free energy of the system.

Two new concepts were introduced to the class in the lesson: the interaction-at-a-distance, and the magnetic field. These ideas were developed through a series of experiments.

Experiment 1. Two boys pulled on a rope in opposite directions. The pupils identified the system of interest as consisting of Bruce, James, and the rope. Interactions between objects in the system included the one between James and the rope and the one between Bruce and the rope. Bruce and James were considered not to interact with each other. *Invention of interaction-at-a-distance:* Next, the teacher pointed out that Bruce and James were really the important objects in the system; that the whole class could think that there was an interaction between the two boys (at a signal, Bruce yanked James with the rope); but that it was not a *direct interaction,* it was a *distant interaction.* The new term was stressed. The rope made the distant interaction possible. The teacher further asked Bruce and James to interact strongly, then weakly, then strongly again.

Experiment 2. The teacher produced two wooden balls that were held together by a strip of rubber tacked to the balls. Five objects were identified in the system: the two balls, the rubber strip, and the two thumbtacks. The pupils identified the direct interactions ball-rubber, ball-thumbtack, and rubber-thumbtack. They identified the distant interactions ball-ball, thumbtack-thumbtack, and end of rubber-end of rubber. The pupils called the interaction weak when the balls were close together, strong when they were far apart, and medium when they were somewhat separated. The strip of rubber made the distant interaction possible.

Experiment 3. The teacher put his hand on the head of one boy. The pupils correctly identified the direct interaction, teacher-boy, and the distant acoustic interactions, teacher-all pupils.

Experiment 4. The teacher repeated Experiment 2 with a long brass spring. The distant interaction between the ends of the spring and the strength of the interaction were identified. The spring made possible the distant interaction between its own ends.

Experiment 5. The teacher produced two large U-magnets mounted to attract one another on roller skates so that they could move easily. The pupils identified the distant interaction between the two magnets in the system. They also determined that the strength of the interaction decreased as the magnets were separated. The interaction was sufficiently strong for the magnets to roll toward one another at a separation of four inches. *Invention of magnetic field:* In response to the teacher's question, "Which do you like better, direct interactions or distant interactions?" The pupils expressed a strong preference for direct interactions. The teacher now told the pupils that most people prefer to think in terms of direct interactions. In the earlier experiments there had been something between the two objects that made possible the distant interaction between them. Was there something now between the two magnets that made possible the distant interaction between them? There was nothing visible. (Curiously enough, no pupil suggested that the air was involved.) Even though the magnetic field was not yet mentioned by name, the children were given the crucial idea of a mediator (an "it") for the distant magnetic interaction. This step constituted what we have called the "invention."

Experiment 6. Discovery of the significance of the magnetic field;

a. Three children came to the demonstration table to find "it" by feeling with their fingers. They did not find "it."
b. Two children came to the demonstration table to find "it" with a wooden ruler. They did not find "it."
c. One child came to find "it" with a nail held at the end of a piece of wire. The nail responded to something!
d. All pupils wanted to explore with the nail. As others had an opportunity to do so, the teacher verbally confirmed the fact that the nail indeed seemed to have responded to something. When the teacher was going to name it, he was interrupted by one pupil who said "I know what 'it' is called. 'It' is a magnetic!" The teacher agreed to the "magnetic," because it occurrec in a magnetic interaction, but proposed the name "magnetic field." Thereafter, the discussion was carried out in terms of exploring to find the magnetic field—the "it" which made possible the distant interaction between the two magnets.
e. Several more pupils explored and found the magnetic field with the nail.
f. As a final step of this experiment, the teacher invited the pupils to find the magnetic field with other objects. Screws, paper, paper clips, a screw driver, jewelry, and coins were used. Some of these objects responded to the magnetic field, some did not.

It is necessary to point out here that the appeal to the children's intuitive preference that was significant in the invention of the field concept was not at all unscientific, but was the necessary first step in the adoption of a new concept. While questions of scientific observation are decided by experiment, questions of interpretation are at first decided by preference in the light of past experience and later by the usefulness of the interpretation in generating discoveries. The magnetic field is a useful *invention*, but it is not essential to describe magnetic interactions (3). Without the invention of the magnetic field, the subsequent explorations with the nail, etc., would have resulted in the discovery of additional distant interactions between the magnets and the nail or the other objects.

There is one feature of the preparatory Experiments 1-4 which should be emphasized. These experiments had been carried out earlier in a somewhat different way, but the distant interactions and the strength of interaction were newly introduced in this lesson. The sequence in which these experiments are carried out is not important. The pupils are not led step-by-step to the magnetic field concept.

"Rather, they are: led in a circle around the magnetic field concept so they may then converge on the center of the circle from several directions." This strategy offers more promise of success.

Now, the lesson described must be placed in a science course. It is essential that the discussion of magnetic fields not be terminated and wrapped-up with the discovery described. Instead, this discovery should in itself be part of a strategy of attack on another more profound concept. In teaching the second grade, the concept of energy is the next higher order of understanding. Springs, rubber bands, dry cells, candles, and air, all these had been introduced earlier. Now magnets are seen as systems in which energy can be stored. The energy concept, in turn, is part of the strategy being developed for teaching about interactions among the objects in a system, a still higher order concept.

The pedagogical point to be stressed in conclusion is that this type of discovery teaching appears to be strongly motivating and rewarding. Yet, the teaching seems also to be reasonably efficient even when compared with a more verbal expository approach. The pupils come to the point where they know they will discover something, and they know what their discovery will mean. Hence, perhaps they did not invent the new concepts, but they did make discoveries.

References

(1) Ausubel, David, *Learning by Discovery: Rationale Mystique*. Urbana, Ill.: Bureau of Educational Research, University of Illinois, 1961.

(2) Bruner, Jerome, *The Process of Education*. Cambridge, Mass.: Harvard University Press, 1960.

(3) Wheeler, J. A. and Richard P. Feynman, "Classical Electrodynamics in Terms of Direct Interparticle Action." *Reviews of Modern Physics, 21*:425, 1949.

35

NOTES ON TEACHING SCIENCE

Robert E. Samples

In some authoritative way, the image of the scientists and the body of knowledge called science has filled the minds of men with visions of antiseptic precision and accuracy. This notion unfortunately exists so strongly that those who teach science in public schools are often either overwhelmed by the "immutable structure" myth or are feverishly engaged in reinforcing this image. The only "flies in the ointment" are the working scientists. They stand so close to the structure of science that they perceive the real nature of the beast. To them science is a temporal, but honest structure that accommodates not only the "facts" of the world, but also the flexible generalizations that have put some order into the chaos.

In short, the true scientist learns to live with change and temporary order. If he is an astronomer, he learns to be able to tolerate ceaseless change, for he is viewing this change from a changing system. If he is a biologist, he must try to understand the order in a mountainside whose millions of trees and shrubs are losing billions of leaves and needles every year and whose existence may be altered by constantly shifting relationships between the only partially predictable weather and nearly whimsical pranks of nature. The physicist looks carefully at information provided him about atoms. He scans X-ray diagrams, spectroscopic pictures from which he hopes to gain more insight concerning the structure of matter, knowing all the while that the instru-

Reprinted from *Science and Children*, 5, March 1968, pp. 28–30.

ments he uses, *made up of atoms,* are being focused on something neither he nor the instruments can see.

What this suggests then is that the scientist looks at the body of knowledge called *Science* as sort of an apartment house that has very few old residents in it. New ones have moved in and out constantly, rooms and compartments have been redecorated, walls have been torn down, others have been built, the form and shape of the whole building is not completely known by anyone. And outside there waits a fantastic quantity of information that wants in.

Does this portray *Science* as immutable and suggest that it has rigid form and only a few are able to withstand the rigor of the structure? Hopefully not. Instead it is hoped that a realistic view of *Science* and the scientist would hold that change is inherently a part of science as a process. Change takes place when the old is partially or completely abandoned by the new. When this happens science grows, for the new knowledge is added to science on top of the foundation formed by the old.

If a teacher of science is not aware of the dynamic kind of "internal remodeling" going on in science, then children learning science from such a teacher can hardly be expected to become fearless in the face of the tentative. There is not *a* solution to a problem but rather there are many. If problems are solved, in the name of science, with a single "right" solution in mind, then *Science* is being abandoned. It is fully important for children to realize that any of the answers that prevail in science are not *absolutely* right but are more currently right than others. And the quality of "more rightness" comes from responsible weighing of the variables on the part of scientists.

Turning now to the child and his confrontation by problems and problem situations, let us discuss his advantages and disadvantages in learning science. As the child stands facing a problem situation he has two paths of solution available to him (Figure A). One is essentially a right-handed or substantive path. The other is a left-handed or metaphoric-intuitive path (Figure B). The substantive side is commonly associated with all bodies of organized knowledge including science. This is the internally consistent, concrete, verifiable, factual route. Thus it has more of a path-like aspect since that which is known establishes the parameters of the route. The metaphoric-intuitive route is the loosely knit realm of generally unstructured experience. It is more of an "I've got a feeling about" route. In Figure B, it is represented as an area rather than a route. This is because there is no way to define the boundaries of the experience that a child brings to bear in attempting to solve the problem. The left-handed side has been traditionally associated with the creative, spontaneously connective world of the poet, artist, and writer. The right-handed side seems

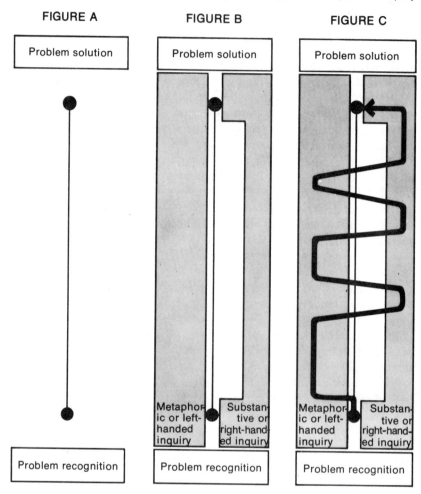

FIGURE A   FIGURE B   FIGURE C

to correlate with prevailing views about scientists and technicians with their worlds of verifiable precision.

In most educational theory, those who teach are charged with the responsibility for preserving both paths toward the solution of problems. The substantive route, we are told, must be built while allowing the learner free access to his left-handed world of unstructured experience. In practice, however, very few teachers, for a variety of reasons, pay more than lip service to the world of children's unstructured experience. This is primarily related to the demands of school systems in the areas of curriculum to be covered, teaching schedules, and the ways the teachers are taught to manage classrooms.

It is true that children have a tendency to ramble in an endless fashion when they begin to talk about things they think are related to the problem at hand. This tendency, when allowed, is usually regarded as a highly inefficient procedure in that it wastes far too much time. In a sense this is true, but the fault lies in the children talking *about* the problem. It is not necessary for children to verbalize the views they have constructed from past experience. Instead it would be far more effective if the children attacked the problem in a way that allowed each of them to focus the problem (as they perceive it) upon their unstructured collection of facts, prejudices, opinions, and myths. A further condition that must be met is that the problem itself should be malleable enough so that it can withstand the undisciplined onslaught of a young mind.

As the student invents the matrix of order that he feels makes the problem more solvable and proceeds to solve it, he too is transformed by his effort. This is better expressed by David Hawkins (1) when he noted that a potter is as transformed by his working the clay as the clay is by the potter. In a sense the child's own intuition is refined and reformed into a more orderly reservoir of experience structured facts, prejudices, opinions, and myths. The real difference is that if the student invents the order through his own effort, the whole array of relationships becomes vitally relevant. If, on the other hand, the student merely mimics what is already known about the problem, then all he could have accomplished is to add a tiny drop-like fact to his left-handed reservoir. In a sense, he has added this drop to a source reservoir that runs the risk of becoming stagnant unless it feeds an on-going river of thought capable of eroding the banks of what the child perceives as unknown.

If a child is allowed access to both paths, how does he seem to progress toward the solution of his problem? (Figure C) In most instances the child attempts to make a collection of substantive, factual information. If he gathers very much, then it's very likely that he is not confronted by a real problem. In addition, this first right-handed start is a response to reward patterns that the child has recognized in the past. Usually after this first short excursion to the right, the child shifts to the left and attempts an ordering of the vast array of intuitions and informal experiences that are available to him. Ordinarily these connected intuitions will suggest a subsolution which may be tested by returning to the problem to gain specific new facts. At this point a "shift" to the right takes place and verification begins. If the problem is at all a challenge to the child, he will not be able to solve it at once. Instead he will make repeated shifts back and forth between the left- and right-handed paths. As the substantive "facts" accumulate, it becomes increasingly difficult for the child to return to the left. This is because any metaphoric connections he makes from that time on must be able to accommodate the wealth of "facts" he has discovered. This involves rather high level processes of abstraction which in fact are very difficult. So rather than persist in returning to his intuition and past experience it is much easier to build on the immediate facts that he has accumulated and gain a solution.

The point of all of this focuses on the view the teacher in such a situation would have regarding science. If science is viewed as a rigorous and immutable substantive structure, then the variety of solutions suggested by children drawing upon their diverse metaphoric-intuitive experiences would seem irrelevant. If, however, the teacher recognizes the responsible flexibility in the structure of science, then the metaphoric-intuitive alternatives will be considered vitally valuable. The important aspect of such a consideration in a teaching situation cannot be overestimated because the determination of relevance is perhaps the most significant intellectual role of the scientist. This role can be assumed by each child to the limits of his ability. But the teacher sets the stage. The teacher's view of science will be an important guide in deciding whether the children will be able to determine the relevance of alternative solutions or whether some external immutable authority shall do so.

Another important factor is the problem itself. Some problems by their very nature require an appeal to authority. For example, the student may be confronted by a "problem" related to the nature of the atmosphere of Jupiter. Such "problems," far too common in science curricula, must involve appellation to the authority of "books" or teachers. Once this is done the child can merely repeat given facts and the problem is apparently solved. Little exercise is given to the mind in determining relevance of solution. Instead, library skills and communciation skills are developed at the expense, in this case, of the child's gaining confidence in the working of his mind. And, in fact, what the child has really learned is how to "psych" the teacher. That is, he has learned to solve the extremely complex social problem of providing adults with what *they* want to satisfy an artificial situation that they constructed. The "solution" could be the atmospheric composition of Jupiter or the date the Vikings landed in the new world and be equally irrelevant.

In learning science, or anything for that matter, a child should be allowed free access to his reservoir of metaphoric-intuitive connections. If this is done, distinctions between the *best* solution and the *only* solution may be made. More important, however, the child will gain insight into the whole universe of relevance. Until this kind of thought activity is allowed and encouraged one can expect that science will continue to be considered as a rigid cubicle where unemotional men talk only of things that can be proven in a language devoid of metaphors.

Reference

(1) Hawkins, David, *The Language of Nature*. New York: Doubleday Anchor Books, 1967.

36

THREE GUIDELINES FOR
ELEMENTARY SCHOOL SCIENCE*

Robert Karplus

I wish I could present to you a comprehensive theory of instruction that might serve as a basis for curricula in science and other areas. Unfortunately, I can't do this; I can only describe some guidelines that have been useful to the Science Curriculum Improvement Study. The teaching objective is to give the students sufficient knowledge and experience so they will have an understanding of the natural environment and an appreciation for original scientific work being carried out by others.

Guideline 1

Two aspects of the teaching program should be distinguished from one another: the experiential (student experience with a wide variety of phenomena, including their acting on the materials involved) and the conceptual (introduction of the student to the approach which mod-

*This article was adapted from papers published in *Curriculum Theory Network,* Winter, 1969–70, and presented to Section 1 (physics) of the 41st Conference of the Australian and New Zealand Association for the Advancement of Science, Adelaide, South Australia, August 1969.

ern scientists find useful in thinking about the phenomena they study). A key problem in planning instruction is how to relate these two aspects to one another, a matter to which I shall return in my third guideline.

Let me list a few examples of what may be done to give the students experience. The observation of magnetized or electrically charged objects interacting without physical contact, of chameleons eating crickets in a terrarium, of trajectories that can be controlled through the launching conditions, and of seeds germinating under certain conditions are useful in helping to form a picture of the broad range of physical and biological phenomena. Also necessary are more elementary experiences with the change in appearance of a liquid sample as it is transferred among differently shaped containers, with the "feel" of specimens of high and low density, with the "disappearance" of solids when they dissolve in liquids, and with the details of surface structure that become visible when a wood or mineral specimen is examined with a magnifying glass. In all these areas it is essential that students experience these directly, and that they have an opportunity to act on the materials and thereby influence what happens.

Supplementing the above is the conceptual approach, which leads to general principles interrelating the phenomena I have just described. Being a physicist, I began my educational activities ten years ago with the notion that force was the fundamental explanatory concept, since force is the cause of motion, and motion is a part of all change. Now I believe that this approach, which is also taken by most physics texts, is not valid. The reason is that observable motion accompanies only a small fraction of phenomena. Thermal, chemical, electrical, optical, and acoustic phenomena do not involve observable motion, hence the force concept is not of direct value in dealing with them. Instead, the broader concept of interaction does apply as an explanatory concept for all these areas, and this concept therefore plays the central role in the SCIS program. The conceptual framework is described in greater detail in each teacher's guide, where supporting concepts such as matter, energy, organism, ecosystem, system, evidence, reference frame, and scientific model are identified.

Guideline 2

Major theories of intellectual development and learning should be drawn upon in curriculum construction, even though they are in conflict with one another. I find it useful to distinguish three major types of theories.

The "learning-by-conditioning" theory views the learner's behavior as a response to a well-planned stimulus. With repetition, practice, and suitable reinforcement, the learner will exhibit the desired behavior. Note that in this therory there is no room for spontaneous or creative expressions by the student. Everything of educational value reflects the inputs accumulated during the teaching program.

The "learning-by-discovery" theory claims that everything of which an individual is capable is latent within him. The educational program must give him opportunities to express these latent tendencies, but should not provide any input that might inhibit or redirect his natural inclinations. Given a sufficiently rich environment, the learner will discover the properties of objects, conditions under which phenomena take place, and general principles relating the isolated incidents and observations in his experiments and investigations.

The "learning-by-equilibration" theory, associated with Jean Piaget, views the individual as capable of mental operations which function in a self-sustaining feedback loop (equilibrium) as he acts on his environment and receives stimuli in return. When the feedback loop is disturbed by events that don't fit the scheme (disequilibrium), changes in the mental operations ultimately lead to more powerful mental operations that can cope successfully with a larger class of events (equilibration).

Guideline 3

By putting together guideline 1 (experience and concepts) and guideline 2 (theories of development and learning), SCIS arrived at a prescription for designing instructional units. We conceive of a learning cycle with three phases: *exploration,* referring to self-directed, unstructured investigation; *invention,* referring to the introduction of a new integrating concept by teacher or by learner; and *discovery,* referring to applications of the same new concept in a variety of situations, partly self-directed, partly guided. Each SCIS teacher's guide describes in detail how the learning cycle relates to the activities of a unit.

Note that the learner is active during the exploration and discovery phases, which occupy most of the teaching time. Experiential input is provided during these phases. He is least active during the invention phase, which should occupy only a brief interval between the other two. Conceptual input is provided during this phase.

Note also how this prescription utilizes the three learning theories. Exploration is in accord with "learning-by-discovery" and "learning-by-equilibration." It allows the learner to impose his ideas and preconceptions on the subject matter to be investigated. If he comes up with a successful new idea, more power to him. If, as is often the case, his preconceptions lead to confusion, the teacher learns about these difficulties. At the same time, the exploration should create some disequilibrium, since not all students can cope with the materials with equal success.

Invention is in accord with the "learning-by-equilibration" theory, as the new idea introduced at that time suggests a way for the learner to resolve his disequilibrium.

Discovery, finally, is in accord with "learning-by-equilibration," and also with the "learning-by-conditioning" view that repetition and practice are necessary for learning. It is essential, however, that the repetition and practice occur largely through self-directed activities by the learner, so that he will actually resolve his disequilibrium by interacting with the experimental materials and by establishing a new feedback pattern for his actions and observations. At this time, the same concepts are applied repeatedly in a wide variety of activities.

These three guidelines are useful to a teacher planning his lessons, as well as to the curriculum developer creating new course materials. After formulating his objectives, the teacher selects the experiential and conceptual inputs that have to be provided for the students; he identifies the elements leading to disequilibrium and conceptual reorganization; and he decides whether highly self-directed exploration, partly guided discovery, or more structured invention is the most appropriate mode for the activity. Over a period of time, the teacher will prepare a program that is balanced in these respects, and that provides for substantial self-direction even at the expense of limiting the course's "coverage."

VIII

Becoming a Better Elementary Science Teacher Through the Synthesis of a Personal Instructional Theory

Teaching is fundamentally concerned with the attainment of maximum beneficial learning for the whole individual. A teacher's role is to insure that learning is efficient and effective in order for students to discover and develop their potentials. A good teacher asks: "How effective am I? How well have I organized the activities for my class? How have I allowed for the involvement of students in planning class activities? How effective is this lesson, demonstration, film, text, or program? How do these lessons contribute to the development of better persons?" In answering these questions, the instructor relies on his training in subject matter, educational psychology, and life experiences.

Stimulating students to be thrilled with learning and to gain a zest for education that will continue for life is a large and difficult task. The great challenge for a teacher is that there is so much to know and learn about academic subjects, human behavior, and education that the work is never done. Becoming an effective instructor is a continuous process. Routine causes boredom. In teaching there is little room for routine since the challenge to maximize the potential of each individual requires constant adaptation, assimilation and innovation by the instructor.

Major portions of this article are reprinted from Dr. Robert B. Sund and Mr. Rodger W. Bybee, "Toward the Teacher's Synthesis of an Instructional Theory," *Colorado Journal of Educational Research*, Fall 1972.

Why Develop a Theory?

Scientists endeavor to construct theories. They use theories to guide them toward insights into the intricacies of nature. A theory is a fantastic intellectual instrument economizing the chores of the mind. For, by knowing relatively little—a theory—the mind knows much. It is through theoretical understanding that it is capable of interpreting and synthesizing volumes of information. A theory provides three fundamental qualities. It:

1. Enables prediction and therefore provides direction
2. Explains phenomena
3. Provides organizational structure

Think for a moment of the implications of knowing the theory of evolution. Given a strata with some fossils, you can predict the types of fossils you will find above and below the layer of exploration. You can explain why the fossils change. And, if you bring fossils up from different layers and somehow become confused as to what fossils came from the lowest strata, you know how to reorganize your findings and put the fossils in the proper order. This would all be impossible without a theory.

"A man without a theory is doomed to make the same mistake twice!" Just as the task of a scientist is to formulate and evolve theories so must teachers build an instructional theory helping them to predict, explain, and organize learning. Beginning teachers start with a few fibers entwined into a theoretical structure. As they progress through myriads of experiences, new awarenesses, and learnings about human behavior, an instructional theory matures. A teacher's instructional theory is never complete, because as he grows and gains insight into human behavior, he evaluates, modifies, and restructures his theoretical framework. The synthesis of a personal instructional theory provides a frame of reference and general direction for educational growth—for becoming a better teacher. Gordon Allport has said, "Becoming is the process of incorporating earlier stages into later; or when this is impossible of handling conflict between early and late stages as well as one can" (1, p. 28). A personal theory of instruction will aid in resolving personal conflicts, provide direction, and establish an over-all schema into which the "earlier stage" can be incorporated.

Becoming an excellent teacher requires a theory that will help you develop fully as a person. Teaching can be exciting because it provides a humanistic laboratory where a teacher can sculpture himself through interpersonal interaction into a better individual. By helping students become what they are capable of the teacher grows as a person. The teacher that helps another toward the actualization of his potential is an individual that *does* something for others and *is* something as a person.

Education has fractioned, divided, and isolated many of the important components of teaching students successfully. Unfortunately, the teacher preparation programs have emphasized these *ad hoc* components. "If you are well planned..." "If you use this curriculum..." "If you understand the child's cognitive stages..." etc. Planning, classroom procedures, methods, and subject matter are important; but they are means, not ends. The results of this atomistic view of education has been the neglect of the primary and crucial variable in the classroom—the teacher as a person. Teachers with an adequate instructional theory include all of the above and have larger goals for their interaction with students.

Educational Forum recently had an article paying tribute to a great French teacher, Emile-Auguste Chartier (known as Alain). The following is an excerpt from that article. It describes a great teacher's instructional theory and personal goals for his students.

> His outstanding contribution as a teacher does not appear to have resided in his educational concepts nor in any particularly successful educational techniques, but rather in a lived and shared philosophy of life, centered on freedom, independence, willed happiness, and the courage to think and live, and in giving his students pride and dignity (2).

The following sections present some areas we feel are important and should be considered as a teacher surveys the terrain and starts to map a personal instructional theory. The healthy personality, a multiple talent approach, and teaching by inquiry can be valuable aids to the individual.

The Healthy Personality

A few years ago the Association for Supervision and Curriculum Development published a book entitled *Perceiving, Behaving and Becoming—A New Focus for Education.* It outlined a general theoretical structure for becoming a fully functioning person and described the implications of this view for teaching. This humanistic approach centers on the individual teacher as a person with a healthy personality rather than a giver of knowledge. It should be mentioned that the healthy personality *is* well-informed. The way the individual views self, others, and the teaching task are the foundations on which the instructional theory is constructed. The teacher's perceptions, beliefs, values, and attitudes guide his interaction with students, selection of curriculum materials, and organization within the classroom. Some of the main tenets of this theory of behavior are:

1. The perceptions an individual has at any given moment determine his behavior
2. Perceptions about self are more important than other existing perceptions
3. Man is always engaged in a continuous striving for self-fulfillment (4)

These principles do not emphasize any one particular domain of education, i.e., cognitive, affective or psychomotor; rather *all* domains are integrated under the three principles.

The role of a teacher under this theoretical framework is continually to help students build their self-concepts. This means the teacher involves students in the learning process so they have successful experiences, feel accepted, are liked, respected, and admired. The theory stresses the necessity of perceiving the individual on the way to his becoming a person and personalizing the learning environment. The instructor must treat every person as an individual with particular needs at a specific place in time on his path to "becoming." The teaching helps him become by being open and nonthreatening, by accepting and liking him, by reducing fear, and by helping the individual discover his identity by building his self-concept. As an individual becomes more secure through acceptance, he is more willing to take risks; and by so doing, he is more likely to be creative. In these times when so many of our students seem to have problems with their identity and self-concepts, the humanistic approach provides an excellent psychological foundation for helping them resolve these problems. As Maslow says, "Every person is, in part, his own project and makes himself" (6).

A Multiple Talent Approach

How is the teacher to help a person build himself? The first need is for the instructor to perceive the individual as a person that is able. The classical view of a person was to think of him as being an unfilled reservoir. The teacher's role was to fill the mind with information and knowledge. Hence, the teacher that presented information and covered more was thought to be a good instructor. This view is absolute. Today the teacher must consider the total person. He should have a holistic and not a fractionated view of the individual.

Guilford, Taylor, and others have shown that a person is a collection of over 120 talents (5; 8). The manifestation and development of these talents contributes to positive perceptions of the self.

Dr. Taylor states that since individuals are a collection of talents —academic, creative, planning, organizing, social, forecasting, communicating, decision making, etc.—a multitalent approach to teaching is required. He means that teachers should attempt to develop a maximum of talents, not just the academic ones. To perceive students as being filled with many talents broadens the perceptions of the teacher and insures better interaction between the teacher and the student. For if you view students through a multiple talent perceptual framework, you see that most of them are in some way above average. Dr. Taylor states:

> If we restrict ourself to cultivating only one talent, we will merely find the top 10 percent to be highly gifted, but if we will seek for the highly gifted in each of several different talents, the number found to be gifted will increase tremendously. In fact, if we cultivate three talents instead of only one, the percent found to be gifted will more than double (will be over 20 percent). Furthermore, if we work in six talent areas, the percent who are highly gifted will triple (will be about 30 percent) (9).

Teachers have traditionally thought that academic talent correlated well with other talents. Taylor has shown this is not true. In fact, some of the most creative individuals may be the poorest academically. No longer can a teacher assume he's a good teacher if he just tries to develop academic ability.

The complexity of developing all the human talents may be frightening. But think for a moment of the beauty of the idea—no student is below average in all talents. Fifty percent of the students may be below average academically. However, if you find a way to manifest the outstanding talents of the academically poor student, he will experience feelings of success, feelings that will affect positively his self-concept and contribute to his expectancy level. He may eventually believe "I can learn and be rewarded for my talents in school." As a result his academic achievement will probably improve.

An Inquiry or Discovery Approach

The teacher's instructional approach should include involvement of the child with materials—an inquiry or discovery approach. Thus, concrete experience with personal meaning is provided. Motivation is a function of personal meaning or nearness of materials to self. This, we feel, has two aspects: first, the personal interest or relevancy and second, the closeness ot the materials in a physical sense, i.e., to be able to touch, manipulate, and interact with objects in the environment.

When direct involvement is combined with recognition of the multiple of potential talents a major step is taken toward recognizing the student as a more complete entity. Through the combination of these approaches success is inevitable. Having success in school develops the self-concept which in turn leads to better mental health for children. These ideas focus on the teacher as a helper or facilitator. The goal is to help each child attain all he is capable of achieving. The synthesis presented can help the teacher produce an environment where every child enjoys multiple options for success.

The Effective Use of Yourself

When techniques, plans, and curriculum materials are combined you are ready to interact with children. The single most important element is the *way* the teacher combines these and builds a helping relationship in the educational environment. The helping relationship is characterized by situations that require the teacher to react immediately. The creative, insightful, and perceptive teacher effectively reacts to the instantaneous needs of the school, classroom, or individual student. The following is quoted from a contemporary science curriculum project: "The problem is I lived half my life before I realized it was a do it yourself job"(7).

An adequate and well-integrated personal instructional theory will insure that you not teach half your career before you realize the important instrument with which you work is yourself. Arthur W. Combs has stated this idea formally: *"Effective helping relationships will be a function of the effective use of the helper's self in bringing about fulfillment of his own and society's purposes* (italics in original) (3).

A theory provides a framework in which past experiences can be organized and, for the individual, provide a personal style in reacting to different educational encounters. In the following quote from Gordon Allport's book *Becoming* "personal theory" could well be substituted for a "consistent line of procedure":

> A personal style is a way of achieving definiteness and effectiveness in our self-image and in our relationships with other people. It evolves gradually by our adapting a consistent line of procedure and sticking to it (1, p. 78).

In summary, the development of a personal instructional theory will help the teacher effectively make predictions, explain and organize the learning environment. The use of self is the single most important element in this interaction. There are other elements such as using inquiry or discovery, emphasizing multiple talents, and developing the healthy personality that will aid the teacher. Remember, teachers do not have to be bad to become better—the choice is yours.

References

(1) Allport, Gordon W., *Becoming–Basic Considerations for a Psychology of Personality*. New Haven: Yale University Press, 1955.

(2) Baslaw, Annette S., "A Great Teacher—Maurois Remembered Alain." *Educational Forum, 36*, January 1972, p. 157.

(3) Combs, Arthur W., et al., *Helping Relationships: Basic Concepts for the Helping Professions*. Boston: Allyn & Bacon, Inc., 1971, pp. 5–6.

(4) Combs, Arthur W., *The Professional Education of Teachers*. Boston: Allyn & Bacon, Inc., 1965.

(5) Guilford, J. P., "New Directions in Education." Presented at the 9th Annual Creativity Workshop, University of Utah, Salt Lake City, Utah, June 16, 1971.

(6) Maslow, Abraham H., "Some Basic Propositions of Growth and Self-Actualization Psychology." In *Perceiving, Behaving, Becoming–A New Focus for Education*, Association for Supervision and Curriculum Development Yearbook, Washington D.C., 1962.

(7) *SENSORSHEET*, Copublication of the Environmental Studies Project and Earth Science Teacher Preparation Project, January 1972.

(8) Taylor, Calvin W., "Multiple Talent Approach Teaching Scheme in which Most Students Can Be Above Average." *The Instructor*, April 28, 1968, p. 27.

(9) _____ "Be Talent Developers as Well as Knowledge Dispensers." *Today's Education*, NEA Journal, December 1968, p. 68.